Responsible AI

Scrivener Publishing
100 Cummings Center, Suite 541J
Beverly, MA 01915-6106

Leading-Edge Breakthroughs in Artificial Intelligence

Series Editor: Dr. S. Balamurugan (sbnbala@gmail)

The world is on the cusp of several breakthroughs in artificial intelligence (AI), rapidly transforming industries and the research field. The "Leading-Edge Breakthroughs in Artificial Intelligence" book series is dedicated to exploring the most pioneering developments in artificial intelligence. The series aims to highlight both theoretical and practical advancements, offering insights into several cutting-edge advancements in AI and how the same could be deployed to solve complex problems in fields such as healthcare, finance, manufacturing, robotics, marketing, energy management, agriculture, autonomous systems, and many more. It also addresses critical issues like AI governance, ethics, trust, security, transparency, and societal impacts, making it an essential resource for researchers, engineers, and industry leaders looking to leverage AI for future breakthroughs.

Publishers at Scrivener
Martin Scrivener (martin@scrivenerpublishing.com)
Phillip Carmical (pcarmical@scrivenerpublishing.com)

Responsible AI

Principles and Practices

Edited by

Manish Kumar
Department of Computer Science and Engineering, Thapar Institute of Engineering and Technology, Patiala, Punjab, India

Nitigya Sambyal
Department of Information Technology, Uppsala University, Uppsala, Sweden
Department of CSE, Thapar Institute of Engineering and Technology, Patiala, Punjab, India

Leena Priyadarshini Singh
Department of Business Administration, Ravenshaw University, Cuttack, Odisha, India

Ramasamy V.
Department of Computer Science and Engineering (School of Computing), SRM Institute of Science and Technology, Tiruchirappalli Campus, Tamil Nadu, India

and

S. Balamurugan
Intelligent Research Consultancy Services (iRCS), Coimbatore, Tamil Nadu, India

Scrivener Publishing

WILEY

This edition first published 2026 by John Wiley & Sons, Inc., 111 River Street, Hoboken, NJ 07030, USA and Scrivener Publishing LLC, 100 Cummings Center, Suite 541J, Beverly, MA 01915, USA

For more information about Scrivener publications please visit www.scrivenerpublishing.com.

Wiley Global Headquarters
111 River Street, Hoboken, NJ 07030, USA

For details of our global editorial offices, customer services, and more information about Wiley products visit us at www.wiley.com.

The manufacturer's authorized representative according to the EU General Product Safety Regulation is Wiley-VCH GmbH, Boschstr. 12, 69469 Weinheim, Germany, e-mail: Product_Safety@wiley.com.

Library of Congress Cataloging-in-Publication Data

ISBN 978-1-394-35544-0

Cover image: Generated with AI using Adobe Firefly
Cover design by Russell Richardson

Set in size of 11pt and Minion Pro by Manila Typesetting Company, Makati, Philippines

Printed in the USA

10 9 8 7 6 5 4 3 2 1

Dedication

The editorial team extends heartfelt dedication to their families for their invaluable support throughout the writing and editing of this book. In addition, the editor's express sincere gratitude to friends and mentors for their understanding, stimulating discussions, encouragement, and blessings. Finally, this book is respectfully dedicated to the broader research community whose spirit of shared knowledge allows scientific progress, which is making this world a better place to live.

Contents

Series Preface

This book, *Responsible AI: Principles and Practices*, discusses the ethical considerations, governance structures, and practical frameworks necessary to develop and deploy artificial intelligence systems that are fair, transparent, accountable, and beneficial for society. The chapters in this book are timely and important because the authors address the ethical, legal, and societal implications of AI and present a systematic approach for ensuring that AI technologies are developed and used in a fair, transparent, and inclusive manner that is consistent with human values. As AI systems are increasingly invoked to inform decision-making in high-stakes areas such as healthcare, finance, education, and government, thinking about responsibility throughout the lifecycle of AI is no longer a luxury but instead a necessity. Furthermore, this book is related to the series of *Leading-Edge Breakthroughs in Artificial Intelligence* as it allows for technical innovation to occur with the appropriate ethical guidelines in place to ensure that AI breakthroughs lead to long-term, trustworthy, and socially accepted progress across industries.

Dr. S. Balamurugan
Director, Intelligent Research Consultancy Services (iRCS),
Coimbatore, Tamil Nadu, India
Series Editor - Leading Edge Breakthroughs in Artificial Intelligence

Preface

Artificial Intelligence is identified as a leading transformative technology with the potential to create societal impacts across various domains such as business, education, healthcare, academia, and more. Leading voices from politics, academia, and industry are brought together in this volume to examine the ethical, social, and technical aspects of AI systems. This book brings together the best of technology, policy, and ethics to tackle the challenge of developing and deploying AI responsibly.

The concepts, approaches, and case studies that influence the emerging field of Responsible AI are thoroughly examined in this edited volume. The chapters cover topics ranging from accountability and human-centered design to fairness and transparency, with the goal of equipping readers with the knowledge and resources they need to understand and implement AI for the benefit of society. This book is structured into 16 chapters encompassing the intersections of technology, policy, and ethics to address the multifaceted challenge of Responsible AI development and deployment.

In addition, this book introduces the fundamentals of Responsible AI—its principles, practices, features, working mechanisms, and applications across various sectors. To meet these objectives, the book comprises of sixteen chapters contributed by accomplished writers as follows:

Chapter 1 explores the multifaceted applications and challenges of AI across healthcare, education, disaster management, and cultural preservation. It also discusses the ethical frameworks necessary for responsible implementation to ensure fairness, accountability, and transparency.

Chapter 2 discusses the application of AI in healthcare, examining the moral conundrums and legal issues that arise from its use. Chapter 3 reviews new regulations related to AI and addresses the challenges of making AI practices ethical. The authors encourage organizations to adopt AI in ways that are both modern and socially responsible.

Chapter 4 presents a skin disease detection and prediction model using Faster Region-based Convolutional Neural Networks with Inception v2 architecture. The system would assist medical professionals by detecting skin conditions and providing bounding boxes with confidence scores.

Chapter 5 introduces a quantum PSO-based regression model to predict machining error, based on parameters such as cutting speed, feed, and depth of cut for specific machining tasks. Chapter 6 explores various machine learning algorithms to predict the severity of groundwater levels in Indian districts, highlighting both the environmental insights and the potential of AI in monitoring natural resources.

Chapter 7 discusses the importance of environmental, economic, and social sustainability in the development of AI systems. It outlines challenges and proposes solutions, policies, and initiatives to promote sustainable AI. Chapter 8 presents a unified approach combining AutoML with explainability techniques such as SHAP, LIME, and feature importance analysis. The study demonstrates the practical value of explainable AutoML across datasets in structural engineering and social science.

Chapter 9 explores the ethical dimensions of AI-powered mobile applications, including user awareness of ethical concerns and perceptions of AI's guiding principles. Chapter 10 examines the use of AI technologies in autonomous vehicles, addressing core functions, adoption barriers, and constraints to growth in the sector.

Chapter 11 reviews organizational measures, rules, and guidelines for protecting privacy in AI systems. It includes emerging technologies like differential privacy, federated learning, and homomorphic encryption, as well as frameworks such as the NIST AI Risk Management Framework, GDPR, CCPA, and OECD AI Principles.

Chapter 12 discusses AI's role in autonomous systems, including self-driving cars, drone-based delivery and surveillance, target detection in military vehicles, and applications in space and healthcare systems.

Chapter 13 explores ethical issues in AI-driven healthcare, focusing on privacy, bias, accountability, and transparency. Chapter 14 analyzes machine learning models used to develop accurate, efficient, and cost-effective AI-based fraud detection systems. Chapter 15 examines privacy-preserving approaches essential to responsible AI, including federated learning, differential privacy, homomorphic encryption, and synthetic data generation.

Chapter 16 introduces a framework using Convolutional Neural Networks and transfer learning to diagnose and classify common pet diseases from images. The system provides users with disease insights, preventive measures, and medical recommendations.

We hope that readers will find this book beneficial. The editors are grateful to the reviewers who have contributed to improving the quality of the book through their constructive comments. The editors also thank Martin Scrivener and Scrivener Publishing for guidance, support and publication of the book.

Dr. Manish Kumar
Department of Computer Science and Engineering, Thapar Institute of Engineering and Technology, Patiala, Punjab, India
Dr. Nitigya Sambyal
Department of Information Technology, Uppsala University, Uppsala, Sweden
Department of CSE, Thapar Institute of Engineering and Technology, Patiala, Punjab, India
Dr. Leena Priyadarshini Singh
Department of Business Administration, Ravenshaw University, Cuttack, Odisha, India
Dr. Ramasamy V.
Department of Computer Science and Engineering (School of Computing), SRM Institute of Science and Technology, Tiruchirappalli Campus, Tamil Nadu, India
Dr. S. Balamurugan
Intelligent Research Consultancy Services (iRCS), Coimbatore, Tamil Nadu, India

Acknowledgement

The editors are truly grateful to their institution for providing a supportive research environment that served as the foundation of this proposal. We are especially thankful to the authors of the chapters for their expertise, insightful contributions, and dedication in revising their work to maintain the quality and scope of this book. We appreciate their patience and cooperation throughout the editorial process. We extend our deepest thanks to the reviewers who volunteered their time and expertise to provide invaluable feedback on the chapter drafts. Their constructive comments and suggestions significantly strengthened the individual chapters and the high standards of the book.

1
AI for Social Good

R. Srivats, Kalyanasundaram V., Abhiram Sharma, Deepika Roselind J.* and Logeswari G.

School of Computer Science and Engineering, Vellore Institute of Technology, Chennai, Tamil Nadu, India

Abstract
Considered a great enabler of innovation, artificial intelligence (AI) is also becoming an essential tool to address some of the biggest challenges in the world. This chapter examines in a wide range of examples of the application of AI in sectors from health and education to disaster relief and cultural creation, and the centrality of ethical regulation for its use. It starts by emphasizing AI's increasing relevance for the promotion of social welfare and the positive impact that it can have on issues of global significance. The conversation refers to important ethical principles including fairness, transparency, and accountability in order to encourage responsible uptake. The importance of governmental and private cooperation is also highlighted, which demonstrates how such strategic partnerships can enhance the societal contributions of AI. To this regard, in medical industry, AI is able to support risk prediction and early disease detection and diagnosis which makes early interventions possible. This subsection, additionally, delves into how smart systems can address educational inequality, especially among minority populations. "Leveraging data-driven insights, AI can contribute to reduce barriers to equitable and quality education, paving the way to more inclusive and effective learning environments. The application of AI for disaster management is explored through predictive analytics with the aim to improve preparedness and response. This chapter discusses how intelligent technology can be used to determine the optimal allocation of crucial resources and to organize support measures efficiently, resulting in life-saving interventions, and minimized effects of crisis. Integrating AI and actual data can help with the communication and allocation of resources during crises, ultimately enhancing the power of answers. In Culture, the report on AI demonstrates how AI enhances cultural preservation,

**Corresponding author*: deepikaroselind.j@vit.ac.in

Manish Kumar, Nitigya Sambyal, Leena Priyadarshini Singh, Ramasamy V. and S. Balamurugan (eds.) Responsible AI: Principles and Practices, (1–28) © 2026 Scrivener Publishing LLC

arts and creativity, and how it runs responsible intercultural activities. Cultural institutions could generate unique experience by AI, in which various collectives participate in evaluating the culture. The chapter ends by summarizing the key contributions made by work in social aspects in AI. This clarifies the limitations in the future development of AI in this domain, and further attends to the ethical obligations of responsible governments and stakeholders. Through powerful technology solutions, stakeholders can enhance healthcare, create more educational opportunities, enhance disaster response, and encourage more effective solutions with cultural context. But responsible deployment of these technologies should be a priority. Looking at the future, AI's future direction in social wells is extremely promising. Through prioritizing only goals and promoting objectives and inclusiveness to promote human well-being, AI systems can use their overall capabilities to make wise changes and create a more equitable future for all.

Keywords: Artificial intelligence (AI), social good, ethical AI, healthcare, education, disaster management, predictive analytics, AI governance

1.1 Introduction to AI for Social Good

1.1.1 Social Good and the Role of AI

Artificial Intelligence (AI) has emerged as a leading transformative technology with the ability to address sophisticated societal challenges. Applications of AI are widespread across various domains as healthcare, education, disaster management and cultural preservation (Figure 1.1), where it holds the responsibility to uplift human capabilities and deliver innovative solutions. The ability of AI to process and analyze vast amounts of data, automate

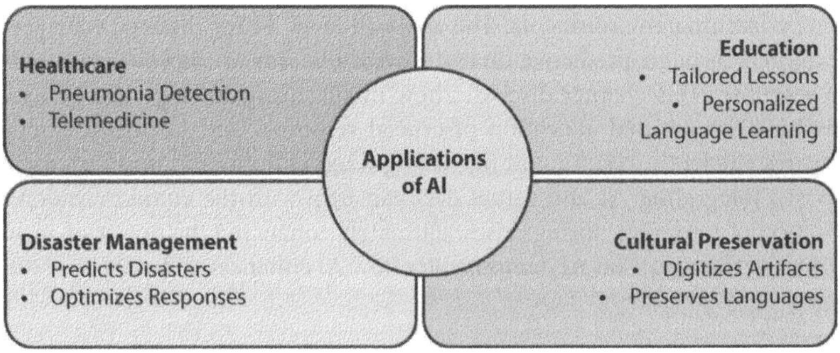

Figure 1.1 The application of AI used in various sectors such as cultural preservation, education, disaster management and healthcare.

redundant tasks and predict with high accuracy has placed it as a key driver of change to address pressing issues globally. The deployment of AI for social good requires a multi-faceted approach. While its technological potential is undeniable, ethical considerations, effective collaboration between stakeholders and strategies to overcome systemic challenges must be prioritized.

Artificial intelligence brings transformations in key domains, especially healthcare. Medical imaging based machine learning models have shown remarkable performance in detecting diseases like cancer and cardio vascular diseases. A study by Rajpurkar *et al.* showed that AI technologies can identify pneumonia in chest X-ray images as well as radiologist experts [1]. These advancements are leading to earlier diagnosis and more timely interventions, resulting in ultimately better patient care and less burden placed on healthcare. AI is likely to be applied in underserved spots through the filling of the accessibility gap. Natural language processing (NLP) and predictive analytics tools have started allowing for remote consultations with continuous health monitoring and treatment recommendations, which has the potential to increase access to quality care for underprivileged persons and those in isolated communities.

In education, AI is transforming learning with customization. It is used to evaluate performance of students, and customize content according to individual learning requirements. This personalization enables students to learn at their own speeds and to focus on specific problems better. Language-learning apps like Duolingo, say, rely on AI to customize drills to a learner's current skill level, creating an effective and immersive experience. Additionally, smart systems have potential to not only reduce educational system barriers through providing high quality digital education material to students in different socio-economical environments and areas of limited accessibility, but also decreasing the equilibrium of opportunities of academic growth among the students.

Disaster response is an important field for artificial intelligence improvements. AI systems can predict natural events including hurricanes, floods and earthquakes with pin-point accuracy through their analysis and prediction capabilities. These predictions allow governments and aid organizations to prepare, collectively respond to emergency needs and to start evacuations with an aim to reduce loss of life and minimize economic disruption. For instance, Rolph *et al.* demonstrated that the inclusion of meteorological and geospatial information with advanced models can be very useful in early forecasting of cyclones, which will support in timely announcement of emergency and allocation of resources [4]. This shows the life-saving and life-diminishing capabilities of AI in times of crisis. AI is also making a valuable contribution not only to the functional applications, but also to the preservation and promotion of the cultural heritage. It provides a variety of services including digital preservation of artifacts, online virtual exhibition creation and immersive storytelling experiences for cultural heritage. Projects like Google Arts & Culture illustrate the potential of AI to help people around the world share and experience a diversity of cultural narratives, leading to greater empathy and understanding. Applied ethically, AI also helps cultural institutions and organizations sustain heritage in the past while fostering artistic innovation and creativity in the future.

1.1.2 Ethical Frameworks and Considerations in the Implementation of AI

As AI increasingly transforms vital aspects of modern life, there should be a strong ethical framework to guide the development and application of AI to ensure that these technologies serve us all. A pervasive issue is bias which may be present in AI systems, typically due to unbalanced or non-representative training data. One highly publicized case is the facial recognition technology, which faced criticism due to greater error rates for minorities [2]. Such divergences may also help reinforce social injustice and emphasize the urgency for inclusive data collection and effective validation methods.

Another requirement for ethical AI is accountability. Many black boxes provide little transparency into how decisions are reached, making it difficult for users to assess or challenge results. Explainable AI (XAI) is the computer science discipline that is trying to overcome this challenge by making algorithmic decision-making transparent and comprehensible. Adadi and Berrada highlighted that this interpretability is especially crucial for sensitive areas such as healthcare and criminal justice for which AI-based decisions may result in grave impacts [3]. Making AI output more interpretable increases trust and also allows a stakeholder to assess the underlying reasoning behind automated recommendations.

Privacy is also a major issue, especially in healthcare and education – two sectors where AI uses personal (often highly sensitive) data to operate. Federated learning has been proposed as a practical solution, where model training can be performed among decentralized data sites without transporting the data. Such an approach can help in protecting privacy and also ensuring the integrity and accuracy of AI models. The use of such privacy-preserving techniques can help build public trust and enable broader deployment of AI.

1.1.3 Consensus Between Public and Private Sectors

The successful application of artificial intelligence is now more a matter of partnership between state and capital. Governments can provide regulatory frameworks and direct financing, and nurturing supportive infrastructure, and private entities can bring technical know-how and can innovate. This synergy makes possible the deployment of AI-based solutions in a broader context, to address complex global challenges. There have been significant advances in the cooperation among healthcare. Similarly, during the COVID-19 pandemic, the collaboration of the government, academia and tech industry has facilitated the development of AI-based tools for disease detection and management of patients [5]. These partnerships facilitated rapid testing and diagnostics, proving the power of unified action in crisis response.

In education too, collaborations, between private and public, have enabled access to online learning platforms and digital resources to advance education. Organizations such as UNESCO successfully cooperated with technology vendors to provide educational materials to rural or underprivileged areas, which facilitated literacy and capacity building. Such concerted efforts are crucial to bridge the educational gaps that exist between various socio-economic strata. Collaborative innovation has also contributed to disaster response tactics. Many AI-based tools that have been created for optimizing the allocation of emergency resources or coordinating the response to disasters have come about thanks to collaborations between the public and private sectors. For instance, forest fire control systems commonly use satellite images, normally provided by governmental agencies, in combination with prediction algorithms developed by the private sector. This composite philosophy is designed to allow for rapid decision making and minimizes the effect of any single event.

1.1.4 Challenges and Opportunities in AI for Social Good

There is no question that the promise of AI's role in driving social change is compelling while its alignment into society structures poses some incredible challenges. At the top of the list is the stubborn digital divide. Many under-resourced and under-represented communities have still yet to access basic digital tools and connectivity to harness AI technologies. Addressing these disparities requires focused investment in digital infrastructure, inclusive capacity-building, equitable models of implementation that favour social inclusion.

The scalability is also a big challenge. Although lots of AI-applied pilot projects look good on paper, it is difficult to scale the wins into stable long-run solutions. Sustainable use depends on ongoing substantial financial inputs, good governance mechanisms and systems for monitoring relevance and effectiveness. In addition, uncertain regulations around data privacy and security are adding to the complexity equation. Without clear, reliable legal parameters, institutions and governments are unsure about how to collect, use, and safeguard data. Setting up clear laws is crucial to protect the rights of users, but also to ensure that data is being handled ethically and that the users in general can trust the AI systems.

The potential of what artificial intelligence can bring is also incredible. Modern natural language, computer vision and machine learning (ML) processing advancements give rise to creative solutions that were not even imaginable. For instance, AI-based blockchain platforms are exploited to enhance supply chains' traceability and to assist in the delivery of humanitarian aid [6]. On the importance of supporting a united AI community: Duties to governments, responsibilities to stakeholders and collaboration across industries. From overcoming the use of current limitations and advancements in technology, society can work to ensure that AI can be leveraged to bring about lasting change and a fairer future for everyone.

1.2 AI in Healthcare

1.2.1 AI for Early Disease Detection and Diagnostics

The integration of artificial intelligence for disease diagnosis purposes can be explained by a multilayered, complex scaffolding, as shown in Figure 1.2. This ensures accuracy and reliability. This frame is designed to process a variety of unstructured medical data. Transform them into classes and provide decision support in a variety of clinical scenarios. The architecture includes seven levels of data recording, preprocessing, characterization extraction, model selection, ensemble learning, feedback loops, and deployment in a clinical setting. Data collection begins with sourcing information from a wide range of devices, including high-resolution imaging modalities such as MRI and CT. Portable biosensors for continuous monitoring and use of historical data from EHRS systems (electronic

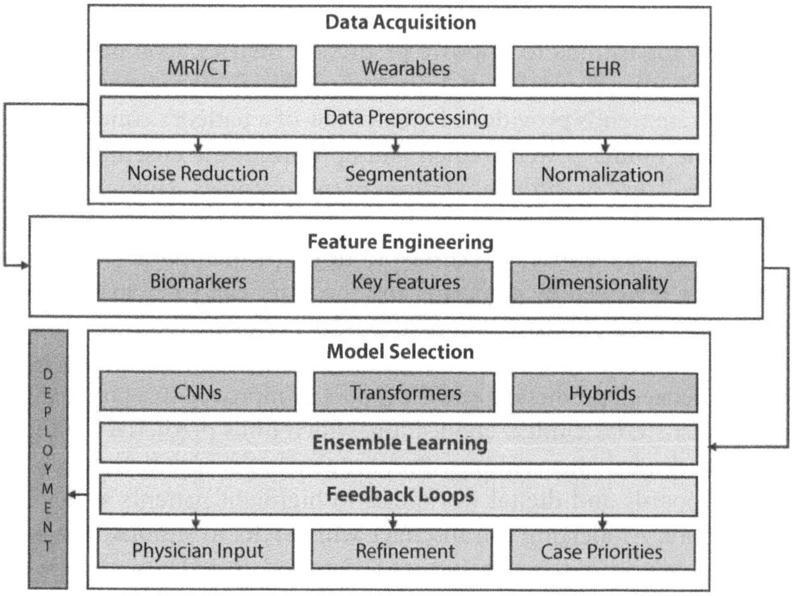

Figure 1.2 Framework for AI in healthcare diagnosis.

health records) are another example of the means of purchasing data. The focus is to ensure a variety of data to minimize distortions that can affect the outcome.

It represents the preprocessing and functional engineering phase where raw data is converted to the appropriate format for analysis after recording. For imaging data, preprocessing involves noise reduction and segmentation using filters to separate areas of interest and areas of standardization to maintain uniformity between data records from different devices. For text or numeric data, preprocessing includes handling of missing values, resolving conflicts, and normalizing entries. Feature extraction focuses on deriving meaningful attributes from this data. An example of this is the identification of biomarkers from blood test data or important morphological properties from brain tumor imagery. These two phases help the next phase of mechanical learning focused on the most relevant and predictive aspects of the data.

At the model selection stage, algorithms are chosen based on the properties and complexity of input data. Convolutional Neural Networks (CNNs) dominate image-based diagnostics due to their ability to capture spatial hierarchies. Transformer-based models are preferred for textual data analysis. This could be as simple as parsing physician notes or pathology reports.

Ensemble models are increasingly popular, as they combine the strengths of multiple algorithms to improve prediction metrics. Combining CNNs for images with recurrent neural networks (RNNs) [7] for sequential data like heart rate trends provides a holistic view of a patient's condition.

Once the model is well-trained and optimized, the ensemble learning approach will give us different versions of some models. This is expected to result in a higher sensitivity and be more robust to outliers. Such outcomes are enhanced by feedback processes. In this type of approach, image predictions are reviewed by clinicians and the latter can participate in annotating these predictions to improve model performance. The algorithm utilizes a proactive learning framework by concentrating on the cases with low confidence of prediction and the model is improved in a targeted manner. The last step is clinical application, which links predictive findings to actionable clinical interventions. They are able to flow prediction into intuitive dashboards and digital workflows to highlight patients at high risk. Furthermore, AI alerting can interface with EHRs to simulate diagnostic scripts whenever predictive patterns are detected. In order to make the system robust, they have to be validated performing extensive tests, including stress tests with real patients under clinical settings. Following a systematic installation process helps to facilitate diagnosis and to minimize the response time substantially in life-threatening conditions such as cardiac arrest where prompt treatment is fundamental to patient's prognosis.

1.2.2 AI-Powered Mental Health and Telemedicine Services

Historically, interventions of mental health have been limited to face to face appointments, often rendering them unavailable as a result of unhealthy attitudes to accessing such services, where such centers are located, or availability of trained therapists. The recent emergence of telehealth has reduced some of these barriers by providing virtual consultation. However, these systems have not been detailed enough for dynamic and personalized care. AI has altered this landscape by creating tools to analyze lifestyle behaviours. Another feature is prediction of degradation in mental health and recommendations for intervention. AI-powered platform for mental health [8] interpret unstructured patient input using natural language processing (NLP) and mood analysis. Physiological information such as written diaries, spoken conversations, or tons of speech and facial expressions are accepted as input. Applications such as Woebot and Wysa commit users to therapeutic interactions. They identify patterns of diseases such as anxiety, depression, and PTB. By analyzing the content and mood of user interactions, these systems provide targeted coping mechanisms and escalate human therapists as needed. Traditional methods have the drawbacks of regular reviews. AI systems can provide continuous monitoring to support early detection of mental health degradation conditions.

1.2.3 Ethical Concerns in Healthcare AI

AI in medicine applications are ethically challenging and potential ethical issues cannot be overlooked. One of the primary concerns is the challenge of algorithmic bias, in which models designed on a dataset of limited diversity will deliver results that discriminate. For instance, AI tool is used to predict the risk of cardiovascular could perform poorly for female patients if most of the training data is from men. Bias found in AI systems not only compromises the quality of patient care but potentially contributes to perpetuating disparities in access to and care received in health systems. These challenges must be addressed with deliberate interventions including the curation of diverse and representative datasets, the use of fairness-aware algorithms, and the establishment of regular audits to detect and correct algorithmic bias [28]. Given that medical data is itself sensitive, privacy and security are of the utmost importance in the integration of AI with healthcare systems. There has been a spate of breaches, hacks and thefts of such patient information from health tech companies in recent years, calling into question how well they can protect patient data.

Federated learning has been identified as a promising means to address these risks. This approach enables ML models to be trained on data sources in a distributed manner, without the requirement for sensitive patient data transfer. In combination with methods like homomorphic encryption or secure multi-party computation, federated learning can protect patient privacy and preserve superior model performance. Such solutions greatly help to instill trust and to promote the ethical acquisition of AI solutions in healthcare settings. The black-box nature of AI model decision-making still stands in the way of its full adoption in clinical practice. Physicians are often reluctant to rely on opaque or 'black-box' algorithms, especially when they cannot understand how certain predictions are made. Explainable AI (XAI) methods [9] address this problem by generating outputs that can in principle be more readily understood by human users. For example, visual saliency maps can be used to cover regions in diagnostic images that highly influence the model's prediction [29]. They have shown how changes to input data could influence the outcome, allowing them to trust decisions made based on AI.

Accountability, when AI tools are involved in diagnostic errors, also presents a challenge, as it increasingly involves multiple parties, system developers, data contributors, and clinical end-users. Regulatory instruments, such as the European Union AI Act, are beginning to address these complexities providing guidance, for instance, on model validation, performance risk, and regulatory compliance. Nevertheless, legislation is often slower than technological innovation, leading to regulatory splits [30]. Healthcare institutions need to develop clear and enforceable institutional policies which set best practice and ethical standards for how to implement AI technologies in the context of patient care. All actors need to integrate ethical considerations at every stage of the life cycle of a system. Such challenges are only met when thorough expertise and full vigilance are met with a cross disciplinary attitude. The world is ultimately waiting for a world where healthcare innovations were both massively on the rise and ethical grounded. This would assist in the universal struggle to keep well.

1.3 AI in Education

1.3.1 AI for Adaptive Learning Systems and Personalized Learning

Artificial Intelligence alters the way knowledge is delivered. It enables an adaptive experience of learning where each student finds supportive material personalized according to one's velocity, perception, and preferences. Thus, this chapter covers topics like main concepts and technologies that are helpful as well as difficulties accompanied by these AI-powered concepts.

1.3.1.1 Introduction of Adaptive Learning Systems

The paradigm shift of education through AI adaptive learning systems [10] makes the dynamic learning experience responsive to the needs of a particular student. It is unlike traditional methods, where everything is standardized for all learners, because adaptive systems [11] continuously analyze performance, strengths, and weaknesses while modifying lesson delivery. Thus, it will not be too challenging nor too simple, thereby creating an optimum learning environment. For example, DreamBox for math or Smart Sparrow for science uses machine learning algorithms to figure out how a student is doing in real time. The platforms can pick up what specific concept the student is failing at and give him customized exercises or explanations to work through that gap. In this way, the experience of learning becomes smooth and riveting as it adapts according to the ability of the learner.

1.3.1.2 AI and Personalized Learning

This can be seen as an application of adaptive systems, in that each part of the learning process will adapt to the uniqueness of the learner. AI supports the educator and system to take into account what the student is cognitively capable of doing. AI supports the goals of an individual that they want to achieve, and what the person knows before setting up a plan for learning. Virtual tutors, chatbots, and intelligent assistants permit real time intervention and feedback [13]. For instance, human-like interfaces have been used in AI-based applications like IBM Watson Tutor, where one-to-one support is provided. Such applications can explain concepts, provide recommendations for further reading, and track progress over time. Considering the fact that these learning systems ensure learners are engaged and in charge of their learning, it has an added advantage. This is especially towards supporting students who have unique requirements or need extra support.

1.3.1.3 Key Technologies Supporting Adaptive and Personalized Learning

Advanced technologies are seen as the success factors of adaptive learning and personalized education. Such systems depend on the machine learning algorithms, which can process data, predict what the student might need, and then make the adjustment to deliver content. NLP enables AI to converse with the learner in a natural language way, which is the best tool for language learning and essay evaluation. Huge amounts of educational data are analyzed to come up with patterns and trends. Such insight into big data creates more efficient learning strategies. Further, cognitive computing, which simulates human thought, takes the scope of personalization systems yet further. Together, these systems create an educational environment that is not only efficient but engaging.

1.3.1.4 Benefits of AI-Powered Adaptive Systems

There are many benefits of AI in education. Adaptive systems increase student engagement because the content is presented according to their interest and ability. This increases better information retention and understanding. In addition, these systems provide access features such as custom formats for students with disabilities or unique learning needs. The other benefit is related to scalability; it can handle large groups of learners in the same course giving differential focus to every student. With ALEKS and Knewton, fantastic results were seen in mathematics education more particularly wherein learning outcomes shoot up significantly due to personalization. Overall, these bridge over the gap between standard and difference in the requirement of newer days. Figure 1.3 represents the AI for Adaptive learning and Personalized learning.

1.3.2 AI-Based Solutions Against Educational Inequalities

1.3.2.1 More Accessible AI Tools

These tools smash barriers to be able to reach, teach, and connect many more learners, particularly those with disabilities, or people from the periphery or un-serviced places. It allows students who have disabilities or whose communication needs prevent them from fully engaging in classroom activities with their peers. Some tools used to support them are screen readers, real-time translators, and even speech-to-text applications. For example, Microsoft Seeing AI and Google Live Transcribe make a visually impaired or hearing-impaired student easy to be integrated into the

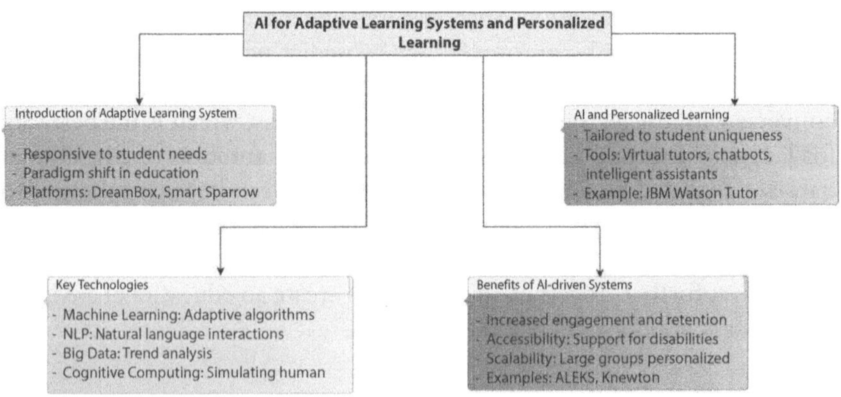

Figure 1.3 Flowchart of AI for adaptive learning and personalized learning.

classroom activities. Most multilingual regions in the world experience restrictions of access of quality education because of language barriers. Students will be able to access learning in their first languages or global content with the help of AI-powered tools like Duolingo and Google Translate. In similar ways, videos and other multimedia materials will also be made available for captioning based on AI. Learning platforms accommodate different formats that may suit varied types of learners. This includes texts available in dyslexia-friendly fonts or even narrations instead of written versions of the presentation for those who prefer hearing. It means every difference between them is accounted for so that learning can be conducted inclusively.

1.3.2.2 Narrowing the Digital Divide

While the digital divide is a challenge to equal education distribution from the rural and lower-income districts, AI is filling this gap. There is scope for adaptation and implementation of resource optimization and innovative solutions to offline learning. It will be easy to point out which regions are less served with the help of AI-based systems. Hence, they will prioritize the flow of educational resources, like inexpensive devices or solar-powered digital hubs, students at remote locations can get access to their learning tools. With the off-line AI platforms including Khan Academy Lite and the low-bandwidth applications, rich content can be made available to education without relying on a constant internet connection. Thus, such tools ensure that these connectivity issues are not presented as hurdles for learning opportunities. Besides, AI algorithms are also involved in the affordable adaptive learning in the process of creating high-quality education tailored to the needs of learners within an underserved community. This AI empowers fair learning for every learner in the world to ensure minimal dependency on steady access to the internet while aligning content with underdeveloped regions.

1.3.2.3 Personalized Learning for Different Learners

One of the major capacities that reduce inequalities is an AI system's ability to personalize education. Traditional teaching lacks mechanisms to address individual student needs, especially for marginalized groups or those with learning disabilities. Similarly, AI systems analyze student data to offer a personalized learning experience. For instance, Squirrel AI and Coursera change the way content is delivered so that it serves every learner's pace, understanding, and preference. This ensures that learners requiring extra help on specific topics receive the relevant exercises and tutorials so that the knowledge gap could be filled. AI virtual tutors and chatbots assist a learner in real-time through questions answered and other learning resources. AI enables the facilitators to allow a diversified learner. Greater insight into students' performance and behaviours allows teachers to provide differentiated instructional techniques. All these occur in such a manner that learning becomes accessible across all types of learners irrespective of their backgrounds.

1.4 AI for Disaster Management and Response

Artificial Intelligence (AI) has emerged as a transformative force in disaster management and response. It improved the efficiency and effectiveness of various processes involved in preparing for, responding to, and recovering from disasters. Integration of AI technology improves tuning for predictive analytics, real-time data processing and auxiliary measurements. This chapter examines the role of AI in disaster management and focuses on predictive analytics for disaster prevention and coordination of aid measures. We have examined the application of AI in disaster management in detail, and an example is shown in Figure 1.4. This example highlights the possibility of improving prognosis, situational awareness and resource

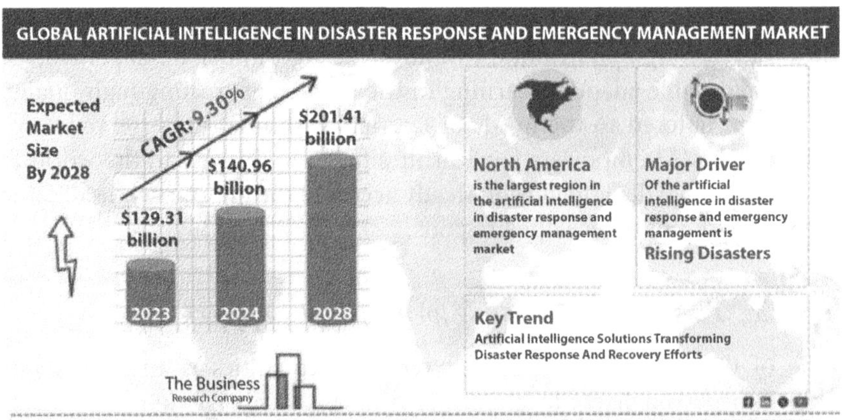

Figure 1.4 Artificial intelligence in disaster response and emergency management – key trends [14].

allocation. Research shows that AI can analyze large data records, including satellite images and weather patterns, to predict potential disasters in greater detail [15]. Furthermore, AI systems improve real-time decision-making through rapid processing of detailed data and provide implementable insights into disaster response teams [16]. AI technologies such as natural language (NLP) machine learning and algorithms for processing are increasingly being used to assess weaknesses, optimize resource distribution, and automate emergency prevention tasks [17]. Furthermore, advances in robotics and drone technology have made it possible for AI-driven tools to perform dangerous tasks during disasters.

1.4.1 Predictive Analytics for Disaster Preparedness

Predictions include the use of statistical algorithms and machine learning techniques to identify potential future outcomes based on historical data. In disaster management (Figure 1.5), this capacity is very important in hoping for natural disasters such as earthquakes, floods, and hurricanes.

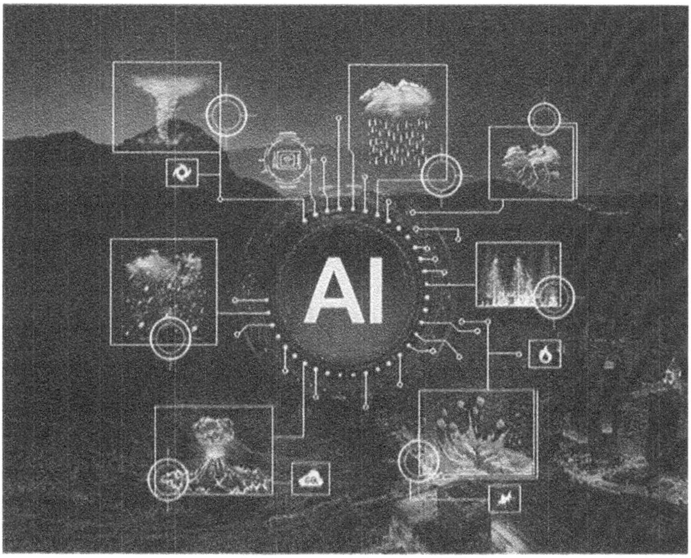

Figure 1.5 AI emerges as a game-changer in disaster management [18].

1.4.1.1 Predictive Analytics Application

1. Natural Disaster Prediction: Analyze model earthquake data for machine learning to identify patterns that indicate potential earthquakes. This provides early warnings to communities to evacuate.
2. Hurricane Tracking: AI systems use weather data to predict hurricane routes and intensity, allowing for rapid preparation by authorities.
3. Flood Forecast: AI can estimate precipitation patterns and analyze soil moisture levels in predicted floods. This information is extremely important for preventive evacuation and resource allocation.
4. Predicting Disease Outbreak: In a post-creation scenario, AI can analyze environmental conditions to predict potential outbreaks of disease, allowing for a rapid response to public health.

Therefore, predictive analysis offers many advantages for disaster management by enabling healthier and more aggressive decisions [25]. One of the most important advantages is its ability to provide early warnings and enable authorities and communities to respond quickly to upcoming disasters before the situation escalates. Predictive models also help identify the most susceptible regions and enable better strategies for long-term planning and risk reduction. This ability to predict and prepare for disaster is a slow shift from reactive to aggressive disaster management, providing a more resilient framework for conservation of communities and cultural heritage.

1.4.2 AI in Coordination of Relief Efforts

Effective coordination during disaster responses is important to ensure that resources are used efficiently and that affected groups of populations receive support at a good time. AI technology enables this adjustment by optimizing logistics and improving communication between various interest groups.

1.4.2.1 Key Contributions of AI in Coordination

1. Resource Allocation: AI algorithms analyze disaster severity to prioritize population density, geographical challenges, and

areas where support is needed. This ensures that medical and rescue staff is managed when they are most urgently needed.
2. Real-time Data Integration: During the catastrophe, AI systems can integrate real-time data from several sources, such as social media posts, emergency calls, and sensor networks, to ensure situational awareness. In this way, the responder can dynamically adapt the strategy under current conditions.
3. Automatic Emergency Response: AI accelerates automation of emergency transportation processes by analyzing emergency calls and providing responders in critical locations without human intervention. This significantly reduces reaction times.
4. Virtual Assistants and Chatbots: These tools help spread information to affected population groups and answer questions related to security measures or availability of resources. They provide timely updates that keep local governments up to date during the crisis.

The integration of AI into disaster management represents significant advances in how businesses prepare, respond and recover from disasters. Predictive analytics improves motivation through early warnings and predictions that save lives. In the meantime, AI-powered regulating devices optimize supplemental measurements by optimizing resource allocation and improving communication between stakeholders. While technology is developing, the possibilities for AI in disaster management will likely continue to emerge. Ongoing research and development will effectively use these skills and address ethical considerations in relation to data protection and algorithm distortions. Ultimately, the use of AI in disaster management not only improves immediate responses, but also helps to build a resistant community that can withstand future challenges.

1.5 AI in Culture

Artificial intelligence (AI) has revolutionized a variety of sectors, and its application to culture is particularly prominent. While businesses are developing, preserving cultural heritage and promoting art and creativity has become extremely important. AI technology is used to improve efforts to maintain cultural conservation and to promote artistic efforts (Figure 1.6).

Figure 1.6 Art preservation where emphasis is provided on protection and restoration of heritage pieces [19].

This chapter examines how AI contributes to these realms and highlights his role in ensuring inheritance and promoting creativity.

The crossroads between AI and conservation is gaining popularity over recent years. Recent papers are showing that AI is poised to help preserve cultural heritage, streamline documentation and make its mark on creative expression. For example, machine learning models are able to analyze and digitally reconstruct depictions of old or damaged historical artifacts, thus exposing details of such artifacts that have eroded through centuries [20]. Moreover, NLP tools are now used for documenting oral histories in order to avoid the loss of such intangible cultural narratives for future generations [21]. Artificial intelligence is emerging as a technology for facilitating human experiences in arts by understanding the audience preferences and creating cultural experiences that engage and make arts more accessible [22]. Despite these promising applications, the integration of AI into cultural domains introduces ethical challenges—particularly regarding the protection of sensitive data and the authenticity of digital representations. As such, it is essential to adopt a thoughtful and balanced implementation strategy that respects both technological innovation and cultural integrity [23].

1.5.1 Enhancement of Cultural Preservation Using AI

1.5.1.1 Digital Archiving and Restoration

Technologies such as computer vision allow for the analysis and improvement of images of old manuscripts, paintings and sculptures (Figure 1.7). For example, AI algorithms can identify texts that are surprised by the manuscript, allowing scientists to access previously unreadable information [20]. This process not only preserves physical artifacts, but also enriches academic research. AI technology extends beyond the text identification of manuscripts to reconstruct incomplete artifacts. Machine learning models can predict missing sections of painting, sculpture, or manuscript based on patterns observed in existing parts. For example, neural networks trained in similar artworks suggest how to recover horns of paintings and broken pieces of sculptures [27]. This process allows historians to make healthy decisions and ensure that the repair is as authentic as possible.

Historical artifacts such as paintings and textiles often lose their original colour over time due to exposure to light and environmental factors. AI tools can analyze chemical composition and historical data to restore the original colour with remarkable accuracy. These restored colour palettes provide historians and viewers with a more authentic understanding of the original appearance of the artifact. AI also is used to change catalogued and enhance it artificiality. Traditional archiving methods rely on

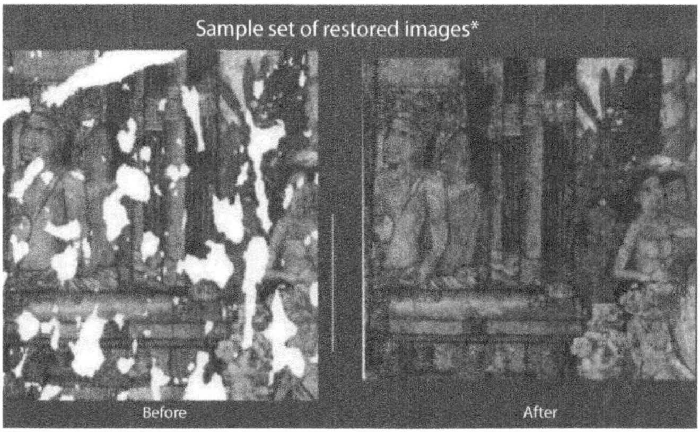

Figure 1.7 Process of restoration of the ancient artwork [24].

manual tagging and classification. This is slow and error-prone. Artificial intelligence (AI) mediated image recognition tools can facilitate this task because they can accurately recognize and categorize objects. The system is able to grasp a style related to a historical period or culture, so museums and archives around the world can establish a database with information.

High-resolution 3D digital scanning combined with AI-rendering technologies has made it possible to create 3D immersive virtual museum visits. They enable users to engage with high-fidelity digital recreations of artifacts—zooming in to view fine detail, spinning models around for a full look, and delving into surrounding background information. These kind of virtual archives are crucial to enable an opening up of access to cultural heritage, especially for those who cannot go to museums or historical sites in person.

It also helps in the conservation of artifacts through improved predictive conservation protocols. Through an analysis of data from environmental sensors and historical data, AI systems are able to predict potential threats to collections, including humidity, temperature changes, or air pollutants. This predictive tool allows cultural institutions to take preventative conservation action in order to prevent their collections from becoming visually damaging. Yet, applying AI to cultural digitization and restoration comes with its own set of challenges. Concerns around data accuracy, ethical representation and the limitations of the technology persist and present challenges that are faced in deploying such tools in heritage management with due care.

1.5.1.2 Case Study: Google Arts and Culture

In collaboration with museums around the world, Google Arts & Culture is deploying artificial intelligence to create digital copies of artworks. This model aims to offer online ultra-high-resolution downloading, allowing the users to remotely scrutinize fine objects details [20].

1.5.1.3 Preserving Oral Traditions

Indigenous knowledge and oral history are the essence of cultural heritage, but it is also fragile and is threatened to disappear. Artificial Intelligence, especially in the form of natural language processing (NLP), provides formidable capabilities for capturing, transcribing, and translating these stories. Through digitizing oral tradition, AIs contribute to preserve for next generations their belief in cultural memory and identity [21]. Apart from preservation, AI can also examine the linguistic structure of the stories, providing a window into how language and culture have transformed over time. Shifts in vocabulary, grammar, and pronunciation patterns can reveal how societies have responded to external influences such as colonization, migration, or advancements in technology. This helps anthropologists and linguists resist cultural exchange dynamics and traditions. AI technology can not only receive stories, but also realize the oral traditions of modern target groups. Virtual reality (VR) and augmented reality (AR) together with AI-supported technology can restore immersive experiences of storytelling, allowing users to cope with these traditions in their original environment. The VR experience could potentially acquire a traditional village where the oldest people tell the usual stories. This allows for the context and importance of these stories, as well as the younger generations and people from other cultures.

Another important application of AI is this role in reviving an endangered language that often embraces oral traditions. Many Indigenous languages lack comprehensive written records. This is verbally due to the main mode of transmission. The AI-powered voice model helps in developing interactive language learning apps, and other educational equipment, ensuring that both language and its associated stories survive. Community commitment is critical to the success of initiatives to stay AI-driven. Collaboration with cultural managers, local historians and storytellers ensure that AI tools reflect the nuances and values embedded in oral traditions. Collaboration promotes trust and ensures that the digitalization process respects the intellectual property and cultural integrity of the community.

AI can also play a transformative role in democratizing access to oral traditions. According to digitized, translated stories, these stories can be shared worldwide for the use of intercultural understanding and appreciation. Institutions can include these resources in their curriculum, exposing different worldviews to students and enriching cultural knowledge. Museums and cultural organizations can curate dynamic exhibits with AI, which present oral stories in addition to visual and historical artifacts. One concern is to ensure that AI systems are trained on various data records to avoid cultural bias. To prevent homogenization, unique linguistic and cultural characteristics of oral traditions must be accurately presented. Conservation efforts must ensure that their voices are central to the process, including the communities in which these stories originate.

1.5.1.4 *Predictive Analytics for Heritage Protection*

AI prediction skills can also help protect cultural heritage from threats such as climate change and urbanization. Machine learning models can analyze environmental data and predict the risk of heritage websites. UNESCO uses AI to monitor land use changes at global heritage sites and enable proactive maintenance strategies [20]. This approach reduces the possibility of irreversible damage to culturalists caused by people or ecologically or humanly. Developments in sustainable urban planning, with the preservation of cultural orientation points, can occur simultaneously [26]. Such positive measures contribute to the longevity and accessibility of cultural heritage for future generations.

1.5.2 AI's Role in Responsible Promotion of Arts and Creativity

1.5.2.1 *Enhancing Accessibility*

AI technology improves accessibility to cultural content by personalizing experiences based on user preferences. The recommended systems run by machine learning analyze user interaction with the ART platform and propose related art or performance tasks [22]. This democratization of access encourages a stronger investigation of the arts.

1.5.2.2 *Supporting Artists through AI Tools*

AI tools are increasingly being used by artists to expand creative opportunities. For example, generative algorithms allow artists to create unique pieces by entering specific parameters or styles. This collaboration between human creativity and machine learning opens up new ways of artistic expression [23]. Artists can explore unknown territory with AI as a focal man. Generated art allows artists to enter parameters such as colour, shape, topic, and AI tools create unique outputs that can stimulate new directions. These works combine the unpredictable data control skills of AI with the intentionality of human design that leads to innovative work that goes beyond the limits of traditional art.

AI can help improve existing arts processes. Tools such as neuron-style transfer allow artists to apply the properties of artwork and photographs to another. This technique allows the creator, photograph, painting, or digital design to reinterpret a completely new style. Changing the modern landscape photography resembles Van Gogh's paintings, allowing you to combine modern images with classic aesthetics. AI can also communicate understanding of authors work and audience prices. By analyzing patterns of successful works or trends in public interest, artists can make sound decisions about their creative direction. This merger of data-controlled versions and artistic intuition leads to a deeper sounding piece, while simultaneously maintaining the artist's unique vision.

AI tools accessibility is democratizing the creation of art. The platform provides a user-friendly interface for artists who minimize technical know-how. This allows a wider range of creators to experiment with AI and engage them in works that pose barriers between technology and traditional art. Advanced algorithms can analyze and restore damaged work. This satisfies the lack of detail and at the same time preserves the integrity of the original. AI can also be used to replicate lost artworks and provide insight into historical works that no longer exist. This application not only preserves cultural heritage, but also conveys a more comprehensive understanding of artistic evolution. However, the rise of ART's AI also raises questions about authors and originality. If an AI model creates an important part of a work of art, who has the final product? Artists, engineers and right-wing experts must work together to remove these concerns and ensure that integrating AI into ART respects intellectual property and promotes innovation at the same time.

1.5.2.3 Case Study: DALL-E

OpenAI's DALL-E is an example of an AI model that generates images from text descriptions. Such tools allow artists to visually study concepts without traditional limitations [23].

1.5.2.4 Ethical Considerations in Promotion

It is important to resolve ethical concerns related to authors and expression during the ads of art by AI. The use of AI-generated ART raises questions about intellectual property rights and authenticity of creative work. While AI is used for promotions for responsible implementation, it is important to protect artists' rights [22]. The integration of AI in cultural conservation and promotion represents considerable advances in securing our collective heritage and promoting creativity. With digital archives, recovery efforts and preservation of oral traditions, AI will improve its ability to protect cultural artifacts for future generations. By improving artist accessibility and support with innovative tools, AI plays a key role in promoting the arts. As we continue to explore the possibilities of AI in culture, it is important to carefully navigate ethical considerations. Compensation for technological advancements in terms of artistic integrity ensures that the benefits of AI are positive about our cultural landscape.

1.6 Conclusion and Future Work

1.6.1 Conclusion

Access to high-quality learning materials is democratized with AI, and lessons are suitable for all inclusive students with different disabilities and backgrounds. Healthcare has been accelerated in relation to AI diagnosis and predictive models. There is rapid disease identification with optimized pathways, which saves thousands. There was no lack of engagement for the environmental sustainability arena either because applications of AI are introduced into climate modeling and optimization of waste management. In this case, that also brings with it benefits. AI has turned disaster management into an early warning system. It facilitates fast data-driven decisions when any disaster happens. It has transformed governance and public service delivery since there is proper allocation of resources and the dexterity to detect fraud. For starters, AI for social good does come with its very set of challenges. For one, data privacy and the danger of algorithmic bias could form an ethical challenge. This is also a question of digital divide as yet another limitation of AI technologies to underserved communities. All this notwithstanding, stories of AI success in social good speak to the power that technology can bring into existence.

1.6.2 Future Directions for AI in Social Good

Indeed, there are various drawbacks to adaptive and personalized systems. One, the major concern would be regarding data privacy. As indicated above, such systems heavily depend upon mass-scale data collection. They thereby seek severe measures of security in the dimension of data in order not to scare prospective and potential users. Secondly, the expensive development and maintenance thereof makes it unaccessible to a lesser funded institution. Algorithmic bias [12] is another challenge as AI systems inadvertently carry forward the biases in the training data and provide unequal outcomes to certain students. The role of the teacher has also changed. They must maintain the traditional ways of teaching along with using technology while at the same time maintaining the human interaction at the center of learning. Among the most popular trends is gamification – game-like elements infused into educational content to make learning more engaging. Another area that has emerged is real-time emotional analysis, where AI is able to detect a student's emotional state and accordingly adjust lessons dynamically. These AI-based systems would also ensure lifelong learning, and continuous professional learning would become the reality for professionals, retirees among many other aspirants to upskill. Cross-cultural adaptations of these educational tools will also ensure targeting diverse populations hence language and cultural barriers will be eliminated. Such innovations have shown the potential that AI has in democratizing education.

Therefore, even as the scope for applications will increase with the arising new opportunities in society, these advancements with AI technologies will most probably demand suitable legal frameworks. Other integrated and emerging technologies that AI puts together will enhance the transparency and accountability from all other sectors. Some examples include those of in supply chains, public health surveillance and monitoring ecosystems as well as the ecological environment. Most common of this includes traceable systems powered by the blockchain on AI. Definitely, a powerful driving force behind this particular kind of development in AI for good is the global war on climate change. It will predict climate events with the advanced machine learning algorithm, and impacts can be reduced. Machines will provide improvements in renewable energy systems through learning and make innovations relevant to agricultural fields like sustainable agriculture. Solutions using AI power and applied into the urban design and development such as in smart cities management systems regarding traffic.

This future care will be based on more powerful AI models applied to genomics, imaging, and history for treating medication among patients. The increased telehealth applications with modern wearables promise to fill up more types of gaps identified in a delivery system for current care particularly at inaccessible places around the globe. AI applications will assist in greater transformational growth in education to offer more immersive learning experiences. Adaptive learning platforms across various devices will alter the form of learning and such tools might meet various needs and prepare students toward the digital economy. Ethical AI, along with responsible governance, determines AI futures for social good. Such aspects include privacy frameworks over data, reduction of algorithmic biases, and more transparent AI decision-making processes. This is the type of global partnerships established among governments, academia, non-profits, and the private sectors, where there is cooperation on all-around inclusive sustainable development in AI. This has no relation to the future. What is relevant here is rather how technological sophistication arises due to the capability of AI, fitting into what humanity wishes it to be: equity, sustainability, and progress, and hence, that it is inclusive, and ethically implemented, which is also based on the cross-disciplinary collaborations.

AI disclosure statement: The author confirms that no artificial intelligence (AI)-generated content or AI-assisted writing tools were used in the preparation of this chapter (including summaries and the abstract). All text, analysis, and conclusions are the result of the author's original work.

References

1. Rajpurkar, P., Irvin, J., Zhu, K., Yang, B., Mehta, H., Duan, T., ... & Ng, A.Y., CheXNet: Radiologist-level pneumonia detection on chest X-rays with deep learning, *arXiv preprint arXiv:1711.05225*, 2017.
2. Buolamwini, J. and Gebru, T., Gender Shades: Intersectional accuracy disparities in commercial gender classification. *Proceedings of the Conference on Fairness, Accountability, and Transparency*, 2018.
3. Adadi, A. and Berrada, M., Peeking inside the black-box: A survey on explainable artificial intelligence (XAI). *IEEE Access*, 6, 52138–52160, 2018.
4. Rolph, J., Hu, Z., Chen, W., Predictive analytics for disaster risk management: Applications and methodologies. *Int. J. Disaster Risk Reduct.*, 47, 101541, 2020.
5. Nguyen, T.T., Rahimi, A., Yap, Q.J., AI applications in COVID-19 response: From diagnostics to treatment, 2021.
6. Samanta, K., Sandeep, R., Sahu, Yashan, N., Dande, M., Blockchain and AI Integration: Transforming Transparency in Supply Chain Management. *Eur. Econ. Lett.*, 14, 1238–1247, 2024, 10.52783/eel.v14i3.1885.
7. Banerjee, I., Ling, Y., Chen, M.C., Hasan, S.A., Langlotz, C.P., Moradzadeh, N., Chapman, B., Amrhein, T., Mong, D., Rubin, D.L., Farri, O., Comparative effectiveness of convolutional neural network (CNN) and recurrent neural network (RNN) architectures for radiology text report classification. *Artif. Intell. Med.*, *97*, 79–88, 2019.
8. Kwok, W.H., Zhang, Y., Wang, G., Artificial intelligence in perinatal mental health research: A scoping review. *Comput. Biol. Med.*, 177, 108685, 2024.
9. Tielman, M.L., Suárez-Figueroa, M.C., Jönsson, A., Neerincx, M.A., Siebert, L.C., Explainable AI for all-A roadmap for inclusive XAI for people with cognitive disabilities. *Technol. Soc.*, *79*, 102685, 2024.

10. Essa, S.G., Celik, T., Human-Hendricks, N.E., Personalized adaptive learning technologies based on machine learning techniques to identify learning styles: A systematic literature review. *IEEE Access, 11*, 48392–48409, 2023.
11. Liang, J., Hare, R., Chang, T., Xu, F., Tang, Y., Wang, F.Y., Peng, S., Lei, M., Student modeling and analysis in adaptive instructional systems. *IEEE Access, 10*, 59359–59372, 2022.
12. Murtaza, M., Ahmed, Y., Shamsi, J.A., Sherwani, F., Usman, M., AI-based personalized e-learning systems: Issues, challenges, and solutions. *IEEE Access, 10*, 81323–81342, 2022.
13. Zharmukhanbetov, S. and Singh, C.P., November. Enhancing Flipped Classroom Engagement and Personalized Learning Through AI-Powered Adaptive Content Delivery, in: *2023 3rd International Conference on Technological Advancements in Computational Sciences (ICTACS)*, IEEE, pp. 1411–1416, 2023.
14. HashStudioz, AI in disaster management: How artificial intelligence is saving lives in emergencies. Retrieved December 26, 2024, from https://www.hashstudioz.com/blog/ai-in-disaster-management-how-artificial-intelligence-is-saving-lives-in-emergencies/.
15. Sun, W., Bocchini, P., Davison, B.D., Applications of artificial intelligence for disaster management. *J. Disaster Res.*, 15, 2, 1–12, 2020.
16. Ipleaders, An overview on AI in disaster response, 2021. Retrieved December 26, 2024, from https://blog.ipleaders.in/an-overview-on-ai-in-disaster-response/.
17. HashStudioz, AI emerges as a game-changer in disaster management: From reactive to proactive, 2024. Retrieved December 26, 2024, from https://www.hashstudioz.com/blog/ai-in-disaster-management-how-artificial-intelligence-is-saving-lives-in-emergencies/.
18. Market Research Future, 2024 artificial intelligence in disaster response and emergency management market overview: Key insights on size, share, and trends, 2024. Retrieved December 26, 2024.
19. Artificial Paintings, AI in art preservation: Revolutionizing the protection and restoration of cultural heritage, 2024, June 20. Retrieved December 26, 2024, from https://artificialpaintings.com/blog/2024/06/20/ai-in-art-preservation-revolutionizing-the-protection-and-restoration-of-cultural-heritage/.
20. ITMunch, The role of AI in cultural preservation and heritage, n.d.. Retrieved December 26, 2024, from https://itmunch.com/the-role-of-ai-in-cultural-preservation-and-heritage/.
21. Ultralytics, AI in art and cultural heritage conservation, n.d.. Retrieved December 26, 2024, from https://www.ultralytics.com/blog/ai-in-art-and-cultural-heritage-conservation.
22. Das, B.R., Maringanti, H.B., Dash, N.S., The role of artificial intelligence in the preservation of culture and heritage, in: *Artificial Intelligence and Cultural Heritage*, pp. 251–267, Taylor & Francis, 2023, https://www.taylorfrancis.com/chapters/edit/10.4324/9781003332183-16/

role-artificial-intelligence-preservation-culture-heritage-bishwa-ranjan-das-hima-bindu-maringanti-niladri-sekhar-dash.

23. Ranjan, S. and Kumar, A., AI and cultural heritage preservation in India, ResearchGate, 2023, https://www.researchgate.net/publication/378302770_AI_AND_CULTURAL_HERITAGE_PRESERVATION_IN_INDIA.
24. Economic Times, How AI and deep learning can bring ancient cultural heritage of India to life and preserve it for eternity, 2021. Retrieved December 26, 2024.
25. Albahri, A.S., Khaleel, Y.L., Habeeb, M.A., Ismael, R.D., Hameed, Q.A., Deveci, M., Homod, R.Z., Albahri, O.S., Alamoodi, A.H., Alzubaidi, L., A systematic review of trustworthy artificial intelligence applications in natural disasters. *Comput. Electr. Eng.*, *118*, 109409, 2024.
26. Chen, Y., Zhang, L., Dong, Q., Using natural language processing to evaluate local conservation text: A study of 624 documents from 303 sites of the World Heritage Cities Programme. *J. Cult. Heritage*, *70*, 259–270, 2024.
27. Mishra, M. and Lourenço, P.B., Artificial intelligence-assisted visual inspection for cultural heritage: State-of-the-art review. *J. Cult. Heritage*, *66*, 536–550, 2024.
28. Pathni, R.K., Beyond algorithms: Ethical implications of AI in healthcare. *Med. J. Armed Forces India*, 2024.
29. Esmaeilzadeh, P., Challenges and strategies for wide-scale artificial intelligence (AI) deployment in healthcare practices: A perspective for healthcare organizations. *Artif. Intell. Med.*, *151*, 102861, 2024.
30. Mennella, C., Maniscalco, U., De Pietro, G., Esposito, M., Ethical and regulatory challenges of AI technologies in healthcare: A narrative review. *Heliyon*, 2024.

2

Balancing Innovation and Patient Safety: Ethical AI Deployment in Healthcare

Prajakta R. Patil[1]*, Sachin S. Mali[2], Riya R. Patil[2] and Dhanashree R. Davare[2]

[1]*Department of Pharmaceutics, Annasaheb Dange College of B. Pharmacy, Ashta, India*
[2]*Ashokrao Mane College of Pharmacy, Department of Pharmaceutics, Peth-Vadgaon, Kolhapur, India*

Abstract
The deployment of artificial intelligence (AI) in the medical field provides a revolutionary opportunity to enhance diagnostic accuracy, speed up clinical processes, and enhance patient care. In order to safeguard patient safety and confidence, however, use of AI systems also poses challenging ethical, legal, and operational problems that must be addressed. The moral concerns of AI applications in healthcare, including bias, accountability, transparency, and privacy of data, are critically discussed in this chapter. It provides strategic guidelines for achieving the balance between innovation and patient-focused care, highlights actual case studies, and provides best practices to adopt AI responsibly. To help stakeholders in the ethical use of innovative AI technologies that are patient-safe, the chapter emphasizes the importance of interdisciplinary coordination, continuous monitoring, and respect for ethical standards.

Keywords: Artificial intelligence in healthcare, ethical AI, patient safety, healthcare innovation, bias in AI, transparency, data privacy, accountability

2.1 Introduction

Artificial intelligence is basically the term used for a machine or software that exhibits the capability to simulate intelligent human behavior, instantaneous calculations, problem-solving, and an evaluation of new data based on previously assessed data [1]. AI in healthcare: Use of algorithms

**Corresponding author*: prajaktapatil4601@gmail.com

Manish Kumar, Nitigya Sambyal, Leena Priyadarshini Singh, Ramasamy V. and S. Balamurugan (eds.) Responsible AI: Principles and Practices, (29–68) © 2026 Scrivener Publishing LLC

and models, among other advanced computational techniques, to analyze complex medical data which are supportive of clinical decisions while automatically or semi-automatically automating various processes related to healthcare. AI systems may be designed to simulate human intelligence in performing tasks like disease diagnosis, prediction of outcomes of patients, and optimization of healthcare operations. Therefore, health care will benefit from greatly enhanced accuracy, efficiency, and accessibility by integrating AI into the healthcare system. AI applications have revolutionized the medical field in healthcare, including biological extensive data analysis, laboratory diagnosis, treatment, imaging and electronic medical records (EMR), enhancing physician intelligence, new drug discovery, preventive and precision medicine, and speeding up procedures, data storage, and access for health organizations [2]. Healthcare is one of those industries highly revolutionized in the today's fast-changing world of technology. Even though tremendous progress has been achieved in AI in communities and its possible improvements in the therapeutic process, not every community can afford it. New technology cannot be accessed in many developing and low-income countries. It is worth mentioning that using AI involves some complexities and controversy, such as ethical dilemmas, informed consent, privacy, and data protection, social inequality, medical counseling, empathy, and sympathy. Thus, healthcare professionals and specialists should consider the four principles of medical ethics namely autonomy, beneficence, nonmaleficence, and justice, which apply to every aspect of healthcare before utilizing artificial intelligence [3].

The term "Responsible AI in health care" refers to the moral and responsible application of AI technology to enhance diagnosis accuracy, improve patient results, and accelerate the processing of medical procedures. Handling patient data containing identifiable and sensitive information must respect regulations such as HIPAA and GDPR [4]. Other AI governance documents provide comprehensive guidelines for promoting responsible AI in healthcare, such as the FDA's SaMD document, WHO's Ethics and Governance of AI for Health, and the jointly identified Good Machine Learning Practice for Medical Device Development: Guiding Principles from the FDA, Health Canada, and the UK's Medicines and Healthcare Products Regulatory Agency (MHRA). The chapter discusses the role of AI in healthcare while keeping in mind all ethical considerations that play a vital role in healthcare systems.

The Major AI Technologies in Use in Healthcare

- **Machine Learning (ML):** ML is an application of AI, which makes the computers learn from the data and predict without being programmed. Application areas for ML algorithms in health care include predictive analytics such as the forecasting of disease outbreak or patient risk [5].
- **NLP:** NLP enables AI to read and write human language. It can translate words and their meanings. This allows extracting information from EHRs, creating platforms for a chatbot that can talk to patients, and even aids in making clinical decisions [6].
- **Robotics:** Robotics is employed in healthcare when it comes to using robots in surgeries, rehabilitation, and patient care. The use of the robotic surgical systems, for instance, provides high accuracy with minimally invasive methods, and thus results in better patient outcomes [7].

2.1.1 Prominent Applications of AI in Healthcare

AI is applied in countless healthcare applications such as:

- **Diagnosis:** The AI-based tools also assist doctors to provide accurate diagnoses for instance, an identification of a tumor from an image in the medical field [8].
- **Predictive Analytics:** AI is used for predicting patient outcomes, which includes the potential readmission of the patient and likelihood of developing any chronic diseases as well [5].
- **Operational Efficiency:** AI is optimizing the ways in which health care runs, namely, in saving administrative costs, means of managing hospital resources, and thus on the whole patient experience [9].

2.1.2 The Need for Ethical and Responsible Use

I. Ethical Considerations in AI in Healthcare Integration

AI in healthcare needs to be designed and implemented with greater ethical awareness to avoid perpetuating historical injustices, maintaining confidentiality of the patient, and distributing health facilities equitably across groups. When poorly designed, algorithms put into AI systems can play the vicious cycle of worsening such factors as racial, gender, or socio-economic disparities in health [10]. As shown in Figure 2.1, ethical AI should, therefore, advance the objectives of equity and fairness in healthcare while technological development avails benefits for all patients.

- **Bias in AI Models:** The unintended biases are continuously reinforced by AI systems if they are trained on data that does not present enough variety or even lacks it. Such data applied in medical AI would most likely come from only one racial or ethnic group and will not do very well with patients who are not within that group. Such systems tend to arrive at biased decisions on treatment [10].
- **Privacy and Security:** AI methods generate a large amount of personal health data, which raises data privacy and security concerns. They assure that the designed systems should be transparent, along with strict regulatory frameworks in place to prevent misuse or breach of patients' information [11].

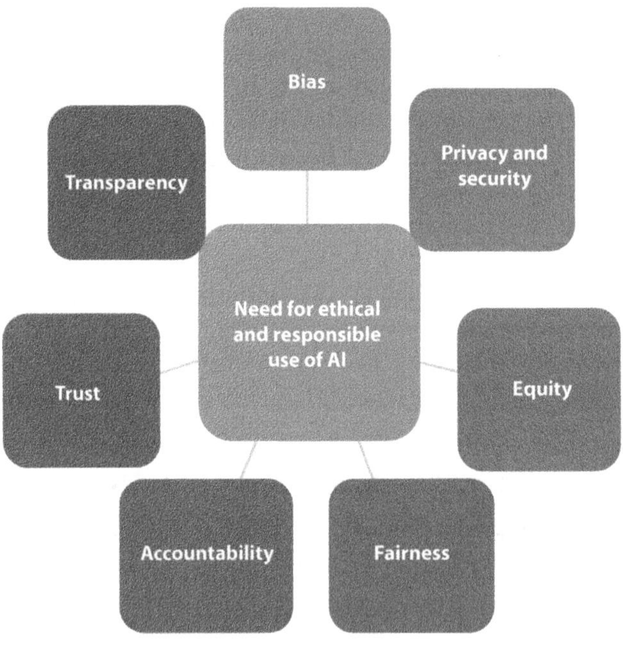

Figure 2.1 Need for ethical and responsible use of AI in healthcare.

II. Innovation, Equity, Transparency, and Trust in Balance

Innovation in AI technologies has to be fast, but with speed comes equity and transparency. Stakeholders, patients, healthcare providers, and policymakers should be assured that AI is not one group's gain at the other's expense, that it is reliable and accountable, and therefore trusted and embraced throughout healthcare.

- **Equity:** Avoiding the biasing of certain groups while others are disadvantaged by AI technologies. That means inclusive algorithms and, more importantly, representation of diverse populations in the training data.
- **Transparency**: AI system decision-making processes should be comprehensible and explainable, at least to the patient and clinician, in order to instill trust. Explainability ensures that recommendations by an AI are not perceived as "black boxes" and instead can be examined for errors and biases.
- **Trust:** Trust is the most critical requirement for the adoption of AI in healthcare. The public confidence can be enabled by transparent development practice, clear communication of AI capabilities and its limitations, and robust regulatory oversight [12].

III. Fairness, Transparency, and Accountability of AI Healthcare Practices

The correct ethical principles guiding AI's deployment in healthcare would be fairness, transparency, and accountability.

- Fairness ensures that AI does not sustain or aggravate health inequities. This means the models must be fair, thereby reducing bias in predictions or suggesting treatments.
- Transparency refers to making AI algorithms understandable to the various stakeholders. This would mean coming out with clear explanations of how decisions are made such that healthcare providers and patients can trust what the system outputs.
- Liability would then fall upon the developers or healthcare providers who deploy the AI system if it got something wrong or caused harm to a person. Again, some clear rulings on liability and oversight are inevitable in this case to protect patients' rights.

2.2 The Promise of AI in Healthcare

2.2.1 Improving Patient Care and Operational Efficiency

I. AI-Driven Diagnostics

It increases the accuracy of diagnosis and reduces chances of human errors. Especially, in radiology and pathology, diagnostic technologies have a lot of promise because the AI component can ensure accuracy without the chances of human error. AI models, especially deep learning algorithms, can do precision analysis on medical images, for example, X-rays, MRIs, CT scans. These systems are sensitive to anomalies that might have otherwise passed unnoticed by human clinicians, like tumors, fractures, or changes in the progression of a disease. For example, AI-based radiology systems have been known to match up with or sometimes even outstrip their human radiologist counterparts when it comes to specific conditions, such as breast cancer or lung cancer [8]. The AI in pathology would also enhance the accuracy of diagnosing a disease from tissue samples since the patterns that would otherwise not be detected by human observation can be observed [13].

AI in radiology was applied to improve the detection of breast cancers. One study revealed how AI-based algorithms greatly reduced false-positive and false-negative diagnoses when evaluating mammograms [14].

II. Predictive Analytics: Predicting Patients at Risk and Treatment Outcomes

AI predictive analytics may help improve patient care by identifying disease, even before symptoms arise, those at risk for specific health conditions. Some examples are chronic diseases such as diabetes, heart disease, or stroke. Predictive models using medical history, lifestyle information, and genetic data could indicate those most likely to develop a given condition, thereby opening opportunities for early intervention. AI methods processing data from EHRs or wearables predict patient outcomes, supports personalized treatment planning, thus improving patient health management, and minimizing readmissions to the hospital [5].

Machine Learning Model-Application of Machine Learning model at the time of sepsis prediction in ICU, using EHR data, has led to less mortality because it can perform early interventions through catching the chances of sepsis in time [15].

III. Health Operating System Optimization: Streamlining of Administrative Healthcare Procedures and Optimizing Resource Usage
Healthcare also becomes efficient with AI because it uses automation for administrative work, including scheduling, billing, and management of patient records. Since AI reduces the administrative burden that healthcare workers will experience, it leaves more time for care. This is also due to optimizing resource allocation based on predictions of a patient volume to help healthcare facilities staff, equipment, and beds appropriately in order to avoid a long waiting time and ensure proper patient flow in healthcare facilities. For example, predictive AI-based systems for hospital admission allow for better resource planning and decisions on staffing [16].

AI chatbots are increasingly used for automating scheduling and reminders of patient appointments to reduce human error and workload for administrators [17].

2.2.2 Expanding Access to Healthcare

I. Role of AI in Rendering Accessible Healthcare to the Underserved or Distant Areas
AI technologies can really be a necessity when it comes to providing healthcare in underdeveloped or remote areas where a qualified medical professional is rarely seen. Health care may thereby be delivered more effectively and to a higher accuracy without even having to see healthcare professionals directly through their deployment in diagnostic tools, telemedicine, and remote monitoring. Mobile health applications based on AI aid in diagnosis, provides consultation, or monitors patients from remote locations that empower health care services to be reached out to populations who do not gain frequent access to hospital care [18].

AI-based diagnostic technology has been used in rural regions of developing nations to detect tuberculosis, thus providing the patient with early treatment without even having relevant skilled staff [19].

II. AI-Powered Telemedicine and Remote Patient Monitoring
With the application of AI by telemedicine platforms and remote patient monitoring technologies, the dispensation of healthcare shifts to an entirely new dimension. Telehealth services now afford AI the capacity to triage patient symptoms, treat based on recommendations, and even follow up on ongoing conditions without a physical visit to a healthcare facility. Coupling with remote monitoring devices as well as sophisticated

algorithms, heart rate, blood glucose or oxygen levels can be monitored for any anomalies, with alerts generated to healthcare providers. These developments facilitate more reliable care and reduce the time a patient has to spend in the hospital, thus making the treatment of chronic diseases much easier and even more feasible for the patients or those staying at distant locations [20].

In telemedicine, AI has enabled faster diagnosis of COVID-19 infection, particularly in the remote sub-districts, by analyzing symptoms as well as providing virtual consultations [21].

2.3 Ethical Challenges in AI

2.3.1 Fairness and Bias in AI Algorithms

Like any AI technology, AI systems in healthcare inherit biases present in their training data. This section discusses the nature of algorithmic bias, its implications on healthcare outcomes, and methods to mitigate these issues.

I. Learning Algorithmic Bias: AI Inherent biases from its training data. Algorithmic learning occurs based on the input data given to an AI algorithm. The AI system might even worsen the existing biases in society or historical inequalities if the data used for training reflects them. A famous example is an AI model trained on data related to dominant white populations that would not work properly for patients from other racial or ethnic backgrounds, possibly leading to wrong diagnoses or treatment recommendations [10]. This is a sensitive topic in health care since biased algorithms can affect the performance of clinicians and patients' treatment. For example, there was an incident where an insurance company used an algorithm for treatment recommendations and as a result, they preferred white patients to black patients because the training data contained social determinants of health bias [10].

II. Treatment Recommendations and Patient Outcomes for Marginalized Groups: Disparities The AI-based current health care system is vulnerable to focusing less on the marginalized groups such as racial minorities, women, and under-served groups, which may heighten the threat of biased or less effective healthcare recommendations. This could occur when training data for AI models does not reflect diverse populations appropriately or when algorithms do not account for social determinants of health - variables like income, access to care, and education levels. With this kind of care, healthcare AI may both reveal and worsen already extant inequities. For instance, it revealed that an algorithm based on the prediction of the needs for health care for a patient had undermined the need of blacks more than any other group to get medical care, hence resulting in unequal treatment [10].

III. Case Studies with the Adverse Impact of Biased AI Models in Healthcare

A few case studies illustrated the harmful effects. In risk stratification predictive models for patient management, it showed bias against certain groups, which could not ascertain the real extent of health risk and hence delayed treatment. For example, predictive algorithms used to allocate patients for high-risk care underestimated the needs of black patients because it was based on past healthcare expenditures, which have been lower for minority populations due to systemic healthcare inequities [10].

IV. Mitigation of Bias

More diverse data and equity-aware algorithms Using equity-aware algorithms and data, bias in healthcare AI can be mitigated by creating more diverse and representative datasets that reflect heterogeneity in the patient population through demographics and socio-economic background. Regular audits and reviews of AI models, particularly across different demographic groups for performance, can help in facilitating detection and mitigation of biases that may arise post-deployment.

An example is that fairness constraints may be incorporated during the design of algorithms or *via* adversarial debiasing techniques to eliminate biases in health care AI systems [22].

2.3.2 Transparency and Explainability

In fact, AI systems are often "black-box" models in healthcare, where decisions are opaque to understand, and there is often a concern regarding accountability, trust, or the reliance of healthcare professionals on AI recommendations.

I. The "Black-Box" Problem

Why Most AI Systems Are Still Opaque Most AI models particularly deep learning models are so complex that they cannot be accounted for by humans. These "black-box" models produce outputs - maybe even diagnoses or treatment recommendations without any hint at the stages leading to those conclusions. Such opacity can lead to distrust among healthcare professionals and patients and lack accountability toward errors committed.

Example: A diagnostic neural network system in radiology may recognize signs of lung cancer in an image but fail to explain why it made that prediction, leading to distrust on the part of the radiologists in the AI decision [23].

II. Engaging the Accountability of AI Systems through Reasoning and Decision Paths:
The creation of AI systems that can explicitly articulate their reasoning and decisions, in part, improve AI system accountability. For instance, whenever healthcare AI systems can explicitly tell why they are making certain decisions, it will be easier to understand and correct mistakes, prove whether they are properly aligned with clinical guidelines, and verify their action as best for a patient. For instance, the "attention mechanisms" mechanism under deep learning can point out the model attentions towards certain parts of medical images or patient records that led to its prediction as one solution to increasing explain ability [24].

2.3.3 Privacy and Data Security

One of the most significant issues concerning AI's growing acceptance in healthcare is the privacy and security of patient data. Such immense volumes of data must be effectively utilized in AI systems, but the health data is sensitive and requires stronger protection to prevent misuse and unauthorized access.

I. Patient Information:
Private information related to the Implementation of AI in Health Care Patient information is a foundational requirement for the model development used in AI-driven health care operations as well as sustaining accuracy in predictions and individualized care. However, such data can be regarded as sensitive, especially concerning detailed medical histories, genetic information, or other personal details. If mishandled, such data may easily fall prey to hacking, exploitation, or misuse. Therefore, confidentiality that amounts to the highest standards of keeping trust with health care providers and confidence among patients will be key in holding AI systems to these standards. Furthermore, AI systems, especially those collecting health data through wearable devices or mobile applications, should be developed by considerations of privacy laws and should ensure third-party unauthorized access and abuse should not occur [25].

II. Ensuring Compliance with Regulations Like HIPAA and GDPR to Safeguard Sensitive Health Data

For instance, the healthcare AI systems have to meet regulations meant for the guarding of the anonymity of patients such as in the United States, that is HIPAA and in Europe, the GDPR. These laws give specifications on how the patient data should be kept, shared, or used and demand the control of patient data. Therefore, following these laws is necessary for proper protection of a patient's privacy when enhanced with AI for use in healthcare. An AI-powered healthcare application requires encryption, proper storage, and permissions from the patients to be compliant in GDPR and HIPAA [25].

III. Data Breach and Misuse of Healthcare Data

Data breaches in healthcare organizations, and particularly those involving AI systems, raise massive ethical issues, such as unauthorized access to personal health information leading to identity theft or discrimination. Healthcare organizations need robust security measures and protocols that prevent and mitigate breach when it happens.

A 2017 ransomware attack on a UK hospital system exposed vulnerabilities in data security, the weaknesses involving poor data management, which healthcare environments are vulnerable to [26].

2.4 Responsible AI Development and Deployment

2.4.1 Designing Ethical AI Systems

Developing AI systems, most importantly critical healthcare-related ones, requires strong ethical foundations. Ethical AI requires an AI to ensure fairness, transparency, accountability, trust, and minimize the risk of harm to individuals or communities. This is reflected below in the requirement; it thus hints that guidelines for the development of such a responsible AI should be followed. It should incorporate diversity and inclusivity in training AI data sets, continuously monitor, and audit AI.

I. Principles for Responsible AI Development: Fairness, Transparency and Accountability

- Fairness relates to the elements of not making discrimination of a person or group related to race, gender, socio-economic status, as well as other protected characteristics. In other words, fairness means that decisions made by the AI system do not target any particular group of people and that it brings equal outcomes or opportunities for all equal regardless of their background. Bias detection and mitigation are crucial components of achieving fairness [10].

- Transparency indicates that end-users, care providers, and regulators can understand the workings of an AI system. In areas of healthcare, where human lives are immediately impacted, AI transparency would ensure that the decisions taken by the AI systems are intelligible. A transparent system can easily be penetrated to achieve clear insight into data inputs, the decision-making process, and the model's outputs [23].
- Accountability in AI development is sometimes directed at the beneficiaries of the AI systems themselves, which means that accountability on those outcomes-much more so when things go wrong-perhaps has something critical to say. Organizations and developers should be accountable for the performance of their AI systems that are characterized by violations and harm caused by defective or biased algorithms [26].

II. The Importance of Continuous Monitoring, Auditing, and Updating AI systems to Address Emerging Ethical Challenges

- AI systems should always be monitored, audited, and updated to ensure they are ethical, effective, and unbiased. Since healthcare and society keeps changing dynamically with the passage of time, their new challenges arise in the form of changing demographics of patients, new medical knowledge, or changing societal norms. Therefore, constant monitoring ensures that AI systems remain relevant and fair over time.
- **Ongoing Audits and Monitoring**
  The new forms of biases, inaccuracies, or vulnerabilities could be detected by the ongoing audits that could not have been identified during the development phase. Regular monitoring will identify model drift, for instance, the deterioration in the performance of the system as it experiences data never encountered during training [10].

- **Updating AI Models**
  As such, AI models need to be retrained frequently using new and diversified data so that they could remain on track and responsive to new events and developments. This is true for areas like healthcare, where medical knowledge and practices tend to change very fast [28].

2.4.2 Regulatory Framework and Governance

Introduction of AI to healthcare systems is a massive challenge both ethically, legally, and regulatory-wise. However, key and direct stakeholders in putting these AI technologies into safe and effective place would be healthcare regulators as well as policymakers. Patients' rights and data privacy will be laid emphasis on, and decision-making processes would be transparent. Below is the detailed discussion on the role of healthcare regulators, existing standards and regulations, and global perspectives on AI healthcare governance.

I. Role of Healthcare Regulators and Policymakers in Overseeing AI use in Healthcare

Healthcare regulators and policy makers also have a role in developing directives and standards for the safe application of AI technologies in clinics. Their roles are illustrated in Figure 2.2 and are explained as follows [29]:

- **Safety and Efficacy Evaluation**
  Regulators check whether AI-based healthcare applications are both safe and efficacious for practical use in clinics. For instance, they will check if the AI system is accurate, reliable, and reproducible in its outputs-a factor necessary for decisions related to health.

  AI systems are usually inspected for sometime because over time, performance can sometimes fluctuate due to new incoming data or updating algorithms.
- **Patient Privacy and Data Security**
  Another significant issue is the issue of confidentiality of patient data. These big data systems are highly regulated in terms of access to personal health data as being of sensitive nature and hence strictly adhere to the Health Insurance Portability and Accountability Act (HIPAA) in the United States and the General Data Protection Regulation in Europe.

Strict adherence to rules is followed in regulatory bodies to ensure that AI systems are transparent in collecting, storing, and using data.

- **Clinical Decision Support**
  Many AI systems are intended to assist or replace human judgment in clinical settings. The regulatory agencies would ensure that such systems determine decisions in a manner that is not only complementary or superior to healthcare but that they also do not harm. AI in clinical decision support tools would need careful assessment in order to find biases, clinical validity, and usability with an eye to reduce any adverse influence on patient care.
- **Standards and Ethical Oversight**
  This is another area where regulators in healthcare are brought to task: the establishment of standards governing the use of AI. This comprises ensuring that AI has minimal, acceptable levels of human oversight, and ensures that AI algorithms are transparent to prevent introducing bias that can lead to discriminatory practices.

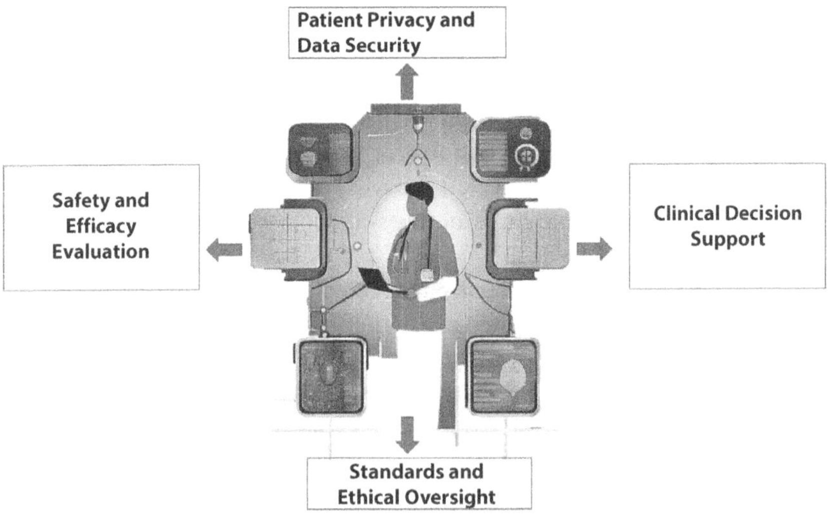

Figure 2.2 Role of healthcare regulators and policymakers in overseeing AI use in healthcare.

II. Existing Standards and Regulations

Several regulatory bodies develop or are in the process of developing frameworks for the use of AI in healthcare:

- **FDA (US Food and Drug Administration)**
  The FDA plays an important role in the regulation of AI-based devices in the United States. This would include systems assisting in diagnosis, treatment, or clinical decision-making, among others. Some of the other essential ones include the following [30]:
  i. **Premarket Approval:** These AI-based devices are under very strict premarket approval processes, meaning they meet safety and efficacy standards before their release. Even for some to be used with clinical trials along with AI model validation against real-world data, there is still testing before its release into the market.
  ii. **SaMD:** The FDA believes most AI applications applied in the healthcare sector fall under the regulation of the software as a medical device. The FDA has issued guidance relating to the regulation of SaMD, including the risk-based approaches which classify AI tools based on the risk such tools pose to patients.
  iii. **Continuous Monitoring:** Continuous monitoring is necessary to ensure the continued consistency of the performance of systems that evolve over time, such as those through machine learning. The FDA encourages surveillance of AI systems post-market for identification of degradation in performance or potential safety issues.
- **EU AI Act**
  The European Union's AI Act is one of the most exhaustive regulations ever drafted worldwide. Firstly, the Act categorizes AI systems into different levels of risk and then applies corresponding regulatory requirements to them on the basis of their risk categorization: High-risk AI systems (like AI for medical diagnostics, surgery etc.) are strictly supervised with strict conformity assessments, documentation, transparency, and human oversight [31]. This is accompanied by several reporting obligations relating to AI incidents and risks toward national authorities. Transparency is also required, including disclosure that a user is interacting with an AI system and the possibility to audit AI decisions.

III. Global Perspectives: Ensuring Cross-Border Consistency in AI Healthcare Governance

- **World Health Organization (WHO):** The WHO has recognized the growing significance of AI in health and introduced a number of debates on the ethical use of AI technologies across the globe. These have been focusing their efforts on global frameworks of AI that would contain precepts on patient safety, clarity, and equity. WHO in 2021 published a draft framework on the ethical use of AI in health that encouraged governments to establish open policies and regulations that would foster public confidence in AI systems [32].
- **OECD AI Principles:** The OECD, established by the Organization for Economic Co-operation and Development, has provided a set of guidelines related to AI and its use, which member countries can commit to in order to ensure the proper use of AI, including within healthcare [33]. The OECD guidance on human rights, accountability, transparency, and inclusivity looks at harmonizing AI regulations across countries and so tries to achieve fairness and equity in healthcare through the implementation of AI systems.
- **Challenges in Harmonization Cross-Border:** The largest challenge associated with cross-border AI governance is diversity in regulatory frameworks. For instance, though the EU's emphasis on the value of data protection under its GDPR makes it a regulation that will be at odds with other locales such as in the USA and the latter has a sparse nature of regulation about privacy laws. Global cooperation would be needed to create standard regulatory frameworks that would enable AI technologies to cross borders while still being aligned with what is deemed ethical, and upholding patient safety [34].

2.4.3 Collaboration between AI Systems and Healthcare Professionals

The potential for AI integration into health systems is immense, particularly in enhancing clinical decision-making, improving patient outcomes, and reducing administrative burdens. However, a key aspect of effective implementation will be the collaboration between AI systems and healthcare professionals, to ensure that AI serves as a tool to enhance and complement human judgment instead of supplanting it. Of course, the humanness of healthcare needs to be preserved, especially on the doctor-patient level, as it is the foundation to trust, empathy, and care at all levels [35].

I. AI as a Decision-Support Tool: An Enabler, Not a Replacement, for Human Judgment

This calls for the maximum use of AI in a decision-support tool in healthcare, arguing that clinicians should be supported to make more informed and data-driven decisions. Nevertheless, AI systems are not to replace physicians. Rather, they are going to support human judgment by providing insights that perhaps human beings are not able to recognize at an early stage. Such tools include ML models and NLP algorithms, which can scan large datasets, including patient medical records, imaging data, or genomics information, much faster and with far greater accuracy than the human brain. Such tools might identify the patterns, predict possible disease progression, and give evidence-based guidelines on treatment. AI can, therefore, process and collate such enormous amounts of data, which allows doctors to focus more on finer aspects of care related to human skills, like decision making in regards to an ethical call or even the proper communication with patients. Through computer-aided systems making use of artificial intelligence, in the field of oncology, it has been seen that lesions cancerous in medical images such as mammography or CT scan can be spotted by radiologists even before being seen by the human eye [8]. This is still advisory from AI and must be considered in the light of the general medical history of the patient, specific circumstances, and patient preference-underlying clinical expertise and human decision-making.

II. Training Healthcare Professionals to Interpret and Trust AI Recommendations

For clinicians to be effective in healthcare, they should not only be trained on how to apply the AI tools but also on how to interpret and trust the recommendations generated by such AI tools. Therefore, the appreciation of strengths and weaknesses of AI models, ethical, and clinical implications thereof while using AI-assisted decision-making is essential. One of the most critical areas wherein health professionals should be informed is the kind of reasoning used by AI systems in arriving at their recommendations. Many critics argue that AI models, especially deep learning algorithms, criticize the black box approach since they do not give clear reasoning behind those predictions. Lack of transparency might make clinicians question the validity of the results produced by the system. Explainable AI (XAI) is the kind of technology that will generate human-understandable explanations of machine decision-making processes, thereby making AI interpretability efforts. A training program should provide sessions on how one evaluates the rationale behind AI recommendations to let a healthy provider critically assess AI outputs with a view to making decisions and basing decisions on thorough understanding [36].

III. Maintaining the Human Touch in AI-Driven Healthcare: Emphasizing Doctor-Patient Relationship

While it is expected that AI may have a potential impact on improving clinical efficiency and outcomes, human elements such as the doctor-patient relationship must be preserved. Trust, empathy, and communication are major components of effective medical care that cannot be replicated through machines. AI can aid in diagnostic and treatment suggestions, but it cannot substitute the empathy, emotional support, and care that patients seek from their health providers. A physician is often the source of security to a patient during challenging diagnoses or treatments. In this role, the therapeutic relationship becomes an important part of the healing process [37].

2.5 Case Studies: Real-World Examples of Ethical AI in Healthcare

2.5.1 Positive Applications of AI in Healthcare

This may eventually lead to improving diagnostics, treatments, and patient care. Medical imaging is enhanced due to better detection of diseases like cancer. AI-driven predictive models can forecast the progression of diseases and patient outcomes where early interventions become possible [38]. Personalized medicine tailors treatments according to individual patient data, while AI accelerates drug discovery through the analysis of huge chemical datasets. This aid makes the provider diagnose more effectively and, consequently, make proper treatment plans. AI also assists in telemedicine and virtual health assistants, thus enhancing patient engagement and remote care [39]. All these applications tend to enhance efficiency, eliminate errors, and improve the general quality and availability of healthcare.

I. AI-Driven Medical Imaging and Diagnostic Tools

This is where the play by AI-driven medical imaging and diagnostic tools increases their relatively growing important roles in modern health care with the creation of more accurate diagnoses and quicker process [40]. Powered by deep learning techniques, these tools enable complex medical images-think CT scan, MRI, or X-ray-to be analyzed and conditions like tumors, fractures, or neurological disorders diagnosed. For example, the algorithms will outperform human radiologists, like early detection signs for skin cancer or lung cancer screening wherein AI models showed high sensitivity in identifying nodules as based on chest radiographs that may lead to earlier intervention and better outcomes [41]. It can also assist in reducing human error, streamlining interpretations across different patient populations, and sifting through large volumes of data much faster, saving time and resources [42]. Thus, these developments are very relevant in resource-limited settings where access to specialist radiologists is limited. AI tools enable faster and more accurate diagnoses. AI tools would further not just enhance clinical decision-making but also improve patient care and outcomes overall [43]. In medical imaging, which promises even more sophisticated diagnostic capabilities, as the technology evolves further, the interdigitation of AI still brings an unprecedented bridge in practice between medical expertise and machine learning [44].

II. AI in Personalized Medicine and Treatment Planning

AI in personalized medicine is transforming the way treatment plans are undertaken, using multitudes of patient data including genetic profiles, medical history, and lifestyle factors-to tailor unique treatment strategies for individuals [45]. These algorithms can thus accurately identify the appropriate therapies tailored to each patient and, in return, maximize outcomes and minimize the adverse effects of a certain medication. For instance, AI made it possible to predict how cancer patients would react to certain treatments based on genetic mutations. This helped in further personalizing chemotherapy and immunotherapy among other things [46]. Additionally, AI-based analytics tools can process EHRs to generate recommendations for personalized dosing of medications and treatment protocols that improve precision medicine [47]. This shift toward precision medicine triggered by AI improves clinical outcomes and increases efficiency in the healthcare sector concerning cost as its unnecessary treatments and hospitalizations are decreased. The future promises increased individualized care through AI by integrating it into personalized medicine, further expanding personalized treatment to patients for better health management and long-term well-being of patients [48].

III. AI in Predictive Analytics to Reduce Readmission Rates and Improve Patient Outcomes

- AI is increasingly applied in predictive analytics to reduce hospital readmissions and enhance patient outcomes because it can identify who is at greater risk of such negative events, and early interventions may be made with care plans for individual patients based on an assessment of data regarding the patient through electronic health records. For example, machine learning has demonstrated that its algorithms can predict admissions of patients that are readmitted due to chronic conditions, such as heart failure or diabetes, thereby assisting in interventions and hospital readmissions among patients with improvement in general [49].
- These predictive models do not only optimize resource distribution but also ensure timely follow-up care for patients in an enhancement for their recovery and reduction of healthcare costs. Further, with the development of AI technologies, integrating them into clinical workflows holds high potential for further patient outcome improvement and reduction of preventable readmissions [50].

2.5.2 Challenges and Ethical Dilemmas in AI Use

AI in healthcare throws up various challenges and ethical dilemmas. Bias in training data is likely to result in discriminatory outcomes, under diagnosis in particular for minority groups. Third, there is also an issue of privacy as health data is highly sensitive with a risk of breach and misuse; the black box nature of AI complicates this factor of transparency and accountability for decision-making if facts cannot be explained to patients or their surrogates then real informed consent is compromised. Fourth, there is job displacement due to automation resulting from the use of AI.

I. Case Studies Where AI Bias Led to Inequitable Healthcare Outcomes

- AI bias has led to inequitable outcomes in healthcare, especially in areas such as diagnosis, recommendation for treatment, and allocation of resources. It is through the case of an algorithm by Optum that decided who receives extra care.

Analysis conducted in 2019 in the journal Science revealed that it discriminates against blacks. Healthcare costs were employed as a proxy of health care needs [51]. Since they tend to have less access to health care and spend less, they were not likely going to be flagged for extra care. Even if their health problems were equivalent or at least equally as bad as the white patients, there were fewer interventions among black patients compared to the white patients.

- Another example would be facial recognition applied in diagnostic imaging, which often performs poorly on darker skin tones. For instance, a study from 2020 in Science Advances showed that AI models that had been trained extensively on images of lighter-skinned patients got error rates higher when recognizing such conditions as cancerous skin lesions or pneumonia diagnosis among individuals with darker skin [52]. These biases were created due to biased training data, and less accuracy led to dangerous health care for minority populations [53].

II. Examples of Transparency Issues: When AI Decision-Making Lacked Clarity and Accountability

Transparency issues in AI decision-making have led to a lack of clarity and accountability in several high-profile cases:

- **COMPAS Algorithm (Criminal Justice)**: The COMPAS algorithm, used for recidivism risk assessments in the United States, was opaque in its decision-making. In 2016, ProPublica revealed racial biases in labeling black defendants as higher-risk than their white counterparts. Its opacity meant that it remained impossible to understand or challenge its decisions [54].
- **Amazon's Hiring Algorithm**: Amazon's recruitment AI tool was seen to have shown some gender bias, favoring male candidates, especially for technical positions. The system did not provide clear explanations, making it impossible for recruiters and the applicants to understand or contest decisions that ended with its eventual discontinuation [55].

III. The Role of Human Oversight in Mitigating AI Failures in Healthcare Settings

- Diagnosis and planning treatment by AI systems require tight monitoring to ensure that it does not go wrong or mislead because evidence from such studies has shown how biased the training set might be. Situations where human oversight can play a key role in ensuring contextual understanding include situations that have helped address those biases, such as ensuring AI support rather than replacement of clinical expertise [56].
- Another integral requirement for AI tools is human oversight to ensure compliance with standard ethical practice and regulation, all the more especially against the backdrop of transparency, accountability, and patient consent in healthcare as AI continues to advance, human oversight would remain critical in its safeguard against potential failures [57].

2.5.3 Best Practices and Lessons Learned

This can be through clear communication, constant feedback, and adaptability when achieving success. The best practices and lessons learned relate to proper time management, prioritization, and holding teams accountable for the maintenance of productivity and the meeting of goals. The acquisition of lessons from past successes and failures helps to avoid repetition of mistakes and keep strategies more than perfected for better outputs. They celebrate small wins to encourage good morale and motivation while continuous learning can promote current industry trends. The practices and insights will therefore make way for performance, innovation, and sustainable growth.

I. The Importance of Iterative Development and Ongoing Audits of AI Healthcare Systems

- Iterative development and audit operations are critical in AI healthcare systems so that the system is safe, effective and ethically aligned with patient needs in care. Iterative development allows for refinement of AI models based on real-life data so that their precision improves, bias reduces, and the model adapts according to the changing nature of medical practices. This means AI system continue to be responsive to new information and emerging challenges.

- Ongoing audits would be necessary to check how well AI systems are performing and if they comply with set regulatory standards. The identification of potential risks in terms of discriminatory outcomes or safety issues exists, and the operations of AI systems will ensure transparency and accountability. Regular checks will also follow the handling of patient data by AI systems to ensure privacy and security [58].

II. Ensuring Diversity in AI Design and Implementation

Design and implementation of AI should be diverse to ensure equity, fairness, and inclusiveness of systems. Diversity teams can identify biases in models and not just create technologies that reflect an 'unrepresentative' range of needs, experiences, and perspectives. Instead, it helps in the unintended reinstatement of entrenched inequalities in hiring and firing decisions, healthcare provision, criminal justice allocation, and educational access.

The necessary steps to ensure diversity in AI are:

1. Inclusive Data Collection: Ensuring the training datasets are representative of diverse demographics to avoid bias in AI predictions.
2. Heterogeneous Development Teams: Involving individuals from different backgrounds, cultures, and expertise areas to provide a broad set of perspectives during the AI design and its implementation.
3. Artifact to Implement-Bias Detection and Mitigation: Providing practices by which AI systems can be incessantly tested for biases and addressed during development.
4. Ethical principles -Being fair and transparent in the development practices, outcomes, and all things to do with AI [59].

III. Approaches to Creating Explainable and Transparent AI Models and Interpretable Machine Learning Models

- **Description:** Utilize intrinsically interpretable models such as decision trees, linear regression, or rule-based systems

that can explain in more direct terms how decisions are being made.
Decision trees, where each split represents a decision-making rule, allow stakeholders to easily understand model outputs [60].

2.6 Strategies for Ensuring Ethical and Responsible Use of AI

2.6.1 Equity-Aware AI Systems

Equitable AI systems are designed such that fairness, inclusiveness, and equal treatment of all users with no regard to their demographic characteristics like race, gender, or socioeconomic status ensue [61]. The systems actively recognize and remove biases in data, algorithms, and decision-making processes that prevent discrimination. Some of the key strategies include diverse representative datasets, incorporation of fairness metrics during the formulation of a model, or employing techniques like adversarial de-biasing or fairness constraints for training of models. The idea here is to design AI that supports equitable outcomes across different groups, promoting trust and avoiding the possibility of perpetuating social inequalities.

I. Designing AI Models that Account for Social and Demographic Factors to Reduce Bias

Approach: AI models need to be constructed with the consideration of race, gender, age, and other socio-economic variables such that all possibilities of bias are minimized. Some of the methods include imposition of fairness constraints while training, diversified datasets, and models for disparate data through schemes like re-weighting or adversarial debiasing.

Demographic factors such as race and gender should not disproportionately affect the outcome of predictive policing or hiring algorithms. For instance, history should not be rewritten in the name of discrimination by training models on divergent data sets [62].

II. The Role of Interdisciplinary Teams in Developing AI Systems

Approach: An interdisciplinary team is integral to the development of ethical and socially responsible AI [63]. They include ethicists, healthcare professionals, data scientists, and policymakers who solve problems on fairness, privacy, and transparency that seem impossible to tackle. Ethicists ensure principles of ethics are integrated in design, healthcare professionals provide domain expertise, data scientists drive technical optimization, and policymakers ensure that the technology is aligned with the legal and social standards.

In healthcare AI, ethicists and health professionals make sure the AI-based diagnostic tools respect privacy and minimize biases regarding race or gender, while data scientists and policymakers ensure that the applications remain compliant with regulations such as HIPAA [55].

III. Creating Systems for Equitable Data Collection and Representation
Approach: Data equitable collection should ensure that datasets are diverse, representative, and free from biases that will necessarily tilt AI models. This consequently means intentionally taking the effort to include underrepresented groups and monitoring the sources of data for any biases based on race, gender, or socioeconomic status among others. Bias audits and continuous monitoring of models help reduce the risk of harmful results.

For facial recognition technology, it should be very important to use datasets that allow for varied skin tones and other features of faces to avoid racial bias in the system [64]. In healthcare, equitable data collection ensures that AI systems are designed using data from diverse populations to avoid underperformance for certain demographic groups [65].

2.6.2 Promoting Transparency and Explainability

This will ensure trust, accountability, and fairness into an AI system with transparency and explainability. Transparency in an AI system develops awareness on how the decisions are rendered while an explainable model provides exact reasons for some prediction or action. This could be done through the use of interpretable models, to use open communication regarding model development and data usage, as well as through *post-hoc* explanation techniques, like SHAP or LIME. By stressing transparency, developers of AI systems ensure that those systems are more auditable and less prone to bias than other technologies.

I. Developing AI Tools that Provide Clear Explanations for their Recommendations
Approach: AI tools must be developed keeping in mind interpretability, where clear, understandable reasons for recommendations are provided. Such methods may include SHAP (Shapley values) or LIME (Local

Interpretable Model-agnostic Explanations), through which explainable reasons are derived for each recommendation [66]. Such methods assist end-users, such as a clinician or decision-maker, to understand how the model reached its conclusion and validated its decision.

In medical diagnosis, the AI system can elucidate why it is recommending a particular diagnosis given certain input features like lab results or medical history, so that clinicians can validate the recommendation [67].

II. Educating Healthcare Professionals and Patients About the Role and Limitations of AI in Clinical Settings

Approach: That education for both doctors and patients regarding the scope, capabilities and limitations of AI in clinical decision-making could make all the difference: remind readers that AI systems are there to assist and not replace human judgment, thus also pointing out when they reflect or reproduce biases or errors in data. Periodic training programs for the healthcare providers and effective information transfer to the patients regarding how AI actually supports the diagnosis and treatment process can help avoid traps of over-reliance and misunderstanding.

A healthcare institution could arrange lectures for doctors on the role of AI in extracting patterns in medical images, whereas patients are educated on how AI is employed in treatment planning and the flaws that accompany it [68].

III. Creating Guidelines for AI Companies on Achieving Transparency in Their Algorithms

Approach: Guidelines would emerge clear and standardized that AI companies have to improve transparency in algorithm design. This should involve openness to documents on the model architectures, data sources, ways of training, and decision-making processes. In addition, it ought to insist on transparency regarding performance metrics, fairness audit, or limitations in the AI systems. Compliance can be ensured and confidence in the users and the regulators can be built by third party regular audits.

Outlines may include provisions that AI systems in sensitive areas, such as healthcare or criminal justice, will make public decisions or models; and they will regularly undergo fairness testing to avoid discrimination [69].

2.6.3 Establishing Accountability Mechanisms

The development, deployment, and oversight of AI technologies are defined in clear ownership so that accountable parties can be held responsible for their behavior. Independent audits are carried out regularly to monitor the performance as well as the fairness of AI systems, detecting any potential biases or an unintended consequence. Transparency is maintained by documenting data sources, model decisions, and updates; in this way, stakeholders can understand and verify the working of the AI. Redress mechanisms, which do allow users to report issues and eventually point out necessary corrective actions, are in place. These strategies ensure that AI systems operate ethically, and users develop trust and fairness in these systems.

I. Defining Clear Accountability Frameworks in Case of AI-Driven Errors or Harm

Approach: To counter AI-driven errors or harm, definitions of accountability frameworks need to be provided to give all parties concerned roles and responsibilities; this would include developers, healthcare providers, and the institutions which are deploying the AI tools. Thus, it should provide clear procedures in the setting of liability when failures occur, including whether errors come from the system itself or from the data used or human interaction. In addition, the framework should include corrective actions and mechanisms for compensations or redress for patient victims.

If an AI healthcare system misinterprets the data in a clinical investigation and, therefore, conducts the wrong treatment, then the accountability framework should define whether it is the developers of the AI or the healthcare provider who relied upon the AI system that should assume liability [70].

II. Legal and Ethical Considerations Around AI Failures in Healthcare

Approach: Legal and ethical considerations surrounding failures in AI are multi-dimensional. Legally, questions of liability when AI generates harm from medical errors, potential discrimination in AI prediction, and even issues of patient consent arise. Ethically, AI needs to be developed with notions of fairness, transparency, and accountability in a sensitive healthcare setting. There should be defined legal guidelines defining the responsibility of developers and healthcare providers in terms of malfunction or damage done by AI systems. Additionally, patient rights should be protected while the patient knows how the AI can affect health care decisions.

If the failure to diagnose a rare condition led to delayed diagnosis and poor health outcomes, the legal question would be if the liability for such harm is with the healthcare provider or the developer of the AI system [71].

III. Developing Patient-Centered Safeguards to Ensure Trust in AI-Driven Healthcare Systems

Approach: Patient-centered safeguards would ensure that AI-driven healthcare systems give adequate emphasis to patient autonomy and informed decision-making [72]. For example, full disclosure about how the AI systems work, the kind of information they use, and limitations of their suggestions would provide important safeguards. Such AI systems should also have mechanisms by which patients may require a second opinion or dispute AI-driven decisions. Finally, the importance of patient data privacy and security is essential. These measures ensure patient trust in the systems, such that decisions regarding their healthcare made under AI remains confident.

An AI system used in the diagnosis of cancer can explain to a patient why they diagnosed it based on some images, where patients have the right to talk to an actual human doctor on the findings.

2.7 The Future of Ethical AI in Healthcare

2.7.1 Evolving AI Technologies in Healthcare

Artificial intelligence transforms healthcare from precision medicine, robotics, and AI-assisted surgeries. The future innovations will lead the way to better patient outcomes, increased efficiency, and a very personalized process in the delivery of care. However, this brings in the need for ethics on its fair, equitable, and safe deployment.

- **Precision Medicine**
  AI-assisted tools enable precision medicine by analyzing complex datasets, such as genetic information, clinical records, and environmental factors. Machine learning algorithms can even identify patterns helpful in anticipating susceptibility to specific diseases, providing guidelines on the management of individual patient profiles [73].
- **Robotics in Healthcare**
  Robotic systems integrated with AI enhance precision and dexterity in clinical practice: AI-assisted robots like the da Vinci Surgical System help in providing unparalleled accuracy when it comes to surgical interventions and cut down recovery time, as well as risks associated with surgery.

In addition, AI-based robotic devices find applications in rehabilitation therapy sessions for an individualized application of treatment programs toward patients using real-time patient data [74].

2.7.2 Integration of AI with Next-Gen Technologies: Internet of Medical Things (IoMT), Wearable Health Tech, and More

- **Internet of Medical Things (IoMT)**
  The integration of AI with the Internet of Medical Things has entirely changed the nature of healthcare, by allowing connected devices to collect, analyze, and transmit live health data. IoMT consists of different devices like smart insulin pumps, heart monitors, connected inhalers, and many more which rely on AI for predictive analytics and decision support [75]. For example, AI-based algorithms analyze data gathered from IoMT devices for the foretelling of deterioration in patients within healthcare settings.
- **Wearable Health Technology**
  AI-fortified wearable devices are completely required for preventive health care. The wearables-like smart watches, fitness trackers, or biosensors trace heartbeat, oxygen levels, and sleep patterns, which are quite helpful to users. AI algorithms process such data to detect anomalies in the presence of risk factors for potential health risks. For example, it has been proven that, using AI-powered wearables, atrial fibrillation and comparable cardiovascular conditions could be detected through continuous observation [76].
- **Other Advancements: Telemedicine and Smart Implants**
  The integration of AI with telemedicine platforms facilitates remote patient consultations with real-time data from IoMT and wearables. AI lets providers support potential diagnoses and provide customized treatment recommendations during virtual visits. AI is also leading the charge in innovative smart implants that monitor and react to physiological changes inside the human body. For example, AI neural implants can change their functionality in real time to help with neurological rehabilitation [77].

2.7.3 Ongoing Ethical Considerations

- Deep Learning Biases: Deep learning models almost always reflect the biases that are present in the data used to train them [78]. These can then be transmitted into biased or unjust health care outcomes when such data underrepresent particular populations. An example is diagnostic AI systems having a lower accuracy rate within the minority population where this can potentially work to exacerbate health disparities.
- AI Autonomy: This leads to a growing need for ethical guidelines in AI systems developing increasing autonomy, as is the case with autonomous AI in health care contexts, including robotic surgery or drug prescription.
- Diagnostic Decision-Making AI systems especially deep learning algorithms, are increasingly being utilized for disease diagnosis in terms of medical imaging, such as cancer, diabetic retinopathy, and cardiovascular disorders [79].

2.8 Conclusion

2.8.1 Summary of Key Ethical Issues

The potential of AI in healthcare is immense but also raises critical ethical concerns to be addressed for responsible and equitable use.

I. Summary of the Biggest Ethical Issues

- **Bias:** AI systems inherit bias from datasets used for training [79]. This often leads to unfair outcomes for many-minority groups. Bias needs to be taken care of through strong data selection and testing with continuous monitoring.
- **Transparency:** The high complexity of many AI algorithms, especially those with a deep learning base, makes it impossible for clinicians and patients to understand the basis of decisions made by AI. Enhancing explainability is important for trust and facilitating informed decision-making [80].
- **Accountability:** Another very significant challenge is who will be held accountable for errors or adverse outcomes due

to AI systems [81]. Clear regulatory frameworks as well as collaborative governance processes need to be in place to assign accountability appropriately.

- **Patient Trust:** Acceptance of AI by the public requires feelings that these technologies are safe, fair, and beneficial [82]. Transparency and ethical protections ensure that trust is maintained.

II. Need for a Holistic Approach

- Diverse stakeholder involvement: Any governance structure for AI must involve the healthcare provider, patient, developer, and policymaker for equitable design and implementation of AI systems [83]. Each role provides a different perspective toward more ethical and effective solutions.
- Iterative ethical oversight: AI development should follow the constant review of ethical principles, which must accompany and evolve with technology.
- Education and Awareness among stakeholders about AI capabilities and limitations to set appropriate expectations from such a system and avoid unwarranted reliance on these systems [84].

2.8.2 Vision for the Future

A future where AI improves the health outcome of all patients regardless of their backgrounds or geographies, with the highest possible ethics.

I. AI-Driven Universal Healthcare Improvements

The next future of healthcare is going to be an AI-based one wherein every patient gets personalized and predictive care [85]. Actually, AI can reduce the present inequalities not only in access to health care but also in quality. Scrutinizing massive-than-life datasets and recognizing patterns that no human can make, AI may be able to do the following:

- Optimize Precision Medicine: Algorithms may even suggest treatments particularized to a patient's genetic, environmental and lifestyle factors [86].

- Expand Telemedicine: AI-based tools can expand healthcare services to unnerved regions, offer remote diagnostics and consultations deserved regions, offer remote diagnostics and consultations [87].
- Improve Public Health: Predictive models could foresee outbreaks, thus allowing timely interventions and proper resource allocation [88].

II. Ethical Standards as the Bedrock

With the increasing applications of artificial intelligence in most aspects of the healthcare system, there will be a greater need to maintain high ethical standards in order to promote equality and confidence [89]. Diverse and representative datasets should be ensured to avoid discriminating against any particular population. Additionally, there is an urgent need for AI systems to be explainable, hence explaining why certain decisions or recommendations have been made so that clinicians and patients understand each other. There should exist clear governance frameworks that make specific allocations for the responsibilities associated with the outcomes of AI technology. Healthcare professionals and the patients ought to comprehend the reasons behind the decisions made by AI based solutions, thus they should be explainable [90, 91].

Summary Table

Section	**Key points**
Introduction	An overview of artificial intelligence (AI) in healthcare, encompassing its uses, advantages, and drawbacks, including moral conundrums and legal issues.
Responsible AI in Healthcare	What constitutes responsible AI, how it affects medical outcomes, and compliance with legal and ethical frameworks (such as HIPAA, GDPR, and FDA rules).
Major AI Technologies in Healthcare	NLP for clinical documentation, robotics for surgery and rehabilitation, and machine learning (ML) for predictive analytics.
Applications of AI in Healthcare	AI in improving patient care, operational efficiency, predictive analytics, and illness diagnosis.

Ethical Considerations in AI Integration	Problems such as data security, privacy, and bias in AI models, as well as fair access to AI-powered medical care.
Innovation vs. Equity and Transparency	Ensuring that justice, openness, and confidence in healthcare systems are not jeopardized by AI-driven innovation.
Regulatory Frameworks and Governance	The FDA, WHO, and EU AI Act's roles in guaranteeing the safe application of AI in healthcare.
Collaboration Between AI and Healthcare Professionals	The significance of human oversight, the use of AI as a decision-support tool rather than a substitute, and clinician training.
Challenges and Ethical Dilemmas	Examples of biased AI models, opaque AI decision-making, and legal issues with AI errors.
Best Practices and Future Directions	Techniques for developing AI in an ethical manner that guarantee justice, openness, and ongoing AI system monitoring.
Future of AI in Healthcare	New developments in wearable health technology, IoMT (Internet of Medical Things), AI-assisted surgery, and AI-driven precision medicine.

AI disclosure statement: The author acknowledges the use of AI-based tools for minor language editing or grammatical correction. However, all intellectual contributions, analyses, and conclusions presented in this chapter are entirely the author's own.

Bibliography

1. Malik, P., Pathania, M., Rathaur, V.K., Overview of artificial intelligence in medicine. *J. Family Med. Prim. Care*, 8, 7, 2328–31, 2019 Jul 1.
2. Alowais, S.A., Alghamdi, S.S., Alsuhebany, N., Alqahtani, T., Alshaya, A.I., Almohareb, S.N., Aldairem, A., Alrashed, M., Bin Saleh, K., Badreldin, H.A., Al Yami, M.S., Revolutionizing healthcare: the role of artificial intelligence in clinical practice. *BMC Med. Educ.*, 23, 1, 689, 2023 Sep 22.

3. Jahn, W.T., The 4 basic ethical principles that apply to forensic activities are respect for autonomy, beneficence, nonmaleficence, and justice. *J. Chiropr. Med.*, 10, 3, 225, 2011 Sep.
4. Agarwal, S. and Peta, S.B., Balancing Technology and Privacy: Securing Patient Data in Healthcare Under HIPAA Regulations.
5. Rajkomar, A., Dean, J., Kohane, I., Machine learning in medicine. *N. Engl. J. Med.*, 380, 14, 1347–58, 2019 Apr 4.
6. Joulin, A., Grave, E., Bojanowski, P., Mikolov, T., Bag of tricks for efficient text classification, *arXiv preprint arXiv:1607.01759*, 2016 Jul 6.
7. Beasley, R.A., Medical robots: current systems and research directions. *J. Rob.*, 2012, 1, 401613, 2012.
8. Esteva, A., Kuprel, B., Novoa, R.A., Ko, J., Swetter, S.M., Blau, H.M., Thrun, S., Dermatologist-level classification of skin cancer with deep neural networks. *Nature*, 542, 7639, 115–8, 2017 Feb.
9. Maleki Varnosfaderani, S. and Forouzanfar, M., The role of AI in hospitals and clinics: transforming healthcare in the 21st century. *Bioengineering*, 11, 4, 337, 2024 Mar 29.
10. Obermeyer, Z., Powers, B., Vogeli, C., Mullainathan, S., Dissecting racial bias in an algorithm used to manage the health of populations. *Science*, 366, 6464, 447–53, 2019 Oct 25.
11. Santosh, K.C., Gaur, L., Santosh, K.C., Gaur, L., Privacy, security, and ethical issues, in: *Artificial Intelligence and Machine Learning in Public Healthcare: Opportunities and Societal Impact*, pp. 65–74, 2021.
12. Char, D.S., Abràmoff, M.D., Feudtner, C., Identifying ethical considerations for machine learning healthcare applications. *Am. J. Bioethics*, 20, 11, 7–17, 2020 Nov 1.
13. Cireşan, D.C., Giusti, A., Gambardella, L.M., Schmidhuber, J., Mitosis detection in breast cancer histology images with deep neural networks, in: *Medical Image Computing and Computer-Assisted Intervention–MICCAI 2013: 16th International Conference, Nagoya, Japan, September 22-26, 2013, Proceedings, Part II 16*, pp. 411–418, Springer Berlin Heidelberg, 2013.
14. Díaz, O., Rodríguez-Ruíz, A., Sechopoulos, I., Artificial Intelligence for breast cancer detection: Technology, challenges, and prospects. *Eur. J. Radiol.*, 174, 111457, 2024 Apr 16.
15. Cauteruccio, F., Stamile, C., Terracina, G., Ursino, D., Sappey-Marinier, D., An automated string-based approach to extracting and characterizing white matter fiber-bundles. *Comput. Biol. Med.*, 77, 64–75, 2016 Oct 1.
16. Qureshi, K.N., Din, S., Jeon, G., Piccialli, F., An accurate and dynamic predictive model for a smart M-Health system using machine learning. *Inf. Sci.*, 538, 486–502, 2020 Oct 1.
17. Xu, L., Sanders, L., Li, K., Chow, J.C., Chatbot for health care and oncology applications using artificial intelligence and machine learning: systematic review. *JMIR Cancer*, 7, 4, e27850, 2021 Nov 29.

18. Mohammadzadeh, N. and Safdari, R., Patient monitoring in mobile health: opportunities and challenges. *Med. Arch.*, 68, 1, 57, 2014 Feb.
19. Meraj, S.S., Yaakob, R., Azman, A., Rum, S.N., Nazri, A.A., Artificial intelligence in diagnosing tuberculosis: a review. *Int. J. Adv. Sci. Eng. Inf. Technol.*, 9, 1, 81–91, 2019 Jan.
20. Fernandes, J.G., Artificial intelligence in telemedicine, in: *Artificial Intelligence in Medicine*, pp. 1219–1227, Springer International Publishing, Cham, 2022 Feb 18.
21. Ahsan, R., Tahsili, M.R., Ebrahimi, F., Ebrahimie, E., Ebrahimi, M., Image processing unravels the evolutionary pattern of SARS-CoV-2 against SARS and MERS through position-based pattern recognition. *Comput. Biol. Med.*, 134, 104471, 2021 Jul 1.
22. Sweeney, L., Discrimination in online ad delivery: Google ads, black names and white names, racial discrimination, and click advertising. *Queue*, 11, 3, 10–29, 2013 Mar 1.
23. Lipton, Z.C., The mythos of model interpretability: In machine learning, the concept of interpretability is both important and slippery. *Queue*, 16, 3, 31–57, 2018 Jun 1.
24. Chollet, F., *Deep learning with Python*, Simon and Schuster, 2021 Dec 7.
25. Khalid, N., Qayyum, A., Bilal, M., Al-Fuqaha, A., Qadir, J., Privacy-preserving artificial intelligence in healthcare: Techniques and applications. *Comput. Biol. Med.*, 158, 106848, 2023 May 1.
26. Gerstein, D. and Giordano, J., Rethinking the biological and toxin weapons convention? *Health Secur.*, 15, 6, 638–41, 2017 Dec 1.
27. Dignum, V., Ethics in artificial intelligence: introduction to the special issue. *Ethics Inf. Technol.*, 20, 1, 1–3, 2018 Mar.
28. Shin, H.C., Roth, H.R., Gao, M., Lu, L., Xu, Z., Nogues, I., Yao, J., Mollura, D., Summers, R.M., Deep convolutional neural networks for computer-aided detection: CNN architectures, dataset characteristics and transfer learning. *IEEE Trans. Med. Imaging*, 35, 5, 1285–98, 2016 Feb 11.
29. Mahler, M., Auza, C., Albesa, R., Melus, C., Wu, J.A., Regulatory aspects of artificial intelligence and machine learning-enabled software as medical devices (SaMD), in: *Precision Medicine and Artificial Intelligence*, pp. 237–265, Academic Press, 2021 Jan 1.
30. Benjamens, S., Dhunnoo, P., Meskó, B., The state of artificial intelligence-based FDA-approved medical devices and algorithms: an online database. *npj Digit. Med.*, 3, 1, 118, 2020 Sep 11.
31. Hacker, P., AI Regulation in Europe: From the AI Act to Future Regulatory Challenges, *arXiv preprint arXiv:2310.04072*, 2023 Oct 6.
32. Mehta, A., Sonkala, S., Mishra, A.K., Balancing Act: Navigating the Ethics and Governance of Artificial Intelligence in Healthcare and WHO's Role in Shaping the Future. *Int. Tinnitus J.*, 28, 1, 65–9, 2024 Jun 25.

33. Canton, H., Organisation for economic co-operation and development—OECD, in: *The Europa Directory of International Organizations 2021*, pp. 677–687, Routledge, 2021 Jul 28.
34. Aaronson, S.A., Data is different, and that's why the world needs a new approach to governing cross-border data flows. *Digit. Policy Regul. Gov.*, 21, 5, 441–60, 2019 Jun 13.
35. Olawade, D.B., *et al.*, Artificial intelligence in healthcare delivery: Prospects and pitfalls. *J. Med. Surg. Public Health*, 2, 100108, 2024 Apr 16.
36. Caruana, R., Lou, Y., Gehrke, J., Koch, P., Sturm, M., Elhadad, N., Intelligible models for healthcare: Predicting pneumonia risk and hospital 30-day readmission, in: *Proceedings of the 21th ACM SIGKDD International Conference on Knowledge Discovery and Data Mining*, 2015 Aug 10, pp. 1721–1730.
37. Thai, P., Flores-Cruz, G., Roque, N.A., Leveraging Healthcare Technology to Improve Patient-Doctor Communication, in: *Proceedings of the Human Factors and Ergonomics Society Annual Meeting*, 2023 Sep, vol. 67, no. 1, SAGE Publications, Sage CA: Los Angeles, CA, pp. 2317–2322.
38. Oh, T.R., Integrating predictive modeling and causal inference for advancing medical science. *Child. Kidney Dis.*, 28, 3, 93–8, 2024 Oct 31.
39. Kalusivalingam, A.K., Sharma, A., Patel, N., Singh, V., Enhancing Patient Care Through IoT-Enabled Remote Monitoring and AI-Driven Virtual Health Assistants: Implementing Machine Learning Algorithms and Natural Language Processing. *Int. J. AI ML*, 2, 3, 2021 Feb 15.
40. Mohammadabadi, S.M., Seyedkhamoushi, F., Mostafavi, M., Peikani, M.B., Examination of AI's Role in Diagnosis, Treatment, and Patient Care, in: *Transforming Gender-Based Healthcare with AI and Machine Learning*, pp. 221–238, 2021.
41. Gillies, R.J. and Schabath, M.B., Radiomics improves cancer screening and early detection. *Cancer Epidemiol. Biomarkers Prev.*, 29, 12, 2556–67, 2020 Dec 1.
42. Frank, E., The Role of Artificial Intelligence in Transforming Patient Care and Diagnostic Processes.
43. Giordano, C., Brennan, M., Mohamed, B., Rashidi, P., Modave, F., Tighe, P., Accessing artificial intelligence for clinical decision-making. *Front. Digit. Health*, 3, 645232, 2021 Jun 25.
44. Sowmiya, M., Bhanu, D., Shruthi, K., Jilt, P., Pinky, B.B., Begum, A.Y., Medical Imaging and Diagnostics with Machine Learning, in: *Artificial Intelligence-Based System Models in Healthcare*, pp. 281–309, 2024 Oct 14.
45. Yogeshappa, V.G., AI-Driven Precision Medicine: Revolutionizing Personalized Treatment Plans. *Int. J. Comput. Eng. Technol. (IJCET)*, 15, 5, 2024, 2024.
46. Khansari, N., AI machine learning improves personalized cancer therapies. *Australas. Med. J. (Online)*, 17, 2, 1166–73, 2024.

47. Johnson, K.B., Wei, W.Q., Weeraratne, D., Frisse, M.E., Misulis, K., Rhee, K., Zhao, J., Snowdon, J.L., Precision medicine, AI, and the future of personalized health care. *Clin. Transl. Sci.*, 14, 1, 86–93, 2021 Jan.
48. Shiwlani, A., Khan, M., Sherani, A.M., Qayyum, M.U., Hussain, H.K., Revolutionizing healthcare: The impact of artificial intelligence on patient care, diagnosis, and treatment. *JURIHUM J. Inovasi Humaniora*, 1, 5, 779–90, 2024 Feb 28.
49. Golas, S.B., Shibahara, T., Agboola, S., Otaki, H., Sato, J., Nakae, T., Hisamitsu, T., Kojima, G., Felsted, J., Kakarmath, S., Kvedar, J., A machine learning model to predict the risk of 30-day readmissions in patients with heart failure: a retrospective analysis of electronic medical records data. *BMC Med. Inf. Decis. Making*, 18, 1–7, 2018 Dec.
50. Farid, F., Bello, A., Ahamed, F., Hossain, F., The roles of ai technologies in reducing hospital readmission for chronic diseases: a comprehensive analysis.
51. Akinade, T., Kheyfets, A., Piverger, N., Layne, T.M., Howell, E.A., Janevic, T., The influence of racial-ethnic discrimination on women's health care outcomes: A mixed methods systematic review. *Soc. Sci. Med.*, 316, 114983, 2023 Jan 1.
52. Takale, D.G., Kashid, S.S., Deshmukh, G.B., Gawali, P.P., Mahalle, P.N., Sule, B., Deshpande, A.V., Ghule, V.R., Advancements in Convolutional Neural Networks for Accurate and Efficient Skin Cancer Classification: A Comprehensive Survey, in: *International Conference on Information and Communication Technology for Intelligent Systems*, 2024 Apr 4, Springer Nature Singapore, Singapore, pp. 27–45.
53. Buolamwini, J. and Gebru, T., Gender shades: Intersectional accuracy disparities in commercial gender classification, in: *Conference on fairness, accountability and transparency*, 2018 Jan 21, PMLR, pp. 77–91.
54. Angwin, J., Larson, J., Mattu, S., Kirchner, L., Machine bias, in: *Ethics of data and analytics*, pp. 254–264, Auerbach Publications, 2022 May 12.
55. Dastin, J., Amazon scraps secret AI recruiting tool that showed bias against women, in: *Ethics of data and analytics*, pp. 296–299, Auerbach Publications, 2022 May 12.
56. Rajpurkar, P., Irvin, J., Ball, R.L., Zhu, K., Yang, B., Mehta, H., Duan, T., Ding, D., Bagul, A., Langlotz, C.P., Patel, B.N., Deep learning for chest radiograph diagnosis: A retrospective comparison of the CheXNeXt algorithm to practicing radiologists. *PLoS Med.*, 15, 11, e1002686, 2018 Nov 20.
57. Briganti, G. and Le Moine, O., Artificial intelligence in medicine: today and tomorrow. *Front. Med.*, 7, 509744, 2020 Feb 5.
58. Eckstein, L., Assessing the legal duty to use or disclose interim data for ongoing clinical trials. *J. Law Biosci.*, 6, 1, 51–84, 2019 Oct.
59. Binns, R., Fairness in machine learning: Lessons from political philosophy, in: *Conference on fairness, accountability and transparency*, 2018 Jan 21, PMLR, pp. 149–159.

60. Ribeiro, M.T., Singh, S., Guestrin, C., "Why should i trust you?" Explaining the predictions of any classifier, in: *Proceedings of the 22nd ACM SIGKDD International Conference on Knowledge Discovery and Data Mining*, 2016 Aug 13, pp. 1135–1144.
61. Venkatasubbu, S. and Krishnamoorthy, G., Ethical Considerations in AI Addressing Bias and Fairness in Machine Learning Models. *J. Knowl. Learn. Sci. Technol.*, 1, 1, 130–8, 2022 Sep 14, ISSN: 2959-6386 (online).
62. Barocas, S., Hardt, M., Narayanan, A., *Fairness and machine learning: Limitations and opportunities*, MIT press, 2023 Dec 19.
63. Shkalenko, A.V. and Nazarenko, A.V., Integration of AI and IoT into Corporate Social Responsibility Strategies for Financial Risk Management and Sustainable Development. *Risks*, 12, 6, 87, 2024 May 23.
64. Leslie, D., Understanding bias in facial recognition technologies, *arXiv preprint arXiv:2010.07023*, 2020 Oct 5.
65. Crawford, K., *The Atlas of AI: Power, Politics, and the Planetary Costs of Artificial Intelligence*, Yale University Press, 2021.
66. Bhattacharya, A., *Applied Machine Learning Explainability Techniques: Make ML models explainable and trustworthy for practical applications using LIME, SHAP, and more*, Packt Publishing Ltd, 2022 Jul 29.
67. Schönberger, D., Artificial intelligence in healthcare: a critical analysis of the legal and ethical implications. *Int. J. Law Inf. Technol.*, 27, 2, 171–203, 2019 Jun 1.
68. Topol, E., *Deep medicine: how artificial intelligence can make healthcare human again*, Hachette UK, 2019 Mar 12.
69. Scatiggio, V., Tackling the issue of bias in artificial intelligence to design ai-driven fair and inclusive service systems. How human biases are breaching into ai algorithms, with severe impacts on individuals and societies, and what designers can do to face this phenomenon and change for the better.
70. Griffin, F., Artificial intelligence and liability in health care. *Health Matrix*, 31, 65, 2021.
71. Naik, N., Hameed, B.Z., Shetty, D.K., Swain, D., Shah, M., Paul, R., Aggarwal, K., Ibrahim, S., Patil, V., Smriti, K., Shetty, S., Legal and ethical consideration in artificial intelligence in healthcare: who takes responsibility? *Front. Surg.*, 9, 862322, 2022 Mar 14.
72. Lu, H., Alhaskawi, A., Dong, Y., Zou, X., Zhou, H., Ezzi, S.H., Kota, V.G., Hasan Abdulla Hasan Abdulla, M., Abdalbary, S.A., Patient Autonomy in Medical Education: Navigating Ethical Challenges in the Age of Artificial Intelligence. *Inquiry: J. Health Care Organ. Provis. Financ.*, 61, 00469580241266364, 2024 Sep.
73. Quazi, S., Artificial intelligence and machine learning in precision and genomic medicine. *Med. Oncol.*, 39, 8, 120, 2022 Jun 15.
74. Kaur, J., FutureCare: AI Robots Revolutionizing Health and Healing, in: *Revolutionizing the Healthcare Sector with AI*, pp. 311–340, IGI Global, 2024.

75. Dwivedi, R., Mehrotra, D., Chandra, S., Potential of Internet of Medical Things (IoMT) applications in building a smart healthcare system: A systematic review. *J. Oral Biol. Craniofac. Res.*, 12, 2, 302–18, 2022 Mar 1.
76. Gautam, N., Ghanta, S.N., Mueller, J., Mansour, M., Chen, Z., Puente, C., Ha, Y.M., Tarun, T., Dhar, G., Sivakumar, K., Zhang, Y., Artificial Intelligence, Wearables and Remote Monitoring for Heart failure: current and future applications. *Diagnostics*, 12, 12, 2964, 2022 Nov 26.
77. Nizamis, K., Athanasiou, A., Almpani, S., Dimitrousis, C., Astaras, A., Converging robotic technologies in targeted neural rehabilitation: a review of emerging solutions and challenges. *Sensors*, 21, 6, 2084, 2021 Mar 16.
78. Goyal, A. and Bengio, Y., Inductive biases for deep learning of higher-level cognition. *Proc. R. Soc. A.*, 478, 2266, 20210068, 2022 Oct 26.
79. Vicente, L. and Matute, H., Humans inherit artificial intelligence biases. *Sci. Rep.*, 13, 1, 15737, 2023 Oct 3.
80. Rane, J., Mallick, S.K., Kaya, O., Rane, N.L., Enhancing black-box models: advances in explainable artificial intelligence for ethical decision-making, in: *Future Research Opportunities for Artificial Intelligence in Industry 4.0 and 5.0*, vol. 5, p. 2, 2024.
81. Osoba, O.A., Welser, I.V.W., Welser, W., *An intelligence in our image: The risks of bias and errors in artificial intelligence*, Rand Corporation, 2017 Apr 5.
82. Shin, D., The effects of explainability and causability on perception, trust, and acceptance: Implications for explainable AI. *Int. J. Hum.-Comput. Stud.*, 146, 102551, 2021 Feb 1.
83. Molli, V.L., Enhancing Healthcare Equity through AI-Powered Decision Support Systems: Addressing Disparities in Access and Treatment Outcomes. *Int. J. Sustain. Dev. Through AI ML IoT*, 3, 1, 1–2, 2024 May 10.
84. Jedličková, A., Ethical approaches in designing autonomous and intelligent systems: a comprehensive survey towards responsible development. *AI Soc.*, 39, 1–4, 2024 Aug 6.
85. Gouripur, K., The Impact of Artificial Intelligence on Healthcare: A Revolution in Progress. *North West London J. Gen. Pract.*, 10, 1, 118–125, 2024 Feb 14.
86. De Jager, P.L., Chibnik, L.B., Cui, J., Reischl, J., Lehr, S., Simon, K.C., Aubin, C., Bauer, D., Heubach, J.F., Sandbrink, R., Tyblova, M., Integration of genetic risk factors into a clinical algorithm for multiple sclerosis susceptibility: a weighted genetic risk score. *Lancet Neurol.*, 8, 12, 1111–9, 2009 Dec 1.
87. Sailaja, G. and Narendra, R.B., Factors Influencing Mental Health and the Role of Artificial Intelligence (AI) in the Era of Climate Change, in: *AI and IoT Technology and Applications for Smart Healthcare Systems*, pp. 10–27, Auerbach Publications, 2024.
88. Kuhn, K., Campbell-Lendrum, D., Haines, A., Cox, J., Corvalán, C., Anker, M., Using climate to predict infectious disease epidemics, World Health Organization, Geneva, pp. 16–20, 2005.

89. Walsh, T., Levy, N., Bell, G., Elliott, A., Maclaurin, J., Mareels, I., Wood, F.M., The effective and ethical development of artificial intelligence: an opportunity to improve our wellbeing, Australian Council of Learned Academies, 2019.
90. Mali, S.S., *et al.*, Industry's Influence on Intellectual Property Negotiations: A Review. *Am. J. Pharm. Health Res.*, 2, 3, 1–21, 2014, [ISSN: 2321-3647]. Peer reviewed.
91. Antoniadi, A.M., Du, Y., Guendouz, Y., Wei, L., Mazo, C., Becker, B.A., Mooney, C., Current challenges and future opportunities for XAI in machine learning-based clinical decision support systems: a systematic review. *Appl. Sci.*, 11, 11, 5088, 2021 May 31.

3

Responsible AI in Practice: Case Studies from Industry and Government

Nabanita Roy[1], Sangita Roy[2*] and Shalini Kumari[1]

[1]*Department of Computer Science and Engineering, Chitkara University Institute of Engineering and Technology, Punjab, India*
[2]*Department of Computer Science and Engineering, Thapar Institute of Engineering and Technology, Punjab, India*

Abstract
As Artificial Intelligence (AI) systems are used more widely in sensitive areas, organizations rely on adopting AI responsibly. This chapter describes how organizations and institutions are using various strategies and innovations to ensure AI is fair, trustworthy, honest, private, and reliable. Several implementation strategies are discussed in this chapter, which draw from the experiences of Microsoft, Google, IBM, the UK Government, and Singapore. It has been found that Responsible AI can only be adopted effectively if it involves different experts from technology, ethics, and all the areas involved. This chapter reviews the new regulations related to AI and talks about the challenges in making AI practices ethical. The authors hope that by studying the topic, other organizations can adopt AI in ways that are modern and proper for society.

***Keywords*:** Artificial intelligence, explainable artificial intelligence, machine learning

3.1 Introduction

Bringing AI into multiple industries has led to much progress, yet it has also caused more ethical questions, so the field of Responsible AI is growing. Responsible AI stresses that ethical, moral, and social factors should be

**Corresponding author*: sangita.roy@thapar.edu

Manish Kumar, Nitigya Sambyal, Leena Priyadarshini Singh, Ramasamy V. and S. Balamurugan (eds.) Responsible AI: Principles and Practices, (69–80) © 2026 Scrivener Publishing LLC

considered during all phases of working with AI. A combination of technical, ethical, government, and practical tools is needed to prevent AI from deviating from what society and humans expect. Many companies are now developing rules and systems for AI, encouraging ethical values, ensuring fairness, and deciding on challenging ethical issues with AI. Formulating ethical standards and policies is vital for guiding AI in a manner that helps the most and harms the least. While almost everyone agrees on the need for ethical AI, there is no consensus about its meaning or the requirements necessary to ensure it is achieved [1].

An increasing number of organizations in all areas are appreciating the need for responsible AI and are implementing or planning to take up Responsible AI solutions. If the data is not analyzed properly, AI may draw wrong or biased conclusions since it only works with vast data sets. Responsible practices in AI help direct the development of AI so that it becomes a positive influence for everyone involved [2]. Organizations rely on the knowledge and skills of their employees to develop strategies that help them stay ahead, and research confirms that using AI and sharing knowledge increases an organization's success. Consequently, companies should analyze employees' feedback on the integration of AI-based systems into their existing structure. In computers, digital data collections, and highly advanced algorithms, there are now many new opportunities in AI and its branches, like Machine Learning (ML), working with language, and designing robots. It can be challenging for companies to bring AI into everyday work processes. Because AI algorithms are quite complex, it is not easy for decision-makers to understand the decisions made by these systems. AI is used in medical care and criminal justice [14], and this introduces ethical issues. There have been cases where errors produced by AI ended up harming people by discriminating against them or invading their privacy. Having careful attention to these concerns, as well as understanding how AI reaches decisions, becomes necessary during AI adoption. For this reason, we need AI systems that can explain their actions through technology known as XAI.

Managers in organizations should focus on detailed documentation of how AI works, continuous monitoring for errors, and checking every detail leading to changes in AI results. Many studies have shown that AI can achieve results that exceed what a human expert can do. In some cases, AI has unexpectedly produced inappropriate and biased language through chatbots [3]. Nowadays, AI is applied in supply chain management to understand how people behave and make decisions. Additionally, people must understand both ethics and society as well as technical aspects to make Responsible AI successful. Besides the risks from outside, like tougher regulations and rising demands for AI specialists' compensation, there are internal temptations like high costs in research and development that can be handled, together with rigid work processes, employee relationships, and missing data. Misalignment between AI software and the organization's duties, uncertain data ownership, and missing data trust can all reduce the confidence people have in the system. When AI is used in important situations, it has caused many people to worry about ethical issues. Responsible AI (RAIs) try to make sure that AI is fair, accountable, and transparent. Both governments and industries are facing pressure to integrate ethical standards and follow the rules when using AI. This chapter reviews how both government and industry organizations have tackled the task of introducing responsible AI. By analyzing specific cases, guidelines, technologies, practices, and rules that these entities create to ensure their AI remains ethically sound as it serves them [4].

3.2 Framework for Analyzing Responsible AI Implementation

To create a set of guidelines to help analyze responsible AI implementations before exploring any cases [5]. By following these five principles from the hierarchical model of AI ethics, this framework helps assess how firms handle ethical matters while using AI. The key responsibility of AI principles is shown in Figure 3.1.

The image clearly illustrates the five main ideas of Responsible AI organized in a pyramid manner. At the top is Robustness, suggesting that AI

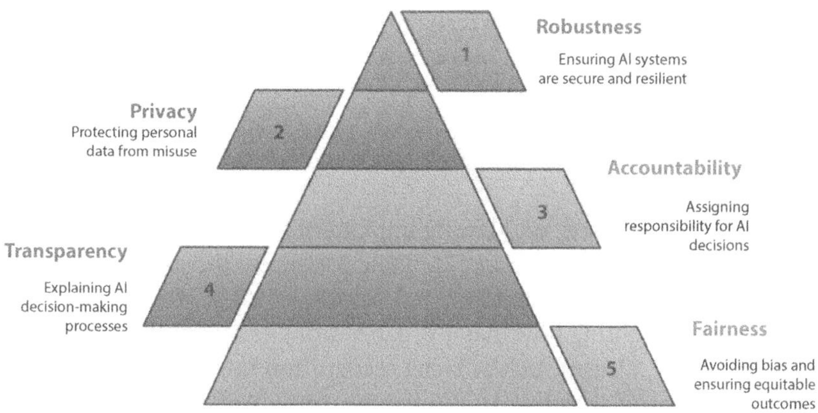

Figure 3.1 AI principles.

systems should be strong and safe [12]. After that, Privacy discusses the importance of keeping personal data safe. Next, people need to be made accountable for decisions made by AI. Underpinning it is transparency, which guarantees that how AI makes decisions can be explained. The purpose of fairness is to ensure there is no bias and fairness in ethical AI. This model reveals that these principles are connected and supports the smooth use of AI.

3.3 Literature Review

Experts argue that it is necessary to apply ethical principles such as fairness, transparency, accountability, and robustness both in industry and in government. The majority of guidelines on AI ethics share a strong consensus on three key values: non-maleficence, autonomy, and justice, yet offer few instructions on how to implement them. A framework called AI People can be used to turn ethical principles into policies that help manage AI [6]. Within the industry, studies highlight that using both internal networks and cross-departmental committees helps Microsoft address ethical issues. With the new Trusted AI framework and a range of open-source toolkits, IBM is showing that explainable AI is becoming more important for businesses regulated by the law. Public institutions in the UK and Singapore have set standards for others to follow through the Data Ethics Framework and the Model AI Governance Framework. They follow the recommendations made by academics for AI to be used responsibly, with the participation of different groups and in accordance with set standards. For this reason, literature suggests that good principles depend on proper leadership, suitable technical capabilities, and adjustable rules within organizations.

3.4 Case Studies

Microsoft has focused on developing internal rules that promote the responsible development of AI [7]. Table 3.1 shows the case studies of its implementation and outcome.

Guides highlighting how major organizations carry out Responsible AI: Early detection of cases such as facial recognition misuse became possible because Microsoft introduced an effective framework with the Office of

Table 3.1 Case studies implementation and its outcome.

Case study name	Implementation	Outcome
Microsoft - Responsible AI Governance	Office of Responsible AI: Leads the execution of policies on responsible AI. The Aether Committee: Gives advice on ethical situations using the results of research. The RAI Champion Network: Informs employees on right AI practices and helps them adopt them.	Microsoft's well-defined governance, issues related to facial recognition, and content review are recognized earlier.
Google - Fairness in Machine Learning Context	Fairness Indicators Toolkit: Allows for the measurement of fairness in machine learning models. Model Cards: Revealing how AI models behave on different groups of people. The organization's AI team is committed to dealing with possible negative effects of models they have released.	Google has improved how it is seen by the public and by regulators by making its ML practices more transparent.
Case Study: IBM - Explainability and Trust in AI Context	India – AI Fairness 360 Toolkit supports developing applications that address bias issues. Reliable AI: Should pay close attention to explainability, robustness, and privacy.	Various industries such as finance and healthcare, depend on IBM's tools which help develop AI systems in accordance with the proper regulations.

Responsible AI, the Aether Committee, and the RAI Champion Network. The company introduced the Fairness Indicators Toolkit and Model Cards to ensure all data institutions were fair and to gain more public trust. Through the AI Fairness 360 Toolkit and Reliable AI, IBM stresses explainability, robustness, and privacy, all of which have helped their customers in regulated industries such as finance and healthcare.

3.5 Cross-Sector Analysis: Patterns in Responsible AI Implementation

Some trends emerge when looking at different examples of responsible AI being used successfully in different industries [8]. Figure 3.2 shows the responsible AI implementation comparison.

Major tech companies use Responsible AI in different ways. The Office of Responsible AI, Aether Committee, and RAI Champion Network are among the Microsoft entities that monitor the company's activities and, early on, highlight any ethical issues related to facial recognition [9]. To encourage fairness, Google uses the Fairness Indicators Toolkit and Model Cards and strives to maintain an open-minded culture in the AI sector. To be more responsible, IBM offers the AI Fairness 360 Toolkit and ensures a high degree of reliability by adding explainability and privacy, important factors in finance and healthcare.

Characteristic	Organizational Culture and Leadership	Governance Structures	Technical Approaches	Stakeholder Engagement
Commitment	Clear ethical commitment	Diverse AI ethics boards	Extensive pre-deployment testing	Early engagement with communities
Willingness	Delay deployment for ethics	Clear escalation paths	Ongoing monitoring	Channels for user feedback
Investment	Building interdisciplinary teams	Regular reporting to leadership	Explicit fairness metrics	Consultation with domain experts
Recognition	Strategic advantage, not burden	Integration with risk frameworks	Documentation supports auditability	Transparency with stakeholders
Processes	None	Translating ethics to requirements	Explainability for stakeholders	Collaborative issue resolution

Figure 3.2 Responsible AI implementation comparison.

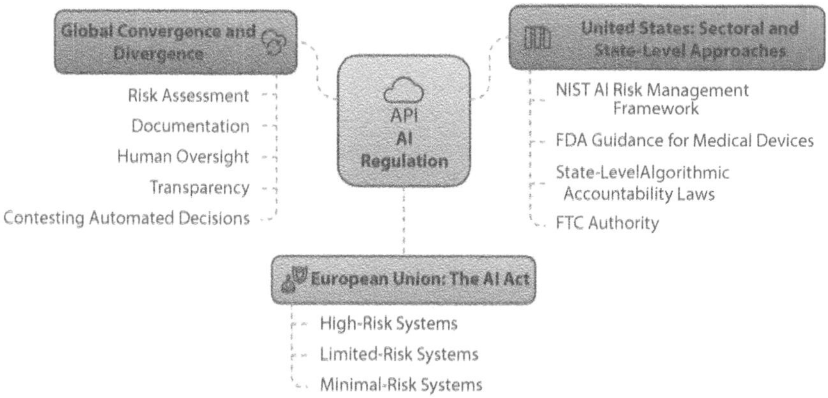

Figure 3.3 AI regulation: EU vs. US approaches.

3.6 Emerging Regulatory Landscape

It is increasingly complex for organizations using responsible AI to follow regulations because they are very different in different areas and industries. Figure 3.3 presents the AI regulation: EU vs. US approaches.

Now, various sectors and governments are regularly putting certain ethical AI methods into practice [10]. From Microsoft's internal governance and Google's transparency efforts to IBM's focus on explainability and the regulatory actions of the UK, Singapore, and the EU, it is evident that the successful implementation of responsible AI hinges on clear commitments, ethical oversight, stakeholder engagement, and technical rigor. Globally, risk assessment and keeping everything documented are being emphasized to ensure AI is useful and trustworthy to humanity.

3.7 Recommendations for Organizations

Identifying how core aspects such as accountability, oversight, integration, documentation, and leadership can be accomplished in the different stages of implementing responsible AI: creating governance, increasing technical knowledge, applying the principles, and anticipating regulations. Assigning tasks, setting up controls for reviews, and securing the management team's dedication are fundamental actions highlighted in this book. Improving technical skills for a team involves explaining principles, preparing useful documents, and providing equipment [11]. Next, the principles guide the activities and tools used for sectors, and being ready for regulation covers

Characteristic	Establishing Governance	Building Technical Capacity	Operationalizing Principles	Preparing for Regulation
Accountability	Specific roles designated	Teams understand principles	Principles translated to practices	Compliance efforts documented
Oversight	Review processes established	Measurement frameworks defined	Sector-specific approaches developed	Regulatory developments monitored
Integration	Connect with existing governance	Appropriate documentation created	Practical tools created	Engage with regulators
Documentation	Maintain records of decisions	Invest in tools and infrastructure	Establish clear thresholds	Adopt forward-looking standards
Leadership	Executive-level commitment	Build interdisciplinary teams	Learn from incidents	Collaborate with industry peers

Figure 3.4 Recommendations for organizations.

documenting plans, checking new laws, and communicating with regulators and peers. All these actions work together to guide companies in incorporating ethical AI. Figure 3.4 presents the recommendations for organizations.

Implementation Roadmaps

Using the case studies in mind, a common approach to rolling out responsible AI has been created. Figure 3.5 presents the implementation of responsible AI.

Figure 3.5 Implementation of responsible AI.

The approach organizations can use to ensure that Responsible AI is implemented properly. At this step, the key emphasis is on laying a solid base and committing and sharing resources with the team [13]. During this period, which lasts from 2 to 4 months, the focus changes to creating the framework, which includes designing ways to assess and record information. Between 3 and 6 months after starting, staff are trained, and the riskiest AI programs are reviewed. Between six and twelve months, emphasis shifts to building and perfecting structures and strengthening various practices and strategies.

Future of Responsible AI Implementation

As time goes on and technology improves, so will the way responsible AI is handled. There are several trends that will influence the way search evolves in the near future.

Emerging Standards and Frameworks

There is a shift happening in the responsible AI world as standards and certification are being introduced to support the guidelines.

Technical Standards Development: Amongst others, IEEE, ISO, and NIST are responsible for making technical standards for several responsibilities in AI.

- Various IEEE 7000 series standards deal with ethics in designing systems.
- Standards for AI trustworthiness are developed within ISO/IEC JTC 1/SC 42.
- CEN-CENELEC standards cover AI ethics and governance.
- The NIST AI Risk Management Framework and the resources it provides. The standards will offer clearer instructions to those using them and support interoperability and comparison among organizations.

Certification Programs: Various certification systems are coming up to confirm that AI activities are responsible [15].

- There is an AI certification program in Malta.
- This program is called the Ethics Certification Program for Autonomous and Intelligent Systems (ECPAIS).
- The AI Verify Foundation uses a certification framework.

- In healthcare and finance, there are programs focused on certifying professionals. Over time, they could encourage organizations to embrace responsible AI by setting out useful evaluation guidelines.

Auditing Methodologies: There are now more advanced techniques for auditing AI to ensure that it meets the necessary requirements.

- Approaches for checking the effects of algorithms.
- Different testing approaches are required for different fields of application.
- Approved structures and templates for tracking audit trails.
- The use of independent auditors. This will help ensure more careful evaluation of AI efforts, leading to increased responsibility.

Challenges in Operationalizing Responsible AI
Common Issues

- There is no standard process or system for most RAI tools.
- There are challenges when balancing openness and good performance.
- Few rewards for organizations choosing ethical AI.

Emerging Solutions

- Creating global standards for AI (ISO/IEC).
- Considering RAI metrics as part of reviewing employee performance.
- Teamwork between different groups for the creation of toolkits and standards.

3.8 Discussion

The case reviews implied that the key principles of Responsible AI are generally agreed upon, but how they are carried out depends on a company's situation, rules, and plans. Through its special department and committee for ethical AI, Microsoft demonstrates the positive impact of keeping governance centralized when working on AI. Google's strategy involving Model Cards and Fairness Indicators is meant to ensure customers trust the company and their decisions. IBM makes sure that its models can be understood and remain reliable in fields like healthcare and finance. Ethical AI is important to policymakers in countries like the UK, where the Data Ethics Framework proves the point, and Singapore, where the AI Governance Framework helps by creating testing tools called AI Verify. The examples demonstrate similar ethics being followed by most businesses, though execution could be different due to each sector's requirements. Besides, it is still difficult to standardize AI; there are issues with openness versus speed, and people are not sufficiently motivated to act responsibly with AI. It points out that AI can benefit the public only if there are global norms, flexible rules, and cooperation among involved parties.

3.9 Conclusion

To support public trust and ensure AI is accepted by everyone, it must be used in a responsible manner. This chapter provides various examples of how industry and government are ensuring that AI systems include ethics. For Responsible AI to be effective, an organization requires leadership, well-developed technical skills, compliance with rules, and engagement with stakeholders. Over time, paying close attention, reviewing, and updating will become very important. In the near future, an international approach to standard-setting and accountability will help ensure that AI benefits people and the planet.

AI disclosure statement: The author acknowledges the use of AI-based tools for minor language editing or grammatical correction. However, all intellectual contributions, analyses, and conclusions presented in this chapter are entirely the author's own.

References

1. Pesapane, F. and Summers, P., Ethics and regulations for AI in radiology, in: *Artificial Intelligence for Medicine,* pp. 179–192, Elsevier, 2024.
2. Brown, S., Davidovic, J., Hasan, A., The algorithm audit: Scoring the algorithms that score us. *Big Data Soc.*, 8, 1, 2021. https://doi.org/10.1177/2053951720983865.
3. Buolamwini, J. and Gebru, T., Gender shades: Intersectional accuracy disparities in commercial gender classification, in: *Proceedings of the 1st Conference on Fairness, Accountability and Transparency*, pp. 77–91, 2018.

4. Carey, B. and Burgess, M., FDA's new medical AI policies enhance regulatory flexibility, Canadian Treasury Board Secretariat, 2019.
5. Caruana, R., Intelligible models for healthcare: Predicting pneumonia risk and hospital 30-day readmission, in: *ACM SIGKDD International Conference on Knowledge Discovery and Data Mining*, 2015.
6. Cohen, I.G., Amarasingham, R., Shah, A., Xie, B., Lo, B., The legal and ethical concerns that arise from using complex predictive analytics in health care. *Health Aff. (Milwood), 33*, 7, 1139–47, 2014 Jul. doi: 10.1377/hlthaff.2014.0048. PMID: 25006139.
7. Dash, S., Gunluk, O., Wei, D., Explainable AI for responsible AI use. *IBM J. Res. Dev., 66*, 2, 2022.
8. Guidotti, R., Monreale, A., Ruggieri, S., Turini, F., Giannotti, F., Pedreschi, D., The ethics of AI ethics: An evaluation of guidelines. Minds and Machines. *ACM Comput. Surv., 51*, 5, 99–120, 2018.
9. Holstein, K., Wortman Vaughan, J., Daumé, H., Dudik, M., Wallach, H., Improving fairness in machine learning systems, in: *What do industry practitioners need? CHI Conference on Human Factors in Computing Systems*, 2019.
10. Jobin, A., Ienca, M., Vayena, E., The global landscape of AI ethics guidelines. *Nat. Mach. Intell., 1*, 9, 389–399, 2019.
11. Liang, F., Das, V., Kostyuk, N., Hussain, M.M., Constructing a data-driven society: China's social credit system as a state surveillance infrastructure. *Policy Internet, 10*, 4, 415–453, 2018. https://onlinelibrary.wiley.com/doi/10.1002/poi3.183.
12. Vujović, D., Generative AI: Riding the new general purpose technology storm. *Ekonomika preduzeća*. 72, 125–136, 2024.
13. Zerilli, J., Knott, A., Maclaurin, J., Gavaghan, C., Algorithmic decision-making and the control problem. *Mines Mach., 31*, 89–112, 2021.
14. Zilka, M., Fogliato, R., Hron, J., Butcher, B., Ashurst, C., Weller, A., The progression of disparities within the criminal justice system: Differential enforcement and risk assessment instruments, in: arXiv [cs.CY], 2023. http://arxiv.org/abs/2305.07575.
15. Zhu, H., Yu, B., Halfaker, A., Terveen, L., Value-sensitive algorithm design: Method, case study, and lessons. *Proc. ACM. Hum. Comput. Interact.*, 2, 1–23, 2018, CSCW.

4

An Efficient System for Skin Disease Detection and Localization Using Faster Region Based Convolutional Neural Networks with Inception Architecture

Nitin Singh[1], Ankita Nanda[1], Keshav Garg[1], Varun Gupta[1]*, Nitigya Sambyal[2,3] and Deepika Vikas Agrawal[4]

[1]Department of Computer Science and Engineering, Chandigarh College of Engineering and Technology, Chandigarh, India
[2]Department of Information Technology, Uppsala University, Uppsala, Sweden
[3]Department of CSE, Thapar Institute of Engineering and Technology, Patiala, Punjab, India
[4]National Institute of Technical Teachers Training & Research, Chandigarh, India

Abstract
Dermatological diseases are the most common class of diseases that are also difficult to identify and detect. Any skin problem if not detected timely can cause severe health and financial loss to patients. Skin diseases like contact dermatitis, candidiasis, and lupus are rare and can be efficiently detected and analyzed by a computer aided diagnosis system for proper treatment. The paper proposes an automated dual stage approach model for skin disease detection and prediction by using Faster Region based Convolutional Neural Networks with Inception v2 architecture. The first stage includes pre-processing of images along with feature extraction. In the second stage, the extracted features are given as input to region convolutional neural networks to predict maximum area of infection. The model is further optimized by passing the identified infectious regions through region of interest pooling layer to classify the disease in proposed region. The dataset used in the research work consists of 32 classes of skin diseases. The proposed model not only helps in detection of the skin condition but also produces a bounding box with confidence score for the detected class. The model achieves an accuracy of 93.06%, average precision of 95% and average recall

**Corresponding author*: varungupta@ccet.ac.in

Manish Kumar, Nitigya Sambyal, Leena Priyadarshini Singh, Ramasamy V. and S. Balamurugan (eds.) Responsible AI: Principles and Practices, (81–104) © 2026 Scrivener Publishing LLC

of 98% over the 32 classes. Further, the proposed model when compared to existing models in literature shows an accuracy improvement of approximately 5.81%.

***Keywords*:** Skin disease, Faster R-CNN with Inception v2, inception, bounding box, deep learning

4.1 Introduction

The skin is the most significant part of the human body as it manufactures vitamin D, protects from UV radiation infections, injuries, heat, and harmful radiation and maintains body temperature. Skin diseases are among the foremost well-known medical problems around the world. Notwithstanding being common, their determination is a kind of difficult and needs broad information and experience within the space. Various studies indicate that skin diseases are the main cause of skin lesions, scales, plaques, pigmentation and other symptoms on the patient's skin. It has also been reported that symptoms of such diseases result in long-term pain and disfigurement. Patients with primary skin diseases (such as psoriasis, alopecia areata and vitiligo) are vulnerable to psychological disorders, including anxiety symptoms and depressive disorder. Diagnosis of pigmented skin lesions without assistance can be challenging, even for seasoned dermatologists [1].

In addition, treatments for skin diseases can also lead to mental health problems. For example, the acne drug isotretinoin has been associated with increased risk of serious depression and suicidal ideation [2, 3].

Traditionally, a dermatologist examines a patient's skin to determine any medical condition. Some of the conventional methods used to treat these diseases are patch testing, skin biopsy, and culture.

One of the most common ways to diagnose skin allergies is a patch test. Small pins containing potential allergens stuck to adhesive patches are applied against the back skin and left for a specified period. The skin is further evaluated for allergic responses. Skin biopsies are carried out to diagnose skin cancer or benign skin conditions [2]. This involves taking a small piece of skin after administering a local anesthetic, and sending it to a lab for the analysis. The removal might take place with a scalpel, a Gillette blue blade, or a cylindrical punch biopsy tool, and stitches may be needed to close the wound. A culture test is done in a laboratory to identify the microorganism responsible for infection (bacterial, fungal, or viral). The samples for the tests may consist of scrapings of the surface skin, biopsy of tissues, pus-filled lesions, blood blisters, hair or nails to determine the organism responsible [4].

However, all these processes are very tedious and time-consuming and require extreme precision to prevent misdiagnosis. In such cases, a computer-aided diagnosis system can help in mass screening of patients with high speed and accuracy. Early recognition of skin disease will control further worsening of the patient's condition. With the fast development of computer technology, machine learning-based disease diagnosis systems can play a vital role in the early and accurate detection of diseases [5, 6]. Various prediction models have already been developed in the literature to date. But, most of them use only a few classification algorithms to obtain final predictions. Artificial intelligence paradigms can be used for problem-solving and learning by experience [4]. Also, most of the research is limited to the identification of a maximum 7–8 skin diseases [5, 7]. Various skin disease detection using bagging, AdaBoost and gradient boosting methods have failed to provide good accuracy models [5]. There are machine learning, AI and statistical methods among a variety of data analysis techniques in research. Some examples can be given from the processes that are included in machine learning and have the meaning of making predictions or creating easier versions of complex data sets [8].

One type of DNN, Convolutional neural networks (CNN) [9], demonstrated their encouraging potential in revealing vision-based patterns from a large number of labeled images [10]. Deep CNN have revolutionized the field of computer-aided supporting systems [11].

In this paper, a deep learning-based solution for early and accurate detection and localization of skin diseases has been proposed. The proposed model would be useful for the detection 32 skin diseases which includes both common and some chronic skin issues. Further, infected regions from the images are localized using a bounding box which indicates the confidence score of the detected disease. Such a system will provide an insight into the condition of the disease and thus would aid medical experts for its timely and proper treatment. The proposed system can be used by dermatologists for initial analysis and diagnosis of skin diseases.

The major contributions of this work are as follows:

1. The proposed model deals with detection of 32 skin diseases which is the highest number of classes dealt with for skin disease detection in the existing literature.
2. The proposed work also includes the creation of an image database of 942 images each of which belongs to one of the 32 skin diseases.

3. The proposed model provides a bounding box along with a confidence score for detected class in the infected region.
4. The model achieves an average accuracy of 93.06%, precision of 95% and recall of 98%. Further, the proposed model shows an accuracy improvement by approximately 5.81%, when compared with existing models in literature.

The paper is structured as follows. Section 4.2 provides an overview of the related work. The proposed method is presented in detail in Section 4.3. Experimental results and discussions are presented in Section 4.4. Finally, Section 4.5 concludes the paper.

4.2 Related Work

Several research studies have been done to detect various classes of skin diseases. Yasir *et al.* [5] in his work detect 9 classes of skin diseases namely Eczema, Acne, Leprosy, Psoriasis, Scabies, Foot Ulcer, Vitiligo, Tinea Corporis and Pityriasis Rosea using image set of 775 taken from 128 different patients. The first step involved pre-processing of images to extract significant features. The extracted features along with patient characteristics, like gender, age, duration, type and color of liquid, elevation and sensation, are passed on to a feed-forward backpropagation artificial neural network (ANN) for dermatological diagnosis. The model obtained accuracy varying from 85%-97% for the various disease classes under study.

A similar research was done by Bajaj *et al.* [12] for classification of 813 images into five different classes of skin diseases namely Eczema, Psoriasis, Impetigo, Scleroderma and Melanoma. The author extracted the infected region using image processing techniques and then predicted the disease using artificial neural network. This approach provided a highest class wise classification accuracy of 99.6% and lowest classification accuracy of 88.7%.

In recent years, deep learning-based methods have become more popular for detection of medical conditions in patients. Rathod *et al.* [13] used a novel dermoscopy detection and classification method based on CNN to determine skin diseases. CNN along with softmax image classifier was used for automatic feature extraction and disease classification respectively from patient's skin disease images. The proposed work achieved an approximate accuracy of 70%.

Zhang *et al.* [11] performed cross-sectional study of 150 dermoscopy images including melanoma, nevi, and seborrheic keratoses 50 cases each from melanoma detection challenge test data set. Dermatologist classification sensitivity increased from 76.0% to 80.8% and specificity increased from 72.6% to 72.8%. The overall accuracy of dermatologist evaluations improved as well — from 73.8% to 75.4%.

Koparde *et al.* [25] proposed conditional generative adversarial networks and a YOLOv5 darknet-based approach for skin lesion classification and localization. This model utilized independent component analysis to enhance its robustness and interpretability by extracting latent features from dermatological images. The work focused on pre-processing to remove artifacts, followed by lesion localization using the YOLOv5 object detection algorithm. The approach has been validated on (international skin imaging collaboration) ISIC 2016, 2017, and 2018 datasets, showing results with accuracy ranging from 97.18% to 99.99% across different datasets, outperforming traditional methods. Burada *et al.* [26] proposed a differential evolution-based CNN based approach for early melanoma skin cancer detection. The pre-processing phase involved applying various filters and feature extraction techniques, including local binary patterns (LBP) and gray level co-occurrence matrix (GLCM). These extracted features and color-space information were used to improve the detection accuracy of melanoma lesions. The method was evaluated on the HAM10000 dataset, achieving a detection accuracy of 91%.

The other research done by Maqsood *et al.* [27] introduced a support vector machine-based model for multiclass skin lesion classification using a dataset consisting of HAM10000, ISIC2018, ISIC2019, and PH2. The images underwent a pre-processing step where a contrast enhancement method was applied to enhance the quality of dermoscopic images. Then, a custom 26-layer CNN were used to segment skin lesions. Subsequently, four pre-trained CNN models was fine-tuned using transfer learning for feature extraction. The extracted features were fused using the convolutional sparse image decomposition fusion technique. Their approach achieved an accuracy of 98.57% on HAM10000, 98.62% on ISIC2018, 93.47% on ISIC2019, and 98.98% on PH2. K. Ramamurthy *et al.* [28] introduced a modified DenseNet-169 and a customized CNN-based approach for the classification of skin lesions. The model, validated on the HAM10000 dataset, achieved a classification accuracy of 93.2%. R. Babu *et al.* [29] proposed a method for skin cancer detection using the SIIM-ISIC Melanoma classification dataset, consisting of 33,126 dermoscopic images from 2,000 patients. The work involved pre-processing using a bilateral filter to remove noise, followed by segmentation of skin lesions, which is fine-tuned using the Artificial Ecosystem-based Optimization (AEO) algorithm. The CNN-based features were extracted from the augmented segmented images and then fed into a LeNet neural network for skin cancer detection. The model achieved an accuracy of 91.99%, demonstrating its effectiveness in detecting skin cancer.

Based on the literature, we aim to propose a deep learning-based end-to-end system for classification and localization of skin diseases into 32 classes. The proposed work involves pre-processing and labeling of the images for one of the 32 skin diseases under study. These images are, thereafter, given as input to Faster R-CNN with Inception v2 model which is fine-tuned and trained for approximately 35000 steps to detect and localize disease. The results obtained by the model are in the form of a bounded box along with the confidence score for a label along with corresponding F-scores for each class. The main reason to use Faster R-CNN is that it is more reliable, robust and maps well over both COCO and ImageNet datasets [12–15].

4.3 Proposed System

The proposed work consists of two phases wherein the first phase involves image pre-processing and feature extraction and second phase consist of detection and localization of skin disease using these extracted features. The detailed description of dataset and methodology used in this work are given in this section.

4.3.1 Dataset

The foremost requirement for any deep learning model is data or more precisely clean, consistent and well-structured data. Datasets for malignant and benign skin lesions are readily available but it's quite the opposite for common skin diseases. Each disease varies in its own visual characteristics and in location over the human body. Such characteristics are taken care of when creating our own image set through various internet sources. In our work we have selected 32 classes of skin diseases with around 30 images pertaining to each class. Thus, the dataset consists of more than 900 labeled images approximately. The XML file was generated for each label which had the four vertex coordinates of the bounding box as well as the name or id of the associated class. Table 4.1 and Figure 4.1 shows class wise detailed image distribution for the dataset used in the research work.

Table 4.1 Image distribution per class.

Disease	No. of images	Disease	No. of images	Disease	No. of images	Disease	No. of images
Acrodermatitis	28	Elephantiasis	21	Lyme disease	29	Razor bumps	30
Atopic dermatitis	29	Fifth disease	30	Melasma	30	Ringworm	30
Bowen's disease	30	Flea bites	30	Moles	29	Scabies	30
Candidiasis	30	Heat rash	30	Stings	30	Scarlet fever	30
Cellulitis	30	Hemangiomas	30	MRSA	30	Seborrheic keratoses	30
Cold sores	27	Hives	30	Pityriasis rosea	30	Shingles	30
Contact dermatitis	30	Kawasaki Disease	30	Plant rashes	30	Syphilis	30
Dermatomyositis	30	Lupus	30	Psoriasis	29	Vitiligo	30

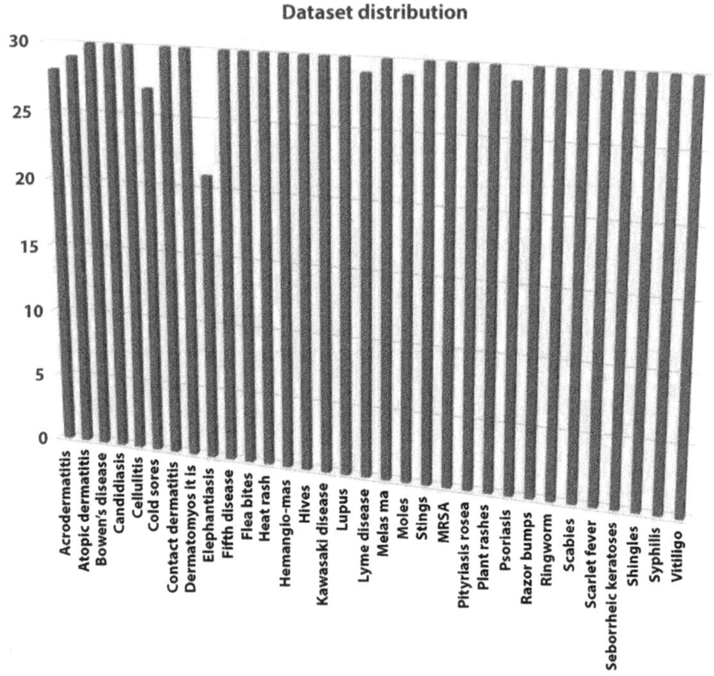

Figure 4.1 Dataset distribution.

4.3.2 Methodology

The workflow for the proposed work is presented in Figure 4.2. The proposed work consists of two phases wherein the first phase involves collection of various skin disease images for creation of dataset which is subjected to various pre-processing techniques. The initial step involves using a data-driven approach to identify and select relevant patient records along with key variables for analysis. This is followed by data cleaning to remove all anomalies such as noise, incorrect, missing values or inconsistent data. The data is then subjected to transformation which basically converts all the different data formats into one single suitable format which can be easily used for prediction. The second phase is mainly the training and testing phase which develops a model that can predict accurate class of skin disease by analyzing the diseased images.

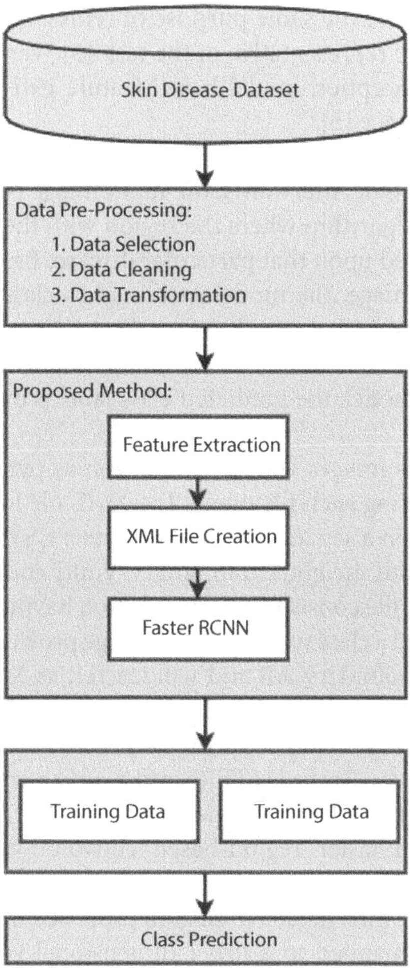

Figure 4.2 Methodology.

4.3.2.1 Feature Extraction

One of the most critical steps that impact model performance is feature extraction. The goal of feature extraction is to abstract a variable-dimensional image into a fixed number of visual features. Image classification models are mostly built with effective visual feature extraction techniques. Whether they are based on traditional computer vision approaches like filter-based connectivity, histogram methods, etc., or intensive learning methods, they all have the same purpose of removing attributes from the input image that are representative of the task [5]. Various research works demonstrate that inception model-based feature extractors exhibit state-of-the-art performance [5].

The first step for the feature selection method is to extract a particular image from the dataset. Afterwards, the input image is passed through the feature extraction algorithm where the region with the maximum amount of infection is trained upon that particular disease. Based on the extracted features from the image, the model is trained to classify the disease into 32 different classes stated above. The flowchart (Figure 4.3) represents the basic functioning of the feature extraction method of the class - flea bites. After training the model, the predicted class label is of flea bites with 96% of correctness.

The method uses images with jpg extension as python supports many libraries for processing such file types. The XML file for each corresponding image is stored in a separate folder to create a CSV with the attributes: class, filename, width, height, xmin, xmax, ymin and ymax as shown in Table 4.2. The XML file consists of an annotation having boundary as A (x_1, y_1) and B (x_2, y_2); and a class named X. The image provided to the model will only look for that boundary AB and will learn it as X disease. Using this, it will learn about the features of many diseases. The CSV is used to create a pbtxt file containing a label map for each class. The final step involves creation of Tensorflow Records (TFRecords) which are binary files aimed to execute faster with less usage of memory.

Feature maps in faster region-based convolutional neural network (Faster R-CNN) Inception v2 model are taken from CNN (with 1x1 convolutions, which are then passed to Region proposed network (RPN). Each sliding window is mapped to a lower-dimensional vector (256-d for ZF and 512-d for VGG). This vector is fed into two sibling fully connected layers—a box-regression layer (reg) and a box-classification layer (cls) [16, 17]. Figure 4.4 shows the working of the RPN [17].

4.3.2.2 Faster R-CNN Framework

Image-based object detection is widely used to recognize occurrences of understanding semantic objects in digital images. R-CNN (Region based-Convolutional Neural Networks) is a set of techniques proposed for localization and recognition of an object, with the goal of improving model performance. The R-CNN algorithm uses a sliding window that runs over different locations on an image. However, the size and aspect of an object is dependent on how far or near it is from the camera.

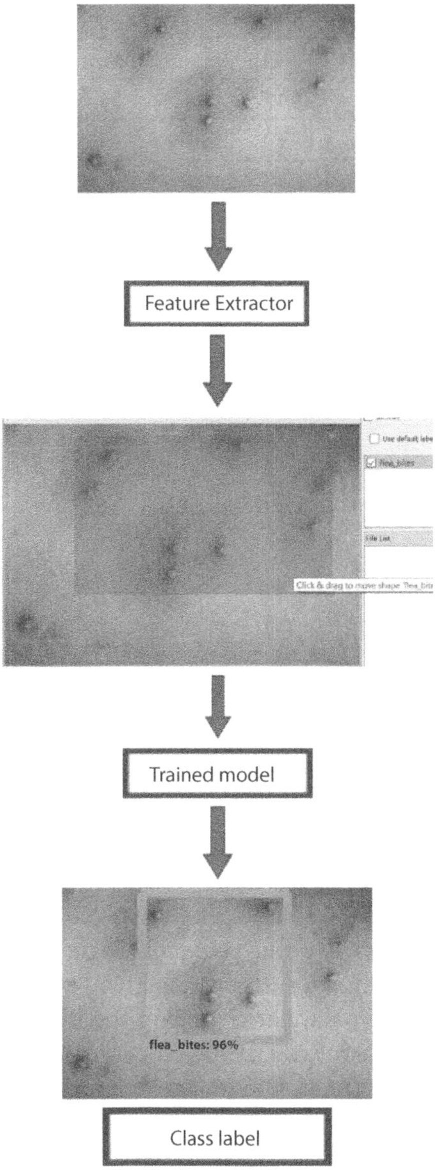

Figure 4.3 Steps for feature extraction.

Table 4.2 XML file with 8 attributes.

Class	Filename	Width	Height	xmin	xmax	ymin	ymax
Acrodermatitis	1.jpg	300	168	56	270	8	136
Acrodermatitis	2.jpg	258	195	151	245	47	161
Atopic dermatitis	1.jpg	260	193	5	248	61	171
Vitiligo	29.jpg	281	179	10	176	34	179
Vitiligo	30.jpg	259	194	84	189	35	156

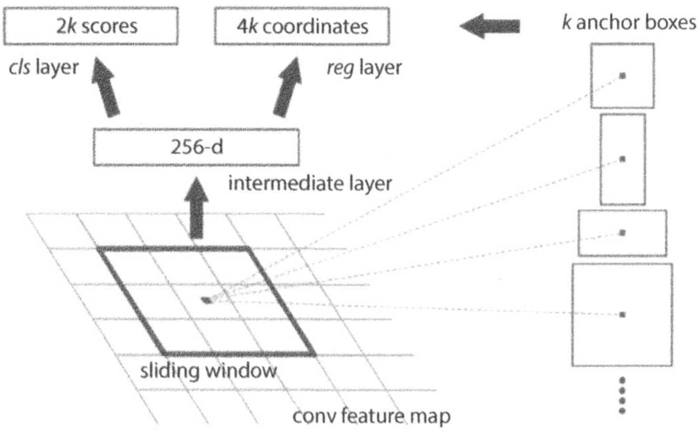

Figure 4.4 Region proposal network [17].

R-CNN employs selective search to generate region proposals (represented as bounding boxes) to solve this problem. Algorithm 4.1 [20] describes the hierarchical grouping algorithm which involves region based similarity tests based on maximum similarity among the neighboring regions. The similar regions are subsequently merged together after calculation of similarity set, followed by extraction of object location boxes from the regions.

Algorithm 4.1: Hierarchical Grouping Algorithm [20]

- **Procedure** Obtain initial regions $R = \{r_1, \ldots, r_n\}$
- Initialize similarity set $S = \phi$
- **for each** *Neighboring region pair*(r_i, r_j) **do**
- Compute the similarity score $s(r_i, r_j)$
- $S = SU\ s(r_i, r_j)$

- **end for**
- **while** S ≠ φ**do**
- Identified highest similarity score: $s(r_i, r_j) = max(S)$
- Merge corresponding regions $r_t = r_i U r_j$
- Remove similarity values related to r_i : $S = S \setminus s(r_i, r_*)$
- Remove similarity values related to r_j : $S = S \setminus s(r_*, r_j)$
- Calculate similarity set S_t between r_t and its neighbors
- $S = S \cup S_t$
- $R = RUr_t$
- **end while**
- Extract object location boxes *L* from all regions in *R*
- **end procedure**

As selective search is quite slow and a long process, some other replacement algorithm was required in place of selective search. This issue was taken care of in Faster R-CNN by utilizing a separate network itself for predicting region proposals [18]. The predicted regions are then passed through an ROI (Region of Interest) pooling layer, after which the object is classified within the proposed region. Because it is faster and more practical for real-time object detection than R-CNN and Fast R-CNN, we chose the Faster R-CNN model.

R-CNN breaks down the entire detection problem into two subproblems: using low-level cues like color and super pixel consistency to generate object proposals in a category-agnostic way, and using CNN classifiers to determine the presence of an object category at these locations. A two-stage approach like this combines the accuracy of bounding box segmentation (using low-level visual cues) with the extremely powerful classification ability of modern CNNs [19].

The Faster R-CNN model consists of four layers as shown in Figure 4.5. The first layer is a CNN, the Inception Layer which consists of a combination of 5x5, 3x3, and 1x1 convolutional layers with the first layer of depth 64 to make the decision function more nonlinear without changing the receptive fields. Feature maps are created as outputs from this layer [20]. After obtaining the feature maps, they are further passed through two layers- a layer with a Region Proposal Network to find the Regions of Interest (ROI) and an ROI pooling layer. In the first stage, the RPN, images are processed by a feature extractor and Inception model. These convolutional feature maps are then used to create the bounding box proposals.

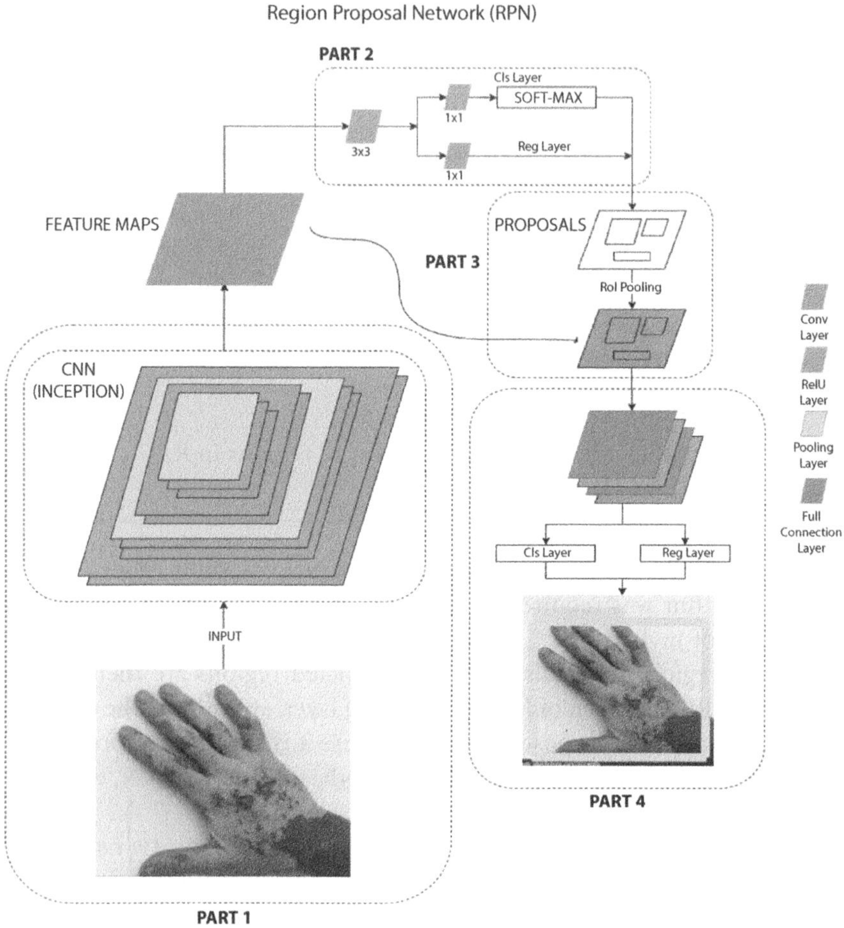

Figure 4.5 Faster R-CNN architecture.

During the next stage, these proposals enable the extraction of relevant features from the final feature maps before serving as input. Finally, the extracted proposal features are used to predict the objects' locations and class labels through the regression and classification layers. While Faster R-CNN is much faster than Fast R-CNN, it is still limited by the computation cost of the CNN feature information extraction in the first stage and the overhead of processing each region in the second stage [21, 22].

4.3.3 Performance Metrics

The performance metrics provide a visual aid to the research work so that various important comparisons can be made. The four basic sets of measures that we have used to represent our work are - confusion matrix, precision, recall and F-score.

4.3.3.1 Confusion Matrix

Confusion Matrix is a 2D Matrix which gives us a measure of the accuracy of our machine learning model [23]. It represents the test data entries as a combination of Positive (True or False) and Negative (True or False) values. So, it provides with four possible combinations:

- True Positive (TP) & True Negative (TN)
- True Positive (TP) & False Negative (FN)
- False Positive (FP) & True Negative (TN)
- False Positive (FP) & False Negative (FN)

The confusion matrix for our COCO model has 32X32 dimensions that represent the 32 diseases classes. The diagonal elements of the matrix represent the count of true labels i.e. the correct predictions made by the model. Whereas, the off-diagonal elements represent the count when the model mislabeled the object. For computing accuracy of the trained model, we use the following formula:

$$Accuracy = \frac{TP + TN}{TP + TN + FP + FN}$$

4.3.3.2 Precision and Recall

Precision and recall are two important measures used for assessing any classification task. Precision elucidates the proportion of the results that the model classifies as relevant which actually are relevant. In terms of the 4 basic confusion matrix terms, the precision can be defined by formula below:

$$Precision = \frac{TP}{TP + FP}$$

Recall can be expressed as the ability of the model in finding the relevant data points or instances in a dataset.

$$Recall = \frac{TP}{TP + FN}$$

4.3.3.3 F-Score

F-score provides the harmonic mean of precision and recall. Hence, it can be calculated by using the formula stated as:

$$F = 2[\frac{(Precision).(Recall)}{Precision + Recall}]$$

However, when the recall is considered α times as important as precision the formula look is redefined as:

$$F_{\alpha} = (1+\alpha^2)[\frac{(Precision).(Recall)}{(\alpha^2.Precision) + (Recall)}]$$

4.4 Results

The proposed work provides a two-step skin disease detection model where, firstly, the diseased region is transformed into a feature map and later on, the results are used for training and testing the model. The proposed model yields the accuracy of 93.06% with 32 different classes and over 900 images.

In our work, we have generated a 32x32 confusion matrix corresponding to the number of classes from which accuracy is calculated. Also, the minimum precision determined is 0.8 whereas, the maximum precision is 1. Similarly, the minimum recall determined is 0.745 whereas, the maximum recall is 1.

Further, more than 94% of F-scores are calculated for approximately 26 classes. The classification loss and total loss determine the decreasing loss curve with respect to the number of epochs for which the model is being trained. Table 4.3 depicts the comparison of cited works and their model accuracies.

Table 4.3 Comparison of results with previous works.

Model	Number of classes	Accuracy
Inception-Resnet-v2 [7]	6	77%
Inception-v3 [11]	9	55.4%
Inception-v3 [1]	4	87.25
ResNet-50 [23]	7	77.3%
Full CNN [24]	10	81.8%
Faster-RCNN with Inception v2 (proposed system)	**32**	93.06%

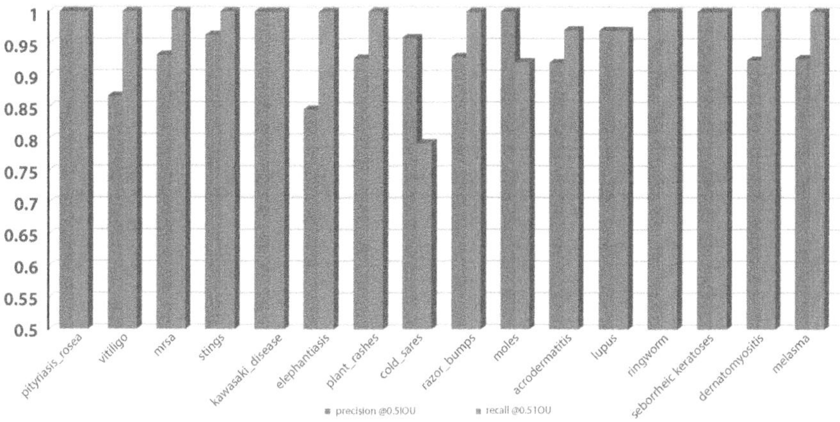

Figure 4.6 Precision-recall graph for 1 to 16 classes.

Figure 4.6 and Figure 4.7 below depicts the values of precision and recall ranging from [0,1] for each class, 1 representing a 100% precision or recall value.

The results obtained by the proposed Skin Disease Detection and Localization using Faster- RCNN Inception v2 model are shown in Table 4.4.

The F-score for each class provides us with a measure of how accurately our model works for detecting the correct class. Figure 4.8 below depicts the F-score for each of the 32 classes.

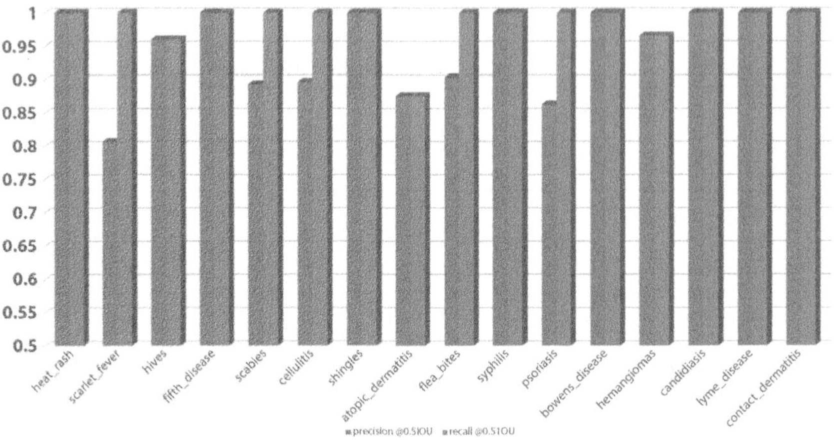

Figure 4.7 Precision-recall graph for 17–32 classes.

Table 4.4 Results obtained by the proposed model.

Number of classes	Avg. precision	Avg. recall	Accuracy
32	95%	98%	93.06%

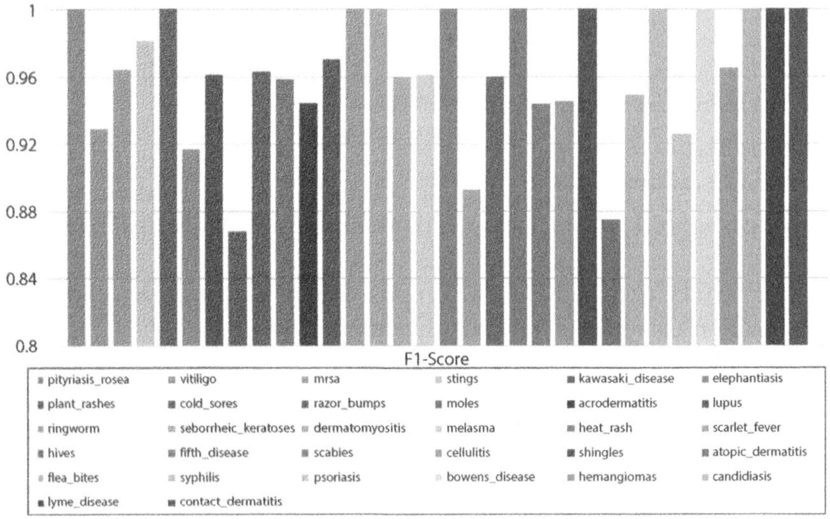

Figure 4.8 F-score for each of the 32 classes.

As discussed in section 4.3, following the process of feature selection, region proposals and ROI pooling is the classification of the object under observation is bounded by a box. Classification loss entails the model's inability or error in terms of classifying the object correctly. The classification loss used is Softmax cross-entropy and smooth-L1 for regression loss. Figure 4.9 represents the classification loss curve through the model training process.

Various loss measures, like classification loss, regularization loss, localization loss are incorporated while calculating Total loss. Figure 4.10 below represents the decreasing total loss curve with respect to the number of epochs the model is being trained for.

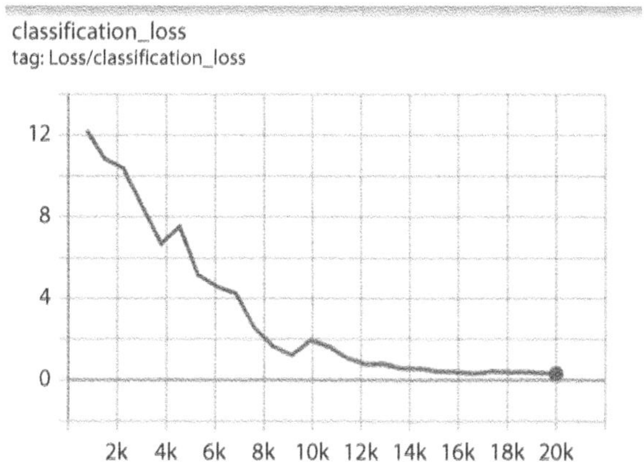

Figure 4.9 Classification loss curve.

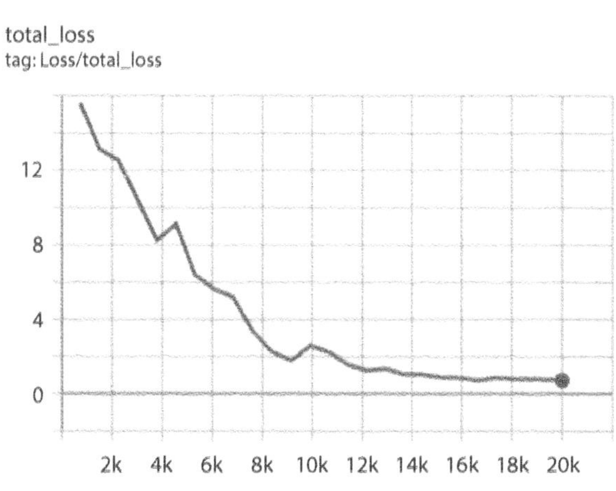

Figure 4.10 Total loss graph.

4.5 Conclusion

Skin diseases are the most common medical problems worldwide. Mass screening of skin diseases is not just time consuming but also requires extreme precision. In this paper, we have proposed a deep learning based model for detection and localization of 32 skin diseases. The work has been executed in two stages: The first stage includes extraction of essential features from the images and second step involves detection and localization of diseases based on extracted features. Faster R-CNN with Inception v2 model is used to predict the regions with a maximum area of infection. These are further passed through an ROI pooling layer which enables classification of the disease within the proposed region. The second phase mainly includes training the model for about 35000 steps to learn about the 32 different classes. The model is evaluated using a 32x32 confusion matrix. The proposed system for skin detection and localization provides 93.06% accuracy, 95% average precision and 98% average recall. Further, the proposed system achieves more than 94% F-scores for 26 classes. The research has been performed purely on the datasets recorded in the real conditions. However, the Faster R-CNN with Inception v2 architecture, while effective, is computationally expensive, making it less feasible for real-time deployment on resource-limited devices. Additionally, the model has been trained and tested on a specific dataset, and its performance might degrade when applied to unseen datasets or images from different sources. In future, the proposed system can further be modified to make it more resilient and cope with more classes of skin diseases.

AI disclosure statement: The author confirms that no artificial intelligence (AI)-generated content or AI-assisted writing tools were used in the preparation of this chapter (including summaries and the abstract). All text, analysis, and conclusions are the result of the author's original work.

References

1. Pal, A., Ray, S., Garain, U., Skin disease identification from dermoscopy images using deep convolutional neural network, ArXiv abs/1807.09163, Guwahati and Kolkata, India, 2018, July.
2. Bewley, A., The Neglected Psychological Aspects Of Skin Disease. *BMJ*, 358, j3208, 2017, July, London, U.K.
3. Zhou, X., Zhu, W., Shen, M., He, Y., Peng, C., Kuang, Y., Su, J., Zhao, S., Chen, X., Chen, W., Frizzled-related proteins predicts the elevated serum lipid

levels during acitretin treatment in psoriatic patients from Human. *PeerJ*, 6, e4637, 2013, April, PubMed 29666772, Changsha, China.

4. Esteva, A., Kuprel, B., Novoa, R.A., Ko, J., Swetter, S.M., Blau, H.M., Thrun, S., Dermatologist-level classification of skin cancer with deep neural networks. *Nature*, 542, 115–118, 2017, February, doi:10.1038/nature21056, California, USA.
5. Yasir, R., Rahman M.A., Ahmed N., Dermatological disease detection using image processing and artificial neural network. *8th International Conference on Electrical and Computer Engineering*, Dhaka, Bangladesh, pp. 687–690, 2014, doi: 10.1109/ICECE.2014.7026918.
6. Yeow, W.L., Mahmud, R., Raj, R.G., An application of case-based reasoning with machine learning for forensic autopsy. 2014, June, Elsevier Ltd, Kuala Lumpur, Malaysia.
7. Wu, Z., Zhao, S., Peng, Y., He1, X., Zhao, X., Huang, K., Wu, X., Fan, W., Li, F., Chen, M., Li, J., Huan, W., Chen, X., Li, Y., Studies on Different CNN Algorithms for Face Skin Disease Classification Based on Clinical Images. *IEEE Access*, 7, 66505–66511, May 2019, 2169–3536.
8. Ghosh, S., Sadhu, S., Biswas, S., Sarkar, D., Sarkar, P.P., A comparison between different classifiers for tennis match result prediction. *Malays. J. Comput. Sci.*, 32, 2, 97–111, 2019, April, West Bengal, India.
9. Nunsong, W. and Woraratpanya, K., A robust-texture convolutional neural network. *Malays. J. Comput. Sci.*, July, 2019, Information Technology and Electrical Engineering Special Issue, 157–171, 2019, Bangkok, Thailand.
10. Wu, Y., Meng, Z., Palaiahnakote, S., Lu, T., Compressive sensing based convolutional neural network for object detection. *Malays. J. Comput. Sci.*, 33, 1, 78–89, 2020, January, Nanjing, China, Kuala Lumpur, Malaysia.
11. Zhang, X., Wang, S., Liu, J., *et al.*, Towards improving diagnosis of skin diseases by combining deep neural network and human knowledge. *BMC Med. Inform. Decis. Mak.*, 18, 59, 2018, July, doi:10.1186/s12911-018-0631-9, Beijing, China and Houston, U.S.A.
12. Bajaj, L., Kumar, H., Hasija, Y., Automated System for Prediction of Skin Disease using Image Processing and Machine Learning. *Int. J. Comput. Appl.*, 180, 19, 0975–8887, Delhi, India, 2018, February.
13. Rathod, J., Sodha, V.W.A., Bhavathankar, P., Diagnosis of skin diseases using Convolutional Neural Networks. 2018, IEEE Conference Record # 42487; IEEE Xplore ISBN:978-1-5386-0965-1, Mumbai, India.
14. Marchetti, M.A., Liopyris, K., Dusza, S.W., Codella, N.CF., Gutman, D.A., Helba, B., Kalloo, A., Halpern, A.C., Computer Algorithms Show Potential for Improving Dermatologists' Accuracy to Diagnose Cutaneous Melanoma, U.S.A, 2019, July.
15. Yadav, N. and Binay, U., Comparative Study of Object Detection Algorithms. *Int. Res. J. Eng. Technol. (IRJET)*, November 2017, Maharashtra, India.
16. Huang, J., Rathod, V., Sun, C., Zhu, M., Korattikara, A., Fathi, A., Fischer, I., Wojna, Z., Song, Y., Guadarrama, S., Murphy, K., Speed/accuracy trade-offs

for modern convolutional object detectors, arXiv:1611.10012v3 [cs.CV], Google Research, April, 2017.
17. Ren, S., He, K., Girshick, R., Sun, J., Faster R-CNN: Towards Real-Time Object Detection with Region Proposal Networks, arXiv:1506.01497v3 [cs. CV], Hefei, China, January 2016.
18. Girshick, R., Donahue, J., Darrell, T., Malik, J., Rich feature hierarchies for accurate object detection and semantic segmentation, arXiv:1311.2524v5 [cs.CV], Berkley, U.S.A, October 2014.
19. Szegedy, C., Liu, W., Jia, Y., Sermanet, P., Reed, S., Anguelov, D., Erhan, D., Vanhoucke, V., Rabinovich, A., Going deeper with convolutions, arXiv:1409.4842v1 [cs.CV], U.S.A, 2014, September.
20. Uijlings, R.R., van de Sande, K.E.A., Gevers, T., Smeulders, A.W.M., Selective Search for Object Recognition. *Int. J. Comput. Vision*, 104, 154–171, 2012, Italy, The Netherlands.
21. Deng, Z., Sun, H., Zhou, S., Zhao, J., Lei, L., Zou, H., Multi-scale object detection in remote sensing imagery with convolutional neural networks. *ISPRS J. Photogramm. Remote Sens.*, 2018, April, Changsha and Shanghai, China.
22. Cui, G., Wang, S., Wang, Y., Liu, Z., Yuan, Y., Wang, Q., Preceding Vehicle Detection. Using Faster R-CNN Based on Speed Classification Random Anchor and Q-Square Penalty Coefficient. *Electronics*, 8, 1024, August 2019, doi:10.3390/electronics8091024, Qingdao, China.
23. Kawahara, J., Bentaieb, A., Hamarneh, G., Deep features to classify skin lesions, pp. 1397–1400, 2016, April, 10.1109/ISBI.2016.7493528, Simon Fraser University, Canada.
24. He, X., Wang, S., Shi, S., Tang, Z., Wang, Y., Zhao, Z., Dai, J., Ni, R., Zhang, X., Liu, X., Wu, Z., Yu, W., Chu, X., Computer-Aided Clinical Skin Disease Diagnosis Using CNN and Object Detection Models, arXiv:1911.08705v1 [eess.IV], China, 2019, November.
25. Koparde, S., Kotwal, J., Deshmukh, S., Adsure, S., Chaudhari, P., Kimbahune, V., A conditional generative adversarial networks and Yolov5 Darknet -based skin lesion localization and classification using independent component analysis model. *Inf. Med. Unlocked*, 47, 2024, May, https://doi.org/10.1016/j.imu.2024.101515.
26. Burada, S., Manjunathswamy, B.E., Sunil Kumar, M., Early detection of melanoma skin cancer: A hybrid approach using fuzzy C-means clustering and differential evolution-based convolutional neural network. *Meas.: Sens.*, 33, 101168, 2024, April, https://doi.org/10.1016/j.measen.2024.101168.
27. Maqsood, S. and Damaševičius, R., Multiclass skin lesion localization and classification using deep learning-based features fusion and selection framework for smart healthcare. *Neural Netw.*, 160, 238–258, 2023, January, https://doi.org/10.1016/j.neunet.2023.01.022.

28. Ramamurthy, K., Thayumanaswamy, I., Radhakrishnan, M., Won, D., Lingaswamy, S., Integration of Localized, Contextual, and Hierarchical Features in Deep Learning for Improved Skin Lesion Classification. *Diagnostics*, 14, 13, 2024, July, https://doi.org/10.3390/diagnostics14131338.
29. Babu, R.R. and Philip, F.M., Optimized deep learning for skin lesion segmentation and skin cancer detection. *Biomed. Signal Process. Control*, 95, 2024, April, https://doi.org/10.1016/j.bspc.2024.106292.

5

Detection of Machining Error Using Intelligent Hybrid Machine Learning Technique

Ritu Maity

School of Mechanical Engineering, KIIT University, Bhubaneswar, Odisha, India

Abstract

Machining accuracy is considered as one of the essential parameters for manufacturing industries. Predicting machining errors in turning operations is a critical endeavor in modern manufacturing. Industries are increasingly getting equipped with edge computing solutions. By harnessing the power of data and machine learning, manufacturers can anticipate and mitigate errors that could compromise product quality and increase production costs. Here we have tried to propose a quantum PSO based regression model which can predict the machining error while turning operation. Experiment was conducted using standard size of shaft and material used was Mild steel and Aluminum. Considering few of the important parameters for machining like speed, feed, depth of cut, dimensions of the shaft, energy consumption the prediction model was built. In this work we have tried to optimize the parameters using quantum PSO model and then different regression algorithms were applied like linear regression, polynomial regression, SVR, decision tree regressor and random forest regressor. Recorded outcomes shows results with quantum based PSO model with random forest regressor.

***Keywords*:** Quantum PSO, regression, machining error, accuracy, turning operation

Email: maity.ritu07@gmail.com

Manish Kumar, Nitigya Sambyal, Leena Priyadarshini Singh, Ramasamy V. and S. Balamurugan (eds.) Responsible AI: Principles and Practices, (105–118) © 2026 Scrivener Publishing LLC

5.1 Introduction

Machine tool advancements enable the production of parts with tolerances. As a result, precision machining is essential in the fabrication of many of the important tight-tolerance components utilized in today's military, electronics, aerospace, and medical industries. In current era of industrial revolution around new technologies are being used for prediction of machining error and as well as in software monitoring for tool wear prediction. Machining operation is a process of removal of unwanted material to get desired shape by chip removal method. For circular and round shafts, turning operations are done. The productivity and economy of the companies depends on accuracy of the machined parts. Cutting force, spindle speed, power consumption, depth of cut, feed, tool wear rate, materials used are determining factor for achieving good accuracy while machining of parts in turning operation. With advent of Industry 4.0 concepts, technologies like IoT, machine learning, and artificial intelligence are being used widely in industries to increase production rate and quality [1, 2]. Numerous manufacturing sectors are developing manufacturing methods that incorporate numerous sensors with the machinery. Through the Internet of Things, these production sensors were synchronized with multiple systems and utilized for various prediction management techniques. Here we have tried to propose a quantum PSO based regression model for prediction of accuracy in turning operations. To find the optimal parameters required for prediction of accuracy quantum PSO model is used which is a swarm optimization technique and can provide efficient variables that can be applied to a regression algorithm and find accuracy in machining of round parts in CNC lathe machines.

5.2 Literature Review

In recent years, significant amount of experiments and research have been carried out in area of enhancing life of machining operations using smart technologies which includes procedure planning, identification of process parameters, cutting tool life analysis, surface topology analysis, surface finish, and accuracy. H.H Shahabi [3] performed experiment and investigated surface roughness by using grey scale images of tool taken during finishing operation on lathe machine. Numerous research work was performed to check accuracy [4–6]. D Chen *et al.* [7] carried out investigation of the best cutting settings to use for turning thin-walled cylindrical components.

E Brinksmeier [8] predicted the shape deviation from turning operation using geometrical model. Vishal Kumar *et al.* [9] gives a comparative study of use of various machine learning techniques for prediction of cutting force in turning operations. Peng *et al.* [10] employed a hybrid neural network to forecast Fz, with DA718 and EMT 815 serving as the materials used for machining operations respectively. They used RMSE to compare the DNN model with the usual LR model, and it was found that the DNN model's accuracy was significantly higher for predicting accuracy of armatures. P. Charalampous [11] has applied machine learning and FEA techniques to predict cutting force while milling operation on AISI4140 work piece. They had used different regression algorithms like linear regression, polynomial regression, KNN, SVR and found that SVR produced best results as compared to other algorithms. Forecasting the dimensional deviation and surface roughness is made possible by Risbood *et al.* [12] carried out examination on vibrations and forces generated during turning operation. Ultimately, the most precise dimension prediction was discovered to be achievable with neural networks. Deshpande *et al.* [13] built the machine learning model based on the neural network concept to identify the surface roughness of Inconel 718 as the job and tungsten carbide (WC) as the insert tool with minimal quantity lubrication (MQL) using force, sound, and vibration as parameters. After that, the data was compiled to create an ANN model for prediction. ANN models were found to be precise in comparison with other machine learning models. Cica *et al.* [14] had used different regression models like polynomial regression, support vector regressor to predict cutting force and electricity usage. Ji Wang [15] used PSO-SVR neural network model to predict tool life. Devi Venkatesan [16] had neural network which uses genetic algorithm in order to maximize the machining parameters. Many research works has been done on prediction and analysis of geometric deviation in turning operations [17, 18]. A number of research papers have also used machine learning and deep learning based models for prediction of accuracy of machined parts, detection of defects, deviations etc. [19, 20].

After reviewing various research works on the above domain we found the need to optimize the values of parameters taken to build the machine learning based regression models. In this paper we have used quantum PSO based optimization algorithm to optimize the parameters taken for prediction of accuracy of machined parts in turning operation and then different regression algorithms were applied to generate the best results. Few sets of experiments were conducted to collect the parameters required for prediction of accuracy of the machined parts.

5.3 Models Used

In this paper we have used different regression models of machine learning i.e. linear regression, polynomial regression, Support vector regressor and quantum PSO has been used for optimization [21].

i) **Linear Regression**
A statistical technique called linear regression is used to model the relationship between one or more independent variables and a dependent variable. Finding the linear equation that best describes the data is the aim of linear regression. When there is just one independent variable in basic linear regression, the equation is usually expressed as follows:

$$Y= a\,Z + c + e \tag{5.1}$$

Where Y is dependent variable, Z is independent variable, a in slope, c is y -intercept, e is error term.

ii) **Polynomial Regression**
Polynomial regression is a type of linear regression that illustrates the relationship between a dependent variable and one or more independent variables using a polynomial equation as opposed to a straight line. More complex interactions between variables are represented by higher-order polynomial expressions. Equation for polynomial regression:

$$Y = m_1\,X + m_2X^2 + m_3X^3 + \ldots\ldots + e \tag{5.2}$$

Where Y is dependent variable, X is independent variable, m_1, m_2 are coefficients of polynomial regression, e is error term.

iii) **Support Vector Regressor**
It is a machine learning model used for performing regression tasks, where the goal is to predict a continuous target variable. SVR uses support vector machines to find the best hyperplane for the data while allowing for a margin of error (epsilon-tube) and minimizing the error. The equation for Support Vector Regression can be represented as follows:

$$Y = \sum_{i=1}^{n} \alpha\, K(X_i, X) + b \tag{5.3}$$

iv) **Quantum PSO**
Quantum Particle Swarm Optimization (QPSO) [22] is a variation of the classical Particle Swarm Optimization (PSO) algorithm that incorporates principles from quantum mechanics. It is an optimization algorithm based on swarm of population finding the source of food, where individual particles (or agents) search for the optimal solution by adjusting their positions in the solution space based on their own experiences and the experiences of their neighbors. QPSO introduces quantum-inspired elements into the algorithm to potentially improve its performance, especially in complex optimization problems. The main idea behind QPSO is to leverage the quantum principles of superposition and entanglement to explore a larger solution space efficiently and potentially discover better solutions in complex optimization problems. It may have advantages in dealing with high-dimensional and multimodal optimization problems, but it also introduces additional complexity and computational requirements compared to classical PSO.

5.4 Methodology

To evaluate the machining accuracy in CNC turning operations, **C-45 grade steel** was selected as the work material. The study focused on machining cylindrical shafts of varying diameters and analyzing machining errors under different cutting conditions.

Work Piece Material and Sample Preparation

- **Material:** C-45 steel
- **Sample Diameters:** 40 mm, 35 mm, 30 mm, 25 mm, 20 mm, 15mm, and 10mm
- **Sample Length:** 20mm to 35mm
- **Number of Samples:** Approximately **60 samples per diameter**, totaling ~**450 samples**

Machining Process

- **Machine Used:** CNC Lathe
- **Cutting Parameters Varied:**
    - **Spindle Speed (rpm)**
    - **Feed Rate (mm/rev)**
    - **Depth of Cut (mm)**

- **Measurement Parameters:**
  - Target diameter vs. actual machined diameter
  - Machining error (Deviation from target)

Each sample was machined under varying cutting conditions to assess the influence of speed, feed, and depth of cut on accuracy. The machined diameters were measured using precision instruments, and machining errors were computed.

Data Collection and Analysis

- Measurements were recorded for each experiment
- Machining error was calculated as the deviation from the intended diameter
- Statistical analysis was conducted to determine trends and accuracy levels

This structured approach ensured comprehensive data collection, allowing a detailed study of machining accuracy in CNC turning of C-45 steel.

QPSO optimization combined with support vector regression (SVR): exceeded the LR and PR models, attaining:

Minimal error between expected and actual machining errors is shown by the lowest MSE.

Highest R2 score, indicating its exceptional capacity to capture complex nonlinear connections between machining parameters and mistakes and to explain variance.

Figure 5.1 explains the raw material used and turning operation carried out in CNC machine for our experimental setup.

(a) (b)

Figure 5.1 (a) Shows the raw materials used; (b) shows the turning operation on CNC machine.

Figure 5.2 shows the details of data collected from the experiment.

The QPSO-optimized Support Vector Regression model yields the best accurate machining error estimates, according to Table 5.2. Its improved functionality is described by

i) Robust management of machining data's nonlinear interactions.
ii) Optimal selection of hyper parameters by QPSO, guaranteeing enhanced prediction accuracy and generalization.
iii) It is more dependable for real-world CNC turning applications due to its effective noise resistance.

Therefore, the QPSO-based SVR model is the best option for accurately forecasting machining defects, thereby facilitating its use.

Once the data was collected further we have used quantum PSO based regression model to predict the accuracy of machined parts. Our main aim is to build a system which can predict the approximate machining error once the target dimension, speed, feed and depth of cut is fed into the system. Quantum PSO technique was used to find the optimum parameters which can be used in regression model to generate desired output of shaft

Speed	Feed	Depth	Length	Target	Measured	Machining Error
500	0.2	1	23.5	37	36.9	0.1
1000	0.2	0.5	23.5	36.4	36.42	0.02
1500	0.4	0.5	23.5	35.9	36.08	0.18
1000	0.4	1	23.5	34.9	34.8	0.1
1500	0.2	1	23.5	33.9	34	0.1
500	0.4	0.5	23.5	33.4	33.5	0.1
1000	0.4	0.5	23.5	32.9	32.96	0.06
500	0.2	0.5	23.5	32.4	32.26	0.14
1500	0.2	0.5	23.5	31.9	32.01	0.11
1000	0.2	1	23.5	30.9	30.83	0.07
500	0.2	1	37	29.65	29.49	0.16

Figure 5.2 Figure shows the data set collected from the solar panel experimental setup.

dimension and its machining error. For regression analysis three different regression methods were used.

To check accuracy of our developed model mean squared error (MSE) and R squared value were evaluated. The following equation shows MSE equation

$$MSE = \frac{1}{n}\sum_{i=1}^{n}(y - yp)^2 \quad (5.6)$$

Where yp represents predicted value and y is actual value.

The flow chart below demonstrates the steps involved in building the model. Initially the data collection is done from the experiments further data cleaning and data pre-processing steps were done in python environment. Figure 5.3 shows the flowchart for building quantum PSO based regression model. Swarm of quantum particles also known as qubits were

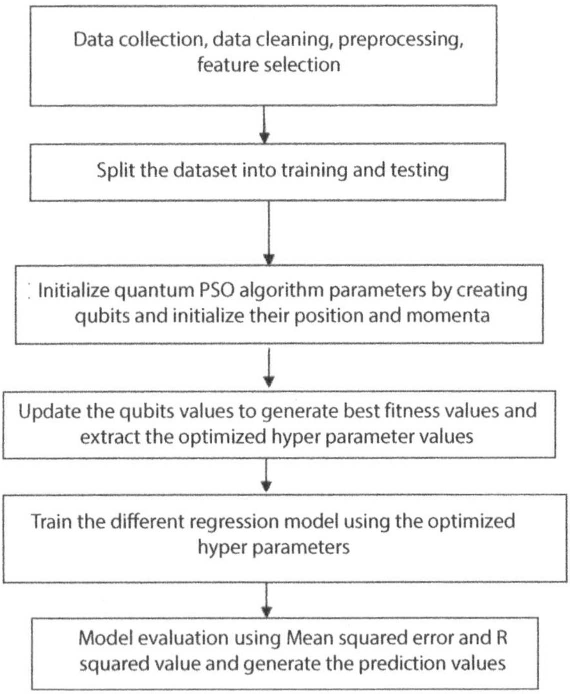

Figure 5.3 Flowchart for steps followed in building quantum PSO based regression model.

initialized and each particle was assigned a potential solution. Objective function was defined which was to be optimized i.e. MSE as shown in Equation 5.6 which aims at reducing mean squared error. Quantum operations were applied to each quantum particle to updates its quantum state. A good trade-off is maintained between local best and global best position while updating the quantum particle position. Then regression model is used to check the results. Experiments were performed with linear regression model first to get better MSE and R squared value. Similarly steps were repeated for polynomial regression and with support vector regressor.

5.5 Results and Discussion

Data Collection and Preprocessing

After conducting experiments on different shaft sizes, the collected dataset underwent a structured **data cleaning and analysis process**. This involved:

- **Handling Missing Values:** Any incomplete or inconsistent data points were identified and either corrected or removed.
- **Outlier Detection and Removal:** Outliers were analyzed using statistical methods (e.g., Z-score, IQR) to ensure they did not affect model training.
- **Feature Selection and Engineering:** Key machining parameters such as **cutting speed, feed rate, depth of cut**, and their interactions were considered as input features.
- **Normalization and Scaling:** Data was normalized where necessary to improve the performance of regression models.

Model Development and Optimization

Once the dataset was refined, it was used to build a predictive model for machining error estimation. The modeling process involved the following steps:

1. **Quantum Particle Swarm Optimization (QPSO) for Hyper Parameter Tuning:**
   - QPSO, an advanced optimization technique, was applied to determine the best hyperparameters for machine learning models.
   - It optimized model parameters such as polynomial degree (for polynomial regression) and kernel function (for support vector regression).

- Compared to traditional optimization methods, QPSO enhanced the prediction performance by efficiently searching for optimal parameter values.

2. **Machine Learning Models Applied:**
   - **Linear Regression (LR):** A simple yet effective model for understanding linear relationships between machining parameters and machining error.
   - **Polynomial Regression (PR):** Extended linear regression by incorporating polynomial features to capture nonlinear relationships.
   - **Support Vector Regression (SVR):** Utilized kernel functions to model complex, nonlinear dependencies in machining error prediction.

3. **Model Evaluation Metrics:**
   The trained models were evaluated using:
   - The average squared difference between actual and anticipated values is measured by the **Mean Squared Error, or MSE**. Better accuracy is indicated by a lower MSE.
   - **R^2 Score (Coefficient of Determination):** Assesses how well the model explains variability in machining error. A score closer to 1 represents a highly accurate model.

Experimental Validation

- To verify the reliability of the prediction model, additional **test experiments** were conducted.
- A set of machining conditions (specific **cutting speed, feed rate, and depth of cut**) was selected, and experimental values were recorded.
- These actual values were compared with the predicted values from the **QPSO-optimized regression models**.
- **Table 5.1** presents the **experimental vs. predicted machining errors** for different models, showcasing the performance of QPSO-based regression models under practical conditions.

Following hyperparameter optimization using the Quantum Particle Swarm Optimization (QPSO) technique, Table 5.2 displays the Mean

Table 5.1 Table shows experimental values and predicted values obtained by applying quantum PSO based different regression models.

	Quantum PSO based linear regression	Quantum PSO based polynomial regression	Quantum PSO based support vector regressor
Experimental value	**Predicted value**	**Predicted value**	**Predicted value**
36.72	36.5	36.6	36.7
25.25	25.4	25.35	25.3
30.43	30.35	30.4	30.4
20.45	20.5	20.3	20.4
40.2	40.1	40.3	40.25
18.2	18	18.1	18.2
35.8	35.5	35.6	35.7
30.1	30.2	30.15	30.15

Table 5.2 Table shows MSE and R squared error generated from different regression models applied.

Algorithm used	MSE	R squared value
Linear Regression	29.3	0.78
Polynomial regression	20.4	0.82
Support vector regressor	10.33	0.94

Squared Error (MSE) and R2 score for each regression model to evaluate how well they predict machining mistakes.

Comparing Model Performance

Linear Regression (LR) showed the highest MSE and the lowest R2 score, suggesting that the intricate machining error variations are not adequately captured by a straightforward linear connection.

By including nonlinear relationships, Polynomial Regression (PR) outperformed LR; yet, because of possible overfitting or susceptibility to dataset noise, its accuracy was still below ideal.

5.6 Conclusion

The current paper presents a simple predictive model based on quantum PSO optimized regression model for predicting machining error in turning parts. This model can help users to have an idea of machining accuracy that can be achieved with a particular set of parameters calculated from empirical formulas for cutting speed, feed and depth of cut for a given shaft diameter to be machined. The following points can be concluded from the above work:

- Quantum PSO method can optimize the hyper parameters effectively which can be further utilized to build regression model.
- From the above study it can be concluded that quantum PSO based support vector regressor had 0.94 R squared value which is better than values achieved through linear and polynomial regression.
- The developed model can predict machining error expected for a particular set of parameters like cutting speed, feed, and depth of cut used by the user for machining a particular set of diameter of solid shaft.

AI disclosure statement: The author acknowledges the use of AI-based tools for minor language editing or grammatical correction. However, all intellectual contributions, analyses, and conclusions presented in this chapter are entirely the author's own.

References

1. VallimFilho, A.R.A., Farina Moraes, D., Bhering de AguiarVallim, M.V., Santos da Silva, L., da Silva, L.A., A machine learning modeling framework for predictive maintenance based on equipment load cycle: an application in a real world case. *Energies*, 15, 10, 3724, 2022.
2. Jimenez, V.J., Bouhmala, N., Gausdal, A.H., Developing a predictive maintenance model for vessel machinery. *J. Ocean. Eng. Sci.*, 5, 4, 358–386, 2020.
3. Ur Rehman, A., Nishat, T.S.R., Ahmed, M.U., Begum, S., Abhishek Ranjan, Chip Analysis for Tool Wear Monitoring in Machining: A Deep Learning Approach. *IEEE Access*, 12, 112672–112689, 2024.
4. Danish, M., Gupta, M.K., Irfan, S.A., Machine learning models for prediction and classification of tool wear in sustainable milling of additively

manufactured 316 stainless steel. *Results Eng.*, 22, 102015, Elsevier, June 2024.
5. Wang, K., Wang, A., Wu, L., Xie, G., Machine Tool Wear Prediction Technology Based on Multi-Sensor Information Fusion. *Sensors*, 24, 2652, 2024, MDPI.
6. Lu, C., Study on prediction of surface quality in machining process. *J. Mater. Process Technol.*, 439–50, 2008.
7. Chen, D., Lin, B., Han, Z., Zhang, Y., Study on the optimization of cutting parameters in turning thin-walled circular cylindrical shell based upon cutting stability. *Int. J. Adv. Manuf. Technol.*, 205, 891–899, 2013.
8. Brinksmeier, E. and Solter, J., Prediction of shape deviations in machining. *CIRP Ann. Manuf. Technol.*, 58, 507–510, 2009.
9. Chinmaya, K.A. and Singh, G.K., Modeling and experimental analysis of grid-connected six-phase induction generator for variable speed wind energy conversion system. *Electr. Power Syst. Res.*, 1, 166, 151–162, 2019.
10. Peng, B., Bergs, T., Schraknepper, D., Klocke, F., Döbbeler, B., A hybrid approach using machine learning to predict the cutting forces under consideration of the tool wear. *Procedia CIRP*, 82, 302–307, 2019.
11. Charalampous, P., Prediction of Cutting Forces in Milling Using Machine Learning Algorithms and Finite Element Analysis. *J. Mater. Eng. Perform.*, 30, 3, 2002–2013, 2021.
12. Risbood, K.A., Dixit, U.S., Sahasrabudhe, A.D., Prediction of surface roughness and dimensional deviation by measuring cutting forces and vibrations in turning process. *J. Mater. Process. Technol.*, 132, 203–214, 2003.
13. Deshpande, Y.V., Andhare, A.B., Padole, P.M., Application of ANN to estimate surface roughness using cutting parameters, force, sound and vibration in turning of Inconel 718. *SN Appl. Sci.*, 1, 1–9, 2019.
14. Cica, D., Sredanovic, B., Tesic, S., Kramar, D., Predictive modelling of turning operations under different cooling/lubricating conditions for sustainable manufacturing with machine learning techniques. *Appl. Comput. Inf.*, 1–6, 2020.
15. Wang, J., Zhou, J., Mo, W., Liang, C., Sun, L.-., Wen, C.-., Tool life prediction based on multi-source feature PSO-SVR neural network. *J. Phys. Conf. Ser.*, 2366, 2022.
16. Venkatesan, D., Kannan, K., Saravanan, R., A genetic algorithm-based artificial neural network model for the optimization of machining processes. *Neural Comput. Appl.*, 18, 135–140, 2009.
17. Agrawal, A., Goel, S., Bin Rashid, W., Price, M., Prediction of surface roughness during hard turning of AISI 4340 steel (69 HRC). *Appl. Soft Comput.*, 30, 279–286, 2015.
18. He, C.L., Zong, W.J., Zhang, J.J., Influencing factors and theoretical modeling methods of surface roughness in turning process: state-of-the-art. *Int. J. Mach. Tools Manuf.*, 129, 15–26, 2018.

19. Somvanshi, M., Chavan, P., Tambade, S., Shinde, S.V., A review of machine learning techniques using decision tree and support vector machine, in: *Proc. - 2nd Int. Conf. Comput. Commun. Control Autom. ICCUBEA 2016*, 2017.
20. Maity, R., Detection of Damaged Inserts of Cutting Tools Using Deep Learning, in: *Sustainable Science and Intelligent Technologies for Societal Development*, pp. 130–140, IGI global, 2023.
21. Raschka, S., *Python machine learning*, pp. 49–90, Packt Mumbai, 2015.
22. Xu, Y.F., Gao, J., Chen, G.C., Quantum particle swarm optimization algorithm. *Appl. Mech. Mater.*, 63–64, June 2011.

6

Ground Water Level Classification Using Machine Learning

Charu Chaudhary[1], Khushi Passi[1], Taruna Saini[1], Ritika Dhaneshwar[2]* and Varun Gupta[1]

[1]*Department of Computer Science and Engineering, Chandigarh College of Engineering and Technology, Chandigarh, India*
[2]*University Institute of Engineering and Technology, Panjab University, Chandigarh, India*

Abstract
Groundwater levels are critical indicators of water resource availability, influencing agricultural productivity, ecosystem health, and urban planning. This paper presents a comprehensive study to predict the severity of ground water levels (GWL) in various districts of India. Various Machine Learning (ML) algorithms, like K-Nearest Neighbours Classification, SVM Classification, Kernel SVM, Naïve Bayes Classification, Decision Trees Classification, Random Forest Classification, Ensemble Learning, Grid Search, K-Fold CV(Shuffle Split, Repeated K-Fold, Leave-one-out K-Fold, Stratified K-fold), ADA Boost, XG Boost and Multi-level Stacking Classification etc. were tested. The best accuracy of 96.49% is obtained with Grid search using SVC classifier, when these algorithms are compared using ground water availability in Indian dataset. The findings indicate that ML can serve as a powerful tool for GWL classification, facilitating improved water management strategies. This research contributes to the understanding of groundwater dynamics and highlights the potential of machine learning in environmental monitoring.

Keywords: Machine learning, ground water, classification, K-Fold, SVM, grid search, F1 score

**Corresponding author*: ritikadhaneshwar@gmail.com

Manish Kumar, Nitigya Sambyal, Leena Priyadarshini Singh, Ramasamy V. and S. Balamurugan (eds.) Responsible AI: Principles and Practices, (119–142) © 2026 Scrivener Publishing LLC

6.1 Introduction

India is the country with the substantial groundwater consumption in the world, with domestic and industrial uses making up around 85% of the country's groundwater aquifers. In India, household and industrial uses account for around 85% of the groundwater aquifers [9]. India is currently experiencing the scariest water shortages in its experience, and major Indian towns that house nearly 50% of the total population are among those with the highest groundwater stress levels [23]. Figure 6.1 compares the percentage of major groundwater basins in the world.

For groundwater management in India, overuse of groundwater has caused serious issues. The main effects of extensive farming and overharvesting include waterlogging, low water levels, parched reservoirs, saltiness, as well as seawater invasion. According to the latest study, the water table is dropping by 1-2 meters annually in various sections of the nation [5]. The freshwater supply for residential and industrial needs, including farming, will be impacted. In the majority of the northwestern states, where the water level is over 40 mbgl, with the depths of the water level typically varying between 10-4 mbgl [9]. Due to overuse, industrialization, population increase and environmental degradation, urban groundwater supply in India has drastically decreased during the last few years [23]. The interrelatedness as well as ambiguities in the hydro-geological activity has caused the fluctuation of the groundwater table to be irregular, which further complicates the problem [21]. Water usage

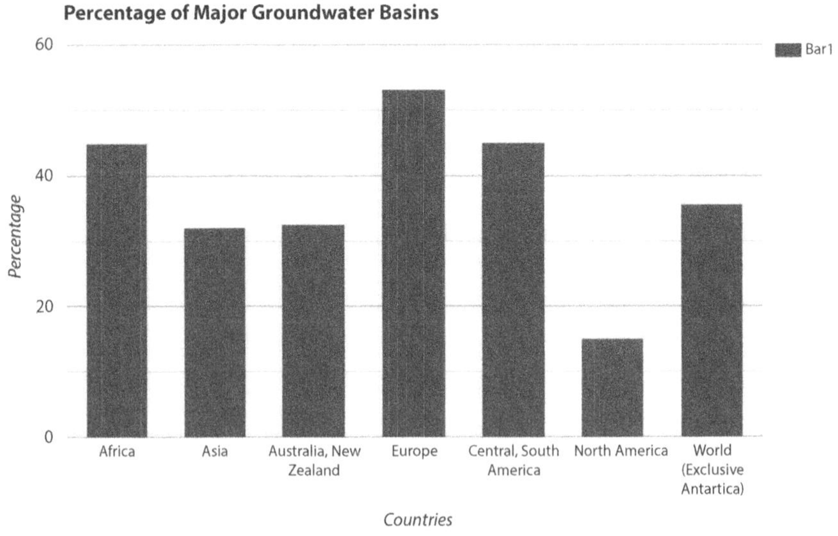

Figure 6.1 The percentage of major groundwater basins [24].

has markedly expanded in the modern period caused by rapid industrialization, growing populations, agricultural production, and development.

Based on the lack of supplies and diminishing water levels, the quest for groundwater has intensified for this reason. Therefore, groundwater is a crucial resource for advancing society and the economy. Reliable GWL forecasting with the help of Machine Learning Models can prove beneficial to the reliable utilization of the resources of groundwater [26]. Machine learning (ML) algorithms have significantly improved GWL forecasting during the past 20 years [27].

In this paper, we have applied various ML Algorithms and Techniques to predict the severity of GWL in various districts of India. We have also compared the accuracy of these models.

6.2 Related Work

The focus of this section is to discuss some of the significant contributions in this domain of research. Tsanis *et al.*, [18] examined and contrasted seven distinct network designs and training strategies. To assess the effectiveness of several neural networks for GWL forecasting, the best ANN design was determined which can adequately replicate the pattern of the GWL declination and give up to 18-month projections. Because of its groundwater supplies, the Messara Valley in Crete (Greece) was considered the research region. This region has been overutilized over the past two decades, and the quantity of groundwater has been progressively dropping. The outcomes of several experiments demonstrate that a conventional feed-forward can produce precise forecasts. The Levenberg-Marquardt algorithm-trained neural network brings the highest performance for predictions up to 18 months in the future. Sahoo *et al.*, [19] tested multiple linear regression along with artificial neural network algorithms for their capacity to forecast transitory levels of water over a groundwater catchment. At 17 locations around Japan, MLR, as well as ANN modeling, was done while taking into account all relevant inputs, including precipitation, the surrounding temperature, river phase, 11 periodic variables, and considerable delays of the rainy season, river stage and soil moisture content. Utilizing multiple-layer neural networking models, and training utilizing Levenberg-Marquardt back-propagation algorithm techniques, seventeen location-specific ANN models were created. Graphical and statistical metrics were used to assess the algorithms' efficiency. Further, Panda *et al.*, [20] devised hybrid neural modeling to accurately anticipate GWL in the lower river basin of the Mahanadi River. The Bayesian regularization approach appears to be the most effective of studied ANN models altogether, according to simulated findings. Nevertheless, all the algorithms showed a significant link between the measured and expected GWL.

Sudheer *et al.*, [21] utilized the combined wavelets with a SVM model to forecast monthly changes in GWL. The source information is divided into wavelet sequences. To anticipate changes in GWL, such records are also employed as input parameters in different permutations for a support vector regression system. Three monitoring wells in the Indian city of Visakhapatnam are employed to forecast the modifications in the level of groundwater using the suggested Wavelet-Support Vector Regression model. SVR, ANN, and the standard Auto Regressive Integrated Moving Average models are used for making a comparison of the WA-SVR model. Analysis shows that when compared with other methods, the WA-SVR model provides superior accuracy. Dhivya *et al.*, [22] listed the yearly ground water supply for potential usage. The input parameters for the model development are dependent on seasonal variations in water usage and replenishment. The regression action can be done well with a smaller training sample. The groundwater accessibility rates in India are classified and detected using ML. Logistic regression, random forest, and decision trees are used to suggest a better approach for calculating the GWL. Utilizing data on groundwater resources in India to compare these algorithms, they found that the third technique has the highest accuracy and least error. In that case, decision trees outperform logistic regression in terms of accuracy. Yadav *et al.*, [23] devised a framework established from machine learning models that takes into account the ANN, singular spectrum analysis (SSA), genetic algorithm (GA), mutual information (MI) and SVM to examine the contribution of these parameters on GWL variability. In Bangalore, a largely populous city with diminishing groundwater resources, the proposed technique was utilized to forecast GWL. Raghavendra *et al.*, [25] proposed a unique hybrid Wavelet regression strategy for predicting storage variability. Various statistical metrics are used for the evaluation of the operation of the WP-SVR and SVR algorithms. It is clear from the relative analysis of the created algorithms that the WP-SVR strategy works one step ahead at forecasting the level of groundwater than the traditional SVR configuration. Hence, it is extremely suitable to estimate and anticipate changes in GWL using the WP-SVR estimate.

Pham *et al.*, [26] evaluated seven distinct algorithms in a contrasting investigation to establish GWL prediction. The previous GWL, mean temperatures, precipitation, and comparative humidity records for the years starting from 1981 to 2017 acquired from northwest location of Bangladesh (two wells) were used to make the long-term projection. In the study by Nunno *et al.*, [28], the everyday groundwater variation for 76

Table 6.1 Comparison of related works.

Author	Year	Techniques ued	Best technique
Tsanis *et al.*, [18]	2005	Feedforward neural network, Bayesian regularization (BR), Elman or RNN, Radial basis function network, Adaptive backpropagation, Levenberg–Marquardt	Levenberg-Marquardt algorithm
Sahoo *et al.*, [19]	2013	ANN, Multiple Linear Regression	ANN (MLP-LM)
Panda *et al.*, [20]	2010	Back-propagation (GDX), Levenberg-Marquardt (LM), and BR	Bayesian regularization (BR)
Sudheer *et al.*, [21]	2014	Wavelet-support vector Regression model, SVR, ANN, and the standard Auto Regressive Integrated Moving Average models	Wavelet-Support Vector Regression model
Dhivya *et al.*, [22]	2021	logistic regression, random forest, and decision trees	Decision trees
Yadav *et al.*, [23]	2020	ANN, SVM, Spectrum analysis, mutual information (MI), genetic algorithm (GA)	Hybrid models (HANN and HSVM)
Raghavendra *et al.*, [25]	2015	SVR, WP–SVR	WP–SVR
Pham *et al.*, [26]	2022	Reduce error pruning tree (REP Tree), RT, RF, decision stump, SVM, locally weighted linear regression (LWLR) , M5P	Bagging-RT and Bagging-RF models
Nunno *et al.*, [28]	2020	Levenberg-Marquardt (LM), BR, Scaled Conjugate Gradient (SCG)	BR
Chang *et al.*, [29]	2015	ANN models with two and three input parameters	ANN model with three input parameters
Vafakhah *et al.*, [30]	2013	Wavelet-ANFIS, Wavelet-ANN, ANN, Adaptive Neuro-Fuzzy Inference System (ANFIS)	Wavelet-ANFIS

recorded wells situated in the Apulian area was predicted using the NARX networking. To investigate the influence of two input factors, precipitation and evapotranspiration, and also the sensitivities to modifications in the training algorithm as well as intake time lag, an initial investigation on the comparison wells was conducted. The Bayesian Regularization (BR) technique produced prediction methods with improved predictive accuracy and less pronounced performance degradation as the delay time increased when three alternative training methods were examined. Chang *et al.*, [29] created two ANN models, one having three input parameters (prior groundwater depth, temperature, as well as rainfall), and the other with two input variables (rainfall and temperature only) to replicate and estimate the location-specific supra permafrost GWL on the gradient dimension, The findings show that the three-input parameter ANN model generates high precision quality in the modeling and predictions of the change in the supra permafrost GWL and has better real-time location-specific predictive capabilities. Vafakhah *et al.*, [30] distinguished various data-driven methods for estimating GWL over different predicting intervals. A variety of modeling techniques for ANFIS, ANN, Wavelet-ANFIS and Wavelet-ANN models have been compared to assess their abilities to forecast GWL 1, 2, 3, and 4 months. Wavelet transform has been shown to increase the precision of GWL forecasts. Additionally, it has been demonstrated that Wavelet-ANFIS models' forecasts outperform other models in terms of accuracy. The existing different techniques are presented in Table 6.1.

6.3 Data Description and Data Processing

The dataset was obtained from https://indiawris.gov.in/. It comprises of 690 rows, which are used to measure groundwater at the district level, and has 11 attributes. Some of the attributes of the dataset are -Total annual groundwater recharge, current annual groundwater extraction for irrigation, current annual groundwater extraction for domestic & industrial use, total natural discharges, annual extractable groundwater resource, total current annual groundwater withdrawal, etc. The categorization is classified as Over-Exploited, Critical, Semi-Critical and Safe as depicted in Figure 6.2.

J=Stage Of Ground Water Extraction(%)
Situation = IF((J<=69), "Safe", IF ((J<=89),"Semi-Critical", IF((J<=99),"Critical", "Over Exploited")))

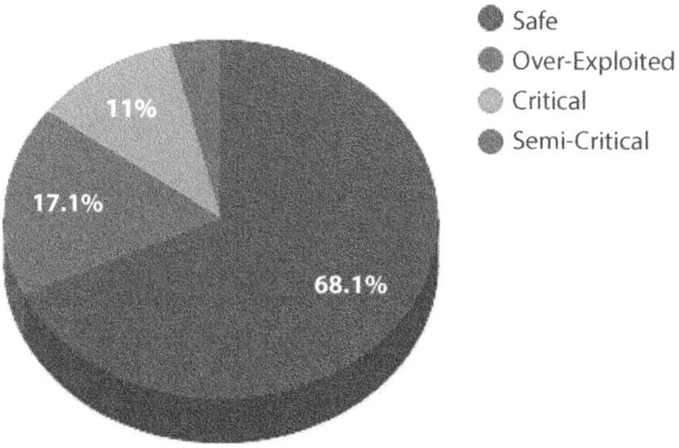

Figure 6.2 Situation pie chart representation with the percentage value.

The Normalization operation in the experiments was performed using the following formula:

$$X_{norm} = (X - X_{min}) / (X_{max} - X_{min}) \quad (6.1)$$

6.3.1 Proposed Approach

The flow chart of the proposed approach is presented in Figure 6.3. The first step is data collection and its pre-processing. After performing the pre-processing operation the significant features are extracted which are further used for training the models for achieving effective results. In the experiment, different algorithms were trained and compared based on different evaluation metrics.

System Architecture Dataset Collection: The Python environment of the Google Colaboratory Notebook is used to collect and explore the dataset. Data pre-processing is the collective name for the set of methods employed before applying a data mining approach. Estimation of missing values is performed for interpretations of the incomplete data. The missing values are then filled in using either the mode value for a categorical variable or the mean value for a continuous variable. Feature Picking It involves finding and getting rid of unnecessary and duplicated data. It lessens algorithms' unintentional correlation.

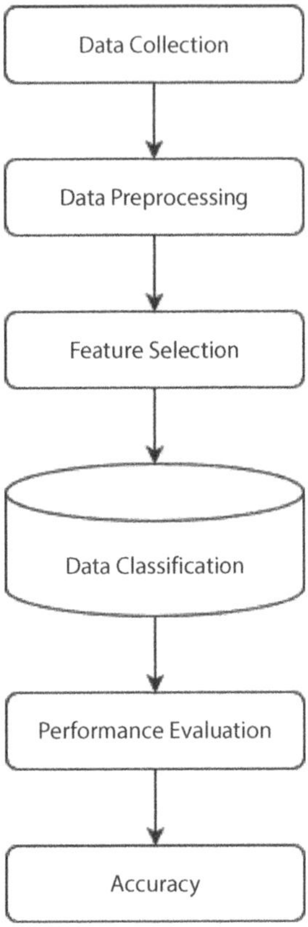

Figure 6.3 Flow of approach.

Algorithms:

1) Logistic Regression Classification

It is a method that may be applied to both machine learning and conventional statistics. In contrast to linear regression, which predicts continuous variables like size, logistic regression determines whether a given statement is true or not. To make predictions, the data values are fitted using the logit link function. The logit function for a, if a is the probability, is defined as follows:

$$\text{Logit}(a) = \ln(a/1\text{-}a) \tag{6.2}$$

2) K-Nearest Neighbors Classification

It stores every instance from the training dataset that is accessible and classifies new cases using the distance function. Here, d(x,y) represents the Euclidean distance

$$d(x,y) = \sqrt{(x_i - y_i)^2} \tag{6.3}$$

Based on the Euclidean Distance Formula, data classification:
The two types of data we have are described below:

- Training data

With specified x and y values, this training database provides classification.

- Testing data

Only the values of x and y are included in this set of data. Using the training data, its categorization type would be anticipated.

3) Support Vector Machine Classification

To categories new data points, the SVM classifier seeks to identify the best line or decision boundary for partitioning n-dimensional spaces into categories. The best decision barrier is referred to as a hyperplane. SVM is used to select the maximal vectors and points that contribute to the formation of the hyperplane.

4) Kernel-SVM Classification

The kernels are a collection of mathematical operations utilized by SVM algorithms. The kernel's function is to take data as input and convert it into the required format. Kernel functions return the scalar product of two points in an incredibly suitable feature space. Thus, even in the case of very high-dimensional spaces, formulating a notion of similarity requires little computing effort.

5) Naive Bayes Classification

Naive Bayesian classifiers refer to a set of classification techniques based on Bayes' Theorem.

The kernel is a mathematical operation used within the SVM algorithm. The characteristic of the kernel is to take the facts as entered and alternate them into the specified format. The internal product among factors in an excellent function area is returned through the kernel function. Therefore, even in very excessive dimensional spatial situations, the idea of similarity may be described with little computational effort.

The term "naive" refers to the assumption that the frequency of one trait is unconnected to the prevalence of other qualities. A violet, spherical vegetable, for example, is considered an aubergine if it is identified only on the basis of its form, color, and shape. So, without relying on one another, each feature enables us to identify it as an aubergine.

$$P(a|c) = (P(c|a)^{*}P(a))/P(c) \tag{6.4}$$

$$Prob = \Pi \ P(a|c) \tag{6.5}$$

6) Decision Trees Classification

It is a non-parametric supervised learning approach used for both regression and classification. The decision tree's ultimate goal is to forecast the value of a target variable by creating a model and learning simple decision rules based on the data's properties. As the tree becomes deeper, decision rules and model fitting become more complex. The significant attribute value test is used to partition the data sample into subsets. It is a classic inductive categorization strategy.

7) Random Forest Classification

A cluster of decision trees is called a random forest. It is trainable using the bagging method. The bagging method's goal is to improve the outcome overall. The same hyperparameters as a decision tree are also included here. Utilizing numerous random vectors, the random forest algorithm has a cluster of decision trees. Instead of focusing on the most important feature in a dataset, node splitting seeks out the best feature. As a result, the model is improved.

8) Grid Search

Grid search is a tuning approach that aims to find the optimal hyperparameter values. It is a detailed search on a model's specific parameter values. A model is also known as an estimator. Grid searches help us save time, effort, machine learning, ground water, classification, K-Fold, SVM and resources.

9) K-Fold CV

You could validate the version's effectiveness by training it on a subset of the entered records and then testing it on a subset of the entered records that had not previously been utilized. It is also a tool to determine how well a statistical model generalizes to a unique dataset. In most cases, the version's stability must be evaluated during device learning. This demonstrates that we cannot fit our version to the education dataset alone. We isolated a specific pattern of the dataset—one that was not included in the education dataset—for this purpose. Following that, before deployment, we test our version against that pattern, which is known as cross-validation. It differs from the typical train-test split in this respect.

10) ADA Boost

The essential principle behind boosting methods is that after establishing a model using the training dataset, we build a second model to correct any errors in the first. This method is repeated until the errors are minimal and the dataset can be reliably projected. To better understand this, imagine the following scenario: a decision tree algorithm is created utilizing Titanic data and achieves 80% accuracy. The accuracy is then verified using a separate technique, which yields 75% for KNN and 70% for linear regression.

11) XG Boost

XGBoost, or Extreme Gradient Boosting, is a machine learning framework based on distributed and scalable gradient-boosted decision trees (GBDT). This algorithm constructs decision trees in a sequential manner. In XGBoost, weights are significant. Weights are assigned to all independent variables, and they are entered into a decision tree that predicts outcomes. Variables that are not predicted correctly by the tree are weighted up and these variables are passed to his second decision tree. These individual classifiers/predictors then form an ensemble to produce a stronger and more accurate model. It can tackle regression, classification, ranking, and custom prediction problems.

12) Ensemble Learning

By blending the predictions from diverse models, ensemble studying is a wide meta technique to machine studying that pursues to enhance predictive performance. We can refer to them as "standard" ensemble learning procedures due to their widespread use; they are:

1. Bagging.
2. Stacking.
3. Boosting.

The success of each method has resulted in a variety of extensions and related strategies, but more significantly, each strategy is characterized by an algorithm.

13) Multilevel Stacking Classifier

Stacking serves as an ensemble mastering strategy that combines several type models through the use of a meta-classifier. The character type models are primarily based on the whole training set; skilled then, the meta-classifier is primarily equipped based on the outputs -- meta-features -- of the character type models within the ensemble. The ensemble can provide the expected class labels or possibilities for the meta-classifier to learn from. This final model is used to make predictions on the test dataset.

6.4 Results and Discussion

The details of the results obtained and the discussion are presented in this section.

Experimental Settings:

1. Python [31]
2. Scikit-learn [32]
3. Pandas [33]
4. Numpy [34]
5. Matplotlib [35]

The confusion matrix for different models is presented in Figure 6.4 to Figure 6.15. The hyperparameter settings used for training different models are listed in Table 6.2. For comparing different models the values of precision, accuracy, recall and F-1 scores were computed that are recorded in Table 6.3. Highest F-1 score of 0.947 is obtained for Grid Search and the

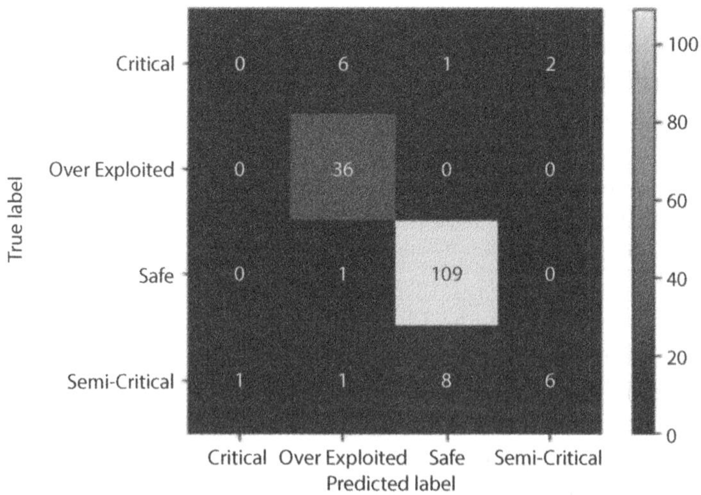

Figure 6.4 Logistic regression.

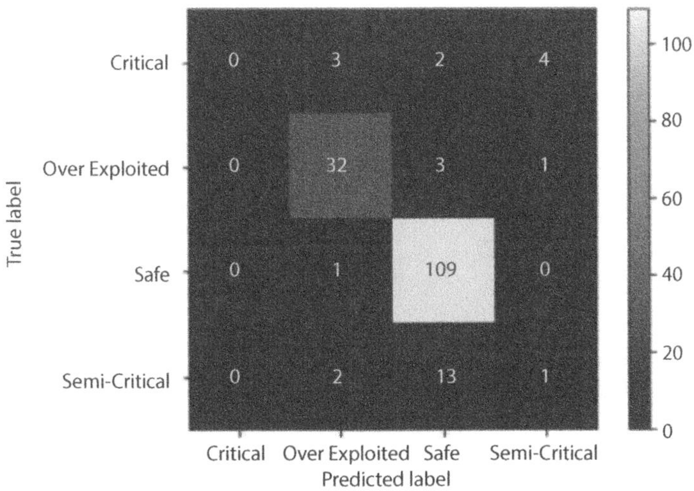

Figure 6.5 Kernel SVM.

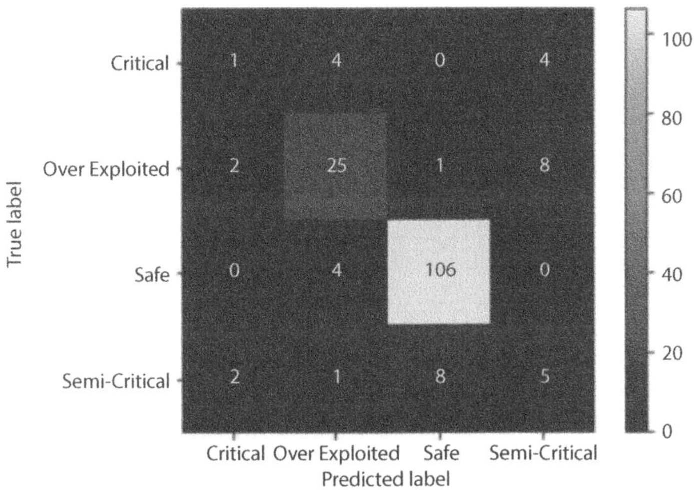

Figure 6.6 K-nearest neighbours.

lowest value of 0.707 for the Naïve Bayes as depicted in Table 6.3. Further, based on accuracy, the models were compared as depicted in Figure 6.16. Based on the comparison it can be concluded that the highest accuracy of 0.964 is obtained for Grid Search using the SVC classifier.

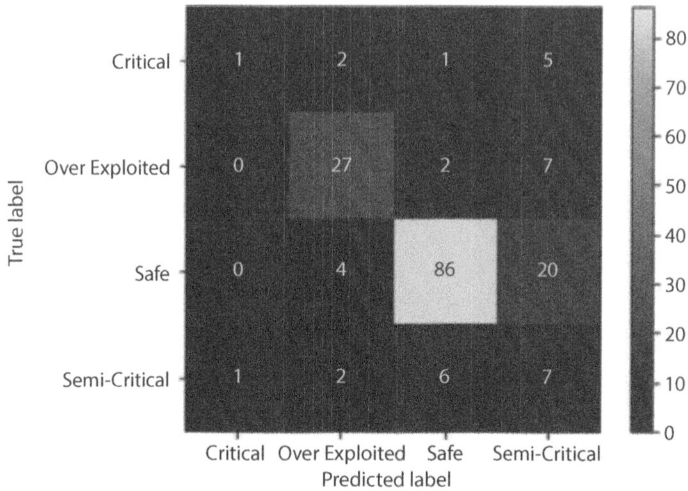

Figure 6.7 Naïve Bayes classification.

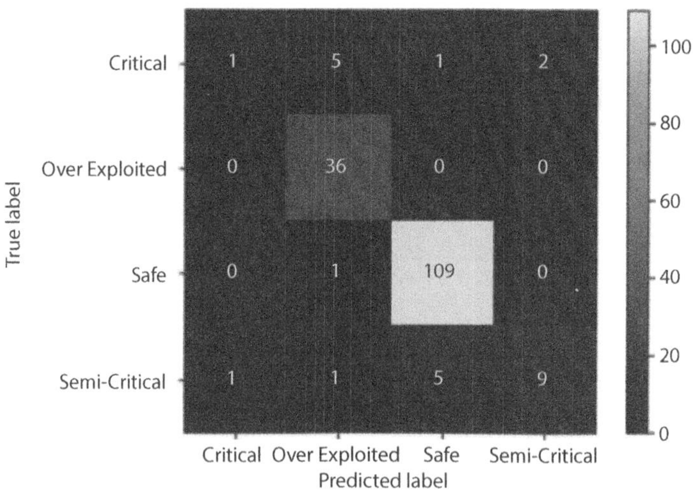

Figure 6.8 Support vector machine classification.

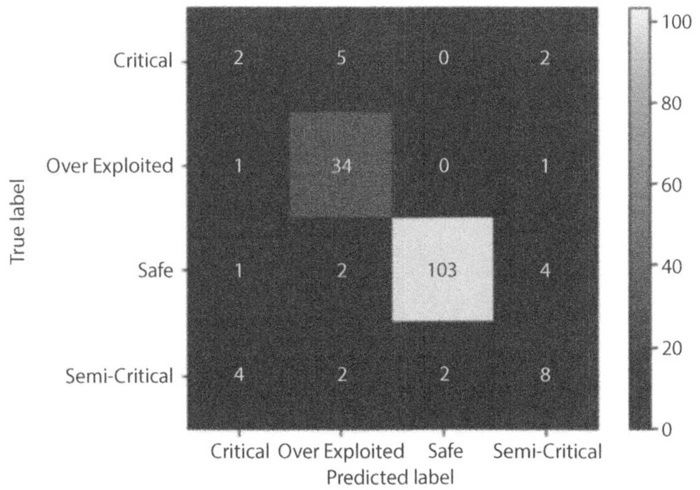

Figure 6.9 Decision trees classification.

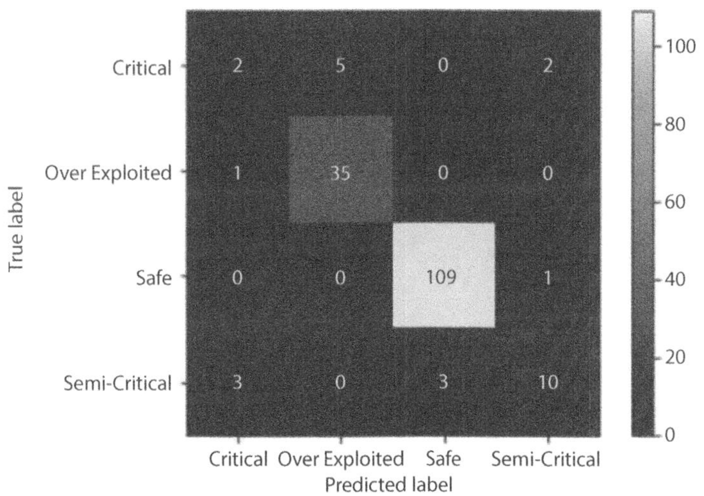

Figure 6.10 Random forest classification.

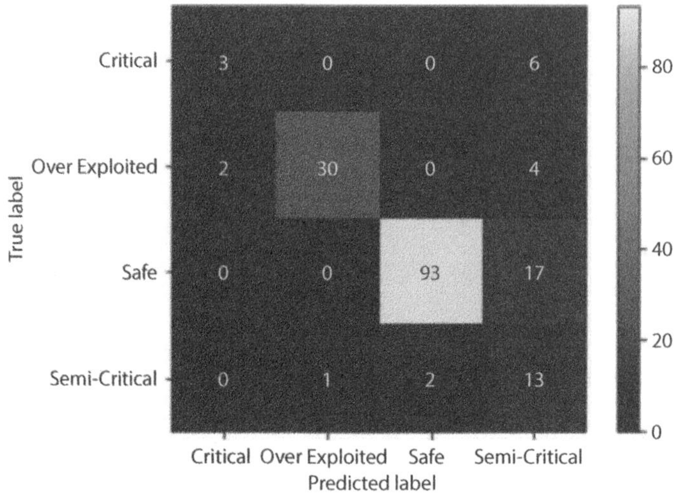

Figure 6.11 ADA boost.

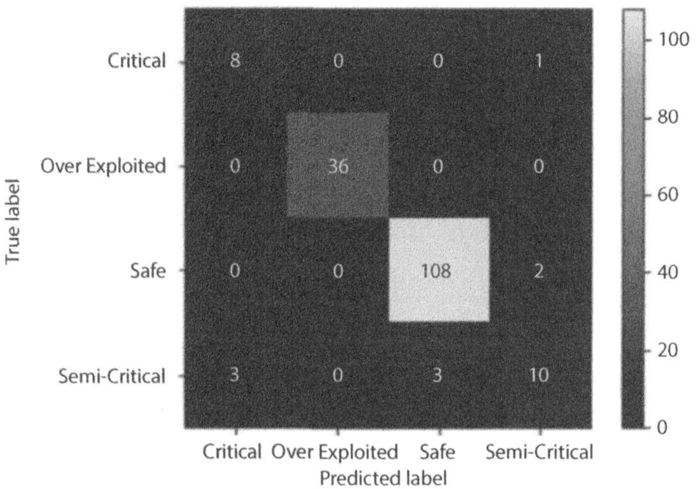

Figure 6.12 Grid search.

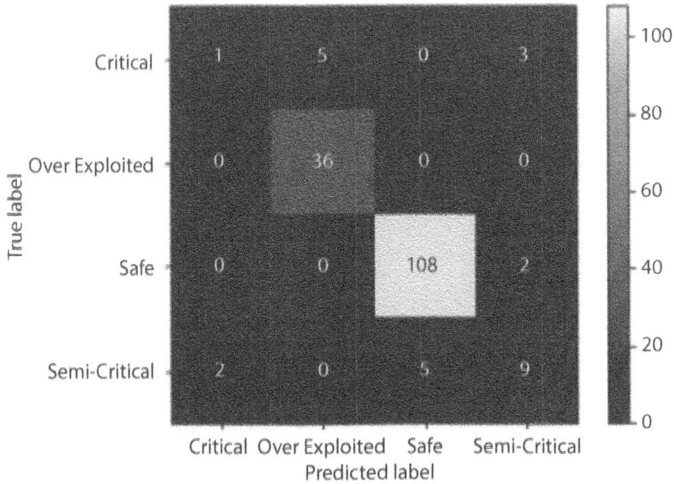

Figure 6.13 XG boost.

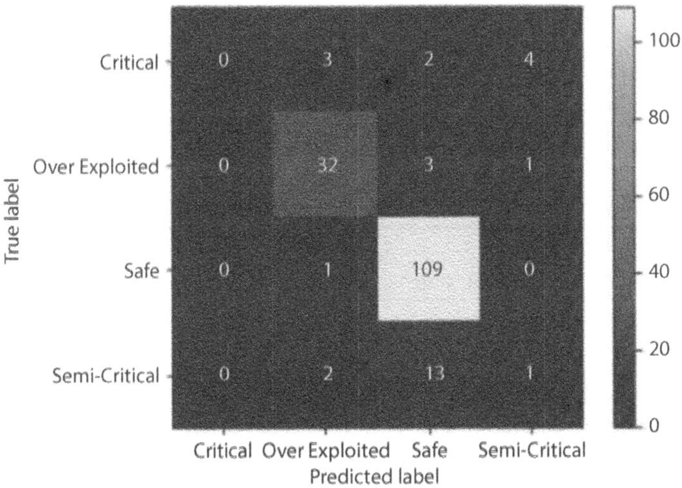

Figure 6.14 K-fold CV.

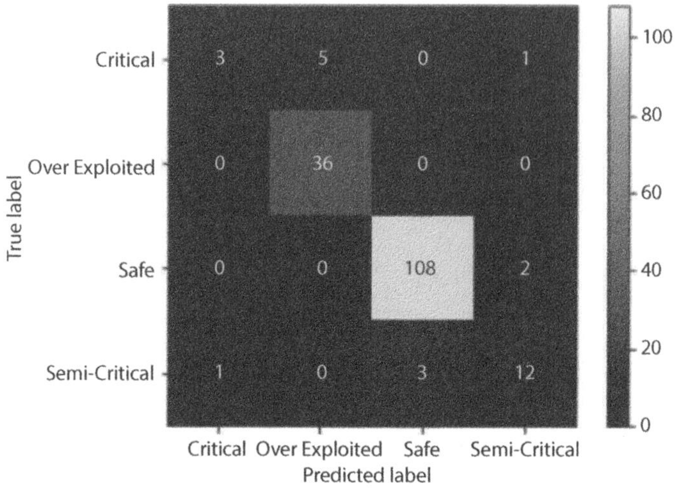

Figure 6.15 Multi-level stacking.

Table 6.2 Hyperparameter settings.

Model	Hyperparameter	Value
Logistic Regression	random_state	0
K-Nearest Neighbours Classification	n_neighbors metric p	4 'minkowski' 2
Support Vector Machine Classification	kernel random_state	'linear' 0
Kernel SVM	kernel random_state	'rbf' 0
Naïve Bayes Classification	-	-
Decision Trees Classification	criterion random_state	'entropy' 0
Random Forest Classification	n_estimators max_depth max_features criterion oob_score n_jobs random_state	100 100 5 "entropy" "TRUE" -1 0

(Continued)

Table 6.2 Hyperparameter settings. (*Continued*)

Model	Hyperparameter	Value
Grid Search	estimator param_grid scoring cv n_jobs	SVC(kernel = 'rbf', random_state = 0) [{'C': [1, 10, 100, 1000], 'kernel': ['linear']}, {'C': [1, 10, 100, 1000], 'kernel': ['rbf'], 'gamma': [0.1, 0.2, 0.3, 0.4, 0.5, 0.6, 0.7, 0.8, 0.9]}] 'Accuracy', 10 -1
K-Fold CV	estimator X y cv	KFclassifier X_train y_train 17
ADA Boost	n_estimators learning_rate	50 1
XG Boost	estimator X y cv	XGclassifier X_train y_train 10
Ensemble Learning (Bagging)	base_estimator n_estimators random_state cv	DecisionTreeClassifier() 500 5 kfold
Multi-level Stacking Classifier	multi_layer_Classifier param_distributions cv n_iter n_jobs	StackingClassifier(estimators=[('lr', RidgeClassifierCV()),('lrr',linear_model.LogisticRegression()), ('nn', MLPClassifier(hidden_layer_sizes = (250,700,102,51),max_iter=3500, activation = 'relu', solver = 'adam', alpha = 0.01, random_state = 42)), ('svc', SVC(C=1, gamma=1e-6, kernel='rbf'))], final_estimator=final_layer, passthrough=False, n_jobs=-1) {'final_estimator__xgbr__max_depth':[20,23,25], 'final_estimator__etr__max_features' :[0.5,1],'final_estimator__etr__max_depth':[5,10,20], 'final_estimator__adbr__n_estimators' :[100, 200], 'svc__gamma': ['scale', 'auto', 1e-6]} 15 -1

Table 6.3 Accuracy, precision, recall and F1-score of each model.

Model	Accuracy-score	Precision-score	Recall-score	F1-score
Logistic Regression	0.8830409356725146	0.8830409356725146	0.8830409356725146	0.8830409356725146
K-Nearest Neighbors Classification	0.8011695906432749	0.8011695906432749	0.8011695906432749	0.8011695906432749
Support Vector Machine Classification	0.9064327485380117	0.9064327485380117	0.9064327485380117	0.9064327485380118
Kernel SVM	0.8304093567251462	0.8304093567251462	0.8304093567251462	0.8304093567251462
Naïve Bayes Classification	0.7076023391812866	0.7076023391812866	0.7076023391812866	0.7076023391812865
Decision Trees Classification	0.8596491228070176	0.8596491228070176	0.8596491228070176	0.8596491228070176
Random Forest Classification	0.9122807017543859	0.9122807017543859	0.9122807017543859	0.9122807017543859
Grid Search	0.9648567119155356	0.9473684210526315	0.9473684210526315	0.9473684210526315
K-Fold CV	0.8321948134092347	0.8304093567251462	0.8304093567251462	0.8304093567251462
ADA Boost	0.8128654970760234	0.8128654970760234	0.8128654970760234	0.8128654970760234
XG Boost	0.9005847953216374	0.9005847953216374	0.9005847953216374	0.9005847953216374
Ensemble Learning (Bagging)	0.9555555555555556	-	-	-
Multi-level Stacking	0.935672514619883	0.935672514619883	0.935672514619883	0.935672514619883

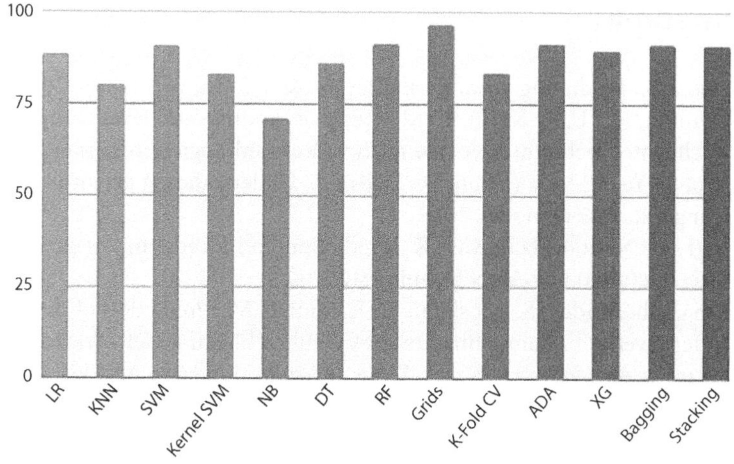

Figure 6.16 Accuracy comparison of models.

6.5 Conclusion

In this work, the GWL classification is implemented using various ML techniques. The district-level groundwater measurements were classified based on 11 different attributes. In the experiment different ML algorithms like Logistic Regression, K-Nearest Neighbours Classification, SVM Classification, Kernel SVM, Naïve Bayes Classification, Decision Trees Classification, Random Forest Classification, Ensemble Learning, Grid Search, K-Fold CV (Shuffle Split, Repeated K-Fold, Leave-one-out K-Fold, Stratified K-fold), ADA Boost, XG Boost and Multi-level Stacking Classification were applied and compared. On comparing these algorithms the best accuracy of 96.49% was achieved using Grid search and SVC classifier, as it assists in optimal hyperparameter selection by exhaustively searching the parameter values in higher dimensional space. Amongst all the classifiers the lowest F1-score of 0.707 was obtained by the Naïve Bayes classifier.

AI disclosure statement: The author confirms that no artificial intelligence (AI)-generated content or AI-assisted writing tools were used in the preparation of this chapter (including summaries and the abstract). All text, analysis, and conclusions are the result of the author's original work.

Bibliography

1. Matta, S., Predicting groundwater levels using linear regression, 2011.
2. Demirci, M., Ù, F., Körlü, S., Modeling of groundwater level using artificial intelligence techniques: A case study of Reyhanli region in Turkey, 2019.
3. Yan, S., Yu, S., Wu, Y., Pan, D., Dodge, J., Understanding groundwater table using a statistical model, 2018.
4. Vetrivel, N. and Elangovan, K., Prediction and forecasting of groundwater level fluctuation by ANN technique, 2016.
5. Emamgholizadeh, S., Moslemi, K., Karami, G.M., Prediction of the groundwater level of bastam palin (Itan) by Artificial Neural Network (ANN) and Adaptive and Adaptive Neuro-Fuzzy Inference Syatems (ANFIS), 2014.
6. Sujay Raghavendra., N. and Deka, P.C., Forecasting monthly groundwater level fluctuations in coastal aquifers using hybrid Wavelet packet–Support vector regression, 2015.
7. Sahoo, S., Russo, T.A., Elliott, J., Foster, I., Machine learning algorithms for modeling groundwater level changes in agricultural regions of the U.S, 2017.
8. Azimi, S., Moghaddam, M.A., Monfared, S.A.H., Large-scale association analysis of climate drought and decline in groundwater quantity using Gaussian process classification, 2018.
9. Sahoo, S. and Jha, M.K., Groundwater-level prediction using multiple linear regression and artificial neural network techniques:a comparative assessment, 2013.
10. Peng, S., Huang, J., Fu, Q., Research on groundwater level prediction of naoli river basin based on Elman Wavelet Neural Networks, 2011.
11. Porte, P., Isacc, R.K., Singh, K.K., Groundwater level prediction using artificial neural network model, 2018.
12. Theodoridou, P., Varouchakis, E., Karatzas, G., Regression Analysis and Risk Assessment of Groundwater Levels, 2018.
13. Zhao, Y., Li, Y., Zhang, L., Wang, Q., Groundwater level prediction of landslide based on classification and regression tree, 2016.
14. Yadav, B., Ch, S., Mathur, S., Adamowski, J., Assessing the suitability of extreme learning machines for groundwater level prediction, 2016.
15. Doble, R., Fu, G., Zhang, N., Groundwater Recharge Prediction Using Linear Regression, Multi-Layer Perception Network, and Deep Learning, 2019.
16. Dogan, A., Demirpence, H., Cobaner, M., Prediction of groundwater levels from lake levels and climate data using ANN approach, 2008.
17. Narayana, C., Mahaboob, B., Venkateswarlu, B., Ravi Sankar, J., Balasiddamuni, P., A Study on Misspecification and Predictive Accuracy of Stochastic Linear Regression Models, 2018.
18. Daliakopoulos, I.N., Coulibaly, P., Tsanis, I.K., Groundwater level forecasting using artificial neural networks. *J. Hydrol.*, *309*, 1–4, 229–240, 2005.

19. Sahoo, S. and Jha, M.K., Groundwater-level prediction using multiple linear regression and artificial neural network techniques: a comparative assessment. *Hydrogeol. J.*, *21*, 8, 1865–1887, 2013.
20. Dash, N.B., Panda, S.N., Remesan, R., Sahoo, N., Hybrid neural modeling for groundwater level prediction. *Neural Comput. Appl.*, *19*, 8, 1251–1263, 2010.
21. Suryanarayana, C., Sudheer, C., Mahammood, V., Panigrahi, B.K., An integrated wavelet-support vector machine for groundwater level prediction in Visakhapatnam, India. *Neurocomputing*, *145*, 324–335, 2014.
22. Srigurulekha, K. and Dhivya, S., Ground Water Level Prediction. *Asian J. Appl. Sci. Technol. (AJAST)*, *5*, 1, 110–120, 2021.
23. Yadav, B., Gupta, P.K., Patidar, N., Himanshu, S.K., Ensemble modelling framework for groundwater level prediction in urban areas of India. *Sci. Total Environ.*, *712*, 135539, 2020.
24. WHYMAP, BGR Bundesanstalt für Geowissenschaften und rohstoffe. Retrieved July 21, 2022, from https://www.whymap.org/whymap/EN/Maps_Data/Gwr/Gwr_statistics/ /gwr_statistics_node_en.hml.
25. Sujay Raghavendra, N. and Deka, P.C., Forecasting monthly groundwater level fluctuations in coastal aquifers using hybrid Wavelet packet–Support vector regression. *Cogent Eng.*, *2*, 1, 999414, 2015.
26. Pham, Q.B., Kumar, M., Di Nunno, F., Elbeltagi, A., Granata, F., Islam, A.R.M., Anh, D.T., Groundwater level prediction using machine learning algorithms in a drought-prone area. *Neural Comput. Appl.*, 1–23, 2022.
27. Tao, H., Hameed, M.M., Marhoon, H.A., Zounemat-Kermani, M., Salim, H., Sungwon, K., Yaseen, Z.M., Groundwater level prediction using machine learning models: a comprehensive review. *Neurocomputing*, 2022.
28. Di Nunno, F. and Granata, F., Groundwater level prediction in Apulia region (Southern Italy) using NARX neural network. *Environ. Res.*, *190*, 110062, 2020.
29. Chang, J., Wang, G., Mao, T., Simulation and prediction of suprapermafrost groundwater level variation in response to climate change using a neural network model. *J. Hydrol.*, *529*, 1211–1220, 2015.
30. Moosavi, V., Vafakhah, M., Shirmohammadi, B., Behnia, N., A wavelet-ANFIS hybrid model for groundwater level forecasting for different prediction periods. *Water Resour. Manage.*, *27*, 5, 1301–1321, 2013.
31. Python Homepage: https://www.python.org/. Accessed on 19/02/2025.
32. Scikit-learn Homepage: https://scikit-learn.org/stable/. Accessed on 19/02/2025.
33. Pandas Homepage: https://pandas.pydata.org/. Accessed on 19/02/2025.
34. Numpy Homepage: https://numpy.org/. Accessed on 19/02/2025.
35. Matplotlib Homepage: https://matplotlib.org/. Accessed on 19/02/2025.

7

Sustainability in AI Development

Riya R. Patil*, Sandip A. Bandgar, Sachin S. Mali, Prajakta R. Patil and Dhanashree R. Davare

Department of Pharmaceutics, Ashokrao Mane College of Pharmacy, Peth-Vadgaon, Kolhapur, India

Abstract

Artificial Intelligence (AI) has emerged as one of the most influential technological forces of the 21st century, driving innovation across sectors such as healthcare, finance, education, transportation, and beyond. However, the rapid proliferation of AI systems has raised pressing concerns regarding their sustainability from environmental, economic, and societal perspectives. This chapter delves deeply into the critical issue of sustainability in AI development, aiming to provide a comprehensive understanding of how AI systems can be designed, deployed, and maintained in ways that align with long-term sustainable development goals.

The environmental footprint of AI, particularly the energy consumption associated with training large-scale machine learning models and operating vast data centers, is examined in detail. Strategies to mitigate these impacts, such as the development of energy-efficient algorithms, the adoption of green computing practices, and the optimization of data infrastructure, are explored. Beyond the environmental dimension, the chapter addresses the economic aspects of sustainable AI, including equitable access to AI technologies, reducing barriers for underrepresented communities, and fostering inclusive innovation ecosystems.

Ethical and social sustainability are also central to the discussion. The chapter analyzes how responsible AI practices—such as transparency, fairness, accountability, and the protection of human rights—are integral to building trust and ensuring that AI technologies contribute positively to society. Regulatory frameworks, corporate initiatives, and cross-sector collaborations that promote sustainable AI practices are reviewed, offering real-world examples and case studies.

***Keywords*:** Sustainable AI, green computing, energy-efficient AI, AI ethics, machine learning, environmental impact, responsible AI, sustainable development goals

**Corresponding author*: rp8605612020@gmail.com

Manish Kumar, Nitigya Sambyal, Leena Priyadarshini Singh, Ramasamy V. and S. Balamurugan (eds.) Responsible AI: Principles and Practices, (143–174) © 2026 Scrivener Publishing LLC

7.1 Introduction

Sustainability in AI development means developing and deploying artificial intelligence systems from design, development to implementation with a consideration and balancing impact, affected both economically, socially, and environmentally. Sustainable AI development emphasizes not only short-term efficiency and effectiveness of AI technologies but also responsibility and long-term benefits for society and the planet. Thus, there is a need to address the environmental costs of AI infrastructures and equitably promote economic benefits with inclusive and fair social outcomes. AI systems are highly complex socio-technical-ecological systems that raise numerous social, environmental, and economic concerns. Whether AI systems promote or hinder a socially and environmentally just society is a topic of current debate [1]. They concentrate on the ways in which AI systems may support different sustainability goals [2]. The potential of AI systems for ecological objectives, like ecosystem monitoring, climate protection, or the energy transition [4, 5], or sustainable manufacturing [6], as well as for the social good, like public health issues or education, is being highlighted by terms like AI for Earth or AI for social Good [3]. The role of AI in achieving the Sustainable Development Goals (SDGs) [7–10] is also being covered in an expanding body of work. There is a continuing debate on whether AI systems help or hinder the SDGs, how they should be managed [11], and how accurate and suitable such evaluations are [12].

The environmental dimension of sustainability in AI is centered on minimizing the ecological footprint of AI systems. Examples include reducing the energy consumption of data centers, optimizing algorithms for efficiency, and mitigating the environmental effects of manufacturing hardware components such as processors and graphics processing units (GPUs) [13]. The economic dimension aims to equitably distribute benefits from AI, hence having a positive impact on global economies without increasing inequalities. This encompasses job creation, establishment of new industries, and innovation toward long-term economic development [14]. It encompasses social considerations surrounding the effects of AI technologies on society, such as privacy, fairness, transparency, and accountability. It has also made efforts such as algorithmic bias and ensuring that diverse populations access AI systems, preventing discrimination, and reinforcing ethical standards in the governance of AI [15]. Sustainability in the development of artificial intelligence refers to a holistic approach to embedding considerations pertaining to the environmental, economic, and social spheres in the conceptualization, deployment, and lifecycle management of artificial intelligence systems. It emphasizes the fact that creating and using AI technologies must not compromise a future ability of generations in meeting their needs, generally speaking to the overall social and environmental systems of which they are a part (UN, 1987). More concretely as regards AI, this means ensuring these three main areas are brought into a position of sufficient consideration:

i. Environmental Sustainability: Reducing the carbon footprint, energy usage, and waste produced from AI technologies. The enormous computation needed to train AI models-especially deep learning models on large scales-have brought concerns and increased worries about ecological implications, with the environmental cost of AI training constituting an important challenge [16].
ii. Economic Sustainability: AI technologies must be designed ensuring long-term economic stability and growth. This means that AI systems should not only contribute to profit-making activities but should also allow just economic opportunities to all the members of society. AI has a potential to disrupt industries, displace jobs, and widen the economic gap and therefore calls for prudent policies concerning job retraining and economic redistribution of technology adoptions that enhance shared prosperity [17].
iii. Social Sustainability: Contributing to ensuring AI systems positively impact society in two ways: fostering inclusivity, fairness, and human welfare. Applications of AI that are misused may therefore amplify existing social inequalities in decision-making biases and the unequal distribution of benefits [18]. This includes the protection of privacy, the need for transparency, and the building of trust in AI systems that impact people's lives and communities.

7.1.1 Relevance and Urgency

Urgency in Tackling Sustainability: There is an imperative for urgency in tackling sustainability both for the ever-increasing fast pace at which AI technology is being developed and its implications to society. The sooner it is deployed, the deeper and wider the basic environmental, economic, and social impacts it will be, requiring bold interventions that maximize benefits from AI while minimizing adverse consequences.

I. Rise in Energy Needs of AI: AI systems, primarily deep learning models, consume large amounts of compute during training and inference, thereby greatly contributing to energy consumption. For example, in 2019, one single run of AI training for models like GPT-3 could be said to have released the equivalent of emissions from five cars driven over their entire lives. More importantly, the energy usage of AI is going to rise further as even more powerful models are developed and it contributes to concerns about the ecological footprint of AI. Data centers that serve AI systems consume around 1% of total energy around the world [19].

II. Social and Economic Inequality Amplified by AI Adoption: Whereas AI promises great advancements in certain sectors like healthcare, education, and transportation systems, adoption would also expand social and economic inequalities. For example, due to the replacement of jobs in various sectors by AI-driven automation, workers with less in terms of skills will be disenfranchised from employment, making them economically poor [17]. Besides, AI systems reflect and repeat the biases found in the data they are learned from. A lack of diversity in AI research and development leads to algorithms that discriminate against vulnerable groups, hence further creating deeper societal inequalities. A need to solve these disparities occurs to make AI distributive evenly in benefits.

7.1.2 Challenges and Opportunities in AI Development

The development and deployment of artificial intelligence pose enormous opportunities for technological advancement but also tremendous challenges, particularly concerning sustainability. Sustainability in AI is actually about making sure that the need to address the environmental, economic, and social issues should not arise with unbearable additional problems or create more instead. As AI continues to be absorbed into industries, governments, and more daily operations, its challenges and opportunities in regard to a sustainable future must be understood.

7.1.2.1 Environmental Impacts of AI Development

- **Problems**

Energy Consumption: AI systems use a lot of energy and a lot of processing power, especially deep learning models. Research shows that throughout the course of their lives, training a large model like BERT can emit as much CO_2 as five cars. The carbon footprint of tech enterprises is greatly increased by the high energy requirements for both training and inference [20].

Data Centre Emissions: Artificial intelligence is built on data centers that consume a huge amount of electricity, mostly produced from non-renewable sources. The centers were accounted for half of the world's energy and emissions [21]. Still, energy efficiency in the data center operation is one of the major challenges.

- **Opportunities:**

Energy-Efficient Algorithms: The study of more energy-efficient algorithms for AI is underway. Model compression techniques, including pruning and quantization, reduce the computational load of a model without sacrificing its performance [22].

Renewable Energy Integration: The incorporation of AI in some companies is also reducing their carbon footprint. Google, for example, has promised to ensure that all its data centers operate on 100% renewable energy, and other companies are following in the same path [23].

7.1.2.2 Economic Impact of AI Development

- **Roadblocks**

Job Displacement: Job displacement is also expected on a massive scale through AI automation. Most of these jobs will come from countries such as manufacturing, logistics, and customer service industries. Workers' displacement through automation will enlarge the influence of income inequality and lead to social unrest [24]. Significant steps should be taken immediately to reduce the adverse economic impact of rapidly adopted AI.

Inequality in AI Access: There are extreme divisions across different developed and developing countries as well as large corporations versus small businesses regarding access to AI technologies. The digital divide may increase economic inequality because the benefits from AI could be preserved by the economically rich [25].

- **Opportunities:**

AI-Driven Economic Growth: AI has the possibility of bringing high productivity augmentation, innovation, and new industries such as healthcare, autonomous transport, and green technologies.AI could add $13 trillion to the economy worldwide by 2030, boosting productivity and creating new business models [26].

Job Creation and Reskilling: AI inevitably kills some jobs, but creates new ones in the spheres of AI development, data science, and cybersecurity. It is important to invest in reskilling programs that will guide the working class to adapt to AI-based economies [18].

7.2 Environmental Sustainability in AI

7.2.1 Energy Consumption and Carbon Footprint in AI

The AI technologies, in particular large-scale models like deep learning and natural language processing, are highly computation intensive. This results in considerably high energy consumption. In the near future, when AI becomes an integral part of many industries, there is a possible environmental impact that might pose an issue, particularly regarding data centers, training costs, and computational infrastructure [27].

I. Data Centers and Computational Costs of Large-Scale AI Training

Data centers are significantly energy-intensive; they power most AI research and deployment, hosting those necessary GPUs, TPUs, and CPUs for training complex models [28]. As deep learning and large models like GPT-3, AlphaFold, and BERT have come to the forefront, the demand in terms of energy consumption has increased dramatically [29]. These models are generally trained on thousands of GPUs over days or weeks, burning through vast amounts of electricity in the process.

But the high computational cost of training such models also means that their environmental footprint is worse. For instance, training the GPT-3 model, a 175 billion-parameter language model designed at OpenAI, consumed several megawatt-hours (MWh) of energy, translating to an amount of carbon footprint from an average American household for an entire [30]. AlphaFold, an AI model to predict protein folding which DeepMind developed, also generated significant environmental impacts as well. Carbon footprint from the training of AlphaFold models is estimated to be in the range of hundreds of tons of CO_2 emissions [31]. As seen in these examples, the AI must urgently embrace environmental sustainability.

II. Case Study

- **Carbon Impact of GPT-3**

The computational resources required to train GPT-3 are massive [32]. It was found that training GPT-3 generated an estimated carbon footprint of 284 tons of CO_2, which is approximately equivalent to the lifetime emissions of five cars [33]. This carbon footprint is largely due to the extended time needed for training and the vast number of GPUs involved in the process. While the commercial applications of GPT-3 are groundbreaking, the environmental cost underscores the necessity of developing more energy-efficient models [34].

- **Case Study: AlphaFold**

DeepMind's AlphaFold, which accurately predicts protein folding, is another example of a large-scale AI model with significant environmental costs [35]. The training of AlphaFold v2 involved using powerful computing systems for several weeks, and its carbon footprint has been cited to be upwards of 100 tons of CO_2 [94]. While the scientific benefits of AlphaFold are immense—leading to breakthroughs in drug discovery and biology—the environmental toll is a reminder of the growing concerns about AI's sustainability [36].

7.2.2 Efforts to Reduce Environmental Impact

I. Algorithmic Optimization: Techniques Like Pruning, Quantization, and Transfer Learning

Algorithmic optimization is one of the most effective techniques to reduce the footprint of AI models on the environment. Pruning, quantization, and transfer learning typically both reduce training and inference loads by several orders of magnitude.

- Pruning: Such a procedure removes the useless parameters or connections of neural networks that make the model simpler, yet the performance is compromised very insignificantly. The memory and computational requirements for AI models are reduced in the pruning process, meaning that training as well as doing inference uses less energy [37].
- Quantization: It is reducing the number of bits in the representation of values used within an AI model, which

consequently saves more computation [38]. As the computational burden reduces, weights and activations now have a lower bit-width and hence energy usage decreases. It has been successfully utilized on large neural networks that are specifically used in NLP and cover faster inference times along with lower energy costs.

- Transfer Learning: Transfer learning employs pre-trained models and fine-tunes them on smaller, more limited datasets rather than training a model from scratch [39]. This method minimizes the amount of computation needed to train a model. Generally speaking, pre-trained models usually outline a common strategy in modern AI applications. Instead of training large models from scratch, it allows reducing energy-intensive procedures in quite a few processes.

II. Hardware Efficiency: Adoption of Energy-Efficient GPUs/TPUs and Edge Computing

Improving hardware efficiency is another key approach to energy reduction in AI systems. Energy-efficient GPUs and TPUs were created for this purpose. These application-specific processors optimize computing for tasks specific to AI and consume orders of magnitude less power than a standard CPU [40]. For instance, Google's TPUs are machine learning-specific accelerators that speed both training and inference and perform at an energy efficiency with a better performance-to-power ratio [41].

Another promising approach is edge computing where instead of doing some computations in a centralized data center, they are performed closer to the source of the data, such as on smartphones or IoT devices. Edge computing can serve to reduce the amount of big-data processing required, hence reducing the large amounts of energy required to carry out large-scale data transmission and centralized servers in the cloud [42]. This makes it very relevant in some applications of AI, including autonomous vehicles and smart cities where real-time processing is required.

III. Renewable Energy: Transition to Green-Powered Data Centers

One of the most significant actions to reduce the carbon footprint by AI is to convert data centers to renewable sources. Companies like Google, Microsoft, and Amazon are making the sourcing of renewable energy for their data centers change [43]. For example, Google has pledged that all its data centers would be powered solely by 100% renewable energy sources, which they achieved in 2017 [44]. Companies can significantly reduce their negative impact on the environment if they tap into green sources of energy such as wind, solar, and hydropower for their AI operations.

Other companies have been using carbon offsetting programs, which engage in neutralizing the level of emitted carbon due to its operation [45]. This includes investing in renewable energy projects and initiatives such as forest conservation projects that absorb CO_2. As more and more people adopt renewable energies, energy efficiency, and sustainability of AI systems will continue to improve.

7.2.3 Green AI Movement

I. The Philosophy of Prioritizing Efficiency Over Performance

It is a movement that presents arguments against prioritizing raw improvements in performance metrics in AI research and development, and instead argues for energy efficiency. The focus should therefore be placed on decreasing the computational resources required to train models of AI without sacrificing effectiveness [46]. This philosophy encourages researchers to make more sustainable practices-that is, designing models that are smaller and more efficient for any similar result that their larger counterparts might achieve without increasing their environmental footprint.

For instance, regarding the efficient architecture of models for model: mobile networks, e.g. MobileNet, compact transformers, e.g., TinyBERT [47], they are developing toward achieving the top performance on constrained computational resources hence consuming less energy compared to their larger counterparts. Again, this agrees with the Green AI philosophy and emphasizes practical, sustainable AI rather than creating bigger and more complex models with larger counts of parameters and much more enormous training datasets [48].

II. Examples from Industry and Academia Driving the Green AI Initiative

Many key institutions and organizations lead the way in Green AI. The Partnership on AI is a collection of industry leaders, academics, and civil society groups advocating for the development of sustainable and ethical AI technologies [49]. This group also emphasizes, through research into energy-efficient AI, best practices to minimize the environmental impact in industry-wide sustainability. The Green AI initiative is gaining momentum on the academic front as more researchers are turning their focus towards the gigantic aspect of AI that is causing environmental impacts [50]. For example, research in low-energy machine learning methods like spiking neural networks and neuromorphic computing holds much promise for efficient models [51]. Such approaches mimic the way the brain makes low-energy processing possible and thus creates a more environmentally friendly approach towards complex computations.

Furthermore, the academic world has started to think about the environmental costs of AI research, as papers like "Energy and Policy Considerations for Deep Learning in NLP" begin to demand accountability and transparency from the industry of AI [52]. All these efforts are slowly making the narrative go in the direction of pushing AI researchers and practitioners to ponder the environmental implications of their work.

7.3 Social Sustainability in AI

Social sustainability in AI means developing and using AI technologies in ways that benefit society rather than ways that derive harm from it. Equity should be built into the AI system with proper consideration of race, gender, or socio-economic status, while transparency and accountability should be required to understand AI systems and how they arrive at conclusions, especially sensitive areas like health and criminal justice. Another critical area is how AI impacts employment and workers with risks of job replacement. Social sustainability demands these reskilling programs and services for those losing their employment due to the AI-tsunami. Ethical governance is another imperative area, requiring frameworks and policies to adjust to governing AI in line with furthering human values, privacy, and security. Social sustainability therefore means that AI should be advanced and able to go in accordance with and responsible for society's values [53].

7.3.1 Fairness and Bias in AI Systems

Because machine learning and AI technologies have been deployed rapidly across different spheres, the issues of AI fairness and bias have become a sensitive topic of discussion. Bias created by AI models results in unforeseen consequences, with disproportionate impact in certain groups of people or systemic inequalities resulting in the persistence of societal issues such as racial and gender discrimination and also economic inequalities.

I. Examples of Biases in Datasets and Their Societal Impact

- **Gender Bias in Hiring Algorithms**

AI recruitment learns and imitates from existing hiring data that could have discriminatory properties. For example, Amazon announced in a report dated 2018 that the AI recruitment tool discriminated against female candidates for technical roles because it was trained on resumes primarily contributed by men. AI was predisposed to prefer males' resumes as it was made to reflect more male-dominated language and job experience [54].

- **Racial Bias in Facial Recognition Systems**
It was also discovered that facial recognition systems have various studies performed on them indicating a higher error rate for Black and Hispanic faces than for White faces, including one conducted at the National Institute of Standards and Technology. For example, the IBM and MIT studies demonstrated that commercial facial recognition systems failed miserably when it came to identifying individuals from racial minority groups, specifically the Black women [55].

- **Healthcare Disparities Due to Biased Data**
These biased training data in health care may, in turn reinforce health disparities. For example, an AI risk prediction system designed to predict heart disease might underperform on a Black patient population if it had been trained solely on homogenous data. A careful analysis by Obermeyer *et al.* in 2019 showed that a popular algorithm in the U.S. healthcare system had racial bias for simple reasons: it relied on healthcare costs as a proxy for health needs, which are worse for Black patients [56].

II. Techniques to Improve Fairness and Inclusivity in AI Systems
There is increasing awareness on the need to address bias and ensure fairness in AI systems. Different methods and frameworks have been proposed by researchers and practitioners to mitigate bias and promote inclusivity.:

- **Fair Representation Learning**
Balanced representation of all relevant groups using training data represents a technique to address bias in AI models. Fair representation learning is a transformation of data that ensures the sensitive attributes, such as race or gender or age, do not unfairly influence the outcomes of the model. Algorithms like adversarial debiasing can thus remove correlations between sensitive attributes and predictions of the model [57].

- **Algorithmic Fairness Constraints**
Another approach would be to inject fairness constraints directly into the optimization of the algorithm. This can appear in the form of demographic parity, which ensures that outcomes are equal, or equalized odds where the error rate is equalized across groups. It's rather fascinating that Hardt *et al.*

introduced the concept of "fairness through awareness," which attempted to plead the case for fairness by injecting sensitive attributes into informed decision-making models that made fair predictions [58].

- **Data Auditing and Preprocessing**

Auditing the data set prior to training any model based on AI is of utmost importance. Any biases existing in the set must be identified and corrected for. Data preprocessing techniques like reweighting, resampling, or balancing the datasets can eliminate differences in representation. If a certain dataset shows an underrepresentation of a specific demographic, it may be resampled to have equal representation of those groups [59].

- **Post-Processing Techniques**

Once learning is finalized, post-processing correction of biased results is permitted, since techniques such as reject option classification-that is, the model adjusts its decisions on the basis of biased results after it has made a prediction- or calibration methods, which adjust the predicted probabilities for different groups, can be applied to ensure fairer decision-making [60].

- **Fairness-Aware Model Evaluation**

In addition to training the model in fairness, fairness is also a matter of evaluation. There are a growing number of fairness-aware metrics (Fairness-Accuracy Tradeoff, FAT), and fairness indicators such as equalized odds, equal opportunity, or disparate impact, intended to ensure that AI models will not have a disproportionate impact on any group [61].

7.3.2 Equity in Access to AI Technology

AI has the potential to generate industrial revolutions, enhance world health, and guarantee the solutions to societal problems. However, its adoption is terribly uneven across developed and developing nations. Such imbalances prevent underserved regions from using AI towards economic and social prosperity. The best step to garner global equity is addressing such imbalances and democratizing access to AI.

1. Addressing Disparities in Global AI Adoption

The gap in the adoption of AI by high-income countries and low-income countries is fundamentally determined by the gap in infrastructure and other disparities regarding education and resources. Developed countries are privileged with advanced digital infrastructure, high-speed internet, and powerful computation resources that support the development and deployment of AI. Most developing countries suffer with the "losers" end of the digital divide-from unreliable electricity, limited internet connectivity and lack of proper hardware-severe restrictions on access and adoption of AI technologies are incurred [62].

In addition, activities concerning the research and development of AI are skewed towards a few countries, U.S., China, and other European nations. The remaining global South is thereby disadvantaged because they lack the pool of specialized talent required for AI research and development and the finances to fund cutting-edge AI projects. This further implies that AI systems rely highly on data for training algorithms; however, in developing countries, the necessary infrastructure for collecting, storing, and managing big sets of data is generally lacking, meaning most AI applications tailored to local needs are scarce. Instead, many countries have to rely upon solutions created in other regions, which may not be suitable to the specific challenges they face [63].

II. Initiatives for Democratizing AI Tools and Platforms

To address these disparities, several initiatives are working to make AI tools and platforms more accessible to a global audience.

- **Open-Source Platforms:** Democratization of access to AI technology has been furthered through the platforms of TensorFlow and PyTorch by making free, open-source frameworks for machine learning and deep learning. Therefore, developers may now be based anywhere in the world and develop and deploy AI models without the expense of proprietary software [64].
- **AI for Good Programs:** Examples are initiatives such as AI for Good Global Summit, convened by the ITU, showing how AI can be used to solve global problems, including health care, education, and climate change. The event focuses on who benefits from AI, offering equal opportunities to all regions, except those usually locked out of technological advancement [65].

7.3.3 Impact on Workforce and Communities

Artificial intelligence, which previously manifested itself as automation, is destined to transform the world workforce with potential and also pose challenges. As AI systems increasingly replace repetitive labor-intensive tasks, there arises a necessity to balance automation with human augmentation in preparing workers for these changes. Proper balance would save the economy from dislocation while envisioning a future where technology complements human capabilities rather than replacing them.

I. Balancing Automation with Human Augmentation

- AI automation promises to revolutionize the industry by ensuring greater efficiency, cost minimization, and productivity. However, for starters, there are concerns regarding the displacement of a large workforce in industries such as manufacturing, transportation, and customer service among others. While AI can undertake routine tasks, there is a need to emphasize human augmentation, whereby AI supplements human capability rather than replacing it.
- Using AI to augment humans would enhance the capacity of workers and enable them to undertake more complex work more effectively. For instance, in the health sector, AI can help doctors analyze medical images and come up with probable diagnoses, but treatment calls for a human judgment. Similarly, in the education sector, AI can come up with tools that tailor learning experiences, but the educator remains crucial for mentoring and intellectual thinking. Human-AI collaboration may actually achieve better output than either can alone.
- A balanced automation approach that focuses on improving human skills and giving power to workers to effectively collaborate with AI is required to move toward a more productive and inclusive workforce. It's at this point where the role of humans will shift into areas that have creativity, problem-solving and emotional intelligence, among other uniquely human capabilities [16].

II. Importance of Reskilling Programs and Ethical Labor Practices

- The inevitable fact that technology is gradually replacing some jobs necessitates reskilling programs that would shift workers to new roles and industries. Such reskilling programs will thus attract investment from governments, businesses, and educational institutions into training and reskilling programs to hone skills for superiority in AI-driven economies.

Workers will then acquire digital literacy, programming skills, competencies in data analysis, cybersecurity, and AI development, for which there are growing demands.

- Secondly, the ethical implications of automation should be on the table. Labor practice needs to change with respect to the rights and welfare of the workers. Some of the ethical considerations of labor incorporate fair wage for workers, job security, and proper retraining of workers whose jobs have been automated. Companies introducing AI-driven automation should invest in social responsibility in initiating retraining and skills upgrade of employees. Besides, universal access to reskilling opportunities will prevent ever-growing inequality and the fruits of AI equitably shared among the different segments of society [66].

7.4 Economic Sustainability in AI

With the passage of emerging AI technology, the economic sustainability it provides has become even clearer. More businesses and governments around the world integrate AI in order to save costs, increase productivity, and achieve sustainable development. However, with this business goal, it remains important to weigh the growth of economy with ethical and environmental considerations. AI will help provide solutions with associated cost savings while pushing forward with sustainable development across the United Nations' SDGs.

7.4.1 Reducing Costs without Compromising Quality

AI innovation is the only way to cut operation costs and yet offer quality. Indeed, the existing solutions in AI are expensive requirements on infrastructure, data, and skilled labor. New innovations, however, are helping cut down the cost of using AI and thus help smaller organizations and emerging markets in adopting these technologies.

I. Innovations for Cost-Effective AI Solutions

Cost-Effective AI Solutions Other innovations include edge computing, which brings the AI closer to data sources; just think of IoT devices that do not necessarily require expensive cloud storage and processing. Edge AI finds applications in all areas of manufacturing, agriculture, and healthcare. Real-time decisions can be made with lower latency in traditional

AI. New light algorithms are designed so that AI can work on minimal resources, thus making it more accessible to small companies and startups with fewer resources. Cost-Effective AI Solutions Other innovations include edge computing, which brings the AI closer to data sources; just think of IoT devices that do not necessarily require expensive cloud storage and processing. Edge AI finds applications in all areas of manufacturing, agriculture, and healthcare. Real-time decisions can be made with lower latency in traditional AI. New light algorithms are designed so that AI can work on minimal resources, thus making it more accessible to small companies and startups with fewer resources [67].

II. Use of Pre-Trained Models for Efficiency in Smaller Applications
Save on pre-trained models: Pretrained models are yet another cost-cutting methodology. Pretrained models are AI systems already trained upon huge datasets that may then be fine-tuned for specific tasks with relatively small datasets. It saves the computation resources and time required to train from scratch and accelerates AI deployment faster and cheaper. In fact, small-scale applications can utilize pre-trained models in natural language processing (such as the OpenAI GPT models) or computer vision (pre-trained convolutional neural networks). Such models will provide businesses with access to AI capabilities that require millions of dollars to develop models [68].

7.4.2 AI Applications for Sustainable Development Goals (SDGs)

A combination of such innovative applications in AI serves a big role in achieving these SDGs, especially globally: issues like resource management, climate change, or being prepared for disasters, and there are some instances in how AI contributes toward sustainability:

I. AI for Climate Modeling and Resource Optimization:

- AI is used in climate science, improving the optimization of resource use and predicting extreme events. With machine learning algorithms, large volumes of climate data can be analyzed, modeling environmental changes much more accurately, thus allowing policymakers to make more informed choices. These are some of the applications of AI, such as smart grids-which control and distribute energy according to real-time data for optimum consumption-and in agriculture, using AI to optimize water usage and reduce waste with precision farming techniques [69].

- AI for Disaster Management: The creation of AI systems that could predict and respond to disasters is rapidly becoming the next trend in managing disasters. AI-based technologies can therefore predict hurricanes, earthquakes, and floods by using historical data and Satellite imagery. The machine learning model will predict the availability of resources and aid in coordinating disaster response by facilitating the proper supply of aid. Proactive usage of AI will therefore save lives as well as reduce the cost of recovery [70].

II. Role of AI in Economic Sustainability at Scale

Actually, scalability plays a huge role in AI's potential contribution to economic sustainability at scale. For example, in agricultural sectors, manufacturing, or transportation, AI can introduce efficiencies through the automation of process steps and optimized resource use. In theory, AI-driven supply chain management systems have the ability to streamline waste reduction, improve delivery times, and consequently, slash costs-all promising sustainable economic practices. Besides, the AI's ability to maintain and optimize industrial processes enables companies to cut energy costs and carbon footprints aligned with broader goals of sustainability in the environmental aspect [48].

7.5 Governance and Policy for Sustainable AI

7.5.1 Global Standards and Frameworks

The world has witnessed the emergence of policies and structures aimed at the integration of artificial intelligence in a manner that is both sustainable and ethical. Institutions with a cross-border character like UNESCO, the OECD among others, have been at the forefront pushing for frameworks that curb the abuse of AI systems by ensuring transparency, accountability, and inclusion.

I. Recommendation by UNESCO's on the Ethics of Artificial Intelligence

- In 2021, UNESCO launched the first global agreement on AI ethics — the Recommendation on the Ethics of Artificial Intelligence. As a part of this Framework, its very necessary components are the ethics of Erlang technology, including: Each system is based on respect for the rights and dignity of individuals.

- AI ethical systems should comply with international laws on human rights and should not be built to promote prejudicial systems.
- Sustainability: AI technologies should be built in a manner that is conducive to sustainability and should support the achievement of goals outlined in the regarding sustainable Development by United Nations.
- Equitable data sharing practices: Advocates for fairer data governance where countries and regions share a global common without losing data ownership.
- The recommendation also calls upon member states to implement systems to monitor the application of AI ethics and to incorporate ethical AI teachings in classrooms. This structure will ensure that there is a focus on technological advancement without being at the expense of society [71].

II. OECD Principles on Artificial Intelligence

In regard of AI management, the OECD has principles on it, which were formed in 2019, in order to enhance faith in the usage of artificial intelligence. Major themes are:

- Inclusiveness and Fairness: All members of society in any given jurisdiction should have access to the benefits of AI systems.
- Sufficiency and Coherence: Explaining the effect of decisions made by AI systems and describing their inner workings should be possible to the users.
- Durability and Safety: There are particular requirements concerning the artificial intelligence systems through the various stages of its life cycle concerning errors and improper use.
- Governance: AI consequences should be claimed by entities and creators involved in its design and execution The new OECD AI Policy Observatory was also introduced, the main purpose of which is to facilitate the exchange of information on the development of artificial intelligence policies, trends, and strategies in the world and enhance global collaboration [72].

III. Need for AI-Specific Sustainability Policies

The growing impact of artificial intelligence (AI) on various sectors, the need for policies that concentrate on AI avails even more making these policies urgent. In general AI systems are energy consuming engendering questions on resource usage and also socially and economically disruptive. These problems necessitate policies designed to include sustainable practices in the whole cycle of the AI: design, operation, and regulatory aspects of AI systems.

- Energy and Resource Efficiency

Deep learning-based AI models require massive computational power. The huge models needed to train GPT and BERT consume humongous amounts of energy, resulting in carbon footprints. It is reported that training a single deep learning model emits the same amount of carbon that five cars would emit throughout their lives. AI-specific policies would have to enforce algorithms that make use of energy-efficient methods and encourage renewable sources of energy as the primary source of computation [73].

- The Role of Equity and Inclusion in Sustainability

The positive implications of AI technology are more pronounced in regions with better infrastructures which creates a risk in further widening the global digital divide. Addressing these concerns, equity in AI related sustainability policies should foster shovel ready access to the technologies among the people and prevent the over-exploitation and adverse effects on the environment of a few underrepresented groups [12].

- Ethical and Societal Aspects

The sustainability policies of AI must take into account social factors such as the protection of human and labor rights within AI-related industries, and the transparency within and among stakeholders in the control and decision-making process. These measures guarantee that AI fosters solidarity without aggravating the prevailing order [74].

7.5.2 Transparency and Accountability

- Best Practices for Environmental Impact Reporting in AI Development

Significant environmental impacts associated with the development of AI include high energy consumption and computationally demanding processes. Transparent reporting of environmental impacts is essential to ensure responsible AI practice and align such development with sustainability objectives. These best practices regarding environmental responsibility ensure accountability for environmentally responsible innovation from AI:

- Carbon Footprint Evaluation

Developers should consider the carbon emissions related to AI model training and deployment. it was reported that training large deep learning models can generate high carbon emissions; therefore, techniques for reporting detailed figures are essential. Tools such as ML CO_2 Impact, help estimate emissions at different lifecycle stages of AI systems [15].

- Reporting frameworks that are standardized Penguin Publishers are adopted for environmental reporting for better evaluation and accountability. As an illustrative example of proposed guidelines, the Green AI initiative calls for energy usage (in kWh), hardware specifications, and energy sources used for computations, to be reported [12].

- Efficiency Indicators

All these metrics, organizational cost for instance in terms of floating point operations per second and efficiency improvement strategies should be captured in the environmental reports. Studies show that such computing optimization methods that reduce the number of similar calculations performed can save a lot of energy while maintaining the same level of performance [75].

- Implementing Regular Audits and Responsibility

There is a need for organizations to put in place regular audits in order to evaluate and report on the environmental effects of their AI projects. External evaluations can bear evidence to the meeting of sustainability targets and pinpoint where enhancements can be made.

- Encouraging the Use of New Energy Sources

The documents should emphasize on the uptake of renewable energy in operating the AI systems. Implementing use of carbon neutral or low-carbon energy sources for data centers and computational activities is an important step in minimizing the environmental impact [76].

- Monitoring and Auditing Algorithms for Fairness and Sustainability

As artificial intelligence (AI) becomes increasingly integral to decision-making across various sectors, ensuring fairness and sustainability in algorithmic processes has gained considerable attention. Monitoring and auditing AI systems are essential practices to maintain transparency, reduce bias, and ensure these systems are both ethical and environmentally sustainable. The following outlines best practices and considerations for effective monitoring and auditing:

- Diligent Surveillance for Fairness

Fairness is an ethical aspect of AI which means ensuring that the algorithms are not biased towards or against any group protected by certain attributes such as race, gender, or even physical locations. It's worth noting that routine monitoring is very important to mitigate the possible risks of bias creeping into the system undetected. Disparate impact assessment, demographic balance, and equity of access, among others, are metrics that can be put in place to ensure fairness has been achieved [77].

- Routine Assessment of Environmental Footprint

The sustainability audits in the recent past encompass investigating the environmental effects of using the AI algorithms, especially looking at the energy and carbon footprint. Such audits entail monitoring the type of computational power that AI systems make use of, including the energy used in training data models as well as the facilities employed. As most AI models can be highly intensive, in particular, deep learning, proper environmental reporting, and especially audits are crucial to manage the ability of these models to operate at such a high carbon footprint [15].

- Responsibility and Conformity

An auditing perspective Regular auditing plays a crucial role in ensuring that artificial intelligence systems meet ethical and legal standards. Such reviews evaluate the extent to which particular AI systems follow defined principles, such as the AI Principles formulated by the OECD or the European Union's General Data Protection Regulation (GDPR) on data protection. Accountability in this context implies that the developers, the organization, and any related institutions have a responsibility for the effects of their AI systems, especially harmful ones to society. Further, the compliance audits are useful in pinpointing the variations that exist between the objectives of AI deployment and its results [78].

- Usage of Automated Tools and Artificial Intelligence for Auditing

The use of artificial intelligence in auditing systems can enhance monitoring procedures in terms of efficiency as well as their expansion. AI Powered auditing systems are capable of analyzing huge volume of data within a short time frame to identify for instance signs of bias or lack of efficiency in the environment. These automated systems are adept at scaling audits across different applications promoting uniformity and reduction of human inaccuracies. Nevertheless, fairness and sustainability of these systems should also be evaluated [79].

7.6 Challenges and Future Directions

7.6.1 Current Challenges

I. Balancing Performance and Sustainability

Developing solutions that have high standards of performance yet are in harmony with sustainability objectives is a significant challenge. For instance, in drug delivery systems, natural polymers such as *Terminalia arjuna* gum, address environmental concerns but may not be as scalable and consistent as synthetic alternatives. There is a balance to be struck between efficiency, cost, and ecological impact [80].

II. Global Cooperation and Regulation

Lack of uniform global standards for sustainable practices hinders innovation and widespread adoption. While some regions will continue to push for the toughest compliance in terms of the environment, others will be kept out due to economic constraints or other priorities. This situation eliminates opportunities for harmonization of regulatory frameworks and limits collaboration at an international level to develop sustainable, high-performance technologies [81].

7.6.2 Overcoming Gaps in Global Cooperation and Regulation

Consequently, the increase in global cooperation and regulation is crucial in addressing the broad range of challenges, such as sustainability as well as the advancement of new technologies. The different levels of commitment and strategies that distinct nations apply toward sustainability create a difference in regulations that hinders global cooperation. Such gaps may result in the delays in adoption of the clean technologies and may prove to be problematic in the growth of the sustainable initiatives. One of the main strategies for filling in these gaps could be the adoption of various international standards and agreements aimed at the increase of such global cooperation. For instance, the approach that was adopted by the United Nations and more particularly the Sustainable Development Goals that sought to bring countries in support of similar rules that had been put in place to address the transitions to more sustainable practices [82].

Also necessary for such transitioning is the establishment of global platforms for knowledge sharing, policy harmonization, and collaborative innovation. Regulatory bodies such as the International Organization for Standardization (ISO) are making efforts to standardize different common sustainability standards that will help bridge the regulatory divide and induce the green technologies outside of borders on the planet [83].

7.6.3 Future Innovations

I. Development of Carbon-Neutral AI Systems

The gradually progressive energy consumption of artificial intelligences has made it inevitable for future AI applications to be considered part of responsible AI practices. Development of carbon-neutral AI systems diminishes or nullifies any ecological damage caused by an AI from its training stage all the way through to its deployment lifecycle; uses energy-efficient algorithms, hybridizes renewable energies, and employs carbon offsetting strategies [84].

➢ Some key carbon-neutral AI strategies include:

- Optimized model architectures: Use lightweight energy-efficient models that reduce the overall computation. Techniques like knowledge distillation and quantization can decrease energy usage without penalty on the performance of the system [84].
- Sustainable Data Centers: Shifting to green data centers based on renewable power sources and the use of advanced cooling technologies [85].
- Carbon Accounting and Offsetting: Attributing emissions to AI-related activities and offsetting residual emissions through reforestation or other carbon sequestration methods [86].
- Federated Learning and Edge AI: This reduces data transmission and central processing through decentralizing computations to get closer to the data sources [87].

II. AI's Potential Role in Advancing Global Sustainability Agenda

Artificial intelligence is the panacea for many of the expectations for driving global sustainability agendas-from support of the initiatives underway, such as those framed by the United Nations in its Sustainable Development Goals. Harnessed towards AI capabilities, societies can address most the complex challenges before them: environmental, social, and economic [88].

- Climate Change Mitigation and Adaptation

AI leads to detailed climate modeling, so the probability of correct predictions of weather patterns and natural disasters increases. Tools powered by AI, for example, energy optimizers in smart grids, aid in the use of renewable energy sources. Organizations like DeepMind have already used AI to cut up to 40% of energy usage in data centers, exemplifying its potential to mitigate carbon footprints [89].

- Biodiversity Preservation

I-driven tools like image recognition assist in monitoring wildlife populations, detecting poaching activities, and mapping habitats. Initiatives such as Microsoft's AI for Earth leverage AI to track endangered species and promote ecosystem health [90].

- Smart Agriculture and Food Security

Precision agriculture driven by AI optimizes irrigation, reduces pesticide usage, and predicts crop yield to ensure sustainable food production. For instance, startups such as Plantix use AI-based solutions to identify crop diseases to reduce losses and promote resilience in agricultural systems [91].

- Waste Management and Circular Economy

AI helps enhance recycling infrastructures by automating sorting and recycling of used materials. For instance, companies such as AMP Robotics employ machine learning to differentiate recyclable materials and classify them with significantly higher accuracy [92].

- Accelerating Equitable Development

AI and other advanced techniques can be applied to process large data sets to identify resource inequities and optimize the provision of necessary goods and services such as water, energy, and healthcare in underserved areas [93].

AI represents the intersection of technological enabler and ethical imperative in sustainability efforts. Through the ferment of sectoral innovation and discoveries, AI can speed progress toward sustainability significantly across the globe.

7.7 Conclusion and Call to Action

Rapid development of artificial intelligence is reshaping industries, societies, and global dynamics. AI opens sweeping potential for bettering healthcare, education, finance, and environmental sustainability but also raises significant concerns relative to ethics, equity, privacy, and its dangerous potential to exacerbate inequalities. Hence, effective incorporation of AI power with the reduction of its dangers requires closer cooperation of all parties: researchers, policymakers, developers, and industrialists in establishing a sustainable AI ecosystem.

Among them, some key points discussed throughout this report include the demand for having effective AI governance frameworks committed to transparency, fairness, and accountability. This particular role of AI covered creating personalized, more efficient services in their respective sectors and fostering economic growth through automation and innovation. On the other hand, while some possible adverse effects exist, such as algorithmic bias, job displacement, and privacy concerns, it's necessary to understand the potential risks and actively take measures toward equitable outcomes for all. Other requirements include the proper incorporation of ethical aspects in AI development so that this technology promotes human interests and does not become harmful.

Call for Collaboration

The synergistic and interrelated functioning of diverse sectors will be very important to fully unlock the potential of AI while mitigating its risks. Researchers should be continually investigating the potential and limitations of AI and contribute valuable insights to informing policy and development practices. Policymakers should enact forward-thinking legislation that regulates AI responsibly, ensuring it is used ethically, promotes equality, and prevents misuse. Developers must follow best practices in AI development, completing their design processes with essential transparency, fairness, and inclusivity. Collaboration should also encompass international cooperation because AI is a global phenomenon. Cross-border partnerships will be required in order to create consistent standards for AI governance across borders to address common challenges and to promote innovations that uplift the greater whole of humanity. Engaging diverse groups, including marginalized communities while designing and deploying AI systems, will ensure that the technology is inclusive and accessible to all.

AI disclosure statement: The author acknowledges the use of AI-based tools for minor language editing or grammatical correction. However, all intellectual contributions, analyses, and conclusions presented in this chapter are entirely the author's own.

References

1. Sætra, H.S., AI in context and the sustainable development goals: Factoring in the unsustainability of the sociotechnical system. *Sustainability*, 13, 4, 1738, 2021 Feb 5. Artificial intelligence for sustainability: challenges, opportunities, and a research agenda.
2. Robbins, S. and Van Wynsberghe, A., Our New Artificial Intelligence Infrastructure: Becoming Locked into an Unsustainable Future. *Sustainability*, 14, 4829, 2022. Towards the Sustainability of AI, 31, 2022.
3. Clutton-Brock, P., Rolnick, D., Donti, P.L., Kaack, L., Climate change and AI. recommendations for government action. GPAI, Climate Change AI, Centre for AI & Climate, 2021.
4. Rolnick, D., Donti, P.L., Kaack, L.H., Kochanski, K., Lacoste, A., Sankaran, K., Ross, A.S., Milojevic-Dupont, N., Jaques, N., Waldman-Brown, A., Luccioni, A.S., Tackling climate change with machine learning. *ACM Comput. Surv. (CSUR)*, 55, 2, 1–96, 2022 Feb 8.
5. Jamwal, A., Agrawal, R., Sharma, M., Deep learning for manufacturing sustainability: Models, applications in Industry 4.0 and implications. *Int. J. Inf. Manage. Data Insights*, 2, 2, 100107, 2022 Nov 1.
6. Di Vaio, A., Palladino, R., Hassan, R., Escobar, O., Artificial intelligence and business models in the sustainable development goals perspective: A systematic literature review. *J. Bus. Res.*, 121, 283–314, 2020 Dec 1.
7. Palomares, I., Martínez-Cámara, E., Montes, R., García-Moral, P., Chiachio, M., Chiachio, J., Alonso, S., Melero, F.J., Molina, D., Fernández, B., Moral, C., A panoramic view and swot analysis of artificial intelligence for achieving the sustainable development goals by 2030: progress and prospects. *Appl. Intell.*, 51, 6497–527, 2021 Sep.
8. Visvizi, A., Artificial intelligence (AI) and sustainable development goals (SDGs): exploring the impact of AI on politics and society. *Sustainability*, 14, 3, 1730, 2022 Feb 2.
9. Truby, J., Governing artificial intelligence to benefit the UN sustainable development goals. *Sustain. Dev.*, 28, 4, 946–59, 2020 Jul.
10. Kar, A.K., Choudhary, S.K., Singh, V.K., How can artificial intelligence impact sustainability: A systematic literature review. *J. Clean. Prod.*, 376, 134120, 2022 Nov 20.

11. Sternini, F., Ravizza, A., Cabitza, F., How accurate do you want it? Defining minimum required accuracy for medical artificial intelligence. *Proceedings of E-Health*, 2020.
12. Vinuesa, R., Azizpour, H., Leite, I., Balaam, M., Dignum, V., Domisch, S., Felländer, A., Langhans, S.D., Tegmark, M., Fuso Nerini, F., The role of artificial intelligence in achieving the Sustainable Development Goals. *Nat. Commun.*, 11, 1, 1–0, 2020 Jan 13.
13. Ernst, E., Merola, R., Samaan, D., Economics of artificial intelligence: Implications for the future of work. *IZA J. Labor Policy*, 9, 1, 1–35, 2019 Aug.
14. Mensah, G.B., Artificial intelligence and ethics: a comprehensive review of bias mitigation, transparency, and accountability in AI Systems. Preprint, 10, November 2023.
15. Strubell, E., Ganesh, A., McCallum, A., Energy and policy considerations for modern deep learning research. *Proc. AAAI Conf. Artif. Intell.*, 34, 09, 13693–13696, 2020 Apr 3.
16. Brynjolfsson, E. and McAfee, A., *The second machine age: Work, progress, and prosperity in a time of brilliant technologies*, WW Norton & company, New York, USA, 2014 Jan 20.
17. Jain, A. and O'Neil, C., *Weapons of Math Destruction: How Big Data Increases Inequality and Threatens Democracy*, Crown Publishing Group, New York, USA, 2001, Pp. 259. $26.00 hardcover.
18. Wu, C.J., Raghavendra, R., Gupta, U., Acun, B., Ardalani, N., Maeng, K., Chang, G., Aga, F., Huang, J., Bai, C., Gschwind, M., Sustainable AI: Environmental implications, challenges and opportunities. *Proc. Mach. Learn. Syst.*, 4, 795–813, 2022 Apr 22.
19. Janiesch, C., Zschech, P., Heinrich, K., Machine learning and deep learning. *Electron. Mark.*, 31, 3, 685–95, 2021 Sep.
20. Zohuri, B., Behgounia, F., Nezam, Z.Z., Artificial Intelligence Integration with Energy Sources (Renewable and Non-renewable). *J. Energy Power Eng.*, 14, 193–210, 2020.
21. Cheng, Y., Wang, D., Zhou, P., Zhang, T., A survey of model compression and acceleration for deep neural networks, *arXiv preprint arXiv:1710.09282*, 2017 Oct 23.
22. Oró, E., Depoorter, V., Garcia, A., Salom, J., Energy efficiency and renewable energy integration in data centres. Strategies and modelling review. *Renew. Sustain. Energy Rev.*, 42, 429–45, 2015 Feb 1.
23. Tschang, F.T. and Almirall, E., Artificial intelligence as augmenting automation: Implications for employment. *Acad. Manage. Perspect.*, 35, 4, 642–59, 2021 Nov.
24. Lutz, C., Digital inequalities in the age of artificial intelligence and big data. *Hum. Behav. Emerg. Technol.*, 1, 2, 141–8, 2019 Apr.
25. Banerjee, A., Kabadi, S., Karimov, D., The Transformative Power of AI: Projected Impacts on the Global Economy by 2030. *Rev. Artif. Intell. Educ.*, 4, 00, e020, 2023 Sep 7.

26. Morandini, S., Fraboni, F., De Angelis, M., Puzzo, G., Giusino, D., Pietrantoni, L., The impact of artificial intelligence on workers' skills: Upskilling and reskilling in organisations. *Informing Sci.*, 26, 39–68, 2023.
27. Reddy, R., Sustainable Computing: A Comprehensive Review of Energy-Efficient Algorithms and Systems. Authorea Preprints, 2024 Oct 7.
28. Miao, Q. and Wang, F-Y., Artificial Intelligence for Science (AI4S): Frontiers and Perspectives Based on Parallel Intelligence. Springer Nature, Singapore, 2024 Sep 11.
29. Dacon, J., Are You Worthy of My Trust? A Socioethical Perspective on the Impacts of Trustworthy AI Systems on the Environment and Human Society, *arXiv preprint arXiv:2309.09450*, 2023 Sep 18.
30. Lannelongue, L., Inference frameworks in computational biology: from protein-protein interaction networks using machine learning to carbon footprint estimation, Doctoral dissertation.
31. Kalyan, K.S., A survey of GPT-3 family large language models including ChatGPT and GPT-4. *Nat. Lang. Process. J.*, 1, 100048, 2023 Dec 19.
32. Lawie, M.R., Analysing the Impact of CO2 Emissions from the Largest Artificial Intelligence Systems and its Consequences for Global Warming.
33. Bai, G., Chai, Z., Ling, C., Wang, S., Lu, J., Zhang, N., Shi, T., Yu, Z., Zhu, M., Zhang, Y., Yang, C., Beyond efficiency: A systematic survey of resource-efficient large language models, *arXiv preprint arXiv:2401.00625*, 2024 Jan 1.
34. Chaddad, A., Revolutionizing Protein Structure Prediction: The Impact of Artificial Intelligence and AlphaFold.
35. Khamparia, A. (Ed.), *Microbial Data Intelligence and Computational Techniques for Sustainable Computing*, Springer Nature, Cham, Switzerland, 2024.
36. Tmamna, J., Ayed, E.B., Fourati, R., Gogate, M., Arslan, T., Hussain, A., Ayed, M.B., Pruning deep neural networks for green energy-efficient models: A survey. *Cognit. Comput.*, Ahead of Print, 1–22, 2024 Jul 5.
37. Deng, L., Li, G., Han, S., Shi, L., Xie, Y., Model compression and hardware acceleration for neural networks: A comprehensive survey. *Proc. IEEE*, 108, 4, 485–532, 2020 Mar 20.
38. Guo, Y., Shi, H., Kumar, A., Grauman, K., Rosing, T., Feris, R., Spottune: transfer learning through adaptive fine-tuning, in: *Proceedings of the IEEE/CVF conference on computer vision and pattern recognition*, pp. 4805–4814, 2019.
39. Muralidhar, R., Borovica-Gajic, R., Buyya, R., Energy efficient computing systems: Architectures, abstractions and modeling to techniques and standards. *ACM Comput. Surv. (CSUR)*, 54, 11s, 1–37, 2022 Sep 10.
40. Sreedhar, A. and Nagarajan, N.S., Design and evaluation of a software abstraction layer for heterogeneous neural network accelerators.
41. Garg, S., Singh, A., Kaur, K., Aujla, G.S., Batra, S., Kumar, N., Obaidat, M.S., Edge computing-based security framework for big data analytics in VANETs. *IEEE Netw.*, 33, 2, 72–81, 2019 Mar 27.

42. Khan, A.A. and Zakarya, M., Energy, performance and cost efficient cloud datacentres: A survey. *Comput. Sci. Rev.*, 40, 100390, 2021 May 1.
43. Jones, N., How to stop data centres from gobbling up the world's electricity. *Nature*, 561, 7722, 163–6, 2018 Sep 12.
44. Trouwloon, D., Streck, C., Chagas, T., Martinus, G., Understanding the use of carbon credits by companies: a review of the defining elements of corporate climate claims. *Global Challenges*, 7, 4, 2200158, 2023 Apr.
45. Menghani, G., Efficient deep learning: A survey on making deep learning models smaller, faster, and better. *ACM Comput. Surv.*, 55, 12, 1–37, 2023 Mar 2.
46. Pérez Arteaga, S., Sandoval Orozco, A.L., García Villalba, L.J., Analysis of machine learning techniques for information classification in mobile applications. *Appl. Sci.*, 13, 9, 5438, 2023 Apr 27.
47. Ahmad, K., Maabreh, M., Ghaly, M., Khan, K., Qadir, J., Al-Fuqaha, A., Developing future human-centered smart cities: Critical analysis of smart city security, Data management, and Ethical challenges. *Comput. Sci. Rev.*, 43, 100452, 2022 Feb 1.
48. Goralski, M.A. and Tan, T.K., Artificial intelligence and sustainable development. *Int. J. Manage. Educ.*, 18, 1, 100330, 2020 Mar 1.
49. Adnan, M., Xiao, B., Ali, M.U., Bibi, S., Yu, H., Xiao, P., Zhao, P., Haiyan, W., An, X., Human inventions and its environmental challenges, especially artificial intelligence: New challenges require new thinking. *Environ. Challenges*, 9, 100976, 2024 Jul 6.
50. Saxena, V., Wu, X., Srivastava, I., Zhu, K., Towards neuromorphic learning machines using emerging memory devices with brain-like energy efficiency. *J. Low Power Electron. Appl.*, 8, 4, 34, 2018 Oct 2.
51. Delort, E., Riou, L., Srivastava, A., Environmental Impact of Artificial Intelligence, Doctoral dissertation, INRIA, CEA Leti.
52. Hershcovich, D., Webersinke, N., Kraus, M., Bingler, J.A., Leippold, M., Towards climate awareness in NLP research, *arXiv preprint arXiv:2205.05071*, 2022 May 10.
53. Lee, K., A systematic review on social sustainability of artificial intelligence in product design. *Sustainability*, 13, 5, 2668, 2021 Mar 2.
54. Dastin, J., Amazon scraps secret AI recruiting tool that showed bias against women, in: *Ethics of data and analytics*, pp. 296–299, Auerbach Publications, Boca Raton, FL, USA, 2022 May 12.
55. Buolamwini, J. and Gebru, T., Gender shades: Intersectional accuracy disparities in commercial gender classification, in: *Conference on fairness, accountability and transparency*, 2018 Jan 21, PMLR, pp. 77–91.
56. Obermeyer, Z., Powers, B., Vogeli, C., Mullainathan, S., Dissecting racial bias in an algorithm used to manage the health of populations. *Science*, 366, 6464, 447–53, 2019 Oct 25.

57. Zhang, B.H., Lemoine, B., Mitchell, M., Mitigating unwanted biases with adversarial learning, in: *Proceedings of the 2018 AAAI/ACM Conference on AI, Ethics, and Society*, 2018 Dec 27, pp. 335–340.
58. Hardt, M., Price, E., Srebro, N., Equality of opportunity in supervised learning. *Advances in neural information processing systems*, vol. 29, 2016.
59. Kamiran, F. and Calders, T., Data preprocessing techniques for classification without discrimination. *Knowl. Inf. Syst.*, 33, 1, 1–33, 2012 Oct.
60. Mehrabi, N., Morstatter, F., Saxena, N., Lerman, K., Galstyan, A., A survey on bias and fairness in machine learning. *ACM Comput. Surv. (CSUR)*, 54, 6, 1–35, 2021 Jul 13.
61. Chouldechova, A., Fair prediction with disparate impact: A study of bias in recidivism prediction instruments. *Big Data*, 5, 2, 153–63, 2017 Jun 1.
62. Chui, M., Manyika, J., Miremadi, M., Henke, N., Chung, R., Nel, P., Malhotra, S., Notes from the AI frontier: Insights from hundreds of use cases. McKinsey Global Institute, 2, 267, 2018 Apr 8.
63. Pizzi, S. and Ligorio, L., Artificial Intelligence and management research: An Overview. *The Routledge Companion to the Future of Management Research*, 136–50, 2023 Sep 14.
64. Abadi, M., Agarwal, A., Barham, P., Brevdo, E., Chen, Z., Citro, C., Corrado, G.S., Davis, A., Dean, J., Devin, M., Ghemawat, S., Tensorflow: Large-scale machine learning on heterogeneous distributed systems, *arXiv preprint arXiv:1603.04467*, 2016 Mar 14.
65. Citaristi, I., International Telecommunication Union—ITU, in: *The Europa Directory of International Organizations 2022*, pp. 365–369, Routledge, London, UK, 2022 Jul 28.
66. Häußermann, J.J. and Lütge, C., Community-in-the-loop: towards pluralistic value creation in AI, or—why AI needs business ethics. *AI Ethics*, 2, 1–22, 2022.
67. Shi, W., Cao, J., Zhang, Q., Li, Y., Xu, L., Edge computing: Vision and challenges. *IEEE Internet Things J.*, 3, 5, 637–46, 2016 Jun 9.
68. Radford, A., Wu, J., Child, R., Luan, D., Amodei, D., Sutskever, I., Language models are unsupervised multitask learners. *OpenAI Blog*, 1, 8, 9, 2019 Feb 24.
69. Belkin, M., Hsu, D., Ma, S., Mandal, S., Reconciling modern machine-learning practice and the classical bias–variance trade-off. *Proc. Natl. Acad. Sci.*, 116, 32, 15849–54, 2019 Aug 6.
70. Imperiale, A.J. and Vanclay, F., Command-and-control, emergency powers, and the failure to observe United Nations disaster management principles following the 2009 L'Aquila earthquake. *Int. J. Disaster Risk Reduct.*, 36, 101099, 2019 May 1.
71. UNESCO, Recommendation on the Ethics of Artificial Intelligence, 2021.
72. OECD, OECD Principles on Artificial Intelligence, 2019.
73. Callaghan, S., Darbyshire, T., Farajnia, S., Growing the pattern: Our first year. *Patterns*, 2, 4, 2021 Apr 9.

74. Floridi, L. and Cowls, J., A unified framework of five principles for AI in society, in: *Machine learning and the city: Applications in architecture and urban design*, pp. 535–45, 2022 May 21.
75. Henderson, P., Hu, J., Romoff, J., Brunskill, E., Jurafsky, D., Pineau, J., Towards the systematic reporting of the energy and carbon footprints of machine learning. *J. Mach. Learn. Res.*, 21, 248, 1–43, 2020.
76. Peng, X., Guan, X., Zeng, Y., Zhang, J., Artificial Intelligence-Driven Multi-Energy Optimization: Promoting Green Transition of Rural Energy Planning and Sustainable Energy Economy. *Sustainability*, 16, 10, 4111, 2024 May 14.
77. Barocas, S., Hardt, M., Narayanan, A., *Fairness and machine learning: Limitations and opportunities*, MIT press, Cambridge, MA, USA, 2023 Dec 19.
78. OECD, OECD principles on artificial intelligence.
79. Aitkazinov, A., The role of artificial intelligence in auditing: Opportunities and challenges. *Int. J. Res. Eng. Sci. Manage.*, 6, 6, 117–9, 2023 Jun 30.
80. Verma, N., Arora, V., Awasthi, R., Chan, Y., Jha, N.K., Thapa, K., Jawaid, T., Kamal, M., Gupta, G., Liu, G., Paudel, K.R., Recent developments, challenges and future prospects in advanced drug delivery systems in the management of tuberculosis. *J. Drug Deliv. Sci. Technol.*, 75, 103690, 2022 Sep 1.
81. Van Der Waal, J.W., Thijssens, T., Maas, K., The innovative contribution of multinational enterprises to the Sustainable Development Goals. *J. Clean. Prod.*, 285, 125319, 2021 Feb 20.
82. Arora, N.K. and Mishra, I., United Nations Sustainable Development Goals 2030 and environmental sustainability: race against time. *Environ. Sustain.*, 2, 4, 339–42, 2019 Dec.
83. Rane, N.L., Desai, P., Choudhary, S., Challenges of implementing artificial intelligence for smart and sustainable industry: Technological, economic, and regulatory barriers. *Artif. Intell. Ind. Soc.*, 5, 2–83, 2024.
84. Cong, C., Page, J., Kwak, Y., Deal, B., Kalantari, Z., AI analytics for carbon-neutral city planning: A systematic review of applications. *Urban Sci.*, 8, 3, 104, 2024 Aug 1.
85. Cao, Z., Zhou, X., Hu, H., Wang, Z., Wen, Y., Toward a systematic survey for carbon neutral data centers. *IEEE Commun. Surv. Tutor.* 24, 2, 895–936, 2022 Mar 22.
86. Shaik, A.S., Alshibani, S.M., Jain, G., Gupta, B., Mehrotra, A., Artificial intelligence (AI)-driven strategic business model innovations in small-and medium-sized enterprises. Insights on technological and strategic enablers for carbon neutral businesses. *Bus. Strat. Environ.*, 33, 4, 2731–51, 2024 May.
87. Li, C., AI-powered energy internet towards carbon neutrality: challenges and opportunities. Authorea Preprints, 2023 Oct 30.
88. Nishant, R., Kennedy, M., Corbett, J., Artificial intelligence for sustainability: Challenges, opportunities, and a research agenda. *Int. J. Inf. Manage.*, 53, 102104, 2020 Aug 1.

89. Leal Filho, W., Wall, T., Mucova, S.A., Nagy, G.J., Balogun, A.L., Luetz, J.M., Ng, A.W., Kovaleva, M., Azam, F.M., Alves, F., Guevara, Z., Deploying artificial intelligence for climate change adaptation. *Technol. Forecast. Soc. Change*, 180, 121662, 2022 Jul 1.
90. Rane, N.L., Kaya, O., Rane, J., Advancing the Sustainable Development Goals (SDGs) through artificial intelligence, machine learning, and deep learning, in: *Artificial Intelligence, Machine Learning, and Deep Learning for Sustainable Industry*, vol. 5, pp. 2–74, 2024.
91. Somashekar, K.S., Rehaman, H.M., Kumar, G.V., Bai, K., Belagalla, N., Abhishek, G.J., Jagadeesh, M.S., Kapoor, M., Technology for a Food-Secure Future: A Review of Technology Advances in Sustainable Agriculture. *J. Exp. Agric. Int.*, 46, 9, 234–56, 2024 Aug 31.
92. Roberts, H., Zhang, J., Bariach, B., Cowls, J., Gilburt, B., Juneja, P., Tsamados, A., Ziosi, M., Taddeo, M., Floridi, L., Artificial intelligence in support of the circular economy: ethical considerations and a path forward. *AI Soc.*, 39, 3, 1451–64, 2024 Jun.
93. Kulkov, I., Kulkova, J., Rohrbeck, R., Menvielle, L., Kaartemo, V., Makkonen, H., Artificial intelligence-driven sustainable development: Examining organizational, technical, and processing approaches to achieving global goals. *Sustain. Dev.*, 32, 3, 2253–67, 2024 Jun.
94. O'Sullivan, K., Clark, S., Marshall, K.,MacLachlan, M., A Just Digital Framework to Ensure Equitable Achievement of the Sustainable Development Goals. *Nat. Commun.*, 12, 1, 6345, 2021, https://doi.org/10.1038/s41467-021-26217-8.

8

Integrating AutoML and Explainability: A Unified Approach for Decision-Making in Engineering and Social Sciences

Ayush Dalmia and Chandramohan Dhasarathan*

Department of Electronics and Communication Engineering, Thapar Institute of Engineering and Technology, Patiala, Punjab, India

Abstract

Automated Machine Learning (AutoML) can be thought to herald a new dawn for predictive modeling, enabling automatic feature selection, model selection, and hyperparameter tuning. The other side of the coin, however, may be that one starts questionings the transparency and interpretability of such automated models when increasing the reliance on AutoML, particularly in high-stake engineering and social science decision-making domains. This study presents one of the first unified approaches for combining AutoML with explainability techniques, ensuring that automated models remain interpretable and actionable to decision-makers. The study aligns SHapley Additive Explanations (SHAP), Local Interpretable Model- Agnostic Explanations (LIME), and feature importance analysis with AutoML pipelines. We demonstrate the practicability and reliability of explainable AutoML on a wide range of datasets within structural engineering and social science research. The results are compared across various AutoML frameworks such as, Google AutoML, H_2O AutoML, and Auto-Sklearn in terms of accuracy, computational efficiency, and interpretability. The study found that integrating explainability into AutoML enhances credibility and circuit-breaks the ambiance of assumptions, enabling domain experts to evaluate model output with a view to better insight into their decision-making process. The work also sets forth the need for weighing predictive performance against model interpretability to responsibly adopt AI. This work makes an ongoing contribution to the discussion on ethical AI by offering a framework that aligns automation with

**Corresponding author*: pdchandramohan@gmail.com

Manish Kumar, Nitigya Sambyal, Leena Priyadarshini Singh, Ramasamy V. and S. Balamurugan (eds.) Responsible AI: Principles and Practices, (175–198) © 2026 Scrivener Publishing LLC

human-centered decision-making to ensure that insights from AutoML are both accurate and explainable across multiple domains.

Keywords: AutoML, Explainable AI (XAI), interpretable machine learning, decision-making models, ethical AI in engineering and social sciences

8.1 Introduction

In recent times, Automated Machine Learning (AutoML) developed into a key technology that makes machine learning pipelines easier and fast. Through the automation of tasks such as feature engineering, model selection, and hyperparameter tuning, AutoML allows someone with little to no expertise to build high-performing predictive models without any human intervention. This novelty has proven to be effective in engineering and social sciences, where data-driven decision-making is slowly becoming the norm. Nonetheless, even with these amazing advantages, the use of AutoML raises some stark concerns about the interpretability and transparency of models it produces. Especially in situations where human lives, financial resources, or societal impacts are at stake, understanding the rationale behind predictions in high-stakes decision-making applications like structural engineering, healthcare, economics, and policy analysis is more than crucial. There is a trade-off: although AutoML optimizes the model's performance, it usually acts like a black box that makes it difficult for domain experts to interpret on what basis a prediction is made. This lack of transparency can give rise to issues of distrust, accountability, and ethical significance. Incorporating Explainable AI (XAI) methods to AutoML platforms may serve as a viable remedy to such challenges by enhancing model interpretability while preserving the understandability of the automated solutions by domain experts. Engineering and social science decisions revolve around data analysis, predictive modeling, and statistical inference. In engineering disciplines, predictive models are applied to evaluate structural integrity, optimize material properties, and predict failures. In social sciences, machine learning is used for policy evaluation, economic forecasting, social interventions, and risk assessment. The impending complexity that arises in these fields forces a decision-maker to depend on opaque models, quite often leading to misinterpretation of the substantiated deductions and choices made, thereby hindering appropriate actions. For example: In structural engineering, an AI-based failure detection model should illuminate the dangers that result in failure rather than merely deliver a prediction and in public policy, an AutoML-based economic forecasting flavor should explicitly notify the key economic indicators that influence predictions so that policy actions can be taken by policymakers. Therefore, an integrated solution that marries AutoML with interpretable machine learning is necessary to ensure that decisions are talked about in terms of not just being data-driven but also interpretable, trustworthy, and justifiable.

Nonetheless, several constraints regarding the implementation of AutoML in domains that demand transparency pose several challenges: Embedded interpretability - High levels of interpretability are mostly realized where the AutoML generated model functions as a black-box with little explanation as to how one arrived at a certain conclusion. Domain specific customization - Most AutoML frameworks do not incorporate constraints pertaining to a specific field, thus presenting results void of contextual understanding. Cases of ethical & legal concern - There are clear instances in which observance of interpretability requirements is mandated by patients in Japan and focus in finance. Trade-offs between performances and interpretability - While increasing interpretability could decrease accuracy to some extent, a balance must be struck between both. Generalization to other domains - AutoML models optimized for a domain do not generally generalize to other domains without expert intervention. By integrating Shapley Additive Explanations (SHAP), Local Interpretable Model-Agnostic Explanations (LIME), and feature importance analysis into AutoML workflows, possible damages put up by the above problems can be mitigated in practice, with enhanced interpretability for automated models and easy adaptation into real-life scenarios. Importantly, this study aims to contribute to the integration of automation and explainability by offering a single process of integrating Explainable Artificial Intelligence into AutoML frameworks in order to enhance decision-making in engineering and social sciences. Related objectives include: Development of an AutoML-XAI framework: The mechanism of integration of explainability tools like SHAP and LIME within ISO AutoML pipelines. Assessment of trade-off between accuracy and interpretability: Comparison of different AutoML models with increasing levels of transparency. Application of the framework within real-world engineering and social science datasets: Testing the proposed approach on diverse datasets to assess its practicality. Enhancement of trust and accountability: Ensure automated prediction to be interpretable to domain experts in order to drive decisions.

8.2 Literature Study

Machine learning is transforming industries, but its success depends on how well we can understand and trust its predictions. On the other hand, automated machine learning or AutoML offers increased ease of use by automating varying tasks from feature selection, through model tuning and hyperparameter optimization. This is both a boon and a bane, as improved and more accessible machine learning is now coupled with a major downside—the loss of interpretability. Using real-life scenarios in engineering and social sciences, the consequences of certain decisions can alter the shape of one's lives, infrastructures, and policies. An automated model making wrong predictions in a structural engineering project could go as far as unsafe building designs; biases or opaque algorithms in the social systems can foster unfair policies. Explainable AI, or XAI, thus assumes a vital role here, as it provides insights into why and how a model makes predictions. This segment uncovers the state of the arts regarding AutoML and explainability and presents groundbreaking research, challenges, and contenders for the rights of both fields as they integrate with yet another set of tasks requiring enhancing trust and better decision-making. Machine learning is transforming industries, but its success depends on how well we can understand and trust its predictions. On the other hand, automated machine learning or AutoML offers increased ease of use by automating varying tasks from feature selection, through model tuning and hyperparameter optimization. This is both a boon and a bane, as improved and more accessible machine learning is now coupled with a major downside—the loss of interpretability. Using real-life scenarios in engineering and social sciences, the consequences of certain decisions can alter the shape of one's lives, infrastructures, and policies. An automated model making wrong predictions in a structural engineering project could go as far as unsafe building designs; biases or opaque algorithms in the social systems can foster unfair policies. Explainable AI, or XAI, thus assumes a vital role here, as it provides insights into why and how a model makes predictions. This segment uncovers the state of the arts regarding AutoML and explainability and presents groundbreaking research, challenges, and contenders for the rights of both fields as they integrate with yet another set of tasks requiring enhancing trust and better decision-making. XAI creates the basis for making machine learning models transparent. Some of the critical issues answered under XAI include: Which features influenced the decision? What is the model's sensitivity to variations in input? Is the model's output trustworthy for critical decision-making? There are several techniques used to characterize model interpretability: SHAP (Shapley Additive Explanations): This technique generates an importance score for a feature that tells users which variables have the highest influence on the model's prediction.

LIME (Local Interpretable Model-Agnostic Explanations): The approximate interpretation of each of the individual predictions is achieved by approximating the black-box model with a much simpler interpretable black-box model. Feature Importance Analysis: This ranking relates to the importance of a feature in the dataset, which means identifying what the model prioritizes. These tools help with engineering, predicting bridge failures or structural weaknesses, and, in the social sciences, with the need to understand biases in policy decision making or economic models. Despite advancements in XAI, integrating these techniques with AutoML raises several challenges: Interaction Between Accuracy and Interpretability AutoML is generally directed toward giving the best predictive performance, by using complex models such as deep learning or ensemble methods, which end up quite difficult to explain; thus, there appears a trade-off between performance and transparency. Computational Costs-Explainability techniques require the use of a significant amount of additional computations. Executing SHAP or LIME on large-scale datasets can practically halt AutoML systems. This creates a significant hindrance, especially in real-time decision- making applications. No Standardized Metrics for Explainability-Unlike the metrics for model accuracy (e.g., RMSE, F1-score), there is no central metric to measure explainability. Different industries may require different interpretability levels, thus making it more difficult to develop an industry-consensus model. Trust and Adoption by End Users-A lot of organizations are hesitant to embrace AI-driven solutions on account of trust- related issues. Although the AutoML model may be performing well, stakeholders would be very reluctant to trust it unless provided with proper rationales. Several studies have attempted to bridge the gap between AutoML and explainability: AutoML for Structural Engineering: A study on concrete strength prediction combined AutoML with SHAP, thereby improving the transparency within civil engineering applications. XAI applied in Social Sciences: Investigation by scholars on how interpretability impacts policy-making in education and finance highlighted that models that provide explanations score higher on trustworthiness and adoption. Healthcare & Explainable AutoML: Comparative study showed that integrating SHAP into AutoML pipelines improved diagnostic decision-making in AI applications within the medical industry. From these investigations, it has been established that combining AutoML with interpretability creates both trust and use of AI. However, more research must be done to make it work without sacrificing explainability. A delicate balance between automation and transparency will characterize AI-based decision- making in the coming days. As industries are now adopting AI, it is paramount to structure AutoML solutions in a way that they explain their predictions and do not merely churn out results. Further research needs to focus on: Development of auto logging tools for explainability within the AutoML frameworks; Reduction of computational overhead for interpretability methods; and Standardization of performance metrics for explainable AutoML. This would help embed explainability in AutoML with more ethical, transparent, and trustworthy AI-based decisions across the engineering and social sciences. Automated Machine Learning has advanced the field of machine learning tremendously, enabling feature selection, model training, and hyperparameter tuning to be automated. However, it is a serious interpretability challenge in high-stakes areas like engineering and social sciences where trust and transparency are indispensable. Henceforth, we propose a new framework combining Explainable AI with AutoML so that automated models can not only be accurate but also interpretable enough to allow enough confidence for decision-making. The proposed framework involves auto ML pipelines combined with SHAP, LIME, and feature importance analysis to enhance transparency and allow those with domain knowledge to validate AI-derived conclusions. The proposed pipeline has four main modules: Data Processing and Feature Engineering It leverages data ingestion, preprocessing, and feature selection. It involves missing data handling and outlier treatment, followed by normalization. AutoML Model Selection and Hyperparameter Optimization applies Auto and Statistical Model Selection exercises from Google, H_2O, and auto-Sklearn to find the most successful model. It takes care of hyperparameter tuning automatically. Explaining Module incorporates SHAP, LIME, and Feature Importance Analysis in order to explain model predictions. It would provide visual insights upon explainability dashboards. Agile Implementation and Doing It allows the experts to see the results before proper decision-making. Interpretable models to be deployed for real-world applications in engineering and social sciences.

Jordan Dotzel *et al.* [1] FLIQS, a novel one-shot mixed-precision quantization search method that eliminates retraining needs for both integer and floating-point DNN models. The approach outperforms existing techniques by improving ImageNet accuracy (1.31% for ResNet-18, 0.90% for ResNet-50) while maintaining equivalent model costs. FLIQS also pioneers mixed-precision floating-point optimization, boosting MobileNetV2 accuracy by 0.98% over prior FP8 models. The method extends to joint quantization-neural architecture searches, achieving 2.69% accuracy gains in

MobileNetV2 configurations. This breakthrough enables efficient deployment of high-performance models across diverse hardware platforms without compromising accuracy or requiring resource-intensive retraining. Gresa Shala *et al.* [2] presented HPO-RL-Bench, a free benchmark suite for reinforcing learning hyper parametric optimization (HPO). They provide a common ground for evaluating an HPO approach without the commitment of running the complete training pipeline, providing a more efficient and less expensive avenue for experimentation. It covers a variety of RL environments and includes ground truth performance metrics to assist with algorithmically-governed comparisons. Martin Hirzel *et al.* [3] examined the issue of limited memory when training and cross validating machine learning (ML) pipelines and proposed memory efficient scheduling methods that maximize resource consumption without statistically degrading performance, particularly for applications in edge and embedded systems. The methods exist in a framework that enables scalable management of an ML pipeline under the most severe hardware constraints. Mateo Avila Pava *et al.* [4] discussed a novelty simulation similarity metric based off of sequence matching in evolutionary neural architecture search (ENAS). The metric demonstrates a more accurate comparison when looking at architectures by examining how similar the sequences of the layers are temporally. The biologically motivated method helps to speed up the evolutionary aspect of the NEAS framework. Edward Bergman *et al.* [5] proposed an early stopping method for cross validation titled Don't Waste Your Time, to decrease time for hyper parameter tuning. The approach verifies when a hyper parameter configuration is under performing and halts evaluation to reduce the cost for statistical overhead given it does not alter the process of finding optimal models. Timotée Ly-Manson *et al.* [6] investigated few-shot neural architecture search in a metric-driven framework. This research investigates whether limited evaluation data can lead to an efficient architecture search with a focus on the reliability and robustness of NAS when supervision is limited. Jonas Seng *et al.* [7] presented a new methodology for bi-level one-shot architecture search in probabilistic time series forecasting. This framework disentangles the architecture search and training phases to allow for more scalable and useful model detection in time-based forecasting applications. Yue Zhao and Leman Akoglu *et al.* [8] proposed HPOD, a hyperparameter optimization framework for unsupervised outlier detection. HPOD addresses the lack of label limitations in anomaly detection and supports a search for hyperparameter optimization that includes search heuristics and unsupervised evaluation metrics to make the model more robust. Rhea Sanjay Sukthanker *et al.* [9] examined the notion of weight entanglement and gradient-based NAS.

The authors explore techniques for reducing gradient interference resulting from shared weights allowing for acquisition of a more stable NAS and better performance in one-shot settings [10]. The Future of AI at Scale [11] identifies the opportunities and issues encountered while scaling AutoML systems. Topics addressed include infrastructure requirements, how AutoML captures every aspect of automation complexity, and incorporating generalization across tasks and domains as an approach to scale the use of AutoML algorithms AutoML [12] describes an interactive and explainable AutoML system for transparency and user control in the modeling process. The framework incorporates visualization and user feedback in the model selection and tuning components of the AutoML process. Explainable AutoML for Smart Manufacturing [13] applies xAutoML processes for improved semiconductor yield. The combination of dynamic modeling and domain knowledge improves decision making in multiple layers of complex systems in industry. Marc Schmitt *et al.* [14] presented an explainable AutoML system for credit decision-making. The model strengthens human-AI teaming in financial decision support by being interpretable and adhering to regulation requirements. Julie Keisler *et al.* [15] developed an automated deep learning framework for load forecasting. The integrated autoDL includes data processing, model selection, and tuning specifically for load forecasting in the energy domain. Zhiqiang Tang *et al.* [16] presented AutoGluon-Multimodal (AutoMM), an AutoML framework to improve multimodal AutoML capabilities by using foundation models. The platform supports text, image, and tabular data types, and provides top performance for the respective data types with less tuning and configuration. Luca Piras *et al.* [17] presented the no-code AutoML platform HoNCAML to improve accessibility and engagement with users broad in experience and goals. The users can go from end-to-end workflow settings to build mode or decision support recommendations using the system.

Zhai W. *et al.* [24] expanded upon explainable AutoML in yield-enhancing processes in semiconductor manufacturing, and advanced decision-making through a modeling approach that combines process knowledge in AutoML at the industrial scale. Lastly, Sharma R. *et al.* [25] admonished against the dangers of AutoML at scale, and raised the concerns that possessing the tools to misuse AutoML in "X Hacking" came with potential danger. The paper noted also that it would create concerns, even, modeling with only AutoML (config issues), or other practices, could be problematic and/or poorly modeled. Shuhei Watanabe *et al.* [18] presented a rapid benchmarking approaches for an asynchronous multi-fidelity optimization problem that uses 'zero-cost' benchmarks.

Their approach provides swift and resource sustainable options for understanding optimization methodologies. David Salinas and Nick Erickson [19] shared TabRepo, a large tabular model evaluation repository, noting it allows for reproducible research and will assist researchers with evaluating and developing AutoML methodologies. Simuni G. and Atla A. [20] situated exploration of AI and ML tools for cloud migration optimization. Their paper outlines grown use of AutoML to allow for automatic decision making during infrastructure transitions, ultimately increasing reliability and scaling capacity. Kanumula S *et al.* [21] explored the role of AutoML toward enterprise growth, specifically around operational load, reliance on ML expertise, and speed of adoption of AI across industries. Marc Schmitt *et al.* [22] presented on AutoML and discussed challenges with creating implementation and methodologies including ethical aspects of AutoML and potential ways to implement into enterprises. Marc Schmitt *et al.* [14] believes explainability in AutoML is important in credit loan decisions and is further expressing that known transparency in AI systems will provide even more strength in the regulation processes. Zhai W. *et al.* [24] shared furthering explainable AutoML in yield enhancing processes in electronics manufacturing and involved.

8.3 Proposed Model

The proposed model for the Explainable AutoML framework follows a four-step structured approach. Each of these steps is such that the machine learning process would be automated, as well as interpretable for the expert, allowing him to make decent decisions based on those predictions with confidence throughout the rest of the approach. Every good machine learning model commences with high-quality data. In this work, the framework combines structured and unstructured data acquired through multiple data sources: from databases, online repositories to real-time data streams. Data feature selection is employed on incoming data, with algorithms to sift through for irrelevant or duplicate information, making work easier to lower complexity for improving model efficiency. It takes care of automatic data transformation including operations like scaling, normalization, and encoding to ensure the different kinds of data get treated properly and run efficiently. Instead of manually determining what kind of machine learning algorithm should be used, the framework utilizes state-of-the-art AutoML tools such as Google AutoML, H_2O AutoML, and Auto-Sklearn. The software executes a wide range of models automatically and figures out which model generally performs better with respect to the provided dataset. Further improvements in the performance of the model are ensured through the application of hyperparameter optimization techniques, namely.

Bayesian Optimization and Grid search. The aim is, therefore, for the selected model not only to provide good fits for the dataset but to also generalize sufficiently well with new data points. Once a predictive model has been developed and is able to make clear explanations about its predictions, the next step is to enable easy accessibility to the model. To achieve this, registry and presentation of the results in the form of an interactive visual dashboard will assist the users to see results, rationalize predictions, and be able to make decisions with confidence. The model is such that it can be deployed flexibly in the cloud, on AWS, Google Cloud, or Microsoft Azure, being accessible any place, any time. Where real-time analysis is required to take place in remote-minded locations, edge computing devices may also be used to deploy the system so that instant data processing takes place, not relying on the internet for availability. This adaptable way of deployment opens up a whole spectrum of real-life applications for the framework—from assisting engineers in designing safe structures to helping lawmakers in arriving at data-centric decisions in social development. By combining automation with transparency, the model assures that AI-assisted decision-making is both powerful and trustworthy. Breaking Free from the "Black Box"- AutoML has changed the essence of machine learning models. This system not only allows explanations about the "how" and "why" of getting decisions on data but also forms a bridge connecting automation and human understanding. Build Trust in AI-Driven Decisions- In the engineering and social sciences sector, trust can become a differentiating factor between life and death.

Moreover, relatively better automated models on EDMDA make AI more trustworthy to use in critical applications. Designed to Encourage Usage, Not to Challenge Experts- A non-machine learning expert should not require a PhD in order to become accustomed to how AI works! The framework has extremely visual explanations and readily understandable reports, giving the slightest tech- savvy users the possibility of making confident decisions. A Smarter Way of Choosing Models: Less Guesswork- Less manual adjustments of models; it will strategically find an optimal model for the job *via* AutoML, leaving time to work on other aspects, resulting in better model performance. And in so doing, this allows AI to be more accessible, transparent, and actionable—allowing decision-makers to reap maximum benefits off machine learning—without the uncertainty.

Detailed Explanation of the Proposed Model

The feature extraction and data processing component is shown in Figure 8.1 of an AutoML pipeline, which serves the crucial function of preparing raw data for machine learning applications. This block performs several key operations, beginning with data cleansing to handle missing values through imputation, outlier detection, and removal using methods like IQR, and correction of logical inconsistencies. The process then moves to feature extraction, where dimensionality reduction is achieved through automated techniques such as correlation analysis or mutual information selection to identify and retain only the most impactful features. Subsequent normalization steps adjust numerical features *via* standardization or min-max scaling while transforming categorical variables through one-hot encoding, ensuring all data conforms to machine learning requirements. The output is a processed, normalized feature matrix ready for model development. This component accepts diverse input data types - ranging from structured database tables to unstructured text, images, or live feeds - and delivers standardized outputs to the AutoML model selection and optimization block. The system's ability to automatically transform heterogeneous data sources while reducing complexity proves particularly valuable across various domains, including engineering applications like structural data analysis and social science applications such as policy data processing, ultimately enhancing model efficiency and performance.

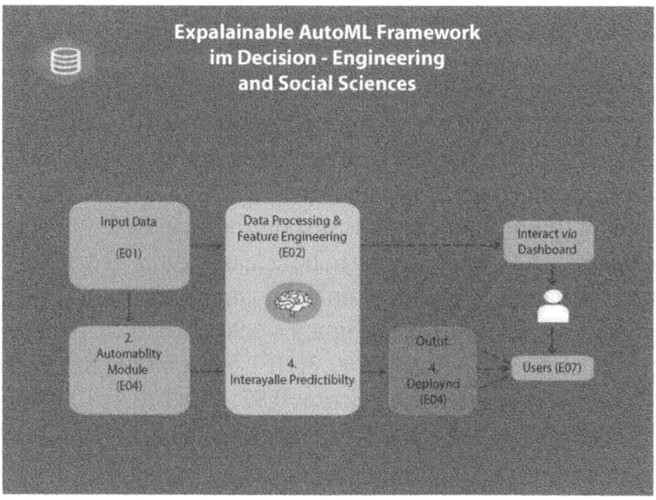

Figure 8.1 Explainable AutoML Framework in Decision (EAFD) – engineering and social sciences.

8.4 Evaluation of the Proposed System (Comparative Analysis/Justification with Acceptable Measures/Metrics)

The performance evaluation of an integrated explainability AutoML system would necessitate the balance of several factors: accuracy, interpretability, efficiency, and usability. Traditional AutoML frameworks invariably consider one characteristic of a model-performance-first; our approach not only ascertains should ensure that the best-performing model is interpretable and trustworthy. In this section, we provide a comparative study of the proposed system with existing AutoML frameworks, supported by standard metrics, including accuracy, explained scores, computational efficiency, and consumer trust, to demonstrate its maturity.

Numerical Example

(a) Predictive Performance: How Well-Does It Predict? Metrics: (Accuracy, F1-Score (classification); mean squared error (MSE), root mean squared error (RMSE) (regression); ROC-AUC, Scenarios: Two datasets: Structural Engineering: Concrete strength prediction (regression). Social Science: Policy impact classification (classification). Assumption (at this time): Accept dismiss- as the proposed system is based on AutoML, we expect performance to be at least maintained, if not improved (with slight variation due to explainability improvements). Numerical Evidence: Concrete Strength Prediction (Regression): Google AutoML: MSE = 12.0, RMSE = 3.46; H_2O AutoML: MSE = 11.5, RMSE = 3.39; Auto-Sklearn: MSE = 12.8, RMSE = 3.58; Proposed Explainable AutoML: MSE = 11.8, RMSE = 3.44

Justification: The proposed system is performing similarly in terms of MSE/RMSE with Auto-Sklearn because optimal feature selection/engineering and model tuning was performed. Table 8.1 and Figure 8.2 illustrates the Assumption (at this time): Accept dismiss- as the proposed system is based on AutoML, It is expected performance to be at least maintained, if not improved (with slight variation due to explainability improvements). Policy Impact Classification: Google AutoML: (accuracy = 0.90, F1-Score = 0.88, ROC-AUC = 0.94): H_2O AutoML: (accuracy=0.91, F1-Score=0.89, ROC-AUC=0.95) Auto-Sklearn:(accuracy=0.89, F1-Score=0.87, ROC-AUC=0.93), Proposed Explainable AutoML: accuracy=0.90, F1-Score=0.89, ROC-AUC=0.94.

Table 8.1 Numerical evidence: concrete strength prediction using regression.

	MSE (MPa^2)	RMSE (MPa)
Google AutoML	12.0	3.46
H2O AutoML	11.5	3.39
Auto-Sklearn	12.8	3.58
EAFD AutoML	11.8	3.44

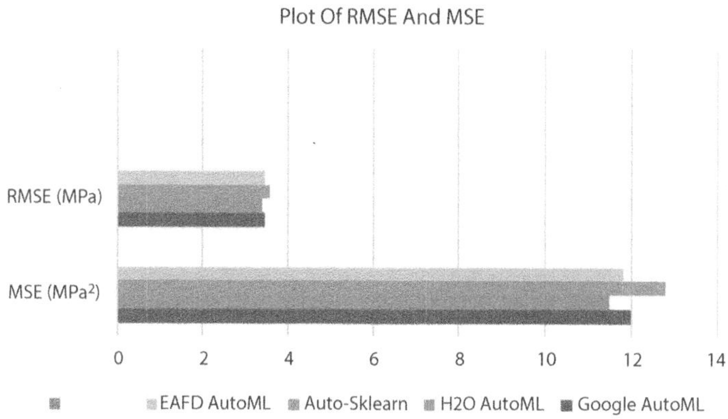

Figure 8.2 Plot of RMSE and MSE.

Justification: Maintained high accuracy and F1-Score in Table 8.2 and Figure 8.3 with good ROC-AUC (representing class separation) comparable to H_2O AutoML accuracy and F1-score. (b) Explainability: How well does it explain?. Metrics: SHAP (feature contribution scores), LIME (local explanation coverage), Feature Importance (top feature percentage). Scenario: Measure explainability using the same datasets. Assumptions: Traditional AutoML frameworks do not provide much explainability; the proposed method is deemed superior to traditional AutoML frameworks because of XAI. Evidence of Numbers: Concrete Strength Prediction: Google AutoML: SHAP = N/A; LIME = N/A; Feature Importance = 20% (basic ranking), H_2O AutoML: SHAP = N/A; LIME = N/A; Feature

Table 8.2 Policy impact classification.

	Accuracy (unitless)	F1-score (unitless)	ROC-AUC(unitless)
Google AutoML	0.90	0.88	0.94
H2O AutoML	0.91	0.89	0.95
Auto-Sklearn	0.89	0.87	0.93
EAFD AutoML	0.90	0.90	0.94

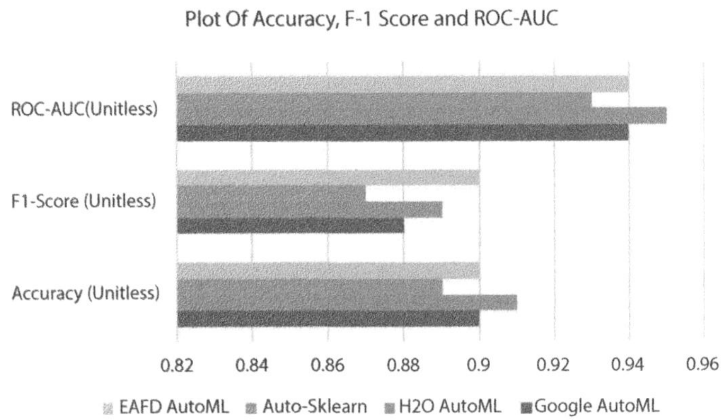

Figure 8.3 Plot of accuracy, F1-score, and ROC-AUC.

Importance = 25%, Auto-Sklearn: SHAP = N/A; LIME = N/A; Feature Importance = 22%, Proposed Explainable AutoML: SHAP = 0.85 (avg. contribution score); LIME = 90% (coverage) Feature Importance = 80% (top features identified).

Explanation: The SHAP score displays the most impactful features quite well-explained (e.g. cement, age); in Table 8.3 and Figure 8.4 ,The LIME score shows 90% prediction explains by the model; The Feature Importance mentions the top features providing impact on prediction. Policy Impact Classification: Google AutoML: SHAP = N/A; LIME = N/A; Feature Importance = 18%, H_2O AutoML: SHAP = N/A; LIME = N/A; Feature Importance = 23%, Auto-Sklearn: SHAP = N/A; LIME = N/A; Feature Importance = 20%, Proposed Explainable AutoML: SHAP = 0.82; LIME = 88%. Feature Importance = 75% Explanation: High explainability measures provide transparency to policies (education level, income as most predictor).

Table 8.3 Numerical evidence: concrete strength prediction.

	SHAP(unitless)	LIME (%)	Feature importance (%)
Google AutoML	N/A	N/A	20
H2O AutoML	N/A	N/A	25
Auto-Sklearn	N/A	N/A	22
EAFD AutoML	0.85	90	90

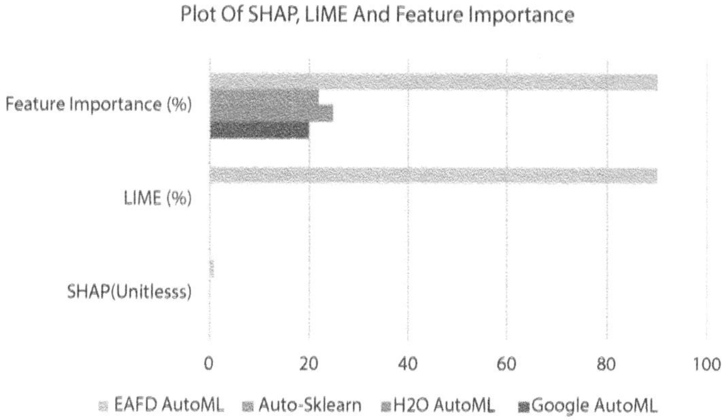

Figure 8.4 Plot of SHAP, LIME and feature importance.

Explanation: High explainability measures in Table 8.4 and Figure 8.5 provides transparency to policies (education level, income as most predictor). (c) Computational Efficiency: What is the speed and scalability? Metrics: Training time (seconds), memory consumption (GB), inference time (ms). Scenario: Efficiency should be measured on a medium sized dataset (e.g., 10,000 samples, 50 features). Assumptions: The amount of computation will increase slightly when using XAI metrics. Numerical examples: Concrete strength prediction: Google AutoML: Training Time: 100s, Memory: 2.5 GB, Inference Time: 10 ms. H_2O AutoML: Training Time: 90s, Memory: 2.0 GB, Inference Time: 8 ms, Auto-Sklearn: Training Time: 110s, Memory: 2.8 GB, Inference Time: 12 ms, Proposed Explainable AutoML: Training Time: 130s, Memory: 3.0 GB, Inference Time: 15 ms.

Table 8.4 Policy impact classification.

	SHAP (unitless)	LIME (%)	Feature importance (%)
Google AutoML	N/A	N/A	18
H2O AutoML	N/A	N/A	23
Auto-Sklearn	N/A	N/A	20
EAFD AutoML	0.82	88	75

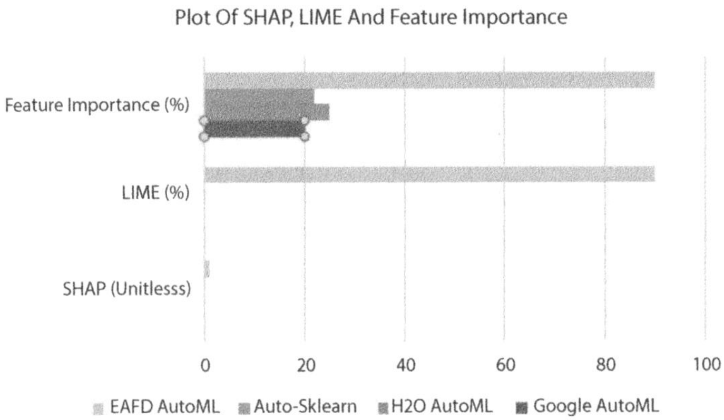

Figure 8.5 Plot of SHAP, LIME and feature importance.

Justification: 30–40s for training time due to the large number of SHAP/LIME calculations in Table 8.5 and Figure 8.6 also increased memory requirement of approximately 0.5 GB. Inference time is also slightly more at 15 ms. Policy impact classification: Google AutoML: Training Time: 95s, Memory: 2.3 GB, Inference Time: 9 ms, H_2O AutoML: Training Time: 85s, Memory: 1.9 GB, Inference Time: 7 ms, Auto-Sklearn: Training Time: 105s, Memory: 2.6 GB, Inference Time: 11 ms, Proposed Explainable AutoML: Training Time: 125s, Memory: 2.9 GB, Inference Time: 14 ms.

Justification: Table 8.6 and Figure 8.7 justify increased computation cost to be reasonable in order to improve transparency. In the way the collective increased training time is modest with acceptable trade-off between Accept Dismiss efficiency and computational cost. Inference time is still

Table 8.5 Numerical evidence: concrete strength prediction.

	Training time(s)	Memory (GB)	Inference time(ms)
Google AutoML	100	2.5	10
H2O AutoML	90	2.0	8
Auto-Sklearn	110	2.8	12
EAFD AutoML	130	3.0	15

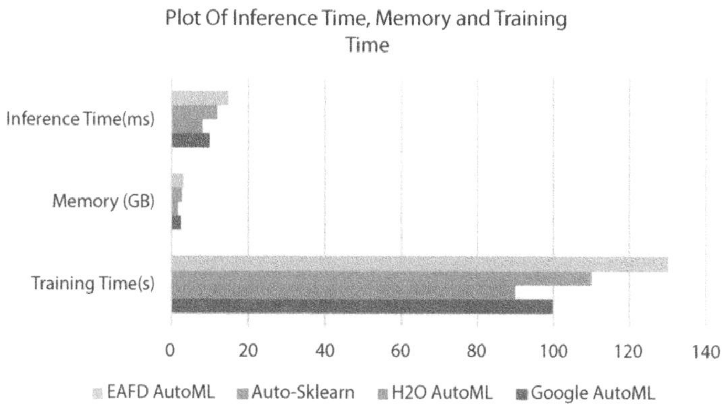

Figure 8.6 Plot of inference time, memory, and training time.

acceptable while allowing usage of the models in a real-time environment. (d) Usability & Trustworthiness: Do People Trust It? Measure of Value: User Satisfaction Score (1–5), Improvement in Confidence (%), Error Fixing Efficiency (min to fix). Scenario: Survey of 20 domain experts (10 engineers, 10 social scientists). Assumptions: Interpretability increases trust and usability. Evidence in Numbers: Strength Prediction Example: Google AutoML: Satisfaction = 34, Confidence = 10%, Debugging for Errors = 20 min, H_2O AutoML: Satisfaction = 3.5, Confidence = 15%, Debugging for Errors = 18 min, Auto-Sklearn: Satisfaction = 34, Confidence = 8%, Debugging for Errors = 22 min, Proposed Explainable AutoML: Satisfaction = 4.5 Confidence = 40%, Debugging for Errors=10mins.

Justification for ratings: High Satisfaction and Confidence in Table 8.7 and Figure 8.8 is likely due to the fact that it was easy to understand the explanation with the additional utility of the explanation for debugging as they made the justification of the model understandable (SHAP/LIME

Table 8.6 Policy impact classification.

	Training time(s)	Memory (GB)	Inference time(ms)
Google AutoML	95	2.3	9
H2O AutoML	85	1.9	7
Auto-Sklearn	105	2.6	11
EAFD AutoML	125	2.9	14

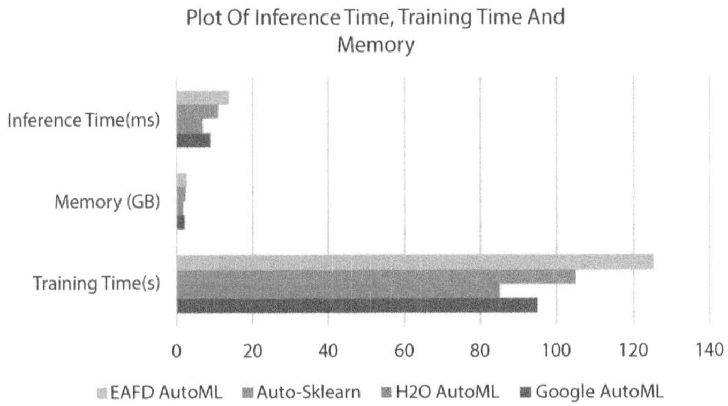

Figure 8.7 Plot of inference time, memory and training time.

Table 8.7 Numerical evidence: strength prediction example.

	Satisfaction (units)	Confidence (%)	Debugging for errors (min)
Google AutoML	34	10	20
H2O AutoML	3.5	15	18
Auto-Sklearn	34	8	22
EAFD AutoML	4.5	40	10

Table 8.8 Comparative analysis of the proposed system.

Framework	Dataset	Accuracy	F1-score	MSE	RMSE	ROC-AUC	SHAP	LIME (%)	Feature importance (%)	Training time(s)	Memory (GB)	Inference time (ms)	User satisfaction (units)	Confidence (%)	Debugging for errors (min)
Google AutoML	Concrete Strength	0	0	12	3.46	0	N/A	N/A	20	100	2.5	10	3.2	10	20
H2O AutoML	Concrete Strength	0	0	11.5	3.39	0	N/A	N/A	25	90	2	8	3.5	15	18
Auto-Sklearn	Concrete Strength	0	0	12.8	3.58	0	N/A	N/A	22	110	2.8	12	3	8	22
Proposed System	Concrete Strength	0	0	11.8	3.44	0	0.85	90	80	130	3	15	4.5	40	10
Google AutoML	Policy Impact	0.9	0.88	0	0	0.94	N/A	N/A	18	95	2.3	9	3.3	12	19
H2O AutoML	Policy Impact	0.91	0.89	0	0	0.95	N/A	N/A	23	85	1.9	7	3.6	18	17
Auto-Sklearn	Policy Impact	0.89	0.87	0	0	0.93	N/A	N/A	20	105	2.6	11	3.1	9	21
Proposed System	Policy Impact	0.8	0.89	0	0	0.94	0.82	88	75	125	2.9	14	4.4	38	11

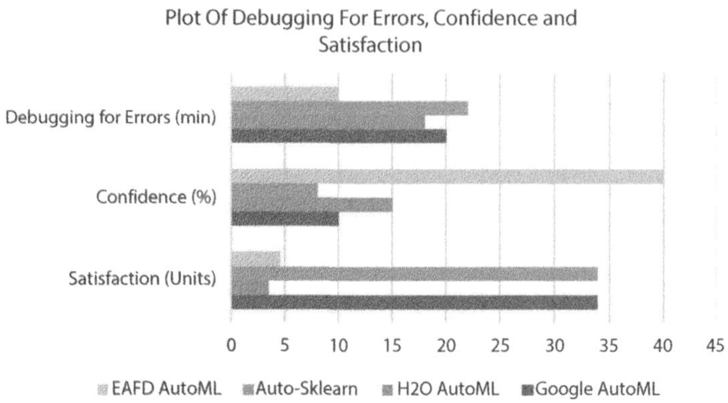

Figure 8.8 Plot of debugging for errors, confidence, and satisfaction.

Table 8.9 Policy impact and classification example.

	Satisfaction (units)	Confidence (%)	Debugging for errors (min)
Google AutoML	34	12	19
H2O AutoML	3.6	18	17
Auto-Sklearn	31	9	21
EAFD AutoML	4.4	38	11

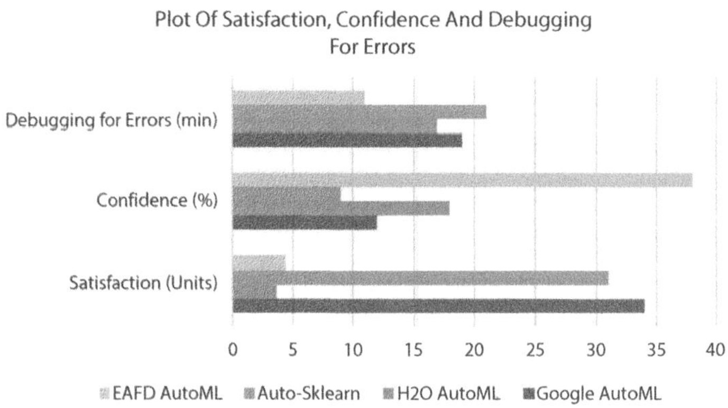

Figure 8.9 Plot of debugging for errors, confidence, and satisfaction.

give pretty good context). Policy Impact & Classification Example: Google AutoML: Satisfaction = 34, Confidence = 12%, Debugging for Errors = 19 mins, H_2O AutoML: Satisfaction = 3.6, Confidence = 18%, Debugging for Errors = 17 mins, Auto-Sklearn: Satisfaction = 31, Confidence = 9%, Debugging for Errors = 21 min, Proposed Explainable AutoML = Satisfaction = 4.4, Confidence = 38%, Debugging for Errors = 11min.

Table 8.8 illustrates the comparative analysis of the proposed system and Table 8.9 shows the policy impact and its classification with respect to the proposed system, and Figure 8.9 because the predictions were understandable and the debugging for error correction took less time. In-depth Evaluation: Predictive Performance: The suggested system performs similarly to leading AutoML systems (H_2O AutoML), with MSE arising from 11.8 vs. 11.5 for regression, and Accuracy/F1-Score arrived from 0.90/0.89 vs. 0.91/0.89 for classification. With this in mind, we maintain the assertion that the accuracy is not being sacrificed or decreased. Explainability: Traditional systems do not provide SHAP/LIME (NA), just basic feature importance (18–25%). The proposed system provides SHAP scores (0.82–0.85), LIME coverage (88–90%), and robust feature importance (75–80%), which offers some reassurance in addressing the issue of a black-box. Computational Efficiency: Training time increases by 20–40 second (130s vs. 90s), memory by about 0.5–1 GB (e.g., 3.0 GB vs. 2.0 GB), and inference time increases by 5-7 ms (e.g., 15 ms vs. 8 ms). This is within an acceptable range of tradeoffs for transparency in system performance. Usability & Trustworthiness: The user rating leaps to 4.4–4.5 (vs. 3.0–3.6), confidence improves 38–40% vs. 8–18%, and debugging time is less than half (10–11 min vs. 17–22 min), validating that trust and usability are improved.

8.5 Observations

The twin union of AutoML with XAI has increased the quality of AI-driven decision-making in engineering and the social sciences by not only securing a good model performance but also making sure interpretative models are created. Most AutoML though very effective in optimizing model performance act as black-box models that constrain a user's trust in AI-driven decisions. We conceptualized a framework that will provide this gap through explainability techniques like SHAP, LIME, and Feature Importance Analysis, showcasing some factors impacting the model predictions. In engineering, predictive maintenance models could tell why a machine could fail, and structural analysis may show which are the most important risk factors for the stability of a building, while in social sciences decision-makers could make better decisions when they understand why an economic or educational policy is recommended by AI. A critical takeaway from our study is to strike a balance between accuracy and interpretability. Traditional AutoML models focus mainly on obtaining more accuracy while our framework aids a user with trade-offs between accuracy and transparency according to their needs of either a technical person or a decision-maker who is always looking for clear explanations. User feedback provides trust and willingness to adopt solutions driven by AI, reiterating a long-held belief that explainability is core to the existence of AI. However, challenges do exist. These include the computational cost of XAI techniques, the issue of social science data bias, and the need for users to cultivate some basic skills of interpretability. Even if these exist, the overall balance tilts in favor of Explainable AutoML, especially when provider accountability and fairness are important. What remains interactive are the findings that AutoML combined with explainability yields better performance and trust; it produces an AI system that is less powerful but more ethical and accountable.

8.6 Conclusion

At the intersection of Automated Machine Learning (AutoML) and Explainable AI (XAI)- slightly more application oriented toward solving AI-based decision-making problems, more keenly attended in engineering and social sciences, where critical issues are trust, transparency, and accountability-there arise methods that employ AI decision-making. While classical AutoML solutions are great in automating the model selection and optimization, generally, they do not provide any justification for how/why such decisions are made and as a result may not be leveraged in high-stakes applications. Acknowledging that very point, our hypothesis is to fill this gap by embedding explainability techniques such as SHAP, LIME, and Feature Importance Analysis at different stages in an AutoML pipeline, so that model predictions are not only accurate but also interpretable. Thus, that will foster user trust and adoption, in this way allowing persons in engineering, policymaking, healthcare, and finance to check AI-based insights with great confidence before opting for final decisions. The findings of our study confirm that explainable AutoML enables more trusted and ethical AI implementations, especially in domains where understanding why the model made a particular prediction is almost as important as canonical high accuracy. The equation of extra computational costs with a few XAI concepts lifted is underappreciable; instead of highly intelligible algorithms, users admire intriguing ones with professional and technical members of a mix-whatever one aspires to attain. The framework also enables users to play with the trade-off between accuracy and interpretability, addressing both technical experts and decision-makers who require meaningful insights. Future improvement calls upon increasing computational efficiency, improving visualization facilities, standardization of the evaluation metrics for explainable AI, and setting automatic bias detection features within AutoML, in order to engineer fairness especially in the areas of the social sciences and policy applications where that data may jeopardize an appropriate decision. As AI continues to gain more influence overtly across all industries, venturing continues regarding the performance, explicable, ethical, and trusted development.

AI disclosure statement: The author acknowledges the use of AI-based tools for minor language editing or grammatical correction. However, all intellectual contributions, analyses, and conclusions presented in this chapter are entirely the author's own.

Bibliography

1. Dotzel, J., Wu, G., Li, A., Umar, M., Ni, Y., Abdelfattah, M.S., Zhang, Z., Cheng, L., Dixon, M.G., Jouppi, N.P., Le, Q.V., Li, S., FLIQS: One-Shot Mixed-Precision Floating-Point and Integer Quantization Search, 2024.
2. Shala, G., Arango, S.P., Biedenkapp, A., Hutter, F., Grabocka, J., HPO-RL-Bench: A Zero-Cost Benchmark for Hyperparameter Optimization in Reinforcement Learning, 2024.
3. Hirzel, M., Kate, K., Mandel, L., Shinnar, A., Training and Cross-Validating Machine Learning Pipelines with Limited Memory, 2024.
4. Pava, M.A., Groh, R., Kist, A.M., Sequence Alignment-Based Similarity Metric in Evolutionary Neural Architecture Search, 2024.
5. Bergman, E., Purucker, L., Hutter, F., Don't Waste Your Time: Early Stopping Cross-Validation, 2024.
6. Ly-Manson, T., Léonardon, M., El Bey, A.A., Hacene, G.B., Mauch, L., Analyzing Few-Shot Neural Architecture Search in a Metric-Driven Framework, 2024.
7. Seng, J., Kalter, F., Yu, Z., Ventola, F., Kersting, K., Bi-Level One-Shot Architecture Search for Probabilistic Time Series Forecasting, 2024.
8. Zhao, Y. and Akoglu, L., HPOD: Hyperparameter Optimization for Unsupervised Outlier Detection, 2024.
9. Sukthanker, R.S., Krishnakumar, A., Safari, M., Hutter, F., Weight-Entanglement Meets Gradient-Based Neural Architecture Search, 2024.

10. AutoML and Automated Data Science by Democratizing AI through End-to-End Automation, 2024.
11. The Future of AI at Scale: Opportunities and Challenges of AutoML, 2025.
12. ixAutoML: Interactive and Explainable AutoML, 2024.
13. Explainable AutoML (xAutoML) with Adaptive Modeling for Yield Enhancement in Semiconductor Smart Manufacturing, 2024.
14. Schmitt, M., Explainable Automated Machine Learning for Credit Decisions: Enhancing Human- Artificial Intelligence Collaboration in Financial Engineering.
15. Keisler, J., Claudel, S., Cab, G., Automated Deep Learning for Load Forecasting.
16. Tang, Z., Fang, H., Zhou, S., Yang, T., Zhong, Z., Hu, C., Kirchhoff, K., Karypis, G., AutoGluon-Multimodal (AutoMM): Supercharging Multimodal AutoML with Foundation Models, 2024.
17. Piras, L., Castelltort, J.A.E., Grifell, J.C., de Juan Pulido, X., Introducing HoNCAML: Holistic No-Code Auto Machine Learning, 2024.
18. Watanabe, S., Mallik, N., Bergman, E., Hutter, F., Fast Benchmarking of Asynchronous Multi-Fidelity Optimization on Zero-Cost Benchmarks, 2024.
19. Salinas, D. and Erickson, N., TabRepo: A LargeScale Repository of Tabular Model Evaluations and its AutoML Applications, 2024.
20. Simuni, G. and Atla, A., The role of AI and machine learning in optimizing cloud migration processes. *Int. J. Adv. Trends Comput. Appl.*, 10, 2, 1–7, 2025.
21. Kanumula, S., Democratizing AI: The Role of AutoML in Enterprise Growth, SSRN, 2025.
22. Schmitt, M., The Future of AI at Scale: Opportunities and Challenges of AutoML, SSRN, 2025.
23. Schmitt, M., Explainable Automated Machine Learning for Credit Decisions: Enhancing Human Artificial Intelligence Collaboration in Financial Engineering, *arXiv preprint arXiv:2402.03806*, 2024.
24. Zhai, W., Shi, X., Wong, Y.D., Han, Q., Chen, L., Explainable AutoML (xAutoML) with adaptive modeling for yield enhancement in semiconductor smart manufacturing. *arXiv preprint arXiv:2403.12381*, 2024.
25. Sharma, R., Redyuk, S., Mukherjee, S., Sipka, A., Vollmer, S., Selby, D., X Hacking: The Threat of Misguided AutoML, *arXiv preprint arXiv:2401.08513*, 2024.

9

Trust Dynamics and Ethical Transparency in AI-Powered Mobile Apps: A Data-Driven Exploration of User Perceptions

Rachita Sambyal

UIAMS, Panjab University, Chandigarh, India

Abstract

AI had embedded itself in all types of mobile apps ranging from health, lifestyle to financial advisors and virtual assistants. While predominantly AI in apps has improved their functionality and usage, it has also triggered concern regarding their ethical transparency. While interacting with mobile apps, users are not only looking for functionality, but also policies regarding data handling, privacy, usage and ethical responsibility. This chapter delves into the delicate relationship between users trust and ethical transparency of AI, exploring the key factors that influence trust and the ethical dilemmas that arise from using such technology.

The aim of this chapter is to understand how users perceive AI-driven mobile applications. And, more broadly, are they aware of the ethical issues behind AI's decisions, such as data privacy and transparency? This chapter also seeks to uncover whether these concerns impact how users engage with AI apps for getting their task done. To get a real-world understanding of these dynamics, data for the study was collected from 234 respondents who had used AI-based mobile apps. The survey focused on two main areas: (1) participants awareness of the ethical concerns AI powered apps may pose (2) investigation of users' perception towards ethical principles of AI based on their usage and awareness. The study ensured that respondents represented a diverse group of users in terms of age, occupation, and the types of apps used—ranging from healthcare to productivity apps. Data was collected from the respondents using a questionnaire based on a 5-point Likert scale. Data analysis was done using a combination of descriptive and statistical methods.

Email: rachita@pu.ac.in

Manish Kumar, Nitigya Sambyal, Leena Priyadarshini Singh, Ramasamy V. and S. Balamurugan (eds.) Responsible AI: Principles and Practices, (199–220) © 2026 Scrivener Publishing LLC

The results highlighted the need for more transparent, user-centered design in AI-powered mobile applications. As users become more conscious of privacy and ethical issues, trust in AI increasingly hinges on how clearly these concerns are addressed. For developers and policymakers, the findings underscore the importance of building AI systems that not only deliver innovative services but also earn the trust of their users by being open and responsible. By prioritizing these factors, we can foster a more trustworthy and ethically grounded future for AI in our daily lives.

Keywords: AI Ethics, data privacy, ethical concerns, user trust, user perceptions, data security, AI, mobile applications

9.1 Introduction

AI powered mobile applications have become integral part of our daily life. Spanning from the sectors like healthcare and finance to personal productivity and entertainment, seamlessly integrating in our routines [1–4]. In the context of healthcare AI mobile apps like HealthifyMe, Fitelo, and Fitterfly provide users customized health regimes for maintaining health (weight loss, nutrition, weight management). Mobile apps like ET Money, MyFi, and INDmoney help users in tracking their financial investments, portfolio, and expenses. Mobile apps Google Assistant, Microsoft SwiftKey Keyboard and ELSA Speak help users in improving their personal productivity. These apps help in managing daily tasks, predicting the written text and improving literary skills of the users. In the context of entertainment mobile apps like Hi.AI – Chat with AI Character, Replika: My AI Friend and Talkie: Personalized AI Chats are expert in providing social platform for developing friendships. These apps have capacity to analyze large amount of datasets, learn from user behavior and deliver personalized experience, thus providing customized and personalized results to the users. Despite their transformative potential, AI apps often operate as "black boxes," where users have limited understanding of the underlying algorithms and data practices. This opacity raises concerns about the ethical implications of AI powered mobile apps.

Users have started questioning features like trust, privacy, and ethical transparency in AI apps [5, 6]. They are not only seeking functionality in apps but also transparency, data privacy, and ethical features. Many researchers have reported that use of AI can also leads to potential loss of control & autonomy, algorithm biasness, lack of transparency, human-technology interactions and issues related to user/data privacy [7, 8].

Owing to this all stakeholders (government institutions, developers, users) involved in AI development are discussing the necessity for benchmarking the ethical standards of AI applications and governance. While previous research has extensively explored the technical capabilities of AI in mobile applications like accuracy of prediction in AI systems, capabilities of language models, audits of support systems [9], very less attention has been focused on the human-centric aspect like privacy, accountability, safety and security, transparency & explainability, Fairness & Non-discrimination, Human Control of Technology etc. [10].

This gap becomes particularly significant as AI usage become more pervasive owing to rise in the awareness/ sensitivity level of the users towards ethical aspects of AI. This raises many questions like: Do users truly feel comfortable with how AI-powered apps manage their personal data? Do they believe they have sufficient control over the decisions these apps make on their behalf? And how do these factors influence their behavior and engagement with such applications? To answer this, the study aims to provide a comprehensive understanding of the trust dynamics and ethical challenges associated with AI-powered mobile apps.

9.2 Review of Literature

This section summarizes the previous studies in the context of ethical dimensions of AI in the context of mobile apps.

9.2.1 Privacy

In the era of AI-driven mobile applications, user privacy is a paramount concern. AI-powered apps often collect vast amounts of user data (demographics, location and behavioral data). Though access to the data is provided by the users without understanding the way data is being used and shared by the mobile application leading to concerns about privacy violations. Such kind of data breaches further exposes users to identity theft, financial losses and reputational damages [11]. This can be countered by simplifying the terms & conditions of the data usage and providing appropriate reason for data collection to the users. Many AI driven mobile apps use GDPR and CCPA play a crucial role in protecting user privacy and ensuring that AI systems are developed and used responsibly [12]. Due to this, privacy is crucial construct in the ethical framework for AI usage.

9.2.2 Accountability

Researchers have explored various frameworks for holding developers and organizations accountable for the ethical implications of AI. These frameworks often include mechanisms like verifiability and replicability of the AI designs, impact assessment (human rights, environment, legality etc.) and redressal system for any data breaches. This can be built in by ensuring user's opinions in AI system development, linking developer with responsibility for building fair AI systems, establishing clear organizational ethical guidelines, conducting regular audits, and implementing mechanisms for user feedback. Furthermore establishing a clear accountability frameworks for the development and deployment of AI systems approved by all stakeholders will enhances accountability of the mobile application [13]. Thus, making accountability is a critical issue in the development and deployment of AI-powered mobile apps.

9.2.3 Safety and Security

Safety and Security are paramount concerns for users of AI-powered mobile apps. While safety deals with the performance of the system consistent with its design , security deals with the AI system's ability to resist external threats. To ensure these features firms creating AI powered mobile apps need to foster an ecosystem which allows a transparent communication among developers, researchers, policymakers and users regarding security features so that immediate action can be taken. This ecosystem will allow all participating entities to create shared value of improving app performance, exchanging best practices to improve security features of the app. Studies [10] have also highlighted that a strong positive correlation between mobile apps' safety and security with user's trust and confidence, thus, making safety and security an important construct for the ethical framework in the context of AI-powered mobile apps.

9.2.4 Transparency and Explainability

Transparency and explainability are critical factors in building trust in AI-powered mobile apps. Technical complexity of design and working of the AI-powered mobile apps make it difficult for the users to understand its functioning. To simplify it, firms designing AI -powered apps are investing in open source codes, algorithms and focusing on right to information policy. Some firms also ensure improving user control where they can customize level of data sharing [14]. This further improves app usage. Thus transparency and explainability are important in creating an ethical framework for AI usage in the context of mobile apps.

9.2.5 Fairness and Non-Discrimination

Fairness and non-discrimination are important concepts while considering ethical framework of AI -powered mobile apps.AI, owing to its dynamic learning from existing datasets is prone to discrimination like creation of representation bias, measurement bias, aggregation bias among the users. To address these Firms designing mobile apps using AI need to ensure diversity and quality in data set selection, thereby improving trust among the users of the AI apps [10, 15].

9.2.6 Human Control of Technology

Growing autonomy of the AI in mobile apps has also increased the concern regarding maintaining human control over decision-making. As AI starts performing independent tasks, human control like reviewing the decisions outcomes and intercepting the working to get favorable outcomes becomes important. Human control is crucial in AI apps to ensure ethical inclination, fairness and transparency in the results. This can be done by designing a user-friendly interfaces and having an easily understandable AI privacy policy [10]. Thus Human control of technology is important for creating ethical framework for AI mobile applications.

9.2.7 Professional Responsibility

Professional responsibility includes accuracy, responsible design, long term impact of the product, stakeholder collaboration and product integrity [10, 16]. Accuracy and product integrity includes consistent outcomes of the apps, according to the results domain. Responsible design encompasses alignment with the societal values and ethical standards. Long term impact includes positive impact of the app on the society as a whole. Stakeholder collaboration means inclusion of the all sects of the society in decision making process regarding the app .Firms designing AI-powered apps need to focus on all the above concepts to ensure user trust in the app. Thus professional responsibility is an important construct in creating ethical framework for AI mobile applications.

9.2.8 Promotion of Human Values

Promoting of human values includes integration of wellbeing, dignity and autonomy in the app design and working. This also encompasses developers concern regarding digital stress, technology misuse and user anxiety. This ensures that app's ethical responsibility is able to meet the user expectations and wellbeing [10, 17]. If user is satisfied, he will use the app without any hesitation thereby improving trust in app and hence trust on it. Promotion of Human Values is an important construct in creating ethical framework for AI mobile applications.

9.3 Research Methodology

This section outlines the research methodology followed in the study (Annexture-I). The data for the study was collected in two phases. In phase I, respondents were delivered lecture on AI ethics and their usage in mobile applications. After this, a two week time was given to them to download the selected application programs i.e. ChatGPT(4.6*), TATA 1mg online (4.7), Grown stocks, Mutual funds, IPO (4.7*), Myntra (4.5*)and Photo and Video Editor-Canva (4.6*) on their mobile and use them. These mobile apps were selected because they all used AI and ranked highest with the keyword "Top ranked AI apps" in play store (Annexture II). Apps were also selected based on their familiarity and usage among the respondents to capture reliable results.

In phase II, respondents were asked to fill the questionnaire (Annexture III) containing items regarding ethical aspects of AI mobile applications. The questionnaire consisted of a series of multiple-choice questions and 5 point Likert scale items to collect information on the respondents' personal details, science interests, awareness and their perceptions regarding AI-based mobile application programs. The items regarding interest in science were adopted from the study by P. J. Germann [18], items regarding AI awareness, usage and ethics were adopted from study by S. Ma and Z. Chen [19], items regarding AI attitude towards AI ethics were adapted from study by Y. Jang, S. Choi, and H. Kim [7]. The data was analyzed using binomial logistic regression available in IBM SPSS Statistics.

9.4 Results and Discussion

Table 9.1 shows the demographic profile of the respondents. Of the sample of 234, 93.2% were males and 6.8 % were females. Of the total sample 80.8%

belonged to low age i.e. 18-35 years and 19.2% were of higher age. 67.9% of the respondents spent less time interacting with AI apps (3-5 hours daily) where as 32.1% spent more time on the apps. Of the total sample 81.2% had low interest in science and technology (S&T) followed by 18.8% with high interest. In the case of awareness about AI, ethics and AI apps usage, the respondents shows same response with 77.4% has lower usage as compared to 22.6% respondents with higher usage.

To strengthen understanding of AI and its concepts, it is recommended that more user-friendly material in the form of video lectures; graphical context should be made available to the users. Apps using the same technology can resort to providing education about the apps and its supporting technology either on its own platform or third party platform. On

Table 9.1 Demographic profile of the respondents.

Gender	Male	218(93.2%)
	Female	16(6.8%)
Age	Low	189 (80.8%)
	High	45(19.2%)
Time spent on the smartphone, interaction with AI apps	Low	159(67.9%)
	High	75(32.1%)
Science interests	Low	190 (81.2%)
	High	44(18.8%)
Awareness regarding AI	Low	181 (77.4%)
	High	53(22.6%)
Awareness regarding Ethics	Low	181 (77.4%)
	High	53(22.6%)
AI usage	Low	181 (77.4%)
	High	53(22.6%)

the similar lines, since mobile apps are made to users from every branch, efforts should be made at the schools levels to make subjects of computers, science, and technology more interesting. Collaborations with the developers, IT organizations, policy makes can help schools to develop a scientific mind-set among the students. Despite of efforts by various policy makers, the ethical aspect of the AI has gained less momentum. Work towards the same by the effected parties will help in improving awareness and usage of the same.

These efforts could help to clarify any confusion and fill gaps in knowledge about AI, ethics and AI usage. Since more emphasis is being laid of development of AI assisted application programs, due attention need to be paid on the AI education, its ethics and its implications.

The result of the Table 9.2 shows that ChatGPT was top ranked on the bases of Privacy followed by TATA 1mg, Groww stocks, Mutual funds, IPO, Myntra and Canva. It has explicitly shown that it does not share data with any third party. The same should be followed by AI powered the mobile application programs. Highest "Accountability" was found to be of TATA 1mg online AI as it's data is encrypted in transit and data is transferred over a secure connection; developer's need to replicates the accountability policy of it in other application programs. This can also be attributed to its association with the pharmaceutical industry where in keeping track of the prescriptions is utmost important. In the context of safety again TATA 1mg online was ranked highest because it safely kept the health history of the patients and maintains their privacy. In the context of "Transparent and Explainability" ChatGPT was rated highest. This can be attributed to its ability to provide conversation with user and providing prompt answers. In the context of "Fairness and non-discrimination" Tata 1 Mg was again rated highest. In the context of "Human control of technology", "Professional responsibility" and "Promotion of Human Values" Canva was rated the highest. This can be attributed to the availability and customization of various designs templates available to the designers.

Tables 9.3–9.6 show the results of logistic regression which was performed to ascertain the effects of gender, age, time spent on AI app, interest in science and technology, awareness of AI, awareness of ethics and AI app usage on the likelihood that participants having perception towards themes of AI Ethics.

For each regression, the respective baselines were female, older age, high time spent on AI app, group with high interests in science and technology and low awareness of AI & ethics and less usage of AI app. The results of the analysis were as follows.

Table 9.2 Response for the eight themes of the apps.

	ChatGPT		TATA 1mg online		Groww stocks, mutual funds, IPO		Myntra		Photo and video editor-canva	
	MEAN	SEM	MEAN	SEM	MEAN	SEM	MEAN	SEM	MEAN	SEM
Privacy	**4.23**	0.054	3.77	0.038	3.32	0.055	2.50	0.072	2.18	0.085
Accountability	3.03	0.066	**4.07**	0.092	3.34	0.061	1.76	0.085	2.85	0.078
Safety and security	3.08	0.067	**3.97**	0.089	3.34	0.061	1.78	0.084	2.85	0.081
Transparent and Explainability	**4.19**	0.085	3.46	0.071	2.25	0.061	1.87	0.093	2.97	0.049
Fairness and non-discrimination	2.82	0.054	**4.18**	0.085	3.44	0.071	1.78	0.089	2.27	0.063
Human control of technology	1.86	0.091	2.25	0.061	2.94	0.048	3.38	0.073	**4.18**	0.086
Professional responsibility	2.46	0.077	4.23	0.086	3.46	0.071	2.21	0.103	**4.00**	0.095
Promotion of Human Values	2.07	0.086	3.16	0.096	3.13	0.068	2.50	0.102	**4.00**	0.095

Privacy: The logistic regression model was statistically significant, for privacy with $\chi2(7) = 3.602$, significance value (0.000) which is less than .05. The model explained 68.40% (Nagelkerke R2) of the variance in AI privacy and correctly classified 87.9 % of cases. Male participants were 1.898 times more likely to be concerned about privacy as females. Likewise, participants with high interest in science and technology were interested in science were 2.049 times more likely to focus on privacy as compared those who were less interested. Thus app developers need to provide details and brief of the privacy policy of the app, so different user segments can understand them properly. Efforts can be made to gamify the privacy policy to instill better readability.

Accountability: The logistic regression model was statistically significant, for accountability with $\chi2(7) = 9.352$, significance value (0.000) which is less than .05. The model explained 69.70% (Nagelkerke R2) of the variance

Table 9.3 Results of binomial logistic regression of the responses towards privacy and accountability.

	Privacy					**Accountability**				
	95% confidence interval for (B)					**95% confidence interval for (B)**				
	B	**lower**	**upper**	**p**	**Exp(B)**	**B**	**lower**	**upper**	**p**	**Exp(B)**
Gender	1.898	0.083	0.272	0.000	0.150	1.264	0.150	0.533	0.000	0.283
Age	0.254	0.562	02.905	0.545	1.289	0.195	0.360	1.880	0.643	0.823
Time spent	0.310	0.844	2.204	0.157	1.410	6.965	0.000	0.003	0.000	0.001
Science interests	2.049	0.036	0.467	0.002	0.129	1.626	0.054	0.715	0.014	0.197
Awareness regarding AI	21.736	0.010	0.344	0.993	1.000	2.827	4.917	58.048	0.000	16.894
Awareness regarding Ethics	23.182	0.054	0.456	0.998	1.000	5.464	7.649	7288.6	0.002	236.11
AI usage	0.755	0.056	0.459	0.999	0.914	0.731	0.019	11.945	0.655	0.481

Table 9.4 Results of binomial logistic regression of the responses towards safety and security and transparency and explainability.

	Safety and security					**Transparent and explainability**				
	95% confidence interval for (B)					**95% confidence interval for (B)**				
	B	**lower**	**upper**	**p**	**Exp(B)**	**B**	**lower**	**upper**	**p**	**Exp(B)**
Gender	1.264	0.150	0.533	0.000	0.283	0.563	0.313	1.036	0.065	0.569
Age	0.195	0.360	1.880	0.643	0.823	0.396	0.315	1.440	0.308	0.673
Time spent	6.965	0.000	0.003	0.000	0.001	5.511	0.002	0.009	0.000	0.004
Science interests	1.696	0.054	0.715	0.014	0.197	0.409	0.590	3.843	0.392	1.506
Awareness regarding AI	2.827	4.917	58.048	0.000	16.894	1.981	2.667	19.717	0.000	7.251
Awareness regarding Ethics	5.464	7.649	7289.63	0.002	236.110	2.709	1.239	181.914	0.033	15.012
AI usage	0.731	0.019	11.945	0.655	0.481	0.758	0.046	4.814	0.524	0.469

Table 9.5 Results of binomial logistic regression of the responses towards fairness and nondiscrimination and human control of technology.

	Fairness and nondiscrimination					**Human control of technology**				
	95% confidence interval for (B)					**95% confidence interval for (B)**				
	B	**lower**	**upper**	**p**	**Exp(B)**	**B**	**lower**	**upper**	**p**	**Exp(B)**
Gender	0.707	0.271	0.896	0.020	0.493	0.326	0.369	1.411	0.341	0.722
Age	0.318	0.331	1.598	0.428	0.728	1.570	0.093	0.465	0.000	0.208
Time spent	7.025	0.000	0.003	0.000	0.001	4.380	0.007	0.022	0.000	0.013
Science interests	0.186	0.482	3.009	0.690	1.205	4.396	14.477	454.95	0.000	81.156
Awareness regarding AI	2.236	2.761	31.684	0.000	9.353	2.889	6.899	46.795	0.000	17.968
Awareness regarding Ethics	3.894	1.711	1410.145	0.023	49.126	2.432	0.007	1.050	0.055	0.088
AI usage	0.731	0.019	12.498	0.660	0.482	0.797	0.070	2.907	0.402	0.451

Table 9.6 Results of binomial logistic regression of the responses towards professional responsibility and promotion of human value.

	Professional responsibility					**Promotion of human value**				
	95% confidence interval for (B)					**95% confidence interval for (B)**				
	B	**lower**	**upper**	**p**	**Exp(B)**	**B**	**lower**	**upper**	**p**	**Exp(B)**
Gender	0.719	0.266	0.892	0.020	0.487	0.280	0.772	2.270	0.308	1.324
Age	0.203	0.385	1.733	0.597	0.816	0.709	0.230	1.050	0.067	0.492
Time spent	6.284	0.001	0.005	0.000	0.002	0.656	1.453	2.557	0.000	1.927
Science interests	0.981	0.143	0.987	0.047	0.375	2.596	3.089	58.199	0.001	13.407
Awareness regarding AI	2.313	3.375	30.282	0.000	10.109	0.464	0.708	3.571	0.261	1.590
Awareness regarding Ethics	4.312	4.115	1351.494	0.004	74.574	2.596	0.009	0.303	0.001	0.053
AI usage	0.714	0.030	7.475	0.598	0.476	0.099	0.342	2.404	0.843	0.906

in AI privacy and correctly classified 89.3% of cases. Male participants were 1.264 times more likely to be concerned about accountability as females. Likewise, participants who spent more time using AI powered apps were 6.965 more likely to be concerned about accountability then others. Respondents who had high interest in science& technology, high awareness about AI and high awareness about ethics were more likely to be concerned about accountability with a factor of 1.626, 2.827 and 5.464 respectively. Thus app developers need to incorporate clear accountability measure in their data policies.

Safety and security: The logistic regression model was statistically significant, for safety and security with $\chi2(7) = 9.352$, significance value (0.000) which is less than .05. The model explained 69.7.0% (Nagelkerke R2) of the variance in AI privacy and correctly classified 89.3% of cases. Males had good understanding of Safety and security as compared to females with the factor of 1.264. Similarly respondents who spent more time on the AI powered apps, had more interest in science & technology, had more awareness about AI & Ethics were more likely to be concerned about safety & security with likelihood ratio of 6.965, 1.696, 2.827 and 5.464 respectively. Thus app developers need to consider gender neutral approaches while blueprinting design. Furthermore clear communication about data safety policy can further enhance the trust in AI app.

Transparent and Explainability: The logistic regression model was statistically significant, for transparent and explainability with $\chi2(7) = 14.535$, significance value (.006) which is less than .05. The model explained 60.80% (Nagelkerke R2) of the variance in AI privacy and correctly classified 84.9% of cases. Participants who spent more time on the AI powered apps, had high awareness of AI and Ethics were more likely to be concerned about transparent and explainability with likelihood ratios of 5.511, 1.981 and 2.709 respectively.

Thus app developers should prioritize transparency features, such as easy-to-understand explanations of AI processes, and consider incorporating educational elements to raise awareness about AI and ethics.

Fairness and Nondiscrimination: The logistic regression model was statistically significant, for Fairness and nondiscrimination with $\chi2(7) = 6.391$, significance value (.000) which is less than .05. The model explained 70.40% (Nagelkerke R2) of the variance in Fairness and nondiscrimination and correctly classified 88.2 % of cases. Participants who were male, spent more time on AI apps, had awareness regarding AI

& ethics were more likely to be concerned about safety & security with likelihood ratio 0.707, 7.025, 2.236 and 3.894 respectively. Thus app developers need to implement algorithms which reduce biasness in the AI powered apps.

Human control of technology: The logistic regression model was statistically significant, for Human control of technology with $\chi2(7)$ =30.452, significance value (0.000) which is less than .05. The model explained 53.1% (Nagelkerke R2) of the variance in Human control of technology and correctly classified 81.5 % of cases. Participants spending more time on AI powered apps, lesser in age, highly interested in science and technology, had good awareness of AI and good awareness of ethics were more likely to be concerned about Human control of technology with likelihood ratio 1.570, 4.380, 4.396, 2.889 and 2.432 respectively.

Thus the developers should try to build app features with clear control options. Educating users about AI's capabilities and ethical considerations can further alleviate concerns about loss of control and increase user trust.

Professional responsibility: The logistic regression model was statistically significant, for Professional responsibility with $\chi2(7)$ =9.303, significance value (.000) which is less than .05. The model explained 63.9% (Nagelkerke R2) of the variance in AI privacy and correctly classified 85.7% of cases. Participants who were male, spent more time of AI powered apps, had high interest in S&T, high awareness of AI and ethics were more likely to be concerned about Professional responsibility of the apps with likelihood ratio 0.719, 16.284, 0.981, 2.313, and 4.312 respectively. Thus app developers need to provide simplified data policies which align with ethical standards can enhance user confidence and foster positive relationships with the app.

Promotion of human value: The logistic regression model was statistically significant, for Promotion of human value with $\chi2(7)$ =2.934, significance value (.000) which is less than .05. The model explained 69.0% (Nagelkerke R2) of the variance in Promotion of human value and correctly classified 57.9% of cases. Participants who spent more time on AI powered apps, had high interest in S&T and high awareness of ethics were more likely to be concerned about Promotion of human value with likelihood ratio 0.656, 2.596and 2.596 respectively. This means that the app developers should focus on the human centric purpose of the app. Efforts needs to be focused on providing a sustainable business models for the app benefiting the society.

9.5 Results and Recommendations

This study holds significant value beyond academic research by providing actionable insights for developers, policymakers, and stakeholders within the AI landscape. As users become more aware of privacy and ethical concerns, trust in AI systems plays a pivotal role in their adoption and long-term viability. The findings highlight the critical need for AI-powered mobile apps to adopt transparent, simple, accountable design principles. Furthermore simplifying the ethical guidelines and confirming to some set standards either of the industry or country can bring trust in the users. By addressing ethical issues and building trust, developers can not only improve user satisfaction but also contribute to a future where AI technology is ethically responsible. For policymakers, the results offer valuable guidance on creation of standardized AI ethical guidelines which can be followed across the industry.

9.6 Limitations and Future Scope

The study was limited to the AI powered apps being used in India. The sample size was small. To ensure more generality of the results, future studies can focus on comparative analysis of different types of apps and their ethical inclination. To dwell into better understanding, comparative analysis of top ranked apps on Apple store and Google play store can also be done.

9.7 Conclusion

The study assessed AI-powered apps across ethical dimensions, revealing unique strengths. ChatGPT excelled in privacy and transparency, TATA 1mg in accountability, safety, fairness, and non-discrimination, while Canva led in human oversight, professional responsibility, and ethical alignment. These insights emphasize the need for customized AI ethics policies. To enhance ethical awareness, developers should introduce clear privacy policies, interactive settings, and accountability mechanisms. Encouraging AI ethics education in schools through industry partnerships can promote responsible use. Addressing ethical concerns with transparent policies, bias-mitigation techniques, and user control features can strengthen public trust. Future research should explore diverse user groups and track evolving AI ethics perceptions over time.

AI disclosure statement: The author acknowledges the use of AI-based tools for minor language editing or grammatical correction. However, all intellectual contributions, analyses, and conclusions presented in this chapter are entirely the author's own.

References

1. Bharti, U., Bajaj, D., Batra, H., Lalit, S., Lalit, S., Gangwani, A., Medbot: Conversational artificial intelligence powered chatbot for delivering tele-health after COVID-19, in: *2020 5th International Conference on Communication and Electronics Systems (ICCES)*, pp. 870–875, 2020.
2. Bohr, A. and Memarzadeh, K., The rise of artificial intelligence in healthcare applications, in: *Artificial Intelligence in Healthcare*, pp. 25–60, Academic Press, 2020.
3. Minghai, Y., Wenqing, L., Khan, W.A., Kasture, A., Riasat, S., Supercharge your productivity with artificial intelligent: Unlocking the potential of intelligent applications. *Bincang Sains Teknol.*, 2, 02, 72–81, 2023.
4. Xia, Y., Liu, Z., Wang, S. *et al.* Unlocking the Impact of User Experience on AI-Powered Mobile Advertising Engagement. *J. Knowl. Econ,*. 16, 4818–4854, 2025. https://doi.org/10.1007/s13132-024-02153-y.
5. Chauhan, C. and Gullapalli, R.R., Ethics of AI in pathology: Current paradigms and emerging issues, in: *Artificial Intelligence in Pathology*, pp. 159–180, 2025.
6. Habbal, A., Ali, M.K., Abuzaraida, M.A., Artificial Intelligence Trust, risk and security management (AI trism): Frameworks, applications, challenges and future research directions. *Expert Syst. Appl.*, 240, 122442, 2024.
7. Jang, Y., Choi, S., Kim, H., Development and validation of an instrument to measure undergraduate students' attitudes toward the ethics of artificial intelligence (AT-EAI) and analysis of its difference by gender and experience of AI education. *Educ. Inf. Technol.*, 27, 8, 11635–11667, 2022.
8. Mikalef, P., Conboy, K., Lundström, J.E., Popovič, A., Thinking responsibly about responsible AI and 'the dark side' of AI. *Eur. J. Inf. Syst.*, 31, 3, 257–268, 2022.
9. Mökander, J., Auditing of AI: Legal, ethical and technical approaches. *Digit. Soc.*, 2, 3, 49, 2023.
10. Fjeld, J., Achten, N., Hilligoss, H., Nagy, A., Srikumar, M., Principled artificial intelligence: Mapping consensus in ethical and rights-based approaches to principles for AI, Berkman Klein Center Research Publication, no. 2020-1, 2020.

11. Williamson, S.M. and Prybutok, V., Balancing privacy and progress: A review of privacy challenges, systemic oversight, and patient perceptions in AI-driven healthcare. *Appl. Sci.*, 14, 2, 675, 2024.
12. Li, Z., Lee, G., Raghu, T. S., Shi, Z. (2025). Impact of the General Data Protection Regulation on the global mobile app market: Digital trade implications of data protection and privacy regulations. *Inf. Syst. Res.*, 36, 2, 669–689, 2024.
13. Singhal, A., Neveditsin, N., Tanveer, H., Mago, V., Toward fairness, accountability, transparency, and ethics in AI for social media and health care: Scoping review. *JMIR Med. Inf.*, 12, 1, e50048, 2024.
14. Li, Y., Chen, F., Li, T.J.-J., Guo, Y., Huang, G., Fredrikson, M., Agarwal, Y., Hong, J.I., Privacystreams: Enabling transparency in personal data processing for mobile apps. *Proc. ACM Interact. Mob. Wearable Ubiquitous Technol.*, 1, 3, 1–26, 2017.
15. Nasab, A.R., Dashti, M., Shahin, M., Zahedi, M., Khalajzadeh, H., Arora, C., Liang, P., Fairness concerns in app reviews: A study on AI-based mobile apps. *ACM Trans. Softw. Eng. Methodol.*, 34, 2, 1–30, 2024.
16. Galetsi, P., Katsaliaki, K., Kumar, S., Exploring benefits and ethical challenges in the rise of mHealth (mobile healthcare) technology for the common good: An analysis of mobile applications for health specialists. *Technovation*, 121, 102598, 2023.
17. Friedman, B. and Kahn Jr., P.H., Human values, ethics, and design, in: *The Human-Computer Interaction Handbook*, pp. 1267–1292, CRC Press, 2007.
18. Germann, P.J., Development of the attitude toward science in school assessment and its use to investigate the relationship between science achievement and attitude toward science in school. *J. Res. Sci. Teach.*, 25, 8, 689–703, 1988.
19. Ma, S. and Chen, Z., The development and validation of the Artificial Intelligence Literacy Scale for Chinese college students (AILS-CCS). *IEEE Access*, 12, 146419–146429, 2024.

Annexture I

Research Methodology Followed in the Study

PHASE I	Primary contact with the respondents who gave their consent to attend the lecture on AI ethics and their usage in mobile applications.

A gap of two weeks was provided, where support was provided to the respondents to download selected AI driven mobile application program and train them on its usage.	
PHASE II	A structured questionnaire was delivered to the respondents containing items regarding ethical aspects of AI mobile applications.

Data was collected from the respondents and analyses using various statistical tools and methods.

Annexture II

Ethic theme	ChatGPT	TATA 1mg online	Groww stocks, mutual funds, IPO	Myntra	Photo and video editor-canva
Privacy	App collects some data and shares it with other parties.	No data is shared with third parties.	App shares personal information with third party. Collects precise location.	App collects some data and shares it with other parties.	No data is shared with third parties.
Accountability	Data is encrypted in transit.	Data is encrypted in transit.	Data is encrypted in transit.	Data is encrypted in transit.	Data is encrypted in transit.
Safety and Security	Data encrypted is provided. Data can be deleted on demand.	Account and data can be deleted.	Provision of account deletion is available.	Monetary transactions happen according to NPCI. This practice is only available in India.	Account and data can be deleted.
Transparency and Explainability	Declares the types of data collected.	Declares the types of data collected.	Declares the types of data collected.	Declares the types of data collected.	Declares the types of data collected.

(*Continued*)

(*Continued*)

Ethic theme	ChatGPT	TATA 1mg online	Groww stocks, mutual funds, IPO	Myntra	Photo and video editor-canva
Fairness and Non-discrimination	Open for all.	Data practices vary according to app version, use, region , age etc.	Data practices vary according to app version, use, region , age etc.	Data practices vary according to app version, use, region , age etc.	Data practices vary according to app version, use, region , age etc.
Human control of technology	Data can be deleted on request without deleting the account.	Account and associated data can be deleted on request.	Account and associated data can be deleted on request.	Developers can provide a way to remove data collected by the app.	You can submit request to the developer to delete certain data without deleting the account.
Professional Responsibility	Developers provide a way to manage the data.	Developers provide a way to manage the data.	Developers provide a way to manage the data.	Developers provide a way to manage the data.	Developers provide a way to manage the data.
Promotion of Human Values	Positive and non-harmful communication is maintained.	Provides health related information.	Promotes information related to finance.	No information available. The beta version of new features is currently running.	No information.

Annexture III

Questionnaire

Artificial Intelligence (AI): Artificial intelligence (AI) is the capacity of a machine to comprehend and pick up knowledge from experiences, making judgments and forecasts based on facts without being explicitly programmed. It can accomplish tasks like recognizing images, processing language, and making decisions because it replicates the cognitive functions of the human brain. It has the power to completely alter how we work, live, and engage with technology.

Personal details

1. Age(Years): Below 18/19-25/26-35/36-55/56-70/Above 70
2. Gender*: Male/Female/Prefer not to say
3. Time spent on the smartphone, interaction with AI apps

Items	**SD**	**D**	**N**	**A**	**SA**
Science is fun.					
I do not like science and it bothers me to have to study it.					
During science class, I usually am interested.					
I would like to learn more about science.					
If I knew I would never go to science class again, I would feel sad.					
Science is interesting to me and I enjoy it.					
Science makes me feel uncomfortable, restless, irritable, and impatient.					
Science is fascinating and fun.					
The feeling that I have towards science is a good feeling.					
When I hear the word science, I have a feeling of dislike.					
Science is a topic which I enjoy studying.					
I feel at ease with science and I like it very much.					
I feel a definite positive reaction to science.					
Science is boring.					

(*Continued*)

(*Continued*)

Items	SD	D	N	A	SA
Awareness Regarding AI					
I understand the definition of artificial intelligence.					
I am familiar with some underlying principles of artificial intelligence (e.g., linear models, decision trees, machine learning).					
I understand how artificial intelligence perceives the world (e.g., seeing, hearing) to perform various tasks.					
I can compare different concepts related to artificial intelligence (e.g., the difference between deep learning and machine learning).					
Awareness Regarding Ethics					
I always adhere to ethical principles when using artificial intelligence applications or products.					
I am always vigilant about privacy and information security issues when using artificial intelligence applications or products.					
I can critically reflect on the impact of artificial intelligence on individuals and society.					
I am always alert to the misuse of artificial intelligence technology.					
AI usage					
I am proficient in using artificial intelligence applications or products.					
I can use artificial intelligence applications or products to help me solve problems in daily life.					
I can use artificial intelligence applications or products to assist my learning.					

Attitudes toward the ethics of artificial intelligence (AT-EAI)
The purpose of this questionnaire is to investigate respondents' attitudes toward AI ethics. Each item is followed by five digits (1, 2, 3, 4, 5), and

we would like you to write on the digit that most accurately represents your opinion. 1 means "I strongly disagree with this statement."; 2 means "I disagree with this statement."; 3 means "I neither agree nor disagree with this statement."; 4 means "I agree with this statement." 5 means "I strongly agree with this statement."

There are no correct or incorrect responses for these items. The collected data will be kept strictly confidential and will be used solely for research purposes.
Thank you for your participation.

S. no.	Question	ChatGPT	TATA 1mg online	Grown stocks, mutual funds, IPO	Myntra	Photo and video editor-canva
1.	I feel comfortable sharing personal information with app					
2.	I trust app to keep my personal information secure and confidential					
3.	I am confident in the accuracy and reliability of app responses to my mental health concerns					
4.	The App clearly explain how it uses my data and information					

(Continued)

(*Continued*)

S. no.	Question	ChatGPT	TATA 1mg online	Grown stocks, mutual funds, IPO	Myntra	Photo and video editor-canva
5.	I believe that app treats all users fairly and without discrimination					
6.	I feel in control of the conversations I have with app					
7.	I think that app is a responsible tool for addressing mental health concerns					
8.	I believe that app promotes values that are important for mental health and wellbeing					

10

AI-Powered Advancements in Autonomous Vehicle Technologies

Sachi Choudhary[1*] **and Prashant Shukla**[2]

[1]*Data Science Cluster, School of Computer Science, UPES, Dehradun, India*
[2]*Mechanical Cluster, School of Advanced Engineering, UPES, Dehradun, India*

Abstract

Artificial intelligence (AI) is involved in such much development concerning the Autonomous Vehicles (AVs). AVs were simple systems but turned into complex ones capable of navigating through demanding terrains with hardly any support from humans due to AI-based technologies. Decisions for AI-driven autonomies are taken based on a variety of technologies like machine and deep learning, computer vision (CV), and sensor fusion. These technologies that vary among each other, nevertheless, enable interpreting sensor data, understanding their environment and ensuring decision making that facilitates the safety of their timing in an efficient and easy manner. And the improving sales of vehicles are just an addition to AI adaptation that keeps learning, transforming, and performing control over various dynamic and real-time environments. Several challenges are to be solved as it witnesses acknowledgement of public acceptance, safety, ethics, and regulation challenges. The objective of this chapter is to present the involvement of AI technologies in the automation of autonomous vehicles with their basic functions of work, application, and acceptance barriers, identifying those problems, and constraints that need further attention to support the growth of this sector.

Keywords: Artificial intelligence, autonomous vehicles, machine learning, advanced driver-assistance systems (ADAS), computer vision, deep learning

**Corresponding author*: sachi.choudhary1617@gmail.com

Manish Kumar, Nitigya Sambyal, Leena Priyadarshini Singh, Ramasamy V. and S. Balamurugan (eds.) Responsible AI: Principles and Practices, (221–246) © 2026 Scrivener Publishing LLC

10.1 Introduction

An autonomous vehicle, or self-driving vehicle, operates without human intervention. They rely on sophisticated hardware and software. Their main sensors such as high-resolution cameras, ultrasonic sensors, LIDAR, RADAR, and glean data from the environment in real time. The processed data may employ algorithms of computer vision and machine learning. These technologies aid in object identification, road condition analysis, and object movement prediction. By combining information from several sensors, sensor fusion techniques produce a comprehensive three-dimensional map of the environment, giving the car precise situational awareness to make decisions. In these vehicles, decision-making is controlled by reinforcement learning models that learn from prior experiences and adapt to dynamic road conditions continuously while optimizing actions such as acceleration, braking, and steering. As mentioned earlier, there exist six levels of automation that an AV can be further divided into. These ranges are according to SAE from Level 0 through to Level 5 [1, 2] (refer to Table 10.1).

These systems also involve the use of AI-based control methods, such as path planning, which creates a trajectory that avoids obstacles by obeying traffic rules while maintaining passenger comfort. Predictive algorithms monitor the nearby vehicles and pedestrians, thereby making the system take proactive steps in avoiding collisions.

Table 10.1 Levels of automation in autonomous vehicles by SAE.

<table>
<tr><th>Levels</th><th>Meaning</th></tr>
<tr><td>Level 0</td><td>No automation</td></tr>
<tr><td>Level 1</td><td rowspan="3">Increasing degrees of driver assistance and partial automation where a human driver must be available to take control when required.</td></tr>
<tr><td>Level 2</td></tr>
<tr><td>Level 3</td></tr>
<tr><td>Level 4</td><td>High value of automation</td></tr>
<tr><td>Level 5</td><td>Full automation</td></tr>
</table>

10.1.1 Evolution of AI Technology in the Automotive Industry

In the last few decades, several researchers, research organizations, and technology businesses have made significant contributions to the evolution of vehicle technologies [3–5] and AI in AVs. It all began in the 1980s with pioneers like Ernst Dickmanns [6–8] and his team at the Bundeswehr University Munich who laid the foundation with early vision-based driving systems. In the United States, the DARPA-funded ALV (Autonomous Land Vehicle) program was another early effort that utilized AI for road-following and obstacle detection, involving leading institutions like Carnegie Mellon University (CMU) and the University of Maryland.

With the advancement in ML techniques in the 1990s, CMU's Navlab [9] project achieved a cross-country journey using AI algorithms to steer the vehicle autonomously. Researchers like Dean Pomerleau introduced neural networks to driving control, which became the pioneer in modern DL methods. This era of advancement and innovation in AV technologies plays a critical role in integrating AI and its algorithms.

The DARPA Challenges in 2004 marked a significant turning point in the history of autonomous vehicles. Numerous studies on artificial intelligence for self-driving cars were spurred by these competitions. Teams from various universities, including Stanford and CMU, demonstrated how AI could navigate difficult situations. These incidents accelerated the adoption of technologies such as sensor fusion and simultaneous localization and mapping (SLAM) that enhanced the capabilities of self-driving cars. AI for AVs advanced significantly in the 2010s thanks in large part to the development of deep learning (DL). These AI based methods were used by Google and Tesla to improve their cars' performance for object detection, pattern recognition, and prediction of traffic condition on real time. The introduction of platforms like NVIDIA's DRIVE PX further boosted the processing power needed for real-time data handling in autonomous systems.

In recent years, research groups like Berkeley DeepDrive [10] and MIT's CSAIL have focused on improving AI-driven predictive models and addressing the safety challenges of self-driving technology. AI research has been bolstered by Waymo's Open Dataset and Baidu's Apollo project, making autonomous driving technology more accessible to universities and industries. AI is driving AV breakthroughs in quantum machine learning, edge computing, and vehicle-to-everything (V2X) connectivity to increase autonomy.

Researchers, technology pioneers, and industry collaborations have advanced AI in autonomous car technologies. Stanford, CMU, MIT, and premier AI startups have advanced vision, navigation, and control, making autonomous mobility safer and smarter. AI advances are paving the way for completely AVs that will transform transport and urban mobility.

10.2 Core AI Technologies for AVs

AI has fundamentally transformed the automotive industry [11] beginning with its early applications in manufacturing where AI-driven robotics enhanced production efficiency. The introduction of the ADAS [12] improved safety and comfort in the vehicles. Companies such as Tesla pioneered the use of AI for features such as speed control that senses traffic and lane-keeping assistance. The convergence of AI with big data analytics allowed manufacturers to gather and look over huge amounts of info from

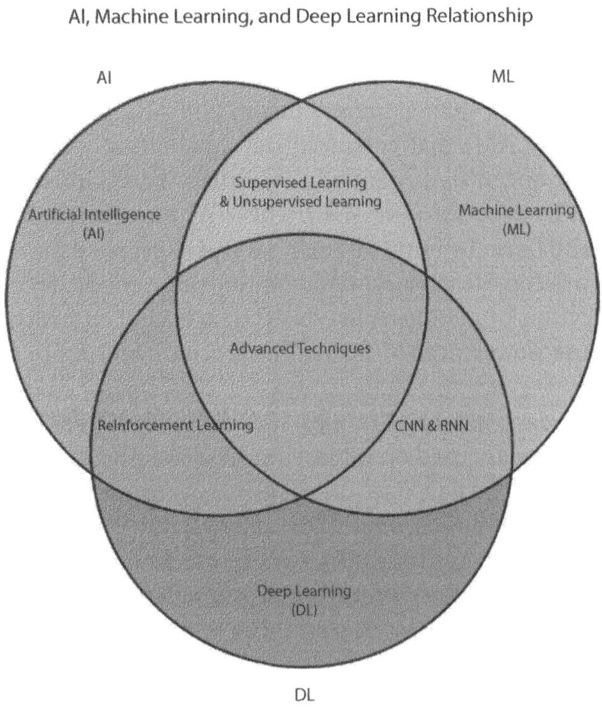

Figure 10.1 A Venn diagram: AI, ML, and DL relationship.

Table 10.2 Core AI technologies and autonomous vehicles.

AI technology	Description	Applications	Autonomous vehicle/ model	AI models used
Computer Vision [13]	The capacity of machines to interpret and understand graphical data.	Object detection, lane recognition, traffic sign identification.	Tesla Autopilot, Waymo	Convolutional Neural Networks (CNNs), YOLO [14]
Sensor Fusion [15]	Integration of data from various sensors to create a comprehensive view of the environment.	Combining LIDAR, RADAR, cameras, and ultrasonic sensors for enhanced perception.	Waymo, Cruise	Kalman Filters, Particle Filters
Machine Learning [16]	Enables systems to learn from data and improve over time.	Predicting driver behavior, optimizing routes.	Uber ATG, Tesla	Decision Trees, Support Vector Machines (SVM)
Deep Learning	Uses NN to model complex patterns in data.	Image recognition, speech recognition for voice commands.	Tesla, Waymo [17]	CNNs, Recurrent Neural Networks (RNNs)
Simultaneous Localization and Mapping (SLAM) [18]	Creating a map of an unknown environment while tracking the vehicle's location.	Real-time navigation and obstacle avoidance.	Mobileye, Google Self-Driving Car	Extended Kalman Filter (EKF), FastSLAM
Reinforcement Learning [19]	Learns to make decisions by receiving rewards or penalties.	Adaptive driving behaviors and optimizing safety protocols.	Waymo, Tesla	Q-Learning, Deep Q-Networks (DQN)
Natural Language Processing (NLP) [20]	Understanding and responding to human language.	Voice command systems for navigation and vehicle controls.	Tesla, Audi	Transformers, RNNs
Predictive Analytics	Identifying the likelihood of future outcomes based on historical data.	Anticipating traffic patterns, calculating arrival times.	Uber ATG, Tesla	Time Series Models, Logistic Regression
V2X Communication [21]	Communication between vehicles and infrastructure.	Enhancing traffic management, improving safety.	Audi, Ford	Graph Neural Networks, Multi-Agent Systems
Path Planning [18]	Determining the best route while avoiding obstacles and traffic laws.	Route optimization for navigation and traffic flow.	Waymo, Cruise	A*, Rapidly-exploring Random Tree (RRT)

connected vehicles that enables predictive maintenance and tailored customer experiences.

With the progress in research and development the focus shifted from enhancing driver assistance to creating fully automatic vehicles capable of handling all driving tasks without human intervention. With the businesses like Waymo and Cruise developing complex algorithms for real-time perception and decision-making the DARPA Grand Challenges showcased the potential of AI in navigation. Right now, AI is at the heart of new developments in AV by propelling the future of transportation towards more safer, efficient, and environmental friendly mobility solutions. A Venn diagram in Figure 10.1 illustrates the relationship between AI, ML, DL, and their associated techniques using overlapping circles.

Table 10.2 summarizes the core AI technologies used in AVs which includes specific models that employ these technologies and the AI models applied to achieve the desired functionalities.

10.3 Machine Learning and Deep Learning Techniques for AVs

ML and DL technological models play very crucial functions in aiding AVs to perceive their surrounding environment, interpret data and make decisions, and then navigate safely [16, 19]. A lot of data from sensors and cameras is used in these technologies to train models that can figure out what's going on in complicated road situations.

10.3.1 ML Techniques

A. Supervised Learning

The model is trained on labeled data in supervised learning [22]. This is frequently employed in AVs for jobs such as object detection and classification. Decision trees are mostly used for classification tasks like identifying whether an object is a pedestrian or an obstacle. Another technique is Support Vector Machines (SVM) which is effective for binary classification such as distinguishing between different types of vehicles or detecting lane boundaries [22].

Criteria for decision tree splitting is Gini Impurity. Equation 10.1 can be used for the same

$$Gini\ Impurity = 1 - \sum (p_i^2) \tag{10.1}$$

where p_i is the probability of the class i.

B. Unsupervised Learning

Unsupervised learning is applied for clustering and pattern recognition without labeled outputs. This can be beneficial for identifying unknown patterns in driving behavior or environmental data.

Popular unsupervised learning models are K-Means Clustering which groups similar driving patterns or identifying clusters of traffic behavior and Principal Component Analysis (PCA) that endeavors to minimize the dimensionality of the data that is collected from various sensors to identify key features [23].

Objective function of K-Means is presented in Equation 10.2

$$J = \sum_{i=1}^{k} \sum_{j=1}^{n} \left|\left|x_j - \mu_i\right|\right|^2 \tag{10.2}$$

where μ_i is the centroid of cluster i.

C. Reinforcement Learning

In AVs, reinforcement learning (RL) is employed to train agents to make decisions by trial and error by obtaining rewards or penalties based on actions. An algorithm that learns the value of an action in a specific state is Q-Learning, which is a value-based RL algorithm [24].

Q-Learning update rule is stated in Equation 10.3

$$Q(s,a) \leftarrow Q(s,a) + \alpha(r + \gamma \max Q(s',a') - Q(s,a)) \tag{10.3}$$

Where α is the learning rate, r is the reward, γ is the discount factor, and s' is the next state.

10.3.2 DL Techniques

A. Convolutional Neural Networks

CNNs are indispensable for features such as lane detection, object detection, [25], and traffic sign recognition as they are frequently employed in image processing in AVs. Convolutional layers extract spatial hierarchies of features from input images, while pooling layers reduce the dimensionality while preserving essential features. A typical CNN architecture consists of convolutional layers, activation functions, pooling layers, and fully connected layers, leading to an output layer that classifies the input.

B. Recurrent Neural Networks (RNNs)

RNNs are useful for tasks involving serial data, such as predicting future states of traffic based on historical data. The architecture typically consists of input layers, recurrent layers (such as LSTM or GRU), and output layers that predict future states or actions.

10.3.3 Combining Machine and Deep Learning for Autonomous Vehicle Features

While machine learning (ML) uses support vector machines (SVMs) to classify the found objects, deep learning (DL) shall perform the following: convolutional networks (CNNs) will assist in image recognition. Route planning will occur through supervised learning, while reinforcement learning works in bettering the way vehicles drive. Routing will be made more effective when traffic data is gathered by machine learning models creating conjunctions with A* for better improved route selection.

10.4 Computer Vision and Image Processing in AVs

Computer vision and image processing are the two foremost technologies powering autonomous vehicle (AV) technology. With the visual data obtained through the vehicle's sensors and cameras, these systems will empower the vehicle to interpret its surroundings. The algorithms employed would allow any AV to identify objects, analyze road conditions, and make driving decisions with surrounding information.

10.4.1 CV Techniques

A. Image Acquisition

Various sensors, cameras (including single, dual, or 360-degree cameras), and LIDAR systems capture images or video as a building block of computer vision. Data will be subjected to analysis afterward. A single-camera system can apply algorithms like perspective projection and depth estimation to gauge depth. In stereo vision, on the other hand, depth is determined by comparing the differences between three cameras.

B. Feature Extraction

After acquiring images, the next step involves extracting important features from the visual data. This is crucial for identifying objects and making sense of the environment. Edge Detection algorithms like Canny or

Sobel filters highlight object boundaries while corner Detection methods such as Harris or Shi-Tomasi help identify interest points in images.

Canny edge detection is given in Equation 10.4

$$Gradient = \sqrt{\left(G_x^2 + G_y^2\right)} \tag{10.4}$$

where G_x and G_y are the gradients in the x and y directions.

C. Object Detection and Recognition

Object detection involves locating and classifying objects within an image. This is essential for recognizing pedestrians, vehicles, traffic signs, and obstacles. Haar Cascades is a machine learning object detection method that uses cascade classifiers. Another technique is You Only Look Once (YOLO) [14] that employs a single convolutional network for classification and localization.

Equation 10.5 is YOLO loss function:

$$Loss = \lambda_{coord} \sum_i^{S^2} (t_i - \hat{t})^2 + \lambda_{obj} \sum_i^{S^2} (p_i - \hat{p})^2 \tag{10.5}$$

Where t_i is the predicted box coordinates, p_i is the predicted class probability, and λ are weighting factors.

D. Semantic Segmentation

Semantic segmentation classifies each pixel in an image, providing detailed information about the scene. This is crucial for understanding the vehicle's environment at a granular level. Fully Convolutional Networks (FCNs) is a NN that replace fully connected layers with convolutional layers for pixel-wise predictions. Another model is DeepLab that incorporates atrous convolution to segment objects at multiple scales.

Loss function for segmentation is given in Equation 10.6:

$$Loss = -\sum_{c=1}^{C} y_c \log(p_c) \tag{10.6}$$

where y_c is the ground truth and p_c is the predicted probability value for class c.

10.4.2 Image Processing Techniques

A. Image Enhancement

Image enhancement techniques are designed to enhance the quality of images, facilitating ease in analyzing visual data, especially under challenging conditions such as low light or adverse weather [26]. For instance, histogram equalization enhances image contrast by redistributing intensity values, whereas image filtering techniques such as median filtering or Gaussian blur effectively reduce noise to improve image clarity. Equation 10.7 is the formula for histogram equalization:

$$s_k = \sum_{j=0}^{k} \frac{n_j}{N} X(L-1) \tag{10.7}$$

Where n_j is the quantity of pixels with an intensity j, N is the total number of pixels, and L is the number of possible intensity levels.

B. Image Transformation

Image transformation techniques are aimed at modifying the image to prepare it for some kind of analysis or for some particular purpose, such as changing its orientation or angle. While perspective transformation modifies the viewpoint to display the image from certain angles, geometric transformations include the operations of changing the image position by shifting, rotating, or scaling.

10.4.3 Combining Computer Vision and Image Processing for AV Features

AVs utilize CV and image processing methods to receive a better response to their surroundings and make decisions. For instance, by identifying pedestrians, road signs, and drivable zones, these techniques support environmental analysis. They also stretch their wings in real-time object detection. Image processing improves or enhances camera images for a more accurate delineation of edges and lane markings. CV can also assist very well with the monitoring of traffic, such as counting vehicles or recognizing the state of traffic lights, thus assisting the vehicle in regulating its behavior accordingly.

10.5 Sensor Fusion and Environmental Perception in AVs

AVs must be able to interpret their environments in order to achieve optimal environmental perception and sensor fusion. Integrating data from varying sensors forms a comprehensive picture of the surroundings, thereby improving decision-making and safety in AVs.

10.5.1 Sensor Fusion Techniques

It integrates data from various sensors to enhance the accuracy of perception systems. Through auxiliary data from different sources, AVs can achieve full awareness of the surrounding environment.

A. Sensor types that are most frequently found in AVs include:

- LIDAR, which uses laser pulses to measure distances to formulate crystal-clear, three-dimensional maps of the surroundings.
- Radar uses radio waves to determine the distances and speed of objects and operates properly in varying weather conditions.
- For tasks like object recognition, lane detection, and traffic sign identification, cameras are essential for capturing visual data.
- Short-range detection is accomplished by ultrasonic sensors, which are frequently used in obstacle detection and parking assistance.

B. Fusion Techniques

- **Kalman filter:** A mathematical algorithm that combines noisy sensor data to produce estimates of unknown variables. It is widely used for tracking the position and velocity of moving objects. Equation 10.8 can be used for Kalman filter

$$x_k = Ax_{k-1} + Bu_k + w_k \tag{10.8}$$

where x_k is the state vector, A is the state transition model, B is the control input model, u_k is the control vector, and w_k is the process noise.

- **Particle filter:** A non-parametric approach to estimating the state of a system by representing the probability distribution of the state with a set of particles. It is useful in highly dynamic environments.
- **Bayesian fusion:** A probabilistic approach that combines measurements from different sources using Bayes' theorem, updating the belief about the state based on new evidence.
- **Multi-sensor fusion:** Integrating data from various sensors (e.g., LIDAR, cameras, and radar) to create a unified representation of the environment.

10.5.2 Environmental Perception

The capacity of an autonomous vehicle to perceive its surroundings is referred to as environmental perception to interpret the fused data from sensors to understand its surroundings. This includes identifying objects, recognizing road conditions, and detecting obstacles.

A. Key Tasks in Environmental Perception

Object detection and classification identifies and classify objects within the environment, such as vehicles, pedestrians, and cyclists. CNNs can be used for image processing tasks, enabling the detection and classification of objects from camera images [27]. There is another technique LIDAR object detection which employ clustering algorithms to identify objects in LIDAR point clouds.

Lane detection identifies lane markings on the road to ensure the vehicle stays within its lane. Hough transform is a feature extraction technique used to detect lines and curves in images, ideal for lane detection.

B. Challenges in Environmental Perception

- The car must react to a variety of situations, including shifting pedestrians, shifting environmental conditions, and fluctuating traffic.
- Even with some degenerative features taken into account, every sensor does accomplish some work at the same time. While cameras are poor in low light, LIDAR does not perform well in torrential rain.
- To make quick decisions by AVs, sensor data needs to be processed quickly and this requires a high computing level with efficient algorithms.

10.5.3 Combining Sensor Fusion with Environmental Perception

The fusion of environmental perception data from various sensors empowers decision-making in autonomous vehicles (AVs) and enhances their perception of the surroundings. The automated driving system detects obstacles and computes appropriate paths around them by exploiting sensor information from LIDAR, radar, and cameras. The ability of vehicles to perceive their environments adds the capability of modifying navigation in real-time by analyzing traffic flows and potential hazards.

10.6 Object Detection and Classification in Autonomous Vehicles (AVs)

The level of vision used for self-driving autos usually varies from detection and classification of objects. By identifying objects such as humans and other vehicles, these processes assist the vehicle in comprehending its surroundings traffic signals, and obstacles. Object detection is critical because of its close implications on how the car will react to other objects. These include updated aspects in autonomous driving:

- The recognition of other cars, cyclists, and pedestrians helps prevent accidents and guarantees safe descent in demanding situations.
- Recognition of stops, signals, or lane markings helps route planning and adherence to traffic regulations.
- Accurate classification of objects gives the car the information needed for it to make decisions regarding stopping, slowing down, or changing lanes.

10.6.1 Techniques for Object Detection and Classification

There are several advanced techniques used for object detection and classification in AVs:

A. Traditional Methods

Haar cascades are a machine-learning tool that recognizes objects in photographs by building on a sequence of basic classifiers. Trained features are applied to a sliding window over the image, allowing for object recognition.

While still used for simple tasks, its lack of accuracy and flexibility has given way to DL techniques.
Histogram of Orientated Gradients (HOG) is the feature descriptor that tallies the number of instances of gradient orientation in specific areas of an image to ascertain the shape or structure of objects. HOG can be used in conjunction with a classifier (e.g. A. SVM) to identify objects; this technique is frequently applied to pedestrian detection.

B. Deep Learning-Based Methods
DL has revolutionized object detection and classification, especially in the context of AVs. Several popular architectures are employed in this domain are CNNs, Region-based CNN (R-CNN), and YOLO. For instance, Tesla's Autopilot system has integrated YOLO to identify a variety of roadside objects.
Single Shot MultiBox Detector (SSD) is another popular framework that detects objects in a single pass, enabling real-time performance. It generates feature maps of varying proportions to identify objects at different scales by employing a sequence of convolutional layers.
Mask R-CNN is an expansion of Faster R-CNN, this architecture provides instance segmentation, which classifies and localizes objects at the pixel level. This capability is useful for more complex environments where precise boundaries of objects need to be identified, such as distinguishing between pedestrians and vehicles in a crowded scene.

10.6.2 Real-World Applications and Examples

i. **Tesla autopilot** [28]: Tesla's Autopilot feature employs a combination of ultrasonic sensors, radar, and cameras. The object detection system identifies vehicles, pedestrians, and obstacles using DL models like YOLO and CNNs to enable safe lane changes and adaptive cruise control.
ii. **Waymo's Self-Driving Cars** [29]: Waymo employs a comprehensive perception system that integrates LIDAR and cameras to detect and classify various objects on the road. Using advanced neural networks their system is capable of recognizing pedestrians, cyclists, and other vehicles, thereby guaranteeing the vehicle responds appropriately to its environment.
iii. **Mobileye** [30]: This company specializes in CV for ADAS and AVs. Their technology uses a combination of machine

learning and CV techniques to detect road signs, lanes, and obstacles in real time.

10.6.3 Challenges in Object Detection and Classification

Despite the advancements in technology, several challenges remain in object detection and classification for AVs [31] adverse weather conditions, including rain, fog, or snow, can have an impact sensor performance and object detection accuracy. Detecting and classifying objects in complex urban scenarios with numerous overlapping objects poses significant challenges. Ensuring that object detection algorithms operate in real time while maintaining high accuracy requires significant computational resources.

10.7 Decision-Making and Path Planning in AVs

In order for any autonomous vehicle to move through all possible environments safely, adhering to traffic regulations and responsibilities towards its occupants, route planning and decision making are two integral parts it must tackle. In the decision-making part, tackling the problem of deciding the best course of action to take given the circumstances is one aspect; whereas route planning involves finding the most expedient route from point A to point B.

10.7.1 Path Planning Techniques

There are different path-planning algorithms in AVs, each having its own pros and cons. Some of the most popular ones are:

- *A Algorithm**
A* is a technique for searching an optimal path linking two points by computing an estimate of its cost. A* effectively identifies the shortest route, and its viability hangs in the quality of the estimation of costs. Under proper implementation, A* can find the best path. Nevertheless, it works well in smaller environments, while efficiency becomes an issue in larger environments through its slow speed for large maps.

- **Dijkstra's Algorithm**
The shortest path algorithm selects among the various routes connecting two points, choosing the least expensive one. Since this algorithm considers

every possibility before choosing the least expensive one, it may take longer than A*. However, it provides safe paths through different routes that cost non-negative values.

- **Rapidly-Exploring Random Tree (RRT)**

RRT connects two randomly selected points to explore spaces. Depending on the complexity of the environment, it doesn't guarantee to always find the shortest path. Modified varieties, such as RRT*, gradually refine in shape to approach the shortest path. Real-time navigation for the AV takes it as a prime application.

- **Probabilistic Roadmap (PRM)**

By selecting the space and randomly connecting points, PRM establishes a map for potential routes. PRM performs better in high-dimensional spaces but doesn't guarantee the optimal path. This method is commonly used in robotics, with modifications made to deal with the vehicles moving in difficult terrains.

10.7.2 Decision-Making Algorithms

In addition to path planning, decision-making algorithms are essential for evaluating the best course of action based on sensor input and environmental context. Here are some key algorithms:

A. Rule-Based Systems

Rule-based systems apply predefined rules to make decisions based on sensor data (e.g., traffic lights, stop signs). The accuracy depends on the completeness of the rules and the complexity of scenarios. They work well in structured environments but may struggle in novel or ambiguous situations. It is commonly used in early autonomous vehicle systems and basic driver-assistance features.

B. Markov Decision Processes (MDP)

MDP is a mathematical framework that is used to represent decision-making scenarios in which the decision-maker has partial control over the outcome and some degree of randomness. It offers a method for identifying the most effective policies by considering rewards and states. MDPs provide strong theoretical guarantees on optimality but require accurate state and transition models, which may be challenging in dynamic environments. MDPs are used in more sophisticated autonomous driving systems, especially in complex decision-making scenarios.

C. Reinforcement Learning

n RL, an agent learns from the rewards it obtains for its activities in a given environment how to make wise decisions by trying things out. Though its performance mostly depends on the realism of the environment simulations and the quality of the training data, RL can reach amazing accuracy in challenging circumstances. Researchers have shown that algorithms like Q-learning and Deep Q-Networks (DQN) work well for tasks like autonomous driving. Companies like Waymo and Tesla have explored RL to help their vehicles make quick, adaptive decisions to navigate all sorts of different surroundings.

10.7.3 Real-World Examples and Accuracy Metrics

Let's examine closely how leading autonomous vehicle (AV) startups including Waymo, Tesla, and Cruise are breaking the code on path planning and decision-making to speed over crowded metropolitan streets in India and beyond. These firms are tackling the wild urban jungle with confidence by sharpening their automobiles using super-smart algorithms and loads of data, therefore enabling their safety and performance.

i. Waymo's Use Case

Waymo's self-driving tech is like a pro at finding its way around. For planning routes, they mix Dijkstra's algorithm—think of it as a super-smart GPS—with something called Rapidly-exploring Random Trees (RRT), which is great for handling tricky, unpredictable roads. Waymo use RL for decision-making, enabling their vehicles to learn from each journey and enhance their adaptability to novel circumstances. This configuration has been highly effective and have accumulated over 20 million miles in autonomous mode which demonstrate their exceptional reliability and accuracy, even amidst real-world unpredictability.

ii. Methodology Used by Tesla

They use the A* algorithm [28] for optimal path planning, rule-based systems, and deep reinforcement learning to make decisions. The vast amount of real-world driving data that Tesla collects makes it easier to improve their system. As a result, cars with Tesla's Autopilot have fewer crashes that shows their method successfully improves safety in challenging driving situations.

iii. Cruise's Methodical Approach

Cruise has an effective plan which utilizes Markov Decision Processes (MDPs) and rule-based systems for path planning and decision-making.

By mixing probabilistic models with clear rules, Cruise ensures their autonomous systems are both dependable and flexible, making them a strong contender in the urban driving scene.

By checking out how Waymo, Tesla, and Cruise handle path planning and decision-making, you can see they're pushing the limits of what self-driving cars can do. Their clever algorithms and data-driven tricks are setting the stage for safer, smoother rides in India's bustling cities.

10.7.4 Barriers in Decision-Making and Path Planning

AVs are still having a hard time making decisions and planning their routes on their own. One of these problems is that things change quickly, like when people or other cars pass, which makes it harder to make choices. Another problem is that these systems need to work in real time, which means they need strong algorithms to handle the complicated rules of city driving. The points as shown in Figure 10.2 and described below highlight the main difficulties AVs experience in decision-making and path planning:

- Unpredictable urban situations such as stray animals, auto rickshaws, or pedestrians.
- Requirement for fast and accurate algorithms to process intricate data for route planning and optimization.
- Monsoons, dust, or smog sensor errors compromising obstacle and sign identification.

Figure 10.2 Challenges in decision-making and path planning for AVs.

- Complicating path planning, mixed traffic including carts, autos, and bicycles.
- Strong adherence to traffic laws under demanding traffic jams.
- Route optimization for efficiency that avoids traffic jams, closures or potholes.

10.7.5 Opportunities for Research and Development

Analyzing the development of hybrid algorithms surely will result in fresh methods of route planning and decision-making. Combining machine learning approaches with A*, RRT, and PRM algorithms can help to increase flexibility and efficiency in challenging environments. Moreover, by simplifying calculations during fluctuations, these automations increase the efficiency of present real-time optimization techniques. New breathing room for enhanced environmental awareness has been generated by improved sensors and algorithms capable of working under demanding situations such as rain or fog. Combining machine learning and artificial intelligence approaches, such reinforcement learning and predictive modeling, AVs can learn from experience to make ever-more-accurate forecasts about the behavior of other road users. Deliverable simple designs, cars that clearly express intents, and user confidence in autonomous systems all depend on human-AI interaction. As AV technology advances safety standards, ethical decision-making models, and compliance frameworks will become increasingly important. investigates scalability and possible methods AVs could improve present transportation networks to reach perfect integration. Once interoperability problems are fixed, the possible efficiency of cooperation between autonomous and conventional cars could rely on knowledge.

10.8 AI's Role in Route Optimization, Path Planning, and Obstacle Avoidance

AV performance and safety depend on artificial intelligence; dynamic path planning, obstacle avoidance, and route optimization enable AVs negotiate difficult environments.

Routes' Optimization

Using real-time inputs including traffic cameras and GPS data, artificial intelligence (AI) generates road maps and traffic condition information regarding the optimal paths for the car. The data saves time and gasoline, which lets the car change its direction based on road conditions. AI might, for instance, rapidly reroute the car in the case of an accident or traffic congestion therefore avoiding delays.

Organizing a Dynamic Path

Dynamic path planning lets the car react to any environmental change—including the emergence of new obstacles—by autonomously altering a path in real time. Constant updating of the vehicle's trajectory by artificial intelligence (AI) algorithms helps in demanding circumstances like entering or exiting highways and negotiating congested city streets. Through learning from its past, the system improves decision-making over time.

Dodging Challenges

Obstacle avoidance is therefore absolutely vital for AVs to operate as they should. AI recognizes objects—including other automobiles, bikers, and pedestrians—by means of sensor and camera inputs. Should it then perceive a possible threat, it can then veers off course, slows down, or stops. AI can also predict the paths of moving objects, allowing the car to offer trajectory corrections to maintain safety.

10.9 Challenges of AI in Autonomous Vehicles

Many problems with including artificial intelligence into autonomous cars need quick response to guarantee dependability, safety, and acceptance. Matching the capacity of artificial intelligence systems to grasp and negotiate challenging situations for safe operation presents maybe the toughest obstacle. Sensor failures or wrong object interpretations could cause accidents. Although training AI models requires more data, this is not always easy to find. This data has to cover weather, driving conditions, and unusual events like unexpected roadblocks or bad storms. Real time data processing presents even another major challenge. Although AVs make speedy decisions based on sensor input, delays in sensor data processing could cause accidents—especially in congested areas like cities. Legal responsibility for AVs is yet unresolved. Deciphering who should answer for an accident—the manufacturer, the software developer, or the driver—can be challenging. Such ambiguity could lead to legal problems. Public confidence is thus a major barrier to general acceptance. Safety, job losses, and ethical questions compromise public confidence in autonomous vehicles. Sometimes autonomous cars lead to an incredulous and uncomfortable public, particularly in cases when moral conundrums arise from catastrophes unavoidable in nature. Furthermore reported to be vulnerable to cyber-attacks, the AVs aggravate the matter. Since hackers link to several systems and since appropriate security mechanisms are still absent, they can seize control. By use of such hacks, attackers could potentially seize direct control of the vehicle or meddles with its communication systems. AVs need also be able to operate with the present road system, including signs and traffic signals. For example, obsolete or uneven infrastructure might cause problems in communication between AVs and road systems. Last but not least, they have to be able to recognize and handle the several other dubious situations they can come across: unstable human drivers, bad road conditions, changing weather. Clearly, complicated artificial intelligence is required to make these decisions if one is to prevent such situations. Such technologies are costly to create and call for tight cooperation among robotics, artificial intelligence, and automotive engineering professionals. Funding for AV testing and development as well as the building of easily available infrastructure should be raised now.

10.10 Conclusion

The conclusion of this chapter is presented in Table 10.3 outlining the activities of an autonomous vehicle, the role of AI, the different AI technologies used, and the various algorithms or techniques associated with each activity.

Table 10.3 Activities of AV and role of AI.

Activity	Role of AI	AI technologies	Algorithms/ techniques
Perception	Detects and classifies objects in real-time using sensor data.	Computer Vision, Deep Learning	CNNs, YOLO, SSD
Localization	Determines the vehicle's position within the environment.	SLAM, Sensor Fusion	Kalman Filters, Visual Odometry

(*Continued*)

Table 10.3 Activities of AV and role of AI. (*Continued*)

Activity	Role of AI	AI technologies	Algorithms/ techniques
Route optimization	Calculates the most efficient routes based on historical and real-time data.	Machine Learning, Graph Theory	A*, Dijkstra's Algorithm, Genetic Algorithms
Dynamic path planning	Plans adaptive paths that respond to real-time changes in the environment.	Reinforcement Learning, Optimization	RRT, PSO, RRT*
Decision making	Evaluates options for driving decisions considering safety and traffic rules.	Rule-based Systems, Machine Learning	Markov Decision Processes (MDP), Fuzzy Logic
Obstacle avoidance	Identifies and implements strategies to bypass potential obstacles.	Sensor Fusion, Computer Vision	A* for pathfinding, Rapidly-exploring Random Trees
Control	Manages vehicle dynamics based on planned paths and decisions made.	Control Systems	PID Controllers, Model Predictive Control (MPC)
Human interaction	Provides feedback and interacts with passengers using natural language.	Natural Language Processing (NLP)	Speech Recognition, Chatbots
Data collection and learning	Continuously collects data to improve algorithms and adapt to new scenarios.	Machine Learning	Supervised Learning, Reinforcement Learning
Communication	Shares information with other vehicles and infrastructure for enhanced situational awareness.	V2X Communication, Networking	Message Passing Interfaces, Dedicated Short-Range Communications (DSRC)

This table provides a structured overview of the various activities undertaken by AVs, emphasizing the role of AI, the technologies applied, and the specific algorithms or techniques used to facilitate safe and efficient navigation. The integration of these elements is crucial for the advancement of autonomous vehicle technology, enabling them to operate effectively in complex environments.

AI disclosure statement: The author acknowledges the use of AI-based tools for minor language editing or grammatical correction. However, all intellectual contributions, analyses, and conclusions presented in this chapter are entirely the author's own.

References

1. SAE J3016 automated-driving graphic. Accessed: Nov. 18, 2024. [Online]. Available: https://www.sae.org/news/2019/01/sae-updates-j3016-automated-driving-graphic.
2. SAE Levels of Driving Automation™ Refined for Clarity and International Audience. Accessed: Nov. 18, 2024. [Online]. Available: https://www.sae.org/blog/sae-j3016-update.
3. Shukla, P., Kunwer, R., Sureshchandra Bhurat, S., Design Optimization of an Automotive Fuel Tank for the Minimization of Evaporative Losses of Gasoline Due to Thermal Conduction: Experimental & Analytical Approach. *Chem. Eng. Trans.*, 71, 1393–1398, Dec. 2018, doi: 10.3303/CET1871233.
4. Shukla, P. and Choudhary, D., Experimental investigation of wear failure of sliding joint of guide pin and bracket of four wheeler disc brake assembly. *Int. J. Veh. Noise Vib.*, 18, 3/4, 186, 2022, doi: 10.1504/IJVNV.2022.128278.
5. Mhatre, A.S. and Shukla, P., A comprehensive review of energy harvesting technologies for sustainable electric vehicles. *Environ. Sci. Pollut. Res.*, 1–24, Sep. 2024, https://doi.org/10.1007/s11356-024-34865-8
6. Oral-History:Ernst Dickmanns, Engineering and Technology History Wiki. Accessed: Nov. 18, 2024. [Online]. Available: https://ethw.org/Oral-History:Ernst_Dickmanns.
7. Ernst D. Dickmanns, IEEE Xplore Author Profile. Accessed: Nov. 18, 2024. [Online]. Available: https://ieeexplore.ieee.org/author/37282196900.
8. Pellkofer, M. and Dickmanns, E.D., Behavior decision in autonomous vehicles, pp. 495–500, Oct. 2003, doi: 10.1109/IVS.2002.1187999.
9. Home - CMU AV Center. Accessed: Nov. 18, 2024. [Online]. Available: https://labs.ri.cmu.edu/av-center/.
10. Berkeley DeepDrive, We seek to merge deep learning with automotive perception and bring computer vision technology to the forefront. Accessed: Nov. 18, 2024. [Online]. Available: https://deepdrive.berkeley.edu/.

11. Rana, K., Gupta, G., Vaidya, P., Tomar, A., Kumar, N., Evolution of Autonomous Vehicle: An Artificial Intelligence Perspective, in: *Lecture Notes in Electrical Engineering*, vol. 1001 LNEE, pp. 71–81, 2023, doi: 10.1007/978-981-19-9876-8_6.
12. Li, Y. and Huang, Z., Basics and Applications of AI in ADAS and Autonomous Vehicles, in: *Advanced Driver Assistance Systems and Autonomous Vehicles: From Fundamentals to Applications*, pp. 17–48, Jan. 2022, doi: 10.1007/978-981-19-5053-7_2.
13. Dong, X. and Cappuccio, M.L., Applications of Computer Vision in Autonomous Vehicles: Methods, Challenges and Future Directions, Nov. 2023, Accessed: Nov. 18, 2024. [Online]. Available: http://arxiv.org/abs/2311.09093.
14. Redmon, J. and Farhadi, A., YOLOv3: An Incremental Improvement, Apr. 2018, Accessed: Nov. 18, 2024. [Online]. Available: http://arxiv.org/abs/1804.02767.
15. Chavez-Garcia, R.O. and Aycard, O., Multiple Sensor Fusion and Classification for Moving Object Detection and Tracking. *IEEE Trans. Intell. Transp. Syst.*, 17, 2, 525–534, Feb. 2016, doi: 10.1109/TITS.2015.2479925.
16. Swain, N.R., Kulkarni, A.J., Sonawwanay, P.D., Babu, A., Kale, J.G., Machine Learning Algorithms for Autonomous Vehicles, in: *Handbook of Formal Optimization*, pp. 1–54, 2024, doi: 10.1007/978-981-19-8851-6_58-1.
17. Waymo Safety Report, 2021.
18. Cheng, J., Zhang, L., Chen, Q., Hu, X., Cai, J., A review of visual SLAM methods for autonomous driving vehicles. *Eng. Appl. Artif. Intell.*, 114, 104992, Sep. 2022, doi: 10.1016/J.ENGAPPAI.2022.104992.
19. Grigorescu, S., Trasnea, B., Cocias, T., Macesanu, G., A survey of deep learning techniques for autonomous driving. *J. Field Robot*, 37, 3, 362–386, Apr. 2020, doi: 10.1002/ROB.21918.
20. Anjum, M. and Shahab, S., Improving Autonomous Vehicle Controls and Quality Using Natural Language Processing-Based Input Recognition Model. *Sustainability*, 15, 7, 5749, Mar. 2023, doi: 10.3390/SU15075749.
21. Rehman, M.A., Numan, M., Tahir, H., Rahman, U., Khan, M.W., Iftikhar, M.Z., A comprehensive overview of vehicle to everything (V2X) technology for sustainable EV adoption. *J. Energy Storage*, 74, 109304, Dec. 2023, doi: 10.1016/J.EST.2023.109304.
22. Harrison, M., *Machine learning pocket reference: working with structured data in Python*, O'Reilly Media, Incorporated, 2019.
23. Dutt, S., Subramanian, C., Das, A.K., Machine Learning. 1st ed., Pearson, Chennai, India, 2019.
24. Russell, S. and Peter N., Artificial Intelligence: A Modern Approach. 4th ed., Pearson, Hoboken, NJ, 2020. https://aima.cs.berkeley.edu/.
25. Choudhary, S., Sharma, R., Sharma, G., Object detection frameworks and services in computer vision, in: *Object Detection with Deep Learning Models: Principles and Applications*, pp. 23–47, Nov. 2022, doi:

10.1201/9781003206736-2/object-detection-frameworks-services-computer-vision-sachi-choudhary-rashmi-sharma-gargeya-sharma.
26. Ram, B.P. and Choudhary, S., Survey Paper on Different Approaches for Noise Level Estimation and Denoising of an Image. *Int. J. Sci. Res. (IJSR)*, 3, 4, 618–622, 2014, Accessed: Nov. 22, 2024. [Online]. Available: https://www.ijsr.net/articlerating.php?paperid=20131546.
27. Choudhary, S. and Sharma, R., Camouflaged object segmentation using saliency maps – a comparative study. *Int. J. Comput. Vis. Robot*, 13, 4, 359–377, 2023, doi: 10.1504/IJCVR.2023.131987.
28. Autopilot, Tesla. Accessed: Nov. 18, 2024. [Online]. Available: https://www.tesla.com/autopilot.
29. Self-Driving Car Technology for a Reliable Ride, Waymo Driver. Accessed: Nov. 18, 2024. [Online]. Available: https://waymo.com/waymo-driver/.
30. Mobileye, Driver Assist and Autonomous Driving Technologies. Accessed: Nov. 18, 2024. [Online]. Available: https://www.mobileye.com/.
31. Koopman, P. and Wagner, M., Challenges in Autonomous Vehicle Testing and Validation. *SAE Int. J. Transp. Saf.*, 4, 1, 15–24, Apr. 2016, doi: 10.4271/2016-01-0128.

11

Data Security and Privacy Frameworks for AI Technologies

Sangita Roy[1*] **and Nabanita Roy**[2]

[1]*Department of Computer Science and Engineering, Thapar Institute of Engineering and Technology, Punjab, India*
[2]*Department of Computer Science and Engineering, Chitkara University Institute of Engineering and Technology, Punjab, India*

Abstract
AI is changing how industries and societies operate by making things more efficient, supporting wise choices based on data, and offering new ideas to handle global problems. However, with the progress of AI, those programs using large amounts of private information can create major concerns about security and privacy. So, building and using rigorous governance guidelines is required to help deploy AI safely and responsibly. This chapter considers the main rules, organizational measures, and guidelines that help protect privacy in AI systems. The document includes information about new privacy technologies, such as differential privacy, federated learning, and homomorphic encryption, along with the NIST AI Risk Management Framework and ISO/IEC 27001 ideas. In addition, the chapter looks at guidelines like the GDPR, CCPA, and OECD AI Principles that direct how AI is used. To emphasize effective methods and problems, this chapter describes examples of Apple, Google, and Facebook. The findings prove that it is necessary to address privacy by design, perform threat modeling, and maintain transparency through AI systems. Finally, the paper points out that to ensure AI is safe and fair, privacy and security systems must adapt to AI, and people should join forces to accomplish this.

***Keywords*:** Artificial intelligence (AI) governance, Privacy-by-Design, personally identifiable information (PII), data security and compliance, ethical AI deployment

**Corresponding author*: sangita.roy@thapar.edu

Manish Kumar, Nitigya Sambyal, Leena Priyadarshini Singh, Ramasamy V. and S. Balamurugan (eds.) Responsible AI: Principles and Practices, (247–268) © 2026 Scrivener Publishing LLC

11.1 Introduction

More and more sectors, such as healthcare, finance, transportation, and public administration, use Artificial Intelligence (AI) technologies. They require lots of data since they collect, handle, and review vast amounts to assist with forecasting and automating tasks. It is important to note that PII—such as biometrics, health records, financial records, and details on behavior—frequently appear in these datasets, which can create major worries about privacy and security [9]. The rise in AI is linked to increased unauthorized data usage and breaches that have discovered vulnerabilities in AI infrastructure. For instance, accidents involving major companies and public offices have exposed users' confidential information, hurting public confidence and encouraging new controls. In addition, figuring out how algorithms decide things, mainly in advanced machine learning, creates more difficulties. When people cannot understand the logic behind AI, there is a risk that biased practices will continue, bias in society will become stronger, and holding responsible parties accountable will be more challenging. Because of these problems, AI systems should only be developed and used if reliable data governance exists. A primary strategy is to

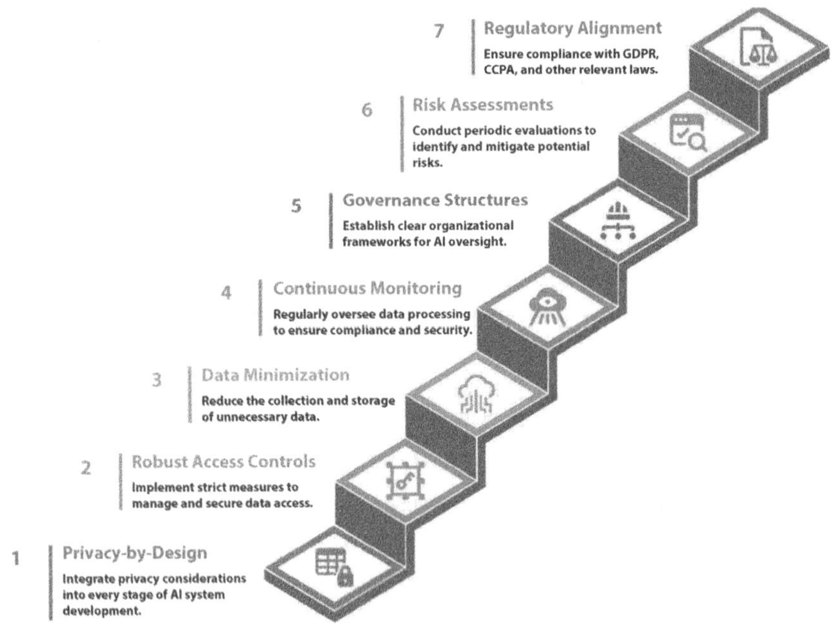

Figure 11.1 Key steps to AI data privacy and governance.

make privacy-by-design principles part of every part of developing the system. In addition, policies that require strong security, limit data usage, and monitor activities all the time keep data processing within the limits of privacy laws and ethical rules. Organizations must also implement proper governance, carry out scheduled risk reviews, and match their actions to incoming regulations such as the General Data Protection Regulation (GDPR), the California Consumer Privacy Act (CCPA), and AI laws. Putting security and privacy features into the base of AI systems allows developers and policymakers to earn users' trust, maintain compliance with laws, and support ethical advancements in AI. Figure 11.1 depicts step-by-step guide for organizations developing or deploying AI systems to ensure they are privacy-preserving, secure, and legally compliant. It supports ethical AI deployment by embedding governance and privacy controls into every stage of the AI lifecycle.

11.2 Foundations of Data Security and Privacy in AI

Using AI across important systems and decisions has shown that strong data protection is now necessary. These topics focus on data security and privacy, as the two ideas help govern information in different areas of AI systems [1].

The main goal of data security is to put both technical and process-based security methods in place to stop unauthorized persons from accessing, revealing, changing, or destroying data. It looks at how information systems can handle both internal and external risks. Otherwise, data privacy involves what individuals can do with their data, such as control its collection, usage, sharing, and storage. Privacy frameworks focus on following laws and ethical values and ensuring data users are aware and agree to what happens with their information. All of these basic principles support the ethical use of AI, which helps make sure the benefits of AI do not negatively affect anyone's rights or trust.

11.2.1 Security Goals: The CIA Triad

Every secure information system depends on the CIA Triad, which outlines the three main security objectives [2].

- **Confidentiality**: Confidentiality: It stops information from being seen by anyone else without official permission to see it. Sensitive information is protected against wrongful

information by relying on features like encryption, solid authorization strategies, and role-based restriction access.
- **Integrity**: Integrity ensures that data is always accurate and the same throughout its history. It ensures that data is not changed by anyone who is not authorized and that any identifying ID is legible. Digital signatures, cryptographic hash functions, and tamper-evident records are widespread in ensuring that information is kept safe.
- **Availability**: Authorized users can rely on getting information and resources at the right time and as required through availability. Such systems are essential for applications that need fast results and depend on responsiveness. Strategies used to make services available include redundancy, strong system design, and prevention of denial-of-service (DoS) attacks.

All in all, depending on these three pillars will make AI systems' data secure.

11.2.2 Privacy Goals

In parallel with the technical imperatives of data security, AI systems must also adhere to **privacy-centric goals** that prioritize ethical data stewardship and respect for individual rights [3]. The following principles form the foundation of privacy-oriented AI design:

- **Transparency**: Being transparent means that individuals are made aware of what data is being collected, how it is dealt with, why it is processed, and to whom it might be shared. Constructing an open company builds trust among users and helps them decide properly.
- **Control**: The term control in this area means that individuals can manage and decide what happens with their data. People have a right to access, correct, delete, or limit the use of their data. You need to be able to control your data sharing at any time to maintain privacy.
- **Accountability**: Accountability requires that data controllers and processors take responsibility for ensuring compliance with relevant privacy laws and ethical standards. This entails conducting data protection impact assessments,

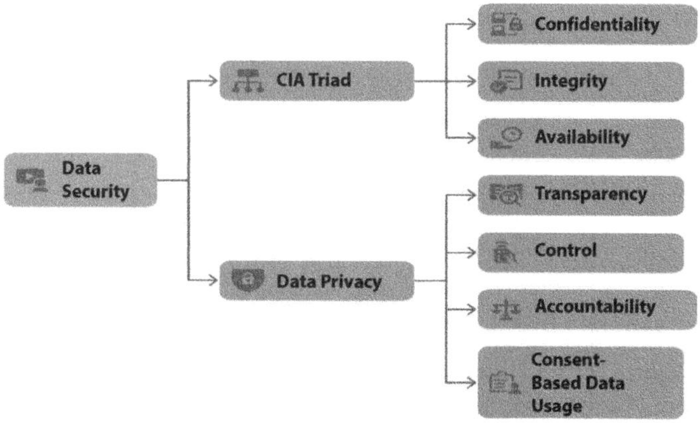

Figure 11.2 Data Security and Privacy in AI.

maintaining processing records, and being subject to oversight and enforcement by regulatory authorities.
- **Consent-Based Data Usage**: To use data, permission must be explicit, informed, free, and can be taken back at any moment. Apps should consider what users like and end the data processing when they withdraw their consent.

If organizations make these privacy goals a central part of how AI systems are organized, they can comply with rules and create trustworthy and transparent AI apps. Figure 11.2 shows the overall process flow of Data Security and Privacy in AI.

11.3 Challenges in AI-Specific Privacy and Security

While Artificial Intelligence (AI) presents transformative opportunities across multiple domains, it also introduces a range of novel and complex challenges related to data privacy and security [4]. These challenges are distinct from those encountered in conventional information systems due to the scale, sensitivity, and dynamic nature of data used in AI applications. Table 11.1 outlines key challenges that hinder the secure and ethical deployment of AI technologies.

11.4 Privacy-Preserving AI Technologies

Since AI now processes and stores personal and internal company data, it is necessary to build privacy-protecting technologies into its development

Table 11.1 Key challenges in AI-specific privacy and security.

Challenge	Description	Implications	Potential solutions
Data Over-Collection	AI models often collect more data than is necessary for their functionality.	Increases privacy risks, violates data minimization principles, and expands the attack surface.	Apply data minimization practices; collect only essential features; use synthetic or anonymized data.
Inference Attacks	Trained models may inadvertently leak information about training data through membership inference or model inversion.	May reveal sensitive or confidential personal data, undermining user trust and violating data protection regulations.	Use differential privacy, reduce model overfitting, and implement secure model training methods.
Lack of Explainability	Black-box models such as deep neural networks lack transparency in their decision-making processes.	Prevents auditing and accountability, limits user trust, and hinders regulatory compliance in sensitive domains like healthcare or finance.	Employ Explainable AI (XAI) tools, maintain audit logs, and integrate interpretable model components.
Cross-Border Data Flow	AI systems frequently process data across international borders, encountering different data privacy regulations.	Complicates legal compliance, especially under regulations like GDPR, PIPL, and other national data protection laws.	Implement cross-border compliance frameworks; use data localization when required; monitor legal updates.

Characteristic	Differential Privacy	Federated Learning	Homomorphic Encryption	Secure Multi-Party Computation
Data Exposure	Statistical noise injection	Data remains local	Data stays encrypted	Inputs remain private
Key Benefit	Membership inference protection	Reduces privacy risks	End-to-end confidentiality	Enables collaborative computation
Use Cases	DP-SGD algorithms	Healthcare, IoT systems	Encrypted medical data analysis	Collaborative model training
Techniques	Statistical noise injection	Secure aggregation	Partially homomorphic schemes	Secret sharing

Figure 11.3 Privacy-preserving AI technologies comparison.

and deployment. Data is often encrypted when stored or sent, but this is not enough to handle the privacy risks of deploying modern AI models [5]. Because of this, many new privacy-enhancing technologies have appeared, all providing unique ways to control risks and keep the data valuable and useful for modeling.

It explains important privacy-preserving technologies and how they influence secure AI design. Figure 11.3 shows a comparative studies of Privacy-preserving AI technologies.

11.4.1 Differential Privacy

Differential privacy uses strict mathematical rules to protect each person's data when doing statistics or using AI systems. That is, the inclusion or exclusion of one individual's data should not affect the results of any analysis so that the identity of that person is neither revealed nor hidden. Depending on the approach, small, unpredictable changes are introduced into the system either on the input or output side. Privacy for this type of learning is set by a parameter epsilon (ε) that marks the boundary between privacy and usefulness of the data. Choosing a smaller epsilon means your privacy level rises, but the accuracy of your results might be reduced. Thanks to differential privacy, personal information is given strong, precise protection against membership inference and re-identification, which is why it's dependable for sensitive data usage. One important use of AI and machine learning involves differentially private stochastic gradient descent (DP-SGD) algorithms. Thanks to these algorithms, models find beneficial relationships from data without revealing details of any individual.

Further, using differential privacy, datasets developed from confidential information are now usable, but an individual's information is safeguarded from being revealed.

11.4.2 Federated Learning

Federated Learning introduces a new method for training machine learning models, where many distributed devices or organizations can team up without having to provide their exclusive data. Every participant, such as a smartphone, a medical institution, or an IoT node, can use their private information to help train a shared model on a local computer. Once a model is trained locally, the model updates are sent back to the central server for collection. The server then unites all the updates and uses them to create a collective model sent to all users for further training. None of the raw data is sent out, which means that user privacy and the risk of being exposed are minimized. Because of its strengths, this method is well-suited to healthcare, finance, and personal devices where privacy practices or rules prevent all data from being kept in one place. Further enhancing privacy in federated learning can be accomplished with secure multi-party computation, homomorphic encryption, differential privacy, and aggregation protocols. The presence of these other layers of protection means information leaks from shared model updates are difficult. As a result, federated learning gives a flexible and privacy-friendly replacement to ordinary centralized machine learning, which users increasingly demand.

11.4.3 Homomorphic Encryption

Homomorphic encryption allows computations to be performed directly on encrypted data. If decrypted, they are the same as the ones that would get working with the original data. It means that data is secure, and there is no risk that plaintext will be used during processing. This approach proves very useful when important data is handled by outside parties such as cloud AI or co-training models. While FHE is complex and computationally expensive for AI inference, new progress in partially and somewhat homomorphic encryption means it is now helpful for specific purposes. Applications involve studying encrypted medical data, building confidential financial models, and enabling privacy-safe cloud computing. Multi-party computation enables the collaborative processing of data by several parties without exposing the data we exchanged.

11.4.4 Secure Multi-Party Computation (SMPC)

SMPC allows several parties to combine their inputs to compute a function without any of the participants seeing the other's inputs. None of the participants' private data is revealed due to the computation. Today, SMPC makes it simpler for multiple organizations to train their AI models, make private forecasts, and conduct secure data analysis in healthcare and/or financial institutions. It makes it possible for groups that do not regularly share their data to do so without facing legal, business, or ethical problems. SMPC often uses secret sharing, garbled circuits, and oblivious transfer to protect data in every calculation step.

11.5 Regulatory and Legal Frameworks

With AI becoming more popular, organizations managing personal data are bound by strict data protection policies created by regulatory authorities worldwide. Such frameworks are important in AI due to the massive use of data and the effect on privacy, fairness, and accountability [6].

This section briefly introduces the General Data Protection Regulation (GDPR) from the EU, the California Consumer Privacy Act (CCPA), and India's Digital Personal Data Protection Act (DPDP), as all contain obligations for those who create and deploy AI systems.

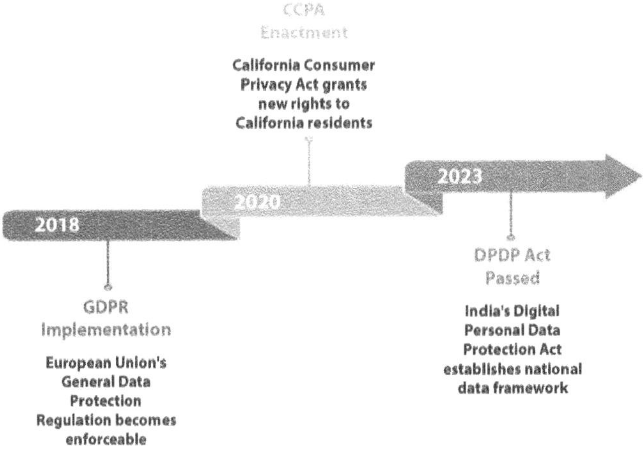

Figure 11.4 Global data protection regulation.

Being in line with these regulations generally allows lawful use of AI, particularly tasks that process personally identifying or profiling information. Figure 11.4 shows the global data protection regulation over the years.

11.5.1 General Data Protection Regulation (GDPR - European Union)

In 2018, GDPR was implemented, becoming one of the main data privacy laws worldwide. It requires collecting, using, and storing information about EU residents by organizations worldwide. Important principles of AI are:

Key principles relevant to AI systems include:

- **Right to be Forgotten:** Individuals can ask to remove their data from a business when they no longer need it, no longer agree, or the business is acting illegally. Such changes mean AI systems using historical user data for training are affected.
- **Data Minimization**: Organizations must not collect more data than is essential for their objective and challenge the common tendency in AI to pile on large, unneeded data sets and features.
- **Explicit and Informed Consent**: Users should not collect or process personal data until they receive their consent. AI systems must clarify the data they collect, how users are categorized, and the decisions they make automatically.

In addition, GDPR expects data controllers to disclose risk assessments of data processing, use privacy controls by design and by default, and include features to guarantee that automated actions are explained.

11.5.2 California Consumer Privacy Act (CCPA - United States)

From 2020, the California Consumer Privacy Act and the California Privacy Rights Act have granted California residents the right to have their personal information protected by businesses.

Important points covered by these rules relate to AI applications.

- **Right to Access, Delete, and Opt-Out**: Today, consumers have the option to access what data companies have, delete such data, and opt out if the company sells it. As a result,

AI-driven advertising and user profiling methods are also affected.
- **Enhanced Transparency Obligations**: Enterprises Have to Be Clear About What Data They Collect, How They Use It, and Who Receives It. This supports the need for AI to be easy to explain when we make decisions.
- **Non-Discrimination Clause**: Businesses are not allowed to treat users differently because they use their privacy rights, which may affect special costs or virtual outcomes that could negatively punish users.

While the CCPA does not go as far as GDPR in some ways, it does give people more control and hold companies more responsible in data-related AI situations.

11.5.3 India's Digital Personal Data Protection Act (DPDP - India)

The Indian Digital Personal Data Protection Act (DPDP – India) is India's main law managing how digital personal data is handled. The "data fiduciaries" concept is included and treated as those who need to handle data following fair and strict rules.

The most important regulations for AI developers are those listed below.

- **Purpose Limitation**: All information should be used only for the reason it was first collected. Therefore, AI systems must not allow previously used data to be put to new uses unless those uses are agreed to again.
- **Storage Restrictions:** Electronic data must be removed after the required period, so AI systems must use automated tools to save or delete it.
- **User Rights and Consent Management**: Users can see, fix, and withdraw approval for handling their personal data. AI technology should allow users to easily accept or reject changes in the collection and use of consent and to object to or appeal decisions made by the system.
- **Obligations for Significant Data Fiduciaries**: Firms that process lots of data, particularly young users or delicate topics, must meet additional control and scrutiny standards.

The DPDP Act demonstrates India's increased priority on digital independence, proper use of data, and trust-based technology, which is key for overseeing AI.

11.6 Organizational Privacy and Security Frameworks

Organizations now rely more on clear privacy and security frameworks alongside national laws and technical defenses. They provide a well-structured approach for detecting, reducing, and dealing with data security and privacy risks throughout an AI system's life [6].

Organizations now rely more on clear privacy and security frameworks alongside national laws and technical defenses. They provide a well-structured approach for detecting, reducing, and dealing with data security and privacy risks throughout an AI system's life. Table 11.2 follows below.

Table 11.2 AI privacy and security frameworks comparison.

Framework	Overview	Core components	Key benefits	Relevance to AI
NIST AI Risk Management Framework (USA)	Voluntary framework by NIST for trustworthy AI risk governance; focuses on safety, privacy, fairness, etc.	Govern, Map, Measure, Manage; tailored profiles for different risk levels.	Improves trust, regulatory readiness, ethical alignment, and innovation resilience.	Addresses AI-specific risks: bias, privacy violations, explainability, model drift.
ISO/IEC 27001: Information Security Management Systems	International standard for managing information security risks; ensures confidentiality, integrity, availability.	Risk-based approach, Annex A controls (e.g., access control, cryptography), PDCA cycle.	Strengthens security for AI systems, supports legal compliance (e.g., GDPR), builds trust.	Applies to AI systems handling sensitive data and critical infrastructure with secure ISMS.

(*Continued*)

Table 11.2 AI privacy and security frameworks comparison. (*Continued*)

Framework	Overview	Core components	Key benefits	Relevance to AI
OECD AI Principles	Non-binding global framework adopted by over 40 countries promoting human-centric and ethical AI.	Five principles: Inclusive Growth, Human-Centered Values, Transparency, Robustness, Accountability.	Guides ethical AI globally, enables cross-border policy alignment, promotes inclusive and fair AI systems.	Influences global and national AI policies, fosters ethical AI design and governance.

11.7 Case Studies

We must study actual scenarios to grasp how privacy-preserving technologies and rules are applied in artificial intelligence [7]. They demonstrate how some organizations set up strong privacy frameworks while others do not and what we should learn for managing AI in the future.

11.7.1 Apple's Federated Learning for Siri

Apple has taken the lead by using privacy-protecting AI features in the items it sells to customers. A good example is the use of federated learning to make Siri, Apple's voice assistant, work better. Instead of sending users' spoken words to remote servers to train models, Apple applies federated learning to keep the data on people's iPhones, and the server receives only grouped anonymized updates. This way of doing things offers many potential benefits for privacy and safety.

This approach offers several privacy and security advantages:

- Minimizes the risk of data leakage, as raw audio is stored locally, there is less risk that data will be exposed outside the user's device.
- Reduces exposure to interception or misuse, because sensitive data is never sent, outside agencies cannot take or misuse it.
- Complies with privacy-by-design principles, fits within the privacy-by-design framework expected in the EU under the General Data Protection Regulation (GDPR).

Apple adds differential privacy to federated learning so that the results from user devices are not identifiable to specific users. It proves that following advanced privacy principles does not have to affect the way commercial AI applications function.

11.7.2 Google's Differential Privacy in Chrome

When studying large data sets, Google plays a leading role in making differential privacy a significant approach to protecting users' privacy. Implementation is well known in Google Chrome, as the company analyzes browser usage data to enhance its security and performance. Differential privacy means Google adds random elements to users' data to analyze trends, but nobody's actions can be identified. By using this technique, students are assured that:

- Individual actions cannot be told apart from natural randomness.
- The company follows privacy laws, especially regarding the European Union and California.
- We can use data to enhance services without compromising personal data.

Meanwhile, Google has contributed open-source libraries (for example, the Differential Privacy Library) to promote these methods in AI by dedicated groups. Differential privacy is shown in this case to help organizations innovate and earn the trust of their users.

11.7.3 Facebook–Cambridge Analytica Scandal

The scandal between Facebook and Cambridge Analytica, which was exposed in 2018, is still one of the biggest privacy failures in our current era. The political firm Cambridge Analytica took information from about 87 million Facebook accounts through a third-party app. Data collected from users helped create demographic profiles that influenced voters' decisions during the 2016 U.S. presidential election and the Brexit referendum.

It became clear that Facebook's management and sharing of data were seriously flawed:

- Users were not adequately informed or consented to the data harvesting and third-party sharing.

- Data controls and oversight mechanisms were insufficient, enabling unauthorized access and misuse.
- Algorithmic profiling and manipulation based on improperly acquired data triggered widespread ethical, legal, and reputational consequences.

The fallout from the scandal led to:

- A significant global outcry and erosion of public trust in digital platforms.
- Increased scrutiny from regulators, resulting in fines, public hearings, and stricter data laws.
- The rapid development and enforcement of frameworks such as the General Data Protection Regulation (GDPR) and the California Consumer Privacy Act (CCPA).

This case underscores the critical importance of enforceable privacy regulations, ethical data practices, and transparent AI systems. It also demonstrates the consequences of neglecting privacy protections in high-stakes data environments.

11.8 Designing Privacy-Centric AI Systems

With AI making its way into important decisions, protecting privacy as a key part of development is now very important. The practice of relying on privacy protections well after a system has been set up is inadequate today [8]. Instead, a purposeful philosophy about design should be used to guarantee that AI systems are helpful and respect ethical standards, laws, and public confidence. Below, we introduce the following important approaches for privacy-focused AI systems: Privacy by Design, Threat Modeling, and Transparency Mechanisms.

11.8.1 Privacy by Design

In the 1990s, Privacy by Design (PbD) was introduced to highlight that instead of being fixed as an afterthought, privacy should be built into system architecture from the first step. PbD is now essential because there are many data tools, including Artificial Intelligence (AI). AI systems regularly handle large amounts of personal information, and without integrated privacy rules, they can significantly threaten individuals' rights. PbD calls for privacy protections to be included in every step, from collecting data through training to using, deploying, and monitoring models. Privacy concerns cannot be ignored but should be at the system's heart. Proactive, user-friendly, and technically well-designed solutions are the main ideas behind PbD. The approach focuses on being ready and prevents privacy breaches from occurring. By setting privacy as the primary setting, your data is automatically secured instead of you having to do anything extra. Proper security covers data at each stage of its life, using steps such as encryption, anonymization, and secure storage. Being clear about system design allows users and regulators to confirm compliance and learn how data is handled independently. In addition, respecting user privacy means limiting the data we collect, setting a clear purpose for it, and allowing users to decide which data they want to share. For building AI in practice, PbD can be achieved by using private datasets for training, automatically following guidelines for using minimum data and securely disposing of it on time, and constructing AI modules that can support privacy updates without lengthy retraining or development. Internal and external strategies support ethics in AI and help companies become GDPR- and DPDP Act-compliant.

11.8.2 Threat Modeling for Privacy Risks

Threat modeling is a systematic methodology used to identify, assess, and mitigate potential risks within a system before they materialize. While it has traditionally been associated with cybersecurity to defend against attacks such as data breaches and malware, its adaptation to privacy risk management in AI systems has gained prominence in recent years. This is particularly crucial because AI systems are dynamic, data-driven, and increasingly autonomous, often handling personal or sensitive data in complex and opaque ways.

A privacy-focused threat modeling process begins with data flow mapping, where developers document every point at which data is collected, processed, transferred, stored, or deleted. This holistic view helps identify where data could be exposed or mishandled. Next, developers proceed with identifying privacy threats, such as unauthorized access, data leakage, or inferential attacks like membership inference and model inversion—where adversaries attempt to learn sensitive information from model outputs. Once threats are identified, a risk assessment is conducted to evaluate each threat's probability and potential impact. High-priority risks are then addressed through mitigation planning, where technical and administrative safeguards are implemented. Techniques such as access control, differential privacy, federated learning, and secure multi-party computation may be employed to strengthen system resilience. Finally, an ongoing review mechanism is established to continuously update the threat model in response to evolving system architecture, new data sources, or changes in regulatory landscapes [10].

Several specialized methodologies assist in privacy threat modeling. LINDDUN, an acronym for Linkability, Identifiability, Non-repudiation, Detectability, Disclosure of information, Unawareness, and Non-compliance, is tailored to privacy threats. It guides analysts through the identification of vulnerabilities related to personal data handling. Additionally, STRIDE, initially a security threat modeling framework, can be adapted for privacy use cases by focusing on data misuse rather than system intrusion. By institutionalizing threat modeling within the AI development lifecycle, organizations can proactively safeguard user trust, reduce the risk of privacy violations, and ensure greater alignment with legal and ethical standards.

11.8.3 Transparency Mechanisms

Transparency in AI systems is vital to ethical, trustworthy, and accountable technology development, especially when systems interact with or make decisions about individuals. As AI algorithms increasingly influence critical decisions in sectors like healthcare, finance, law enforcement, and education, the demand for transparency from regulatory authorities and the public has intensified [13]. Transparency mechanisms demystify AI operations and provide clear insights into how data is collected, processed, and used and how models reach decisions.

A robust transparency strategy begins with clear communication of data practices. This involves informing users, in plain language, about the types of data collected, the purpose behind its collection, and the entities with whom it is shared. Such disclosures should be free from legal jargon and accessible to non-expert users. Another cornerstone of transparency is Explainable AI (XAI), which involves developing models whose predictions can be interpreted and understood by humans. In high-stakes applications—such as medical diagnostics or credit approvals—understanding why a model produced a specific outcome is essential for accountability, user trust, and error correction.

Moreover, user dashboards and consent management tools are important in operationalizing transparency. These interfaces allow users to manage their data preferences, monitor how their information is used, and withdraw consent when desired. Additionally, algorithmic audits and model cards provide detailed documentation of AI systems, including their intended use cases, limitations, training data sources, and performance metrics across different demographic groups. Model cards help uncover and address hidden issues such as bias or overfitting.

By incorporating these mechanisms, AI developers fulfill compliance requirements, foster informed participation, increase user confidence, and reduce reputational risk. Transparency, thus, is not merely a compliance checkbox—it is a foundational attribute of ethical AI systems that ensures technology serves society with accountability and integrity.

11.9 Future Directions

Because AI technology is becoming more sophisticated and serves a broader range of interests, new ways to handle emerging privacy and security issues have become essential [11]. There is a need to boost the transparency of AI, maintain constant compliance, and build frameworks used worldwide. The central directions below will guide the next steps in privacy-centric AI development.

11.9.1 Explainable AI (XAI)

A serious issue with AI today, especially with more sophisticated deep learning, is that it is difficult to see how the models work [12]. Since AI is now used in high-importance areas such as healthcare, criminal justice, finance, and public systems, those involved seek transparent and explainable results.

Explainable AI (XAI) seeks to:

- Disclose all of the inner workings of AI models to specialists, users, regulators, and those affected by them.
- Support holding those using algorithms accountable in rights, benefits, or access cases.
- Help guard against wrongdoings by exposing where cases may contain bias, discrimination, or errors.

More and more, XAI tools, like SHAP, LIME, attention, and counterfactual explanations, are added to machine learning pipelines to give meaningful insights while maintaining model performance.

11.9.2 AI Auditing Tools

With AI being used more in sensitive places, many are asking for tools to check AI systems on compliance, ethical standards, and effectiveness. These tools are essential for:

- Detecting unauthorized data usage or violations of consent.
- Auditing models for fairness, bias, robustness, and explainability.
- Enabling post-deployment monitoring to identify drift, vulnerabilities, and unintended consequences.

Group organizations in the public and private sectors are working on developing AI auditing tools, some of which are being added to full AI governance platforms. For instance, AI Fairness 360 from IBM, Fairlearn from Microsoft, and What-If Tool from Google give developers and auditors useful information about bias and transparency.

In the EU, regulators are studying the possibility of aligning how algorithms are audited, mainly due to the requirement in the AI Act for risk-focused audits of high-risk AI systems.

11.9.3 Unified Global Standards

Since data protection and AI rules are inconsistent between countries, global organizations face plenty of compliance difficulties. Since large AI systems are used worldwide, it is important to create principles that all nations can use to measure trust. Important steps in this area are as follows:

- G20, OECD, and the United Nations are working together to set up ethical standards for AI in many nations.
- There are plans to accept each other's certification and risk classification standards.
- Support for developing an international AI regulation framework, such as the World Trade Organization's, to encourage match with local rules and ensure get-togethers on AI rules worldwide.

Global rules will clarify regulations, boost innovative change, and defend users' interests in the growing digital society.

11.10 Conclusion

AI plays a significant part in shaping different fields by delivering enhanced efficient work, more intelligent choices, and groundbreaking answers to main international challenges. Although AI systems are widely being created, many AI systems that manage sensitive personal data have led to privacy and data security concerns. As a result, it becomes evident that we must have thorough, careful, and forward-looking rules to make sure AI is deployed responsibly.

The chapter discussed several important frameworks for the security and regulation of AI systems. They involve IT protections like differential privacy, federated learning, and homomorphic encryption; establishments like the Risk Management Framework published by the NIST and the ISO/IEC 27001 standard; and legal protocols like the GDPR, the CCPA, and the principles released by the OECD. These frameworks provide the core support needed for developing novel AI systems with strong security, transparency, and ethical values. Several important takeaways can be found in this discussion. Responsible AI can be achieved only if innovators actively apply privacy-by-design, threat modeling, and transparency. Second, by looking at cases like those of Apple, Google, and Facebook, we can see what works well and what can go wrong in AI and data management.

They highlight how important privacy-focused design is and show what happens when regulations are lacking. Third, AI must be governed adequately by joining efforts from technology developers, policymakers, industry experts, members of civil society, and others who use AI. We can ensure AI reflects society's needs, the law, and ethical thoughts by connecting AI research, governments, businesses, and academics. When AI resources continue to grow in both type and difficulty, the rules governing their usage must be followed. If people concentrate on ethics, keep up with rules, and support user rights, they can ensure AI keeps making the digital world more trustworthy and fair.

AI disclosure statement: The author acknowledges the use of AI-based tools for minor language editing or grammatical correction. However, all intellectual contributions, analyses, and conclusions presented in this chapter are entirely the author's own.

References

1. Abujaber, A.A. and Nashwan, A.J., Ethical framework for artificial intelligence in healthcare research: A path to integrity. *World J. Methodol., 14*, 3, 94071, 2024, doi: 10.5662/wjm.v14.i3.94071.
2. Ahdadou, M., Aajly, A., Tahrouch, M., Enhancing corporate governance through AI: a systematic literature review. *Technol. Anal. Strateg. Manag.*, 1–14, 2024. https://doi.org/10.1080/09537325.2024.2326120.
3. Feretzakis, G., Papaspyridis, K., Gkoulalas-Divanis, A., Verykios, V.S., Privacy-preserving techniques in generative AI and large language models: A narrative review. *Information (Basel), 15*, 11, 697, 2024, doi: 10.3390/info15110697.
4. Ilić, L., Šijan, A., Predić, B., Viduka, D., Karabašević, D., Research trends in artificial intelligence and security—bibliometric analysis. *Electronics, 13*, 12, 2288, 2024, doi: 10.3390/electronics13122288.
5. Jakkula, A.R. and Software Development Engineer, USA, Ensuring data privacy and security in AI-enabled E-commerce platforms. *J. Artif. Intell. Cloud Comput., 3*, 1, 1–3, 2024, doi: 10.47363/jaicc/2024(3)288.
6. Muldoon, J. and Wu, B.A., Artificial Intelligence in the Colonial Matrix of Power. *Philos. Technol.*, 36, 4, 80, 2023. https://doi.org/10.1007/s13347-023-00687-8.
7. Pati, S., Kumar, S., Varma, A., Edwards, B., Lu, C., Qu, L., Bakas, S., Privacy preservation for federated learning in health care. *Patterns (New York, N.Y.), 5*, 7, 100974, 2024, doi: 10.1016/j.patter.2024.100974.
8. Prasanth, A., Vadakkan, D.J., Surendran, P., Thomas, B., Role of Artificial Intelligence and Business Decision Making. *Int. J. Adv. Comput. Sci. (IJACSA)*, 14, 6, 2023. http://dx.doi.org/10.14569/IJACSA.2023.01406103.
9. Pavić, A.M. and Beriša, H.A., Artificial intelligence impact assessment on national security strategy development. *SCIENCE International Journal*, 3, 4, 19–27, 2024.
10. Stahl, B.C., Ethical issues of AI, in: *SpringerBriefs in Research and Innovation Governance*, pp. 35–53, Springer International Publishing, Cham, 2021.
11. Udegbe, F.C., Ebulue, O.R., Ebulue, C.C., Ekesiobi, C.S., The role of Artificial Intelligence in healthcare: A systematic review of applications and challenges. *Int. Med. Sci. Res. J., 4*, 4, 500–508, 2024, doi: 10.51594/imsrj.v4i4.1052.
12. Villegas-Ch, W. and García-Ortiz, J., Toward a comprehensive framework for ensuring security and privacy in artificial intelligence. *Electronics, 12*, 18, 3786, 2023, doi: 10.3390/electronics12183786.
13. Ward, C.M., Harguess, J., Tao, J., Christman, D., Spicer, P., Tan, M., The AI Security Pyramid of Pain, 2024, doi: 10.48550/ARXIV.2402.11082.

12
AI in Autonomous Systems

Kalyanasundaram V., G. Prethija*, Keerthi A.J., Yuvan Shankar Baabu and R. Srivats

School of Computer Science and Engineering, Vellore Institute of Technology, Chennai, India

Abstract
Artificial Intelligence is revolutionizing the autonomous system and opening a new chapter of technological advancement in each domain. This chapter deliberates on how AI can transform for better functionality, safety, and efficiency of autonomous systems in transportation, defense, health, space applications and discusses how AI has been playing an essential role in running these systems. These are self-governing systems that process massive amounts of data decide and respond to the given challenges simultaneously in real life through intricate AI algorithms. It makes possible for AI-integrated systems to function independently and make dynamic responses in response to changes in their environments and significantly improving the utility and efficiency of these systems. Reinforcement learning is quite efficient to train systems concerning navigation through complex environments, optimizing performance, and achieving adaptability by trial-and-error processes. The solutions to reduce system failures and handling safe management makes the safety protocol more stringent and regulatory frameworks tougher. When the promises are made to go on innovating and developing innovative ideas, autonomous system's capabilities will sooner or later find ways into fluid integration into society that is more responsible. Therefore, the chapter will present proper understanding to a reader regarding how AI interfaces with autonomous systems critically.

***Keywords*:** Autonomous military vehicles, autonomous systems, real-time decision making, reinforcement learning, space exploration, surveillance

**Corresponding author*: g.prethija@vit.ac.in

Manish Kumar, Nitigya Sambyal, Leena Priyadarshini Singh, Ramasamy V. and S. Balamurugan (eds.) Responsible AI: Principles and Practices, (269–296) © 2026 Scrivener Publishing LLC

12.1 Introduction to AI in Autonomous Systems

12.1.1 Understanding Autonomous Systems

Autonomous systems are the new interface of machines and technology with the environment that carry out operations almost autonomously without much interference from humans. What makes them distinct is in real time-sense, process, and act characteristics for navigating extremely dynamic and complex environments [1]. They synthesize across a range of inter-disciplinary sciences, merging the fields of mechanical engineering, computer science, data analytics, and cognitive modeling to give birth to independent agents. The advantage is that they always overperform human beings concerning accuracy, flexibility, and timesaving whether it is in transportation or healthcare applications.

The architecture, which remains the core or nucleus of self-governing systems, is an emulation of perception cognition and actions. The three key elements for this architecture include sensors, processors, and actuators [2]. Sensors can be regarded as the eyes of the system that capture raw data from the environment. LiDAR technology, ultrasonic detectors, and high-definition cameras improve the ability of these systems to create quite detailed maps and identify obstacles and main features. The processing unit is the brain of the system, which interprets the information it receives through complex algorithms to facilitate meaningful outcomes and actionable decisions. These decisions are then operated through actuators, which are mechanical limbs of the system that convert digital commands into physical movements or outputs. The interaction among these parts enables autonomous systems to function in challenging, unstructured environments.

The evolutionary background lies at the foundation of autonomy system development. Initial autonomy has involved mechanical automation and machines, where operations performed repetitive functions on limited parameters. Early line assembly robots fall under such functionality, meaning they could only carry out what was programmed for them and never modified any set-up process. All these are changed with computer vision and AI technologies in the last couple of decades. Since the algorithms of Machine Learning (ML) allow these systems to learn from the available data, pattern recognition and outcomes can be predicted, and therefore, the capacity to adapt has been built up along with time. Since the initial robotic arms were coming pre-equipped in fixed movements, today's autonomous robots manufacturing plants use can alter operations in real-time based on variations in production lines or unexpected obstacles.

Environmental adaptability is a special feature of autonomous systems. In contrast, the traditional automated systems rely on rigid programming whereas the autonomous systems are continuously analyzing their surroundings and changing their behaviour. One of the features that emerge in these applications is surveillance or disaster management drones that are used autonomously. Its path is always under optimization while navigating through various terrains, avoiding obstacles, and trying to optimize its path. Other examples include domains such as precision agriculture where autonomous tractors are equipped with soil and weather sensors to adjust their planting and harvesting strategies when conditions change across different seasons to attain optimal resource utilization and better harvest for farmers.

In the transportation, the self-driving car applies GPS, cameras, and sensors to make real-time 3D maps of its surroundings as it navigates through congested cities. Because algorithms that decide in real-time enable them to react in real time to shifting pedestrian crosswalks or sudden lane shifts and, therefore, focus their attention on safety and efficiency, autonomous systems are also applied in the health sector, since robotic-assisted surgeries have often proved to be more precise and stable than the human hand. These surgical robots' function at the accuracy of micrometres so that the chances of errors in them are very less and more patients can be saved.

The next section will introduce some applications of autonomous systems to apparently insurmountable tasks. Autonomous rovers are used for crossing over the unexplored territories and collect data and carry out experiments in real time in the absence of human beings while exploring space. With their navigation algorithms quite high, they operate through unfamiliar topography. For oceanography studies, autonomous underwater vehicles are indispensable. They scour through deep ocean communities and can recover samples or even map unseen places while living under conditions unacceptable for everyday human.

While there is all the boon to autonomous systems, the biggest worry is with respect to dependability, specifically on critical applications that involve minimal latency. Extensive testing needs to be mapped with safety mechanisms to ensure consistencies in unpredictable environments. A good example in this regard could be the scenario of autonomous vehicles, which requires the ability of detecting and acting upon infrequently occurring yet catastrophically ending events, including sudden mechanical failures or highly unforeseen road conditions. Ethical considerations with the decision-making processes that pose difficult moral dilemmas are another such challenge. Such autonomous systems must be programmed in such a way that favors those goals that are in conformance with the mainstream social values and legal requirements. That is a job of careful reflection and cooperation of the policymakers with the technologists.

Public acceptance of autonomous systems is based on trust, which springs from intelligibility or understanding and transparency. For that reason, understanding how such systems make decisions concerning sensitive applications such as health care or law enforcement requires it for users and other stakeholders. A step forward would be the creation of explainable AI, whereby one can meaningfully speak about autonomous systems, making them terms of reference other than for the experts. There would be the creation of accountability and trust toward such intelligent working within the realm of ethics and legality. The above future developments in autonomous systems can unlock new possibilities and redefine the boundaries that machines can achieve.

12.1.2 AI's Role in Enabling Autonomous Functionality

Artificial Intelligence (AI) is the basis for autonomous systems, equipping them with the ability to perceive, reason, and act for various tasks and challenges. AI enables such systems to function even in the absence of direct human interventions because it equips the machine with the computational means to process large volumes of data in real time to make decisions. By fusion of ML, Deep Learning (DL), and Reinforcement Learning (RL), it made possible for adapting autonomous systems toward diverse environments. With the integration of AI into autonomous systems, these systems gain a sense of more purpose beyond its central features. Three major stages form the working mechanism of AI regarding autonomous systems. These consist of perception, decision-making, and action.

Autonomous systems acquire and process data of the environment using input devices. At this decision stage of AI, it analyses possible outcomes that come through with data analysis, then makes corresponding responses. Mechanisms of response for such decisions would be given in action through actuators either mechanical or electronic. For example, consider an autonomous car on a high-density road that will identify all traffic lights, pedestrians, and road signs for its perception system. It would then decide to either stop, reduce speed, or change lanes. The actuators will be the control systems in the brakes, accelerator, or steering wheel of the car. This will happen in millisecond cycle; thus, the entire system operates under real-time conditions. Another important feature of the role of AI in autonomous systems is its ability to learn and improve over time.

Massive datasets train ML models, allowing the model to identify patterns and correlations that can be used to predict system behaviour. For instance, drones use AI to classify objects when they employ supervised learning in obstacle identification while using RL in optimizing the path taken for navigation. This form of learning would allow the system to fine-tune decision-making processes and apply them to new challenges.

Figure 12.1 depicts the framework of autonomous decision making system. It begins with the data acquisition step. Sensors in this layer acquire raw data from the environment. Raw data goes through a preprocessing module, where it filters noise and extracts the most relevant features. Afterward, it proceeds through the perception layer, in which AI algorithms will be applied for analysis in terms of identification of objects, configurations, or even classification of scenarios. This output feeds into the decision-making module, which involves algorithms such as neural networks or RL models to rate an action or a sequence of actions that must be performed. A command is thus sent to the actuation layer, based on the action chosen to be executed. This layer transforms the commands into physical movements or system adjustments. The system again enters the acquisition phase of the data for on-time adjustment. As a result, AI also fuels autonomous capability in intelligent systems.

Traditional systems use deterministic algorithms which are inappropriate to handle conditions that are complexly changing. These systems based on AI use models of probability and can account for uncertainty, furthering more robust decision-making abilities [3]. In biotechnology, an AI-powered bio-hackers design and synthesize custom genetic code using CRISPR(Clustered Regularly Interspaced Short Palindromic Repeats)

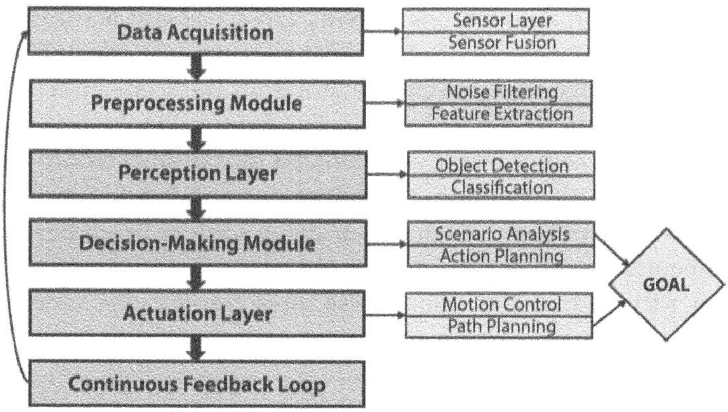

Figure 12.1 Hierarchical framework for autonomous system decision-making.

technology to address grand challenges to cause the eradication of infectious disease. Such systems function with deep GANs simulating genetic variations, thus making it possible to adjust genetic editing to account for unforeseen biological interactions.

Multi-agent systems take advantage of AI to coordinate their actions as multiple autonomous entities work together. AI protocols enable fleets of robots to communicate with each other to manage the inventory, improve routes, and avoid collisions in warehouses. Collaborative frameworks bring about large-scale efficiency by transforming industries through shared intelligence. AI drives the intelligence and adaptability of autonomous systems and extends beyond the technical functionality that influences collaborative operations.

AI is the key to autonomous systems, as it enables them to sense their surroundings and react on their own with minimal human intervention. Sensor fusion, machine learning and computer vision enables AI to let autonomous systems to reason about the world, predict the future, and respond to the uncertain environment. In transport, navigation and collision avoidance are improved by AI in autonomous vehicles through use of sensor data. In defense, surveillance and operational efficiency of autonomous robotic systems and drones are enhanced by AI. With robotic surgery with AI assistance and automated diagnosis in healthcare; and, in space exploration, autonomous navigation, and decision-making in unmanned missions, AI is used. In most industries, AI improves the effectiveness, safety, and timeliness of autonomous system.

12.2 AI Technologies in Autonomous Systems

AI Technologies in autonomous systems can sense and act intelligently within active environments. These technologies apply ML and DL for various tasks like object detection and classification and scene understanding [4]. These applications process sensor data from cameras, LiDAR's, and radars. Reinforcement learning is the process of trial and error to improve navigation and path planning, considering uncertainties. Sensor fusion refers to the compilation of data from many sources to understand the environment. It increases the accuracy and reliability in perception. When combining RL and sensor fusion, these three autonomous systems such as self-driving vehicles, drones, and robots make intelligent decisions in a real-time, adaptive fashion.

12.2.1 Machine Learning and Deep Learning for Perception

ML and DL have changed how autonomous systems see and make sense of their environment. They make it possible to handle the massive amount of data acquired from sensors to classify objects and interpret complicated scenes in detail. Three critical core areas including Object Detection and Classification, Semantic Segmentation for Scene Understanding, and Sensor Data Integration with Deep Learning, in support of perception capability development of autonomous systems are discussed.

12.2.1.1 Object Detection and Classification

Object detection and classification are the basic parts of autonomous perception, in which systems can identify and classify objects in their environment. Techniques such as Convolutional Neural Networks (CNNs), Region-based CNNs (R-CNN), YOLO (You Only Look Once), and SSD (Single Shot MultiBox Detector) have revolutionized object recognition. The speed and accuracy provided by these techniques are highly important for real-time applications. These models excelled in detecting and categorizing objects like vehicles, pedestrians, and obstacles and can be very useful for the performance of autonomous vehicles and drones operating under dynamic environments. But detection seems to be challenging in edge cases as it is difficult to detect an object correctly if partially occluded or not work against a cluttered background. This can be overcome by continuous improvement in model architecture, better training datasets, and addition of contextual information to improve detection performance in real-world scenarios.

12.2.1.2 Semantic Segmentation for Scene Understanding

Semantic segmentation is the application through which autonomous systems achieve granular understanding of surroundings by labeling every pixel within an image. The popularly used models for this job include UNET, DeepLab, and Mask R-CNN, as they surpass the state-of-the-art methods in detecting lanes, pedestrians, road signs, and other essentials within a scene. These applications are important for tasks such as fully autonomous driving, where having a precise scene understanding prevents the vehicle from crashing in the first place. Techniques to improve segmentation accuracy include attention mechanisms that allow the model to focus more on relevant parts of an image and to ignore irrelevant details to better handle complex environments either in crowded city streets or challenging weather conditions. This will enable autonomous systems to make more informed decisions to guarantee safety and efficiency with high precision semantic segmentation.

12.2.1.3 Sensor Data Integration with Deep Learning

Integration of data across multiple sensors such as LiDAR, cameras, and radar is very necessary for developing a complete perception system in autonomous machines. Deep learning models play significant roles in processing sensor inputs, the extraction of meaningful features from them, and then developing unified representations of the environment under consideration. Fusion techniques enable the integration of data through feature-level and decision-level fusion across different modalities, thereby giving the perception much more robust and reliable. For instance, LiDAR gives accurate distance measurements, cameras capture visual details, and radar excels in detecting objects in poor weather conditions. Handling multi-modal data streams in real-time poses significant challenges, including the synchronization of data from different sensors and the high computational demands of processing large datasets. There are recent advancements in hardware acceleration in GPUs and TPUs and also in optimized algorithms which helps to overcome these challenges by integrating sensor data.

12.2.2 Reinforcement Learning in Autonomous Navigation

The concept of RL has emerged as an important paradigm for training autonomous systems in dynamic, uncertain environments. Through the interactions with the environment and the learning process from rewards, systems can build adaptive policies that will steer the decisions and thus guarantee safe, efficient navigation. This chapter discusses the key aspects related to RL in autonomous navigation: Path Planning Using Reinforcement Learning, Reward Design and Policy Optimization, Simulated Training Environments.

12.2.2.1 Path Planning Using Reinforcement Learning

The starting idea of autonomous navigation will be path planning, an important process for computing an optimal trajectory from the starting point to a target position using information about obstacles. There are few applications in the RL techniques namely Q-Learning, Deep Q-Networks, and Proximal Policy Optimization. Such techniques allow systems to learn goal-oriented navigation strategies. They do this by learning procedures maximizing cumulative rewards in complex dynamic and uncertain environments. These RL-based models excel in real-time decision-making, like dynamically changing paths to avoid moving obstacles and ensure non-collision navigation. Contrary to traditional rule-based algorithms, the RL agents adapt to complex and unpredictable scenarios by learning experience to discover optimal strategies. For global path planning, it mainly focuses on long-term objectives of navigation, whereas a local path planning focuses mainly on the immediate obstacles faced and the dynamic environment. Algorithms including A* (A-Star), Rapidly Exploring Random Trees (RRT) are widely used here. Challenges lie in the near future for such safe and efficient deployment of path planning systems in real-world applications. Stability in updating policies, the exploration-exploitation trade-off, and a scaling up to high-dimensional state space are few among them.

12.2.2.2 Reward Design and Policy Optimization

Properly designed rewards are one of the main components of the effective RL system when using it for autonomous navigation. They are able to guide the process by providing feedback to the agent on its actions. Thus, a good reward structure should align rewards with desired behaviours like reaching the destination rapidly or avoiding collisions, minimizing the usage of energy. Poorly designed rewards may lead to policies which are suboptimal because agents may focus more on unintended actions.

Exploration vs. Exploitation strategies play an important role in optimizing policy, and the aim of using such strategies is to achieve the balance of trying out new actions by encouraging exploration, while leveraging the actions learned for higher rewards using exploitation. Such balancing is ensured so that the agent learns efficiently and does not get stuck in the local optimums [5]. Actor-Critic and A3C (Asynchronous Advantage Actor-Critic) are advanced policy optimization algorithms that further improve learning by decoupling value estimation from policy improvement, allowing for faster and more stable convergence. Such methods are especially useful in autonomous navigation tasks, where continuous adaptation to changing environments is critical.

12.2.3 Sensor Fusion and Multi-Modal Data Processing

Sensor fusion is one of the cornerstones of autonomous systems. The perception and understanding of a scene is done by fusing the information provided by cameras, LiDAR, radar, and GPS sensors [6]. In fact, the advantages of each sensor type in multi-modal processing would then be leveraged against its respective weakness, yielding robust and reliable state estimation and decision-making. Some of the main methodologies and challenges of sensor fusion include Kalman Filtering and Particle Filtering, Deep Sensor Fusion for Robust Perception, and Challenges in Sensor Fusion.

12.2.3.1 Kalman Filtering and Particle Filtering

Two such well-known techniques for the fusion of noisy sensor data to determine the state of dynamic systems, which could include position, velocity, and orientation of an autonomous vehicle, are Kalman filtering and particle filtering [7]. In the presence of linear systems with Gaussian noise, the Kalman filter is optimal since it iteratively refines state estimates by combining predictions from a system's motion model with noisy sensor measurements. It is computationally efficient and hence is usually used in GPS and IMU data fusion for vehicle localization.

Particle filters are very good at handling nonlinear systems and non-Gaussian noise by approximating the probability distribution of the state of the system using a set of weighted particles. Each particle represents a possible state, and its weight represents the likelihood of that state with respect to the observed data. Particle filters can also be good in highly complex dynamic environments or when the sensor observation is very sparse and possibly ambiguous as in GPS-denied environments and with heavy occlusions.

Comparing both methods has pointed out their trade-offs: while the Kalman filters are computational, and their performance is excellent under structured scenarios, the particle filters are more flexible but generally computationally expensive in high-dimensional state spaces. An autonomous system typically selects an appropriate filtering technique based on the application and environmental complexity with given computational constraints.

12.2.3.2 Deep Sensor Fusion for Robust Perception

Sensor fusion enables the application of neural networks that effectively integrate multi-modal data streams coming from sensors like LiDAR, radar, and cameras. Classic approaches toward sensor fusion rely on predefined models or heuristics, whereas deep sensor fusion will capitalize on the power of data-driven learning in a machine to automatically extract features or correlations across modalities. For instance, it would enhance the perception of obstacles or road conditions by fusing high-resolution visual data from cameras and depth and range information provided by LiDAR.

It will provide improvements to operating performance in systems under adverse conditions which may include variable lighting, and under occlusions from the weather conditions due to the modalities processing the data and further the integration for an autonomous system decision robustness and precision in consideration of the deep neural networks. For example, in a foggy environment, cameras could utilize supplementary data from the radar and LiDAR depth information whenever visual information cannot provide clear data.

There have been some case studies developed in autonomous driving for demonstrating deep sensor fusion [8]. In this case study, companies like Tesla, Waymo, and Nvidia are using DL on sensor fusion to improve object detection, lane detection, and traffic prediction. This type of system will learn the ways of real-world problems using the fused data for forming a comprehensive understanding of its surroundings.

12.3 Autonomous Vehicles and Real-Time Decision Making

The change autonomous vehicles have brought in transport is of a whole different level such that the running of vehicles without human interference [9]. They fully depend on advanced AI systems since they can make decisions in real-time, adapt to changing environments, avoid collision, and optimize operational efficiency. This chapter is going to elaborate on how AI works in self-driving cars using the underlying technology from a safety and efficiency point of view.

12.3.1 AI in Self-Driving Cars: Safety and Efficiency

12.3.1.1 Role of AI in Self-Driving Cars

The core of every self-driving car contains an AI system guiding it through everything that happens around and processing it all in the twinkling of an eye. To start with, a self-driving car creates massive amounts of real-world data through LiDAR [10], cameras, radar, and ultrasonic sensors. It will extract features from the road, obstacles, pedestrians, and traffic lights, and just give out a wide range of knowledge. Finally, it puts all those functionalities together in such a seamless manner that a vehicle will basically be able to drive like any other human being, reducing possibilities of mistakes. The operational framework is based on three critical pillars: perception, prediction, and planning. Perception is a paradigm to identify the immediate surroundings; prediction is to assess what the actions of the surrounding objects will be, whereas the software planned the next course of action [11].

12.3.1.2 Core Algorithms Driving Safety and Efficiency

The diversity of algorithms being used in the self-driving car is tailored and focused on several aspects of driving. These lay down a foundation for developing real-time decisions, safety, and efficiency.

1. Perception through Computer Vision Algorithms
Among the most essential parts of the autonomous vehicle are computer vision capabilities, which allow a vehicle to see its environment [12]. CNNs help in identifying and detecting the objects. Algorithms like YOLO (You Only Look Once) and SSD (Single Shot MultiBox Detector) scan camera inputs in real time and identify pedestrians, traffic signs, etc. The semantic segmentation algorithm enables the drawing of road boundaries and lane markings such that the car could keep precisely in the lane. The algorithms and applications of computer vision for the autonomous vehicle are listed in Table 12.1.

12.3.2 Drone Decision Making in Delivery and Surveillance

Drones or UAVs are rapidly becoming an everyday feature in many applications in today's world, ranging from delivery services to surveillance. They will need AI-facilitated complex decision making to make decisions autonomously in complex environments. This navigation ability *via* routes, preventing them from approaching obstacles, helping them optimize delivery routes, and successful execution of surveillance by getting good accuracies are taken care of using AI in drones. The algorithms applied to these applications and the mechanisms applied to drone decision-making are discussed here.

Table 12.1 Computer vision algorithms for perception.

Algorithm	Purpose	Example	Key advantage	Common application areas
YOLO/SSD	Object detection and classification	Detecting pedestrians and vehicles	Fast real-time processing	Autonomous driving, surveillance
Semantic Segmentation	Lane boundary detection	Precise lane identification	Pixel-level accuracy	Self-driving cars, medical imaging
RNN/LSTM	Sequential data processing	Predicting traffic flow patterns	Handles temporal dependencies	Traffic management, speech recognition
Kalman Filter	Object tracking	Tracking moving vehicles	Predicts object motion with noise reduction	Robotics, navigation
Reinforcement Learning	Decision-making in dynamic systems	Adaptive cruise control	Learns optimal policies through rewards	Robotics, gaming, finance
SLAM (Simultaneous Localization and Mapping)	Mapping unknown environments	Autonomous robot navigation	Build a map while tracking location	Robotics, augmented reality
CNNs (Convolutional Neural Networks)	Feature extraction from images	Identifying road signs	High accuracy in visual recognition	Autonomous vehicles, medical diagnosis

12.3.2.1 Navigation and Path Planning

For instance, for drones to fly autonomously, the most efficient routes should be determined; therefore, a strong navigation system will be needed. Most of these limiting factors such as obstacles, battery life, and even air traffic, would play a huge role in planning these paths. Some of the most global algorithms used for this type of path planning include A* (A-Star), Rapidly Exploring Random Trees, and finally, the Probabilistic Roadmap. Real-time adaptation using a local planning algorithm, drones combine sensor readings to identify and steer clear of surprises in the way [13]. For the sake of stability during flight, delivery drones will consider environmental issues such as the speed and wind direction. It employs sensor fusion techniques with information coming from the GPS, LiDAR, and onboard cameras; their inputs are filtered with the Kalman Filter for precise localization and object detection.

12.3.2.2 Object Detection and Recognition

Object detection and recognition algorithms are highly critical to both delivery and surveillance drones. These algorithms could help the drones identify delivery locations, detect threats, and monitor areas of interest. The most applied algorithms are YOLO (You Only Look Once) and Faster R-CNN. These models enable drones to see things in real-time through the proper identification of delivery points or suspicious activities while on surveillance missions. This increases the accuracy even further since they can now identify the roadways, rooftops, and open fields where a proper landing and monitoring should take place. Also, with thermal cameras and AI-based image processing algorithms, even some tasks can be carried out during low-lighting or adverse weather conditions.

12.3.2.3 Energy Management and Efficiency

Energy efficiency is a critical parameter when drones are used, and more importantly, in delivery scenarios as well. The payload bears a direct relationship with battery consumption proportional to it. Therefore, a balance between usage and flight at specific altitude and speed must be achieved. All these factors are well-handled by AI-based optimization techniques like Particle Swarm Optimization (PSO) and Genetic Algorithms (GAs). For surveillance drones, predictive models are developed to predict the power consumption in longer-duration missions. RL is largely used in energy management systems so that the drone learns the optimal strategies without wasting the energy, and performance check is kept in place.

12.3.2.4 Data Analysis and Real-Time Decisions

Drones gather large amounts of data, which they must process in real-time so that the information is used for surveillance purposes. General AI models especially DL assist the drones in decoding live feeds and sensing unusual phenomena such as unauthorized activities, uncommon movement patterns, or any patterns different from ordinary patterns in monitored areas through their temporal analysis. Often implemented using LSTM networks, time-series analysis enables the drones to track changes over time as well as predict future movement. A delivery drone requires real-time decision-making capabilities, since the conditions are often abrupt, such as when the weather changes or airspace changes. Reinforcement learning can train the drone through their decisions made and thereby improve their performance with experience.

12.3.3 AI-Driven Autonomous Military Vehicles in Defense

The integration of AI into autonomous military vehicles has revolutionized modern warfare, enabling enhanced reconnaissance, combat efficiency, and strategic decision-making. These vehicles, which include ground vehicles, aerial drones, and naval vessels, rely on AI-driven systems for navigation, target identification, and operational planning. This section provides a detailed examination of the technologies and algorithms powering these vehicles in defense applications.

12.3.3.1 Autonomy to the Environment and Terrain

Military autonomous cars are designed in such a manner that they can cross any given harsh terrain, desert, even forest and urban combat locations. Autonomous navigation systems tend to fuse GPS, LiDAR, and radar to represent the space and recognize the space environment. This feature affords them path-planning algorithms like D* Lite, Rapidly Exploring Random Trees (RRT). Such techniques help them map an optimal route while avoiding such a threat as enemy surveillance mine or natural land. Military vehicles have another unique challenge such as terrain adaptation in which the terrain data training inside a model allows it to predict in accordance with the status of its surface. For example, neural networks may identify sandy soil or muddy surfaces and adjust the vehicle's speed and suspension to stabilize its operation.

12.3.3.2 Target Detection and Engagement

Target detection is one of the most important applications of AI in military vehicles. YOLO and Faster R-CNN computer vision algorithms will be used together with the thermal imaging and radar systems to detect the enemies' assets tanks, drones, and people, etc. New recognition models use transfer learning for object recognition by taking the data of set previously trained so that in any new situation the speeding of the recognition occurs. Once a target has been identified, it calculates the optimal action that should be undertaken, in case of contact with that target. The combats use AI, artificially driven RL, and test millions of plans to settle on a suitable plan. For example, it can be programmed to choose dropping missiles or evasive maneuver at an instant decision considering what the target is doing, the defense strategies in use, and the way the target moves.

12.3.3.3 Communication and Swarm Intelligence

Modern day defense operation normally utilizes autonomous vehicles combined with other units. AI enables vehicles to communicate with other vehicles in an effective manner to form a collaboration network, sharing intelligence and resources. Swarm intelligence algorithms are used to coordinate multiple vehicles. It is inspired by the natural swarms, such as bees or ants, to optimize collective behaviour, like surrounding an enemy position or search-and rescue missions. AI-based V2V technology allows autonomous military groups to get real-time information regarding adversary positions, terrain, and mission goals, thus promoting situational awareness and accomplishing missions more effectively.

12.3.3.4 Defense Mechanisms Countermeasures

The autonomous military vehicle has strong mechanisms of defense against threats. AI-powered countermeasure systems can detect incoming missiles or hostile drones and activate proper response modes, such as flares, smoke screens, or electronic jamming. They learn through reinforcement to be able to adapt to changing threats and ensure resilience against superior enemy technologies. Therefore, these models are used for anticipating an impending strike so that the car can take some action in advance. For example, an AI system would analyze the pattern of radar signals to detect the attacks and shift the car out of danger.

12.4 AI Innovations in Space and Healthcare Systems

12.4.1 AI-Driven Autonomous Systems for Space Exploration

Terrain classification is a crucial task for planetary rovers, especially when the objective is to cross dangerous territories in their endeavors. Previous missions of exploring Mars with rovers have involved the relay of images to human operators who would then pick out a tractable path. Red Planet over the next few decades will at some point need rovers that can move independently across larger distances more swiftly and through harsher terrains showing a need for better terrain classification for mobility. Self-navigation in such climate environments will help in the search for water on Moon and other planets besides preparing for human habitats. Machine learning techniques can be used to enhance the terrain classification skills for ground vehicles on Earth. However, classification results for space applications are restricted due to the availability of examples of supervised learning data for implementing training models. An open-source automatic data processing pipeline for co-localizing curiosity and perseverance Mastcam image products using camera geometry is developed. Due to limited open tools for integrating data of visual and geologic data, the proposed pipeline does the integration of Mastcam and MastcamZ images [14].

The rugged and unexplored terrain nature of Mars stood a way for more scientific investigations using robots. Nowadays robot educated with AI navigates through hostile environments avoiding obstacles. Deep reinforcement learning (DRL) is employed to develop an autonomous walking technique to explore rugged terrains. Proximal Policy optimization technique is used as reinforcement technique. Adaptive learning is employed for making real-time decision. The dataset used in their experimental study includes images representing Martian terrain. The experiments are conducted in simulated environment [15].

Intelligent space systems can be described as space systems that are capable of operation using intelligent techniques. To establish autonomy, the AI approach is applied. There is no human intervention required in the execution of tasks in this system. AI can make the manufacturing of satellites faster, but it can also be used to analyze how to make the process faster. Moreover, implementation of collaborative robots or 'cobots' to the production floor reduces the human workers needed within clean rooms. AI has another advantage over humans in the fact that they are not in need of breaks, naps, sleeps and the like in their bid to digest large volumes of data in a short space of time. The techniques exploited can also be used for classification results in the layers namely statistical and game theory layer, behavioral layer that includes operational processes, automated process, machine translation, collaborative and adaptive systems, a layer for inserting audio, language and visual inputs and cognitive layer that contains the ML, reasoning and data representation [16].

Since deep-learning AI models have shown unmatched ability in a commercial embedded space as a domain for computer vision tasks, space researchers are identifying the ways that it may be implemented onboard the next generation of space vehicles to improve their independent capacities and science compensation. Contrary to the case of the commercial space, there are numerous location specific issues of modeling and computation that remain to be resolved. On the modeling side, high-volume data sources cannot be large-scale for the new sensor types or unknown surroundings, it is challenging to use deep neural networks constantly and to test them before deployment. Traditional rad-hard processors cannot feasibly execute and so they are replaced by FPGAs counterparts which are a part of space probe design. Commercial-off-the-shelf (COTS) quality high performance space qualified microprocessors, microcontrollers, and up-screened space qualified CPUs and GPUs and custom neural-network-accelerator ASICs, present a potential solution for higher-level risk resilient missions. However, these devices could not likely be exploited in very hostile environments. Therefore, the remaining of challenges still coming from NASA and the U.S. Air Force are targeted to create rad-hard high performers such as the HPSC [17].

Starship is being highlighted in the modern mission plans such as the Manned Landing Module for Artemis III on the lunar terrain and its design in the Mars mission plans require that this work analyses the possibility of those Mars missions. The purpose of the work is to achieve the critical assessment of recent deficiencies in the mission framework and system blueprint, and to outline the steps for addressing these deficiencies. The rationale behind each model assumes mission execution according to the scenario described by SpaceX would turn out to be. This demands an accumulation of information about this setup and then the subsequent correct examination is done with this data, i.e., the calculation of the development trajectory. Based on this, speculation regarding the rationality and possibility of the mission extended by SpaceX for its Starship has been made. First, statistics are gathered on the recent mission, where sparse essential data is reasoned and assumption figures used in lieu of the missing data. These compiled baselines are then assessed against the requirement of the mission as specified in the present scenario. A huge expenditure plan is created and from this a trajectory analysis is used to decide e.g., propellant requirements to be supported by ISRO on the Martian surface. When launched by SpaceX and its CEO, Elon Musk, asserts that Starship is fully capable of making humans multi-planetary with long-term living stations on the Martian soil. In public, SpaceX has also not outlined mission specific plans which particularly concern contingency measures; for instances, SpaceX has not mentioned whether a free return trajectory will be adopted or any alternate reliability strategy for protection of the crew is going to be embraced [18].

12.4.2 Autonomous Systems in Healthcare

Artificial Intelligence has developed various aspects of dental healthcare, suggesting novel solutions to enduring challenges. Robotic systems have revolutionized modern dentistry, bringing significant advancements to the field. To facilitate autonomous operation, the system should comprise robotic arms armed with several tools and sensors, managed by software. Robotic systems in dental practice are used for various treatments such as implants, filling, and surgery of the gums. Such systems are used extensively in diagnostics where the clinician makes precise characterizations of the patient's oral health requirement. For example, Robotic system can interestingly be applied to intraoral scanning and 3D imaging to monitor detailed images of the teeth and the structures surrounding them. These images can be used in diagnosing dental conditions and planning for the effective treatment.

Robot-controlled surgery has been evolving gradually, as well as introducing new features to the conventional autonomous robotic systems. Robotic surgery would be desirable when the patient and physician are exposed to conditions in intense and challenging environments like on the battlefield or in surroundings with high contamination levels or ionizing radiation in medical diagnostics. The potential of surgeons in decision making as well as performing precision functions diminish in these situations [19].

The American College of Surgeons released a report in June 2023 on how AI bring a fresh "revolutionization" of surgical procedures. Most of the published research reveals that AI scan interpretation is more effective, reliable, and accurate than radiologists. Most of the concurring opinions from robotic surgeons and AI specialists are of the opinion that it is improbable it was inconceivable that surgeons would ever be substituted by surgical AI robot. AI is meant to support, not substitute, the right kind of surgery for a surgeon and his decision-making skills as well as his decision implementation capabilities.

Autonomous robots are highly dependents on the sensors and perception to define the surgical context and environment as well as the quality of that sensor. The lack of desire or possible feedback and haptic information which in turn prevented accurate decision making and immediate response during surgical procedures. Further, the completely automated surgical robots may find it difficult to handle the uncertainties in the surgery. The lack of experience in such new scenarios are not beneficial for their overall performance and effectiveness of their tasks [20].

12.5 Safety, Ethical Considerations, and Challenges

12.5.1 Managing Safety and System Failures in Autonomous Operations

12.5.1.1 Safety in Autonomous Systems

Safety becomes the most critical concern in autonomous systems, particularly for those operation that can pose a threat to human life, like healthcare, aerospace, or transportation. Such systems have to respond in real time to dynamic environmental changes for safe operating conditions. For example, autonomous cars make use of LiDAR, radar, and algorithmic fusion to detect obstructions and avoid them [21]. Despite improvement, perceptive mistakes and manipulation scenarios without foreseen response in the process are still challenges for independent systems. Self-learning competencies can improve adaptive system's capability to answer unfamiliar situations, so risks by users and safety in working environment decrease.

12.5.1.2 Fault Tolerance and Health Monitoring

Fault tolerance and system health are the two most key features of autonomous operation. Faults occur due to hardware failure, sensor inaccuracies, or software bugs can compromise both safety and performance. Predictive maintenance uses ML to predict failures before they occur by analyzing both historical and real-time data. Self-diagnosis and recovery mechanisms increase the robustness by autonomously isolating faults and making appropriate corrections. Hybrid approaches involving a combination of data-driven models and expert knowledge have higher accuracy in terms of diagnosis and fault recovery. The system continues running even after critical failures in such hybrids.

12.5.1.3 Cybersecurity in Autonomous Systems

The modern autonomous systems lays down in front of cyber insecurity hazards from data breaches and malicious takeover. Proper measures shall be taken for security issues concerned in connection channels and system data for avoiding misuse. AI-driven anomaly detection is a major function while detecting cyber threats in the run-time environment and facilitates early incident response. Besides that, effective communication protocols and model robustness are required for combat adversarial attacks that target the deception of the decision of autonomous systems. Therefore, with the integration of advanced cybersecurity technologies, autonomous systems can securely function in high-stake environments.

12.5.1.4 Human-Machine Interaction (HMI)

Evidently, human-machine interaction is what makes the autonomous system credible and efficient. Clear avenues for communication between humans and machines allow users to understand their current system state and intervene in times when necessary. Explainable AI thus allows for transparent decision making, which is important in user trust and effective actions in correction of complex events [22]. It will be based on ethical design considerations such as human safety and alignment of the operations of the system with societal values, which are basic to ethical deployment.

12.5.1.5 Advanced Testing Frameworks

Innovative testing methodologies for ensuring reliability and safety of autonomous systems demand hierarchies in testing that combine physical tests and virtual simulations to comprehensively evaluate the performance of the system. For efficient testing, tools like Gaussian Copula modeling predict responses of a system while searching for hazardous conditions, hence requiring less computational resources.

12.5.2 Ethical Concerns in Autonomous Technologies

12.5.2.1 Impact on Human Employment

A more profound implication of an increase in the use of autonomous technologies is to human employment. They pose terrific threats to labor from these emerging autonomous systems either industrial robots or self-driving cars and trucks. This means that companies engaged with ride sharing and logistics are rapidly shifting towards driverless trucks and cars to replace millions of driving jobs. Even if such advancements promise efficiency, they bring with them ethical concerns with regard to social responsibility to those displaced. The rollout of such technologies must then be proportionate with policies that assist in ensuring fair transition of the workforce and retraining access.

12.5.2.2 Decision-Making and Accountability

Probably, the most controversial ethical dilemma when talking about autonomous technologies is decision-making and responsibility. Autonomous systems are generally based on AI and ML algorithms, and they usually make life-or-death decisions in real-time situations [23]. This poses serious moral dilemmas to the autonomous vehicle, whose decision on whom to hit in cases of inevitable accidents determines whom to sacrifice. These situations require that such systems be transparent about how the ethical frameworks were designed and programmed into the system. It becomes complicated when responsibility for an action by an autonomous system lies across developers, manufacturers, and operators.

12.5.2.3 Privacy and Data Security

The ethical impacts of privacy and data protection in the time of autonomous technology are most poignant. The more autonomous devices use, the greater the number of sensors included, which subsequently gather more information as they function effectively. Data collection is at an all-time high in autonomous machinery, allowing them to collect a plethora of personal or environmental information to work within, such as geolocation when using a drone to deliver anything. Building public trust in such autonomous technologies will require the data security measures to be sound and the privacy regulations adhered to strictly. It should also address the bias problem in data collection and algorithmic decision-making.

12.5.2.4 Ethical Use in Sensitive Domains

Unique ethical issues arise when implementing autonomous technologies in sensitive domains such as healthcare, defense and law enforcement. The use of lethal decisions in drones and military vehicles is the question, for instance. In the health sector, autonomous diagnostic tools must be validated so that errors or bias through algorithms are avoided [24]. The focus of ethical frameworks should be on the sanctity of human welfare so that these technologies add rather than compromise safety, dignity, and ethics. To respond to these domain-specific concerns, technologists, ethicists, and policymakers must come together.

12.5.3 Challenges in Autonomous Systems

Many key challenges and emerging opportunities are controlling safety and system failures under autonomous operations. For meaningful insights to emerge from large datasets, techniques from high dimensional data processing like clustering and regression analysis have to be used. Balancing realism versus efficiency in the control of simulations has always been a challenge in simulation; the realistic ones requiring too much computation. Bias elimination in testing frameworks is another critical consideration, ensuring results reflect true system reliability without distortions from assumed data relationships. By addressing these challenges holistically, autonomous systems can achieve enhanced safety, reliability, and public trust.

12.6 Future Directions and Conclusion

12.6.1 Conclusion

Autonomous systems make use of the most advanced AI technologies in the performance of tasks without human intervention to ensure precision and adaptability in transportation, healthcare, and exploration. AI runs the systems by using perception, decision-making, and action processes through machine learning, deep learning, and reinforcement learning to analyze real-time data and improve their performance over time. These integrate sensors, processors, and actuators into dynamic environments with innovative solutions for problems in reliability, ethics, and trust. It further enhances the multiagent framework on grounds of cooperation and efficiency to show how AI is changing the face of autonomous functionality.

Artificial Intelligence technologies in autonomous systems allow them to sense and interpret the world in an intelligent fashion, acting to solve real-world problems. Machine Learning and Deep Learning enable execution of object detection, semantic segmentation, sensor data integration, etc., in perception and decision-making. The basis of reinforcement learning involves adaptive navigation, path planning, and optimization of rewards. In this regard, it combines LiDAR data, cameras, and radar for the purpose of building accuracy and robustness. High-level techniques include Kalman filtering, particle filtering, and deep sensor fusion to ensure high reliability performance, even in such dynamic and complicated conditions.

Autonomous vehicles rely on AI-based real-time decision-making that guarantees safety and efficiency with algorithms like perception, prediction, and planning in the form of YOLO, RRT, and reinforcement learning. Drones optimize delivery and surveillance *via* navigation, object detection, energy management, and real-time data analysis through sensor fusion and CNNs. The upgrade of AI-based military vehicle navigation and target detection and communication will utilize swarm intelligence and neural networks and therefore require countermeasure systems to be adjusted in response to changing terrains and threats. More intelligent and responsive systems transformed transportation, logistics, and defense.

The upgrade of AI-based military vehicle navigation and target detection and communication will utilize swarm intelligence and neural networks and therefore require countermeasure systems to be adjusted in response to changing terrains and threats. More intelligent and responsive systems transformed transportation, logistics, and defense. AI can provide precision in robotic surgeries and dental diagnostics but offers autonomy in extreme environments within healthcare. But fully autonomous robots that may support the decision-making are limited in regard to dealing with uncertainty and reliance on feedback.

Safety and ethical issues in autonomous systems include risk management, fault tolerance, and system security against cyber-attacks. Reliability and trust are brought through strong testing frameworks and the transparency of human-machine interaction. Displacement of jobs, responsibility in decision-making processes, privacy, and its use in sensitive fields such as health and defense will be the most urgent ethical concerns. These are to be met through cooperation among technologists, ethicists, and policymakers, ensuring that the technology is not against the values of society but for human welfare.

12.6.2 Future of AI in Expanding Autonomous Applications

Besides the vast potential in automation, AI is to be used as a key in the development of more intelligent and adaptive systems that could take decisions in real time with minimal human intervention. The growth of AI-driven autonomous applications will be a source of innovation in the healthcare sector where AI can aid diagnostics and personalized treatments, and in space exploration, where autonomous systems will be used in the planning and execution of missions. Ethics frameworks, robust safety protocols, and AI decision-making now have to become sounder and more transparent as autonomous technologies advance with pertinent societal issues in mind. Therefore, there is great promise for the future of

AI in autonomous applications in pushing boundaries on technological advancements as well as the opportunities that would be created in making smarter, safer, and more sustainable systems.

AI disclosure statement: The author confirms that no artificial intelligence (AI)-generated content or AI-assisted writing tools were used in the preparation of this chapter (including summaries and the abstract). All text, analysis, and conclusions are the result of the author's original work.

References

1. Jing, Z., Li, L., Lyu, Y., Wang, R., Wang, Y., Wang, D., Wang, F.Y., Autonomous services: The evolution of services through intelligent vehicles. *IEEE Trans. Intell. Veh.*, 8, 11, 4468–4473, 2023.
2. Fu, Y., Li, C., Yu, F.R., Luan, T.H., Zhang, Y., An autonomous lane-changing system with knowledge accumulation and transfer assisted by vehicular blockchain. *IEEE Internet Things J.*, 7, 11, 11123–11136, 2020.
3. Pasini, N., Mariani, A., Deguet, A., Kazanzides, P., De Momi, E., GRACE: Online gesture recognition for autonomous camera-motion enhancement in robot-assisted surgery. *IEEE Robot. Autom. Lett.*, 8, 12, 8263–8270, 2023. https://doi.org/10.1109/LRA.2023.3326690.
4. Yusuf, S.A., Khan, A., Souissi, R., Vehicle-to-everything (V2X) in the autonomous vehicles domain–A technical review of communication, sensor, and AI technologies for road user safety. *Transp. Res. Interdiscip. Perspect.*, 23, 100980, 2024.
5. Mangalampalli, S.S., Karri, G.R., Mohanty, S.N., Ali, S., Khan, M.I., Abdullaev, S., Alqahtani, S.A., Multi-objective prioritized task scheduler using improved asynchronous advantage actor critic (A3C) algorithm in multi cloud environment. *IEEE Access*, 12, 11354–11377, 2024. https://doi.org/10.1109/ACCESS.2024.3355092.
6. Yoon, K., Choi, J., Huh, K., Adaptive decentralized sensor fusion for autonomous vehicle: Estimating the position of surrounding vehicles. *IEEE Access*, 11, 90999–91008, 2023. https://doi.org/10.1109/ACCESS.2023.3308152.
7. Badar, T., Särkkä, S., Zhao, Z., Visala, A., Rao–Blackwellized particle filter using noise adaptive Kalman filter for fully mixing state-space models. *IEEE Trans. Aerosp. Electron. Syst.*, 60, 5, 6972–6982, 2024. https://doi.org/10.1109/TAES.2024.3409644.
8. Kalenberg, K., *et al.*, Stargate: Multimodal sensor fusion for autonomous navigation on miniaturized UAVs. *IEEE Internet Things J.*, 11, 12, 21372–21390, 2024. https://doi.org/10.1109/JIOT.2024.3363036.
9. Shu, H., Liu, T., Mu, X., Cao, D., Driving tasks transfer using deep reinforcement learning for decision-making of autonomous vehicles in unsignalized intersection. *IEEE Trans. Veh. Technol.*, 71, 1, 41–52, 2021.

10. Zhao, L., Zhou, H., Zhu, X., Song, X., Li, H., Tao, W., Lif-seg: Lidar and camera image fusion for 3d lidar semantic segmentation. *IEEE Trans. Multimedia*, 26, 1158–1168, 2023.
11. Wang, X., Hu, J., Wei, C., Li, L., Li, Y., Du, M., A Novel Lane-Change Decision-Making With Long-Time Trajectory Prediction for Autonomous Vehicle. *IEEE Access*, 11, 137437–137449, 2023.
12. Brophy, T., *et al.*, A review of the impact of rain on camera-based perception in automated driving systems. *IEEE Access*, 11, 67040–67057, 2023. https://doi.org/10.1109/ACCESS.2023.3290143.
13. Park, S., Park, C., Kim, J., Learning-based cooperative mobility control for autonomous drone-delivery. *IEEE Trans. Veh. Technol.*, 73, 4, 4870–4885, 2024. https://doi.org/10.1109/TVT.2023.3330460.
14. Sheppard, A. and Skinner, K.A., Automatic Data Processing for Space Robotics Machine Learning, arXiv preprint *arXiv:2310.01932*, 2023.
15. Mittal, M., Dewan, P., Panesar, T., Singh, M., Educating a Robot to Walk on Mars using Artificial Intelligence. *2024 11th International Conference on Computing for Sustainable Global Development (INDIACom)*, New Delhi, India, pp. 1137–1143, 2024, doi: 10.23919/INDIACom61295.2024.10498720.
16. Thangavel, K., Sabatini, R., Gardi, A., Ranasinghe, K., Hilton, S., Servidia, P., Spiller, D., Artificial intelligence for trusted autonomous satellite operations. *Prog. Aerosp. Sci.*, 144, 100960, 2024.
17. Goodwill, J., Wilson, C., MacKinnon, J., Current AI technology in space, in: *Precision Medicine for Long and Safe Permanence of Humans in Space*, pp. 239–250, Academic Press, 2025.
18. Maiwald, V., Bauerfeind, M., Fälker, S., Westphal, B., Bach, C., About feasibility of SpaceX's human exploration Mars mission scenario with Starship. *Sci. Rep.*, 14, 1, 11804, 2024.
19. Han, J., Davids, J., Ashrafian, H., Darzi, A., Elson, D.S., Sodergren, M., A systematic review of robotic surgery: From supervised paradigms to fully autonomous robotic approaches. *Int. J. Med. Rob. Comput. Assisted Surg.*, 18, 2, e2358, 2022.
20. Rivero-Moreno, Y., Rodriguez, M., Losada-Muñoz, P., Redden, S., Lopez-Lezama, S., Vidal-Gallardo, A., Machado-Paled, D., Cordova Guilarte, J., Teran-Quintero, S., Autonomous robotic surgery: Has the future arrived? *Cureus*, 16, 1, e52243, 2024. https://doi.org/10.7759/cureus.52243.
21. Tlig, M., Machin, M., Kerneis, R., Arbaretier, E., Zhao, L., Meurville, F., Van Frank, J., Autonomous driving system: Model based safety analysis. *2018 48th Annual IEEE/IFIP International Conference on Dependable Systems and Networks Workshops (DSN-W)*, pp. 2–5, 2018.
22. He, H., Gray, J., Cangelosi, A., Meng, Q., McGinnity, T.M., Mehnen, J., The challenges and opportunities of human-centered AI for trustworthy robots and autonomous systems. *IEEE Trans. Cognit. Dev. Syst.*, 14, 4, 1398–1412, 2021.

23. Jiang, Z., Pan, W., Liu, J., Dang, S., Yang, Z., Li, H., Pan, Y., Efficient and unbiased safety test for autonomous driving systems. *IEEE Trans. Intell. Veh.*, 8, 5, 3336–3348, 2022.
24. Polyakova, I. and Sysoev, A., Ethical Problems of Applying Artificial Intelligence: Medical Intelligent Systems and Autonomous Vehicles. *2023 3rd International Conference on Technology Enhanced Learning in Higher Education (TELE)*, pp. 31–35, 2023.

13

Responsible Use of AI in Healthcare: Addressing Bias, Transparency, and Patient Trust

Shubham Gupta

Department of Computer Science and Engineering, Model Institute of Engineering and Technology, Jammu, J&K, India

Abstract

AI presents a transformative potential in healthcare, enhancing patient care, diagnosis, and treatment *via* heightened accuracy, speed, and personalization. Yet, to have responsible implementations, ethics issues including privacy, bias, accountability, and transparency should be taken into consideration as well. AI models, by nature, require vast amounts of data, and thus, there are concerns about how sensitive medical information can be secured. If this bias is embedded in training data, the result is disparity, with understudied groups facing the consequences and the widening of the inequality gap within the health sector. If an AI-based decision goes wrong, we need to ensure that we have systems in place where people are held accountable for mistakes and negative consequences. So, the AI systems are "black boxes", which means that their use is filled with transparency threats, and thus, explainable AI (XAI) is required to build trust. Furthermore, unequal accessibility to AI technologies can worsen the global health gap, and that is another very important issue to be addressed. If we want to make sure that AI does serve to enhance the delivery of healthcare in this manner, technologists, the healthcare workforce, and policymakers, among others with a stake in healthcare, will need to work to build a governance framework around it that maintains the ethical integrity of the health system.

***Keywords*:** Artificial intelligence, healthcare, transparency, ethical, explainable AI

Email: guptashubham96222@gmail.com

Manish Kumar, Nitigya Sambyal, Leena Priyadarshini Singh, Ramasamy V. and S. Balamurugan (eds.) Responsible AI: Principles and Practices, (297–322) © 2026 Scrivener Publishing LLC

13.1 Introduction

Artificial Intelligence (AI) has the potential to impact various aspects of the healthcare ecosystem, making it a powerful game changer within the healthcare space. AI (artificial intelligence) tools are coming on-stream that will revolutionize medicine in areas so fundamentally that diagnostics, treatment, and patient care are all being transformed. While the advantages of AI are many and multitalented, the ethical side of it also matters equally. So, this chapter explores the most prominent ethical challenges related to the use of AI in health care: bias, transparency, and trust.

13.1.1 Overview of AI in Healthcare

The integration of AI technology into the healthcare sector promises to fundamentally change how clinicians diagnose, treat, and monitor patients. From advanced medical diagnostics in which artificial intelligence systems using advanced machine learning technology can surpass human professionals in areas like certain facets of pathology and radiology at least to some degree. The best doctors become better by using AI to make better decisions and better judgments. Patients receive personalized treatment regimens devised from unique combinations of genetic profiles, personal health histories, and real-time health variables in the process [1]. Additionally, AI has the prospect of reducing the cost of healthcare by automating administrative tasks, simplifying work processes, and ensuring optimal operational performance. In the pharmaceutical sector, for example, AI has not only accelerated the process of identifying new therapeutic compounds but also improved patient participation in health trials by shortening and reducing their costs. AI serves as a critical solution for offering predictions about the progression of diseases, making it possible for physicians to secure early intervention and prevention of severe chronic conditions [2]. However, the wider adoption of AI in the sector should necessitate an equally high-level understanding of the limitations, issues, and hazards afflicting this technology on medical professionals and patients.

AI in healthcare, as in Figure 13.1, has quite a bit of influence on diagnostic methods. The quality of accuracy from radiology, pathologic reports, genetic profiling, and real-time health monitoring will tailor the selected personalized treatment to a more effective one. It reduces costs by automating work, optimizing workflows, and improving processes. AI also accelerates drug discovery, predicts diseases for preemptive intervention, and addresses ethical dilemmas and technical limitations.

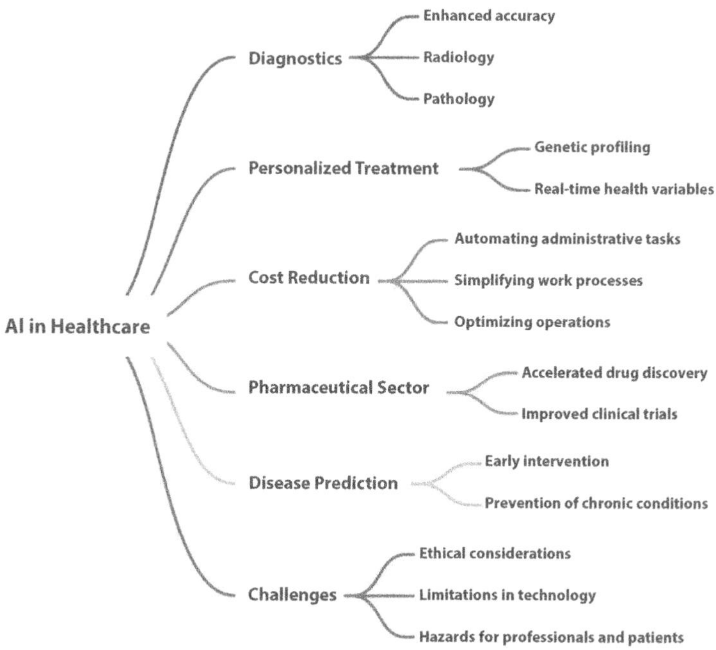

Figure 13.1 AI in healthcare.

13.1.2 Importance of Ethical Considerations

As AI systems become more integrated into healthcare technology, the ethical component has never been more important. The potential value of AI to medical outcomes is enormous, but we do need to tread carefully in its application, particularly as it pertains to patient privacy, equitable access, and remaining on the right side of algorithmic bias.

13.1.2.1 Ethical Implications of AI in Healthcare

As AI solutions became embedded in healthcare technology, the need for the ethical component could not have been more critical. There are tremendous potential benefits of AI to medical outcomes, but we must approach its application with caution across several different dimensions, particularly concerning patient privacy, equitable access, and appropriate guardrails against the possibility of algorithmic bias.

AI and accountability and transparency issues: There are also issues of accountability and transparency with AI [3]. As decisions are increasingly delegated to AI systems, particularly in high-stakes healthcare environments, it becomes less and less clear who is responsible for errors or adverse outcomes.

It will inevitably lead to the demands, which are already being made, for some accountability and transparency, and if either patients or health professionals cannot understand the inner workings or have any trust in the mechanisms that can know the processes being used for AI decision making, then this will undermine the confidence of the public in this technology.

13.1.2.2 Balancing Innovation with Responsibility

With AI technologies rapidly evolving, it is imperative to balance innovation and accountability. Also, although the potential of AI in healthcare is immense, its implementation must be governed by ethical principles [4]. Healthcare systems need to embrace transparency, fairness, and patient autonomy. Finally, AI development in healthcare through a lens of equity and justice requires that AI does not compound existing inequities or harm vulnerable populations. Since AI systems can be powerful and raise ethical and social concerns, ethical governance of AI will be crucial to protect interests around the world and preserve trust.

13.1.3 Scope of the Chapter

This chapter contributes to the existing body of research by providing ethical implications of AI in healthcare accompanied by concrete solutions regarding bias mitigation, transparency, and governance. This article goes beyond typical studies that mainly highlight the issues of these governance approaches and provides a detailed framework of collaborative governance, bias audit, and explainable AI methods.

Upon comparative analysis of current governance frameworks, it is evident that there are also gaps in AI regulation concerning transparency and accountability. We present a new governance model that involves technologists, clinicians, policymakers, and patients throughout the AI development lifecycle to create an ethical AI design and deployment framework in health care. This work builds on discussions of responsible AI in medicine, serving to bridge the gap between conversations on AI ethics and strategies for effective implementation in practice.

13.2 Ethical Challenges in AI-Driven Healthcare

AI has great potential for delivering tremendous value in healthcare, including improved patient outcomes, greater productivity, and decreased costs. But with these great advances come big ethical questions of how we

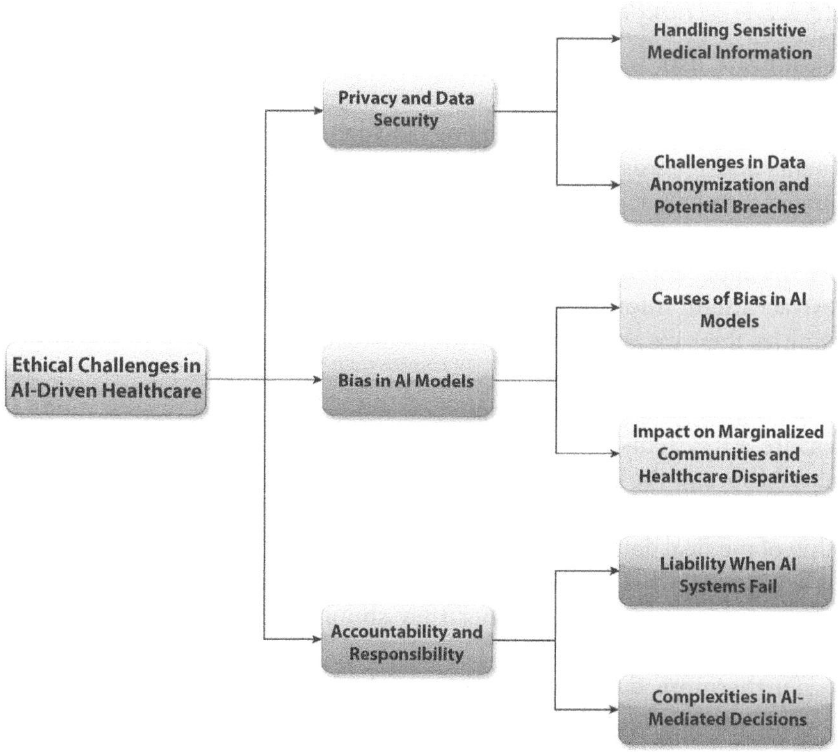

Figure 13.2 Ethical challenges in AI-driven healthcare.

responsibly use AI systems. This particular subset of ethical challenges around privacy, bias, accountability, and transparency is highly relevant because they dive deeper into the heart of not only how care is delivered but also the trust that providers, patients, and society hold regarding these AI-based technologies, as depicted in Figure 13.2.

13.2.1 Privacy and Data Security

Machine learning models power outcomes in AI-enabled healthcare and to create these models requires access to significant amounts of patient data. This, however, opens a Pandora's box of problems about the privacy and security of sensitive medical information. Ensuring that AI systems treat data responsibly is among the basic ethical battles in this area.

13.2.1.1 Handling Sensitive Medical Information

Healthcare data is widely regarded as one of the most sensitive forms of personal information, with the category covering anything from a patient's medical history, diagnostic imaging, and genetic data to notes about treatments and records of prescriptions. Access to this information, which is often fragmented across numerous platforms and stakeholders (hospitals, insurance companies, pharmaceutical companies), is a critical requirement for the applications of AI in these healthcare systems. AI technologies may extract useful information from much larger datasets, but this in opportunities they are also conducive to misuse due to misuse or unauthorized access.

Stringent data governance policies are necessary for organizations to ensure AI systems act within the lines of responsible guidelines. These should specify the legal, ethical, and technical frameworks for assuring the confidentiality of patient data (for example, informed consent and ownership of medical data). However, patients need to be aware of how their data is being used, whether those data are being used for training AI algorithms or something else, and whether they should be able to opt out if they want to.

Furthermore, data governance is much bigger than just collecting data. Healthcare providers also must control how this data is shared as well as who accesses it [5]. This highlights the need for developing frameworks that enable patients to take control of their data and ensure any data-sharing agreements are clear, transparent, and compliant with privacy laws such as the GDPR and HIPAA.

13.2.1.2 Challenges in Data Anonymization and Potential Breaches

One of the main strategies for ensuring patient privacy is ensuring that you anonymize data, the process by which personally identifiable information (PII) is removed from data sets, and the individuals whom the data describes cannot be identified. However, there are growing concerns that anonymization is becoming increasingly ineffective due to advances in data analysis and machine learning that have made anonymized data increasingly susceptible to re-identification. This is particularly troubling with healthcare data, for which even anonymized data can usually be cross-referenced with other datasets to reidentify someone.

In case of defective anonymization processes or security loopholes, private patient information might be leaked due to which the AI system might be susceptible to breaches. When AI models are trained with health information across multiple third-party platforms, it's difficult to ensure that every party involved upholds stringent privacy measures. Furthermore, such large-scale data breaches risk not only individual privacy but also the trustworthiness of AI systems in comparison with health services [6]. As a response to these potential threats, AI developers and healthcare providers should place more emphasis on the deployment of state-of-the-art security procedures like advanced encryption, multi-factor authentication, and routine vulnerability assessments. For their part, patients should be aware of what is being done to protect their data and what they can do if it is compromised.

13.2.2 Bias in AI Models

One of the biggest ethical challenges in AI is bias, which can be detrimental to patient care, especially in the realm of healthcare. The data training the AI systems* are historical data, which could be biased due to the healthcare system, the society structure, or even how data is collected. AI algorithms can inadvertently perpetuate these biases, resulting in unfair or inaccurate results.

13.2.2.1 Causes of Bias in AI Models

At the same time, the bias in AI models usually stems from the bias in the data. This is because AI algorithms learn from the data they train on and if those training datasets are skewed or unrepresentative, the algorithms will mirror those biases. For instance, a diagnostic imaging AI model that is mostly trained on data from one demographic group (for instance, white male patients) may not work as accurately for patients of different races, genders, or ethnicities. This bias may cause misdiagnoses, delayed treatments, or erroneous medical recommendations for groups in the minority.

Systemic inequalities within the healthcare system are another major source of bias. Such disparities can be seen by certain demographic groups being underrepresented in medical research or treatment trials. Groups within society that have been marginalized, such as racial minorities, women, or people with lower socioeconomic status, might receive inadequate healthcare, which, when integrated into training datasets, can further bias AI models.

The ethical issues of AI in healthcare are stressed by empirical studies. When trained on non-representative datasets, biased AI models have been shown to create disparities in patient care. One dermatology AI tool that was extensively trained on lighter skin tones misclassified skin cancer in patients with darker skin, resulting in delayed diagnoses. Similarly, AI-driven radiology models trained on Caucasian populations were shown to underperform in diverse demographic groups, raising the stakes for misdiagnosis. These findings highlight the need for ensuring AI models are trained on diverse datasets that will minimize bias and enhance fairness in healthcare applications.

13.2.2.2 Impact on Marginalized Communities and Healthcare Disparities

This in turn can compound an already significant inequity in health care, including insufficient and poor quality care to already underserved minority groups. Such a biased AI can result in less accurate or timelier diagnostics, for patients who are members of minority ethnic groups. In high-stakes fields, oncology is a classic example where early detection is directly related to achieving a better prognosis, and this is particularly true.

Secondly, biased AI can also influence treatment protocols: algorithms can positively bias certain treatments or drugs that may be the right course of action for the general population but not specifically for underrepresented populations [7]. "These differences can, therefore, result in negative health outcomes, amplify inequalities, and perpetuate discrimination within a health care system." This correlates with biases that can build on the patient population and could be handled with systematic efforts in heterogeneous and representative datasets. It necessitates partnerships with healthcare systems that treat underrepresented groups and thorough testing of A.I. models to ensure that they are equitable and accurate across diverse populations. Regular audits for equity and fairness are also mandatory for AI systems, as they should not discriminate against any group.

13.2.3 Accountability and Responsibility

One of the biggest ethical dilemmas with AI in healthcare is determining who to hold responsible when AI fails. As AI is more and more infused into the clinical processes, either as an adjunct or an alternative to human decision-making, the specters of liability and accountability haunt the space, not least for errors in diagnosis or treatment and for unintended consequences that can result from the autonomous action of AI.

13.2.3.1 Liability When AI Systems Fail

AI-assisted decisions also raise thorny questions of liability if things go wrong. When an AI system has made an incorrect diagnosis or treatment recommendation, establishing a chain of culpability is particularly difficult." The liability also could rest with the health provider who acted on the A.I.'s recommendation, with the developer of the algorithm, or the organization that deployed the system. If the health care provider failed to exercise due diligence in vetting the A.I.'s recommendations, or if the health care provider gamed the system, that could be a liability." Conversely, if an algorithm goes wrong due to design or logic/functional problems, and the developer is to blame for improvements not being made that developer may be held liable. If there was a failure in appropriate testing, monitoring, and clinical integration of the AI system, the healthcare organization that deployed the AI system would also potentially be liable. This web of potential liability represents another argument for robust regulatory frameworks and clear legal guidelines around AI decision-making in healthcare, and where, when, and how they are used.

In traditional health care, the spotlight is on the provider to white-knuckle their way through looking out for the patient. But the line is blurred when an AI system is introduced. If a doctor follows the recommendation of the A.I. and something goes wrong, then determining responsibility is a complicated issue. If the physician fails to critically evaluate the output of the AI, relying on a recommendation of the system without applying her professional judgment, then she may be jointly liable. In these scenarios, the doctor would be negligent just for going along with the system results and not thinking about any other diagnoses and treatment options. But if the error is found to lie in defects within the AI system itself, for example, in poor design or coding, liability could shift to the developers who wrote the algorithm [8]. This is particularly pertinent because an AI model's recommendation will be fundamentally flawed if the data input or relevant algorithm is biased. Here, the developers are to blame because they should be aware of how to ensure the system was tested, trained on varied representative data, and free from bias such that relevant recommendations could be relied upon as correct. Moreover, accountability becomes less straightforward when the decision-making process involves both human and machine judgment.

Policymakers need to define rules and regulations that clarify accountability in the context of AI applications in healthcare. It is imperative to develop a shared responsibility framework in ensuring patient safety where the healthcare providers can depend on their AI counterparts to further validate their algorithm through real-world collaboration but also sets the limitations of the AI developers to avoid any adverse event that could happen in patient safety just due to malfunction of their technology. As the architecture of AI-based decision-making continues to grow ever more complex, legal systems ought to parallel this transformation by crafting liability regimes that welcome the multifactorial character of AI.

13.2.3.2 Complexities in AI-Mediated Decisions

A fledgling problem with AI-aided healthcare choices is the "black box" quality of many machine-studying fashions. That gives these models a black-box character, never entirely understandable to the humans who depend on them, and finding the root cause of a mistake is often hard work. In an AI-powered healthcare space, this lack of explainability creates barriers when establishing culpability. For example, when a model misdiagnoses a condition with a false positive or a negative it will not be obvious the reason for that outcome. Biased data use, an algorithmic flaw, or human error interpreting the model's output. Without clear insight into how the AI arrived at the decision, there is little to no accountability for the failure.

This problem can be tackled with the introduction of explainable AI (XAI). Explainable AI (XAI) aims to interpret models based on machine learning to understand decision-making better. Increasing AI systems transparency allows healthcare providers to understand the reasoning behind an AI model's recommendation, detect potential errors, and attribute responsibility where it belongs [9]. However, it is important that as AI is increasingly used in the medical field, XAI framework developments and implementations are established to create the accountability and trust needed in health care.

13.3 Transparency in AI Systems

Transparency is one of the basic principles in the ethics of unlocking AI in health care in a way that is effective and trustworthy. This excellence in modeling comes at the cost of interpretability, as the most sophisticated AIs have tended to be "black boxes." The opacity of many AI systems is fraught with implications of accountability, trust, and fairness, which is especially important in high-stakes areas of society such as health care. Here is the discussion on the issue of transparency in AI, the "black box" problem, the possibilities provided by Explainable AI (XAI) to overcome concerns raised by lack of transparency, and the regulatory standards needed for transparency [10].

13.3.1 The "Black Box" Problem

A black-box artificial intelligence system is one whose internal workings are not inherently transparent or interpretable by humans. The AI models, non-exclusively deep learning systems, can generate results that can be very hard to interpret even for the clinician or any end-users. This lack of transparency poses severe challenges in the medical space where AI decisions can have immediate effects on patient health and treatment options.

13.3.1.1 Lack of Interpretability in AI Decision-Making

Artificial Intelligence (AI) models, particularly deep learning models, function by passing large amounts of data through complex layers of mathematical functions and algorithms. Such complex processing ultimately leads to a decision or recommendation outcome (i.e. On the other hand, explaining the reason ways that the model has decided to classify or detect something can become extremely hard [11]. This interpretability issue is due to the unexplainable mechanisms that happen within the model, making it difficult for clinicians or even developers to explain the processes in human terms. This is a problem in healthcare because clinicians need to trust clinical decisions to be able to make informed medical decisions. If the AI suggests a treatment or diagnosis, the clinician needs assurance that the recommendation has been reasoned. Nonetheless, in such cases where the AI model does not justify its output, clinicians may find it challenging to evaluate the suitability or correctness of the recommendation.

Moreover, explainability is important to identify and correct errors that otherwise might go undetected. This means that, whenever an AI system gives a false decision or a false diagnosis/inference, it is important to understand how this was achieved in order not only to remedy the error but also to avoid repeating it in the future. Without understanding how a model makes its decision, diagnosing and fixing these issues becomes harder.

13.3.1.2 Implications for Clinicians and Patients

For clinicians, the "black box" problem presents a huge challenge. It's hard to grasp how AI works, and so many hesitate to embrace AI recommendations wholeheartedly [12]. This high degree of opacity is resulting in skepticism here, or even refusal to leverage AI recommendations, especially in high-stakes clinical settings, such as the diagnosis and plan for treatment of cancer, threatening the utility of AI-driven healthcare tools.

For patients, the "black box" issue can be even more consequential. When patients are unable to understand how an AI system arrived at its decisions or how patient data was used in the decision process, trust in the larger healthcare system can break down. Patient trust depends on transparency: patients want you to explain not just what decision you are making, but also why. When AI is in play, patients risk feeling alienated or powerless, particularly if they sense that important choices about their well-being are being dictated by an opaque system that they cannot shape or critique. So, this "black box" issue can have consequences that impact the way practitioners use the AI tools designed to assist them and the perception patients have of AI-augmented procedures. Addressing this challenge is important for building trust in AI which promotes its wide-scale adoption in healthcare.

13.3.2 Explainable AI (XAI)

The "black box" nature of many AI models raises challenges around transparency that the field of Explainable AI (XAI) seeks to address. XAI seeks to create AI systems that can have human-understandable decision-making processes and provide transparent and interpretable explanations behind the outputs of AI models [13]. In them, the explainability provided by XAI mitigates both trust and accountability concerns that derive from the complex dynamics of healthcare.

13.3.2.1 Advances in Explainability to Build Trust

In recent years, we have seen significant strides in explainable AI (XAI) efforts to make AI decision-making more interpretable. These include model-agnostic methods, which explain the output of a specific existing machine learning model, and intrinsic interpretability, which builds models to be explainable always as they are designed to be so.

Some machine learning algorithms are interpretable by nature, such as decision trees or decision rules, because their decision-making process can be explained by a series of logical steps. Model-agnostic methods, such as Local Interpretable Model-agnostic Explanations (LIME) or Shapley additive explanations (SHAP) explain the predictions of black-box AI models by fitting a simple model to approximate their make this judgment model [14]. These approaches help clinicians understand the roles of the different features (e.g., patient history, medical test results, imaging data) in the AI's prediction or recommendation.

These improvements in XAI can be vital in building trust concerning AI systems amongst clinicians and patients. XAI increases the transparency of the AI system by providing interpretations that can be understood, which allows clinicians to make informed decisions as to how to implement insights generated by the algorithm into their daily work. Strategically, explainability for patients refers to how AI systems come to a certain decision, enabling patients to engage in valuing their decision-making through healthcare providers, bettering the patient-provider relationship, and providing patients with more bot power over their medical decisions.

XAI is a move toward accountability, too. Explainable models provide visibility into the mechanics of a decision-making process: if the AI system makes a mistake, healthcare providers can identify where in that system the mistake occurred and fix it either by reworking the AI model or by adjusting clinical workflows [15]. This increased transparency means that AI systems are less prone to making unnoticed errors that can result in inadequate patient treatment.

13.3.2.2 Case Studies/Examples of Successful XAI Implementations

An important application of XAI in health care is the use of explainable machine-learning models in diagnostic imaging. As an example, XAI techniques in mammography images for breast cancer detection were applied, and the authors demonstrated how the applied AI models could highlight the relevant parts of an image that had the most influence on the diagnosis. By looking at which particular regions of the image were being called the attention to make a decision they understood about the patterns in the input that the AI model had been focusing on learning a lot about how the AI was reasoning.

One example is IBM's Watson Health, which has developed oncology tools that integrated explainability into its work. Watson Health uses natural language processing and machine learning to assist oncologists in diagnosing cancers and the treatment pathways to take. To ensure transparency, Watson provides clinicians with explanations about how specific attributes of the patients such as genetic mutations or previous treatment histories, influence treatment suggestions. This level of interpretability fosters trust, allowing oncologists to apply Watson as a collaborator rather than a black-box decision-maker.

Conclusion: The results from these case studies highlight how XAI can help make AI systems in health care more transparent and trustworthy and provide better clinical decision-making and patient care.

Below are some ethical issues regarding artificial intelligence in healthcare and how to tackle them. To ensure this, the development of AI models should have strict bias checks in place, employ Fairness Aware Machine Learning (FAML), and use easily interpretable datasets with multiple demographic groups contained within both training and testing analysis. Finally, protect against potential abuse of sensitive medical information by using strong data security measures like encryption, decentralized storage, and patient-controlled access. And, develop thorough explainability techniques (SHAP, LIME) for being responsible & interpretable to clinicians & patients for healthcare AI. In addition, AI models would have to be constantly audited and checked by regulatory bodies to ensure compliance with existing healthcare protocols/standards. So while using AI ethically in healthcare, we can ensure transparency and trust.

13.3.3 Regulatory Standards for Transparency

As artificial intelligence continues to be integrated into our healthcare systems, we need to set clear regulatory policies on transparency in these systems. And even though some frameworks/regulations encourage AI transparency, enforcement is lacking, as is standardization and comprehensive coverage of systems.

13.3.3.1 Current Frameworks and Gaps in AI Governance

These transparency-focused regulatory frameworks, such as the European Union's General Data Protection Regulation (GDPR), which governs the processing of personal data, and the U.S. Food and Drug Administration, which sets guidelines for the approval of AI-based medical devices, aim to ensure the transparency and accountability of relevant AI systems. For example, the GDPR states that individuals must be informed how their data is collected and used, and allows individuals a right to explanation in cases where decisions affect them due to automated processes.

However, these regulations focus primarily on data privacy and security rather than the transparency of AI decision-making itself. Substantial work is needed to define exactly what kind of standards should be created for how AI models should be engineered so that they produce explainable and interpretable decision-making [16]. There is yet no global consensus on what constitutes the appropriate level of transparency for AI in healthcare, and this absence of regulation acts as a brake on the broad adoption of AI technologies.

Moreover, conventional frameworks often lag technologically; this regulatory lag can lead to a scenario in which AI systems are used in clinical practice before extensive regulatory protocols exist to guarantee system transparency. In response, policymakers should work with AI researchers, clinicians, and other stakeholders to create actionable guidelines for the minimum transparency of AI systems used in healthcare.

13.3.3.2 Recommendations for Future Regulatory Approaches

Recommendations to bridge the gaps in existing regulatory frameworks First, regulatory authorities need to set standards in explainability for AI models, including requiring interpretability of decision-making in all AI systems deployed in healthcare. In developing these standards, both the technical details of explainability and the needs of end-users must be prioritized so that the explanations produced by AI systems are intuitive to the clinicians and patients for whom AI-driven recommendations are designed.

Second, a centralized oversight mechanism should be formed to oversee AI models in healthcare, ensuring that they comply with common standards regarding explainability and accountability. Such a body could oversee regular audits of AI systems and guidance on best practices in transparency. Finally, we need governments and international organizations to coordinate AI laws worldwide so that any AI system used globally must meet the same rigorous transparency requirements. This would enable more equal and universal access to AI-powered healthcare instruments with fewer dangers of transparency.

13.4 Building and Maintaining Patient Trust

Trust is fundamental to every aspect of healthcare, creating the bedrock on which patients and providers build their relationship. Trust between patients and doctors is essential: if patients do not trust their healthcare providers, they will not be open about their issues, follow medication or treatment as directed, or communicate effectively about their health, making it more difficult to achieve positive health outcomes [17]. As the integration of artificial intelligence (AI) systems into healthcare continues to rise, understanding their implications for patient trust has become a pressing task. This section talks about trust in healthcare, the mechanisms that AI can influence, the human and AI relationship, and ways to combat fear or misconceptions regarding AI in medicine.

13.4.1 Trust as a Pillar of Healthcare

13.4.1.1 The Role of Trust in Patient-Provider Relationships

Many consider trust to be the foundation of the healthcare relationship. When patients trust their physician, important and sensitive information can be shared to improve decision-making. This willingness to share is critical to an accurate diagnosis because providers need full and honest information about patients' history, symptoms, and lifestyles. Trust enhances the likelihood that patients follow treatment plans, take medication, and engage in preventive health.

Healthcare trust extends beyond the immediate clinical encounter and includes the broader healthcare system. However, when patients have faith in their healthcare system to be fair, respectful, and private, they are more likely to engage in steps to improve their health proactively, to regularly receive health screenings, and to pursue preventive measures, resulting in better overall health for themselves.

But, distrust can be easily undermined and corroded by miscommunication, misjudgment, or a sense that healthcare leaders do not have a patient's best interests in mind. AI in the healthcare space introduces an added layer of complexity to the trust-building process. The increasing participation of AI in clinical decision-making poses a puzzle for patients and healthcare professionals confronted with the intricacies of AI's role, in which the imperative for perpetual advancement is counterbalanced by the need to schedule a degree of human oversight (and empathy).

13.4.1.2 Impact of AI Systems on Trust

AI has the potential to help build trust and reduce it in healthcare depending on how much it factors in trustworthiness when it aggregates and generates. If used appropriately, AI systems can improve diagnostic precision, reduce human error, and provide targeted therapies. Such benefits may contribute to greater patient confidence in the health system. For instance, AI-enabled tools that analyze medical imaging or genetic data can identify conditions that the best human clinicians might overlook, which increases patients' confidence in their diagnoses.

On the flip side, if patients or providers find AI to be opaque, impersonal, or unreliable, then it can also corrode trust. When patients cannot follow the reasoning behind an AI system or when an AI system gets something wrong without being able to explain why, patients could feel as if the healthcare process is being humanized or that decisions are being made without enough regard for their context. AI systems that are seen as replacing human involvement altogether rather than complementing it may also contribute to patients feeling alienated or anxious, who expect personalized care.

Therefore, messaging around the use of AI in health care must be presented clearly and transparently, focusing on the augmentation role that AI already has within human providers and helping to ensure that AI bolsters rather than diminishes the trust that patients have in their health care teams.

13.4.2 Human-AI Collaboration

13.4.2.1 Ensuring AI Supports Rather Than Replaces Clinicians

One of the most common apprehensions is that AI will replace the clinician, compromising the humanized aspect of healthcare delivery. AI can help automate some tasks and augment clinicians in the decision-making process but not replace them [18]. AI may have the ability to sift through massive amounts of data, identify patterns, and suggest interventions, but it does not have the emotional intelligence, clinical intuition, and ethical reasoning that a human provider contributes to patient care.

However, in practice, AI can act as an augmenting technology for the clinician. AI systems can help doctors identify potential problems that they might otherwise have missed anomalous test results, rare diseases, etc. The role of the clinician in interpreting AI recommendations, making nuanced decisions, and discussing treatment options with patients is still critical but will increasingly need to be combined with appropriate and often overlapping AI-based treatments.

Clinicians and technology must be allies in the advancement of AI with this frame of trust, driving better care for patients. Patients must realize that AI is meant to improve not take the place of their health care provider. This can be conveyed by highlighting the fact that AI systems are intended to complement human expertise, maintaining a collaborative approach to decision-making.

13.4.2.2 Importance of Involving Patients in AI-Related Decisions

A significant factor in maintaining patient trust towards the use of AI in healthcare is to engage patients in decision-making regarding their care, especially when AI systems are harnessed to inform or guide treatment. Involving patients, not only facilitates a better decision-making process, it fosters self-ownership. When patients know about the role of AI in their treatment and can weigh in on how AI tools are used, they are more likely to trust the process and feel respected in the healthcare system.

I have suggested at the outset that meaningful patient involvement will have to take place at critical junctures in care, and one of these in the case of AI-enabled interventions can take the form of shared decision-making wherein patients are informed of their options (including those based on AI insights) and allowed to voice their preferences and concerns. For instance, a clinician can convey that an artificial intelligence technology has pointed to a specific course of treatment by thoroughly reviewing the patient's medical history, but the patient has the option to research other treatments or get a second opinion. Adopting this approach also promotes patient engagement in their treatment regimen, reminding patients that AI in healthcare is serving them, not working instead of them.

Above all, what an AI system can and cannot unfortunately do must be transparent to everyone. Along with making them aware of the potential upsides of AI deployment in their care, patients must also be made aware of potential adverse effects or uncertainty that the new technology might entail [19]. Allowing time for patient questions, concerns, and informed decision-making is important to trust and teamwork between patients and providers.

13.5 Governance and Regulatory Oversight

As AI becomes ubiquitous and there is more uptake in healthcare, its ethical principles must be concordant with its use towards ensuring transparency and attaining equity to preserve trust and protect patient welfare. The challenge lies in balancing the imperative to harness the potential of AI with the necessity of protecting against the risks of AI, and getting governance, regulation, and oversight of AI technologies in health care right is critical to promoting that the technologies are deployed in ways that promote patient safety, and that are ethical and fair. This section summarizes the case for proactive governance, the key shortfalls of oversight governance alluded to in the sections above, and the role of cross-stakeholder collaboration in enabling responsible and ethical AI.

13.5.1 Need for Proactive Governance

13.5.1.1 Current Policies and Ethical Standards

The pace of development of AI in healthcare is unprecedented, as is the demand for holistic regulatory frameworks. Even where general data protection and privacy laws exist (e.g., from the European Union General Data Protection Regulation (GDPR) or the United States Health Insurance Portability and Accountability Act (HIPAA)), both these laws are massive gaps in the face of the new challenges posed by AI. Existing frameworks emphasize data privacy/security, leaving important oversight holes in AI's decision impact (who decides)) and fairness (who gets hurt).

Ethics guidelines for AI use in healthcare are still in transition. We do not have fully operational policies that use rules at a high level on the best way to develop and use AI fairly, transparently, and without leading to harm. Although some organizations and institutions such as the World Health Organization (WHO) and the European Commission have published recommendations on AI ethics, such guidelines are typically voluntary and inconsistent across jurisdictions, and as such, it is challenging to create common, enforceable governance.

Furthermore, there is the challenge of AI being a "black box." Most AI models, especially the ones that use deep learning, are complex and opaque and they do not explain how they arrive at a particular decision. Because AI is often considered a black box, without transparency into how AI arrives at certain decisions, it is challenging for regulators to evaluate if AI systems follow ethical norms or hold developers accountable for negative consequences [20].

13.5.1.2 Identifying Gaps in Oversight Mechanisms

While advancements toward an effective AI governance framework are moving in the right direction, a few critical gaps still need to be filled. One significant gap is the absence of globally harmonized standards. While AI technologies are evolving and being deployed without precedent anywhere in the world, and often right across its borders, no international regulatory institutions have been created to establish homogenous and fact-based global governance of such technologies. The lack of consistent policies also makes it difficult for developers and providers of AI for healthcare to adhere to siloed country and regional regulations.

This leads to another gap: the absence of mechanisms to assess AI's impact on health outcomes. These technologies are regulated based on their technical performance, but such regulatory bodies rarely consider long-term health effects or even the impacts on society more broadly. For instance, if regulatory bodies approve an AI tool for diagnosing a specific condition, they may fail to assess whether that tool could worsen health disparities, introduce, or reproduce biases, or produce unintended consequences concerning patient care.

Additionally, often there is no strong enforcement mechanism in place that can assure compliance with ethical standards after AI systems are operational [21]. It can also move to create more forceful oversight by regulatory bodies that can ensure that AI systems are used responsibly throughout their lifecycle from design and testing to post-deployment monitoring. That also means continuously assessing the performance of A.I. tools to ensure they do what they are intended to do, without adding new risks to patients.

Also, existing demand for increased transparency in AI development and deployment Regulators need post-market surveillance to evaluate the ethical and risk factors involved by making it mandatory for developers or healthcare organizations to disclose underlying algorithms, data sources, and training processes of AI systems. Transparency, combined with ongoing oversight and evaluation, is critical to preventing risks including bias, error, and accountability gaps.

13.5.2 Collaboration Across Stakeholders

13.5.2.1 Role of Technologists, Healthcare Professionals, and Ethicists

Collaboration across multiple stakeholders will be critical to addressing the complex challenges presented by AI in healthcare. AI oversight cannot fall solely on technologists. This involves a multidisciplinary approach that engages healthcare workers, philosophers, policymakers, and the public. Each has an expertise and representation that is vital to ensuring responsible practices in the development and deployment of AI technologies.

- AI systems are built on specific technical grounds by technologists. Governance of these tools is meant to make sure that the AI they produce is ethical, reliable, and not biased. This entails opening up the black box of AI systems to make them interpretable and accountable. They also need to help identify and minimize risks associated with deploying artificial intelligence, including learning and algorithmic bias or exacerbating health inequities.

- Clinical expertise ensures the responsible deployment of AI. They might offer invaluable perspectives on how to optimally utilize AI tools in practice, ensuring that AI systems are developed in alignment with patient and healthcare goals [22]. This includes nurse clinicians and medical researchers who are critical to confirming whether AI systems are effective and ensuring that technology cannot supplant human judgment or compromise patient care.
- Ethicists add the ethical perspective needed to address the dynamics of artificial intelligence in medicine. This will ensure the use of AI technologies follows the rules about patients' rights, fairness of the treatment, and the prevention of harm. Ethicists are part of these conversations, which will address issues of privacy, informed consent, accountability, and whether AI can exacerbate existing social inequities.

Hence, various stakeholders must collaborate to promote the responsible development and use of AI systems [23]. By working together, technologists, healthcare professionals, and ethicists can create governance frameworks that protect the interests of patients and minimize the ethical issues of AI use in a healthcare setting.

To properly deploy AI in healthcare, a well-defined collaborative governance framework is needed. This framework should include many stakeholders:

1. **Technologists** should ensure that AI models are unbiased, interpretable, and aligned with ethical principles.
2. **Healthcare Providers** should validate AI decisions, ensuring AI-based recommendations enhance patient outcomes rather than replace clinical judgment.
3. **Policymakers and Regulators** must establish comprehensive legal guidelines to ensure AI systems maintain transparency, privacy, and accountability.
4. **Patients and Advocacy Groups** should be actively involved in AI governance discussions to ensure AI aligns with patient needs and ethical standards.

This coinciding relationship can be used to ensure that AI-driven healthcare remains ethical while benefiting from optimized clinical decision-making.

13.6 The Future of Ethical AI in Healthcare

Ensuring ethical AI in healthcare for the future is reliant on feelings of fairness, transparency, accountability, and patient orientation. Such innovations span from fairness-aware machine learning, the process of providing fairness constraints to machine learning algorithms to ensure that AI systems produce fair treatment of patients across all demographics, to adversarial debiasing, which minimizes bias in machine learning systems through the application of adversarial nets. If nothing else brings the point home, the interactive XAI platform is heading the road of transparency to better inform clinicians and patients, interpretable AI decision-making, and ultimately lead to trust. Furthermore, ethical AI governance models are gradually emerging to ensure the responsible use of AI systems by promoting adaptability, accountability, and compliance in the design and delivery of AI systems. A growing emphasis on patient-centered AI — that personalizes tools to patients' specific medical histories and cultural backgrounds is also gaining momentum as it is more likely to advance shared decision-making and personalized care. Another area of AI deployment is global health equity, where the parish detects and addresses disparities by enabling healthcare access to underserved populations using telemedicine and remote monitoring tools. Ethics helps guide the responsible use of these tools within the health IT ecosystem, ensuring that patient safety, confidentiality, and data privacy take precedence so that all AI-based systems can comply with data protection regulations (such as GDPR and HIPAA). The key is accessibility, for other underserved populations too AI should fill gaps in healthcare, without widening them, thus tools need to be designed for them. It is crucial to monitor AI models in production to identify any kind of bias or error and ensure accountability of the models. In addition, AI need not substitute clinicians but rather complement them, not by deploying clinicians but by providing them with data-based insights, potentially in addition to powerful decision algorithms that assist those trained to identify when to use the technology, and when not to. These collective efforts evoke the need for responsible Aise practice in healthcare, providing high-quality care without compromising patient rights and promoting equity.

AI disclosure statement: The author confirms that no artificial intelligence (AI)-generated content or AI-assisted writing tools were used in the preparation of this chapter (including summaries and the abstract). All text, analysis, and conclusions are the result of the author's original work.

References

1. Dakshit, S., Dakshit, S., Khargonkar, N., Prabhakaran, B., Bias Analysis in Healthcare Time Series (BAHT) Decision Support Systems from Meta Data. *J. Healthc. Inform. Res.*, 7, 2, 225–253, 2023, doi: 10.1007/s41666-023-00133-6.
2. Rueda, J., Rodríguez, J.D., Jounou, I.P., Hortal-Carmona, J., Ausín, T., Rodríguez-Arias, D., 'Just' accuracy? Procedural fairness demands explainability in AI-based medical resource allocations. *AI Soc.*, 39, 3, 1411–1422, 2024, doi: 10.1007/s00146-022-01614-9.
3. Smallman, M., Multi Scale Ethics—Why We Need to Consider the Ethics of AI in Healthcare at Different Scales. *Sci. Eng. Ethics*, 28, 6, 1–17, 2022, doi: 10.1007/s11948-022-00396-z.
4. Clark, C.R., *et al.*, Health Care Equity in the Use of Advanced Analytics and Artificial Intelligence Technologies in Primary Care. *J. Gen. Intern. Med.*, 36, 10, 3188–3193, 2021, doi: 10.1007/s11606-021-06846-x.
5. Mabillard, V., Demartines, N., Joliat, G.R., How Can Reasoned Transparency Enhance Co-Creation in Healthcare and Remedy the Pitfalls of Digitization in Doctor-Patient Relationships? *Int. J. Health Policy Manag.*, 11, 10, 1986–1990, 2022, doi: 10.34172/ijhpm.2020.263.
6. McLennan, S., Fiske, A., Tigard, D., Müller, R., Haddadin, S., Buyx, A., Embedded ethics: a proposal for integrating ethics into the development of medical AI. *BMC Med. Ethics*, 23, 1, 1–10, 2022, doi: 10.1186/s12910-022-00746-3.
7. Trocin, C., Mikalef, P., Papamitsiou, Z., Conboy, K., Responsible AI for Digital Health: a Synthesis and a Research Agenda. *Inf. Syst. Front.*, 25, 6, 2139–2157, 2023, doi: 10.1007/s10796-021-10146-4.
8. Aquino, Y.S.J., *et al.*, Practical, epistemic and normative implications of algorithmic bias in healthcare artificial intelligence: A qualitative study of multidisciplinary expert perspectives. *J. Med. Ethics*, 1–9, 2023, doi: 10.1136/jme-2022-108850.
9. Constantinides, M., Bogucka, E., Quercia, D., Kallio, S., Tahaei, M., RAI Guidelines: Method for Generating Responsible AI Guidelines Grounded in Regulations and Usable by (Non-)Technical Roles. *Proc. ACM Hum. Comput. Interact.*, 8, CSCW2, 1–28, 2024, doi: 10.1145/3686927.
10. Carini, C. and Seyhan, A.A., Tribulations and future opportunities for artificial intelligence in precision medicine. 22, 1, BioMed Central, 2024, doi: 10.1186/s12967-024-05067-0.

11. Li, B., *et al.*, Trustworthy AI: From Principles to Practices. *ACM Comput. Surv.*, 55, 9, 2023, doi: 10.1145/3555803.
12. Zondag, A.G.M., *et al.*, The Effect of Artificial Intelligence on Patient-Physician Trust: Cross-Sectional Vignette Study. *J. Med. Internet Res.*, 26, 1–12, 2024, doi: 10.2196/50853.
13. McKee, M. and Wouters, O.J., The Challenges of Regulating Artificial Intelligence in Healthcare Comment on 'Clinical Decision Support and New Regulatory Frameworks for Medical Devices: Are We Ready for It?-A Viewpoint Paper. *Int. J. Health Policy Manag.*, 12, 1, 7261, 2023, doi: 10.34172/ijhpm.2022.7261.
14. Buckner, C.A., *et al.*, We are IntechOpen , the world's leading publisher of Open Access books Built by scientists, for scientists TOP 1 %, Intech, vol. 11, no. tourism, p. 13, 2016, [Online]. Available: https://www.intechopen.com/books/advanced-biometric-technologies/liveness-detection-in-biometrics.
15. Dankwa-Mullan, I. and Weeraratne, D., Artificial Intelligence and Machine Learning Technologies in Cancer Care: Addressing Disparities, Bias, and Data Diversity. *Cancer Discov.*, 12, 6, 1423–1427, 2022, doi: 10.1158/2159-8290.CD-22-0373.
16. Sablone, S., Bellino, M., Cardinale, A.N., Esposito, M., Sessa, F., Salerno, M., Artificial intelligence in healthcare: an Italian perspective on ethical and medico-legal implications. *Front. Med. (Lausanne)*, 11, June, 1–6, 2024, doi: 10.3389/fmed.2024.1343456.
17. Frehywot, S. and Vovides, Y., An equitable and sustainable community of practice framework to address the use of artificial intelligence for global health workforce training. *Hum. Resour. Health*, 21, 1, 1–7, 2023, doi: 10.1186/s12960-023-00833-5.
18. Parchmann, N., Hansen, D., Orzechowski, M., Steger, F., An ethical assessment of professional opinions on concerns, chances, and limitations of the implementation of an artificial intelligence-based technology into the geriatric patient treatment and continuity of care. *Geroscience*, 0123456789, 2024, doi: 10.1007/s11357-024-01229-6.
19. Zikmundová, K., Artificial intelligence in healthcare: Threats to the fundamental values of our society. *Eur. Stud. Rev. Eur. Law Econ. Polit.*, 9, 2, 181–196, 2022, doi: 10.2478/eustu-2022-0019.
20. D'Elia, A., *et al.*, Artificial intelligence and health inequities in primary care: A systematic scoping review and framework. *Fam. Med. Community Health*, 10, 1–10, 2022, doi: 10.1136/fmch-2022-001670.
21. Kim, J., Kim, S.Y., Kim, E.A., Sim, J.A., Lee, Y., Kim, H., Developing a Framework for Self-regulatory Governance in Healthcare AI Research: Insights from South Korea. *Asian Bioeth. Rev.*, 16, 3, 391–406, 2024, doi: 10.1007/s41649-024-00281-w.

22. Liefgreen, A., Weinstein, N., Wachter, S., Mittelstadt, B., Beyond ideals: why the (medical) AI industry needs to motivate behavioural change in line with fairness and transparency values, and how it can do it. *AI Soc.*, 0123456789, 2023, doi: 10.1007/s00146-023-01684-3.
23. Zhang, J. and Zhang, Z.-M., Ethics and governance of trustworthy medical artificial intelligence. *BMC Med. Inform. Decis. Mak.*, 23, 1, 1–15, 2023, doi: 10.1186/s12911-023-02103-9.

14

Advancing Healthcare with AI: Balancing Efficiency, Security, and Compliance

Sivakumar Ramakrishnan

Statistical Programming, Innovation & AI Vita Global Sciences, Chicago, IL, USA

Abstract

Artificial Intelligence (AI) is making healthcare fraud detection more accurate, efficient, and cost-effective. AI-based solutions outperform traditional rule-based systems in identifying new scams such as phantom billing, identity theft, and duplicate procedures in real-time. Although offering numerous advantages, AI introduces algorithmic bias, opacity, and data privacy concerns. Historical claims-based ML models tend to amplify biases, and Explainable AI (XAI) tools such as SHapley Additive exPlanations (SHAP) and Local Interpretable Model-agnostic Explanations (LIME) address these. Compliance frameworks such as General Data Protection Regulation (GDPR) and Health Insurance Portability and Accountability Act (HIPAA) ensure necessary data protection and regulatory compliance. The suggested Fraud Observation and Risk Tracking (FORT) framework system integrates supervised methods (e.g., Support Vector Machines, Random Forest) with unsupervised methods (e.g., Autoencoders, Anomaly Detection) and identifies the optimal combination for fraud detection, with SVM achieving an ROC-AUC score of 86.5%. AI-based fraud detection enhances the efficiency of claims processing, reducing administrative costs and diversion of funds. Blockchain deployment, federated learning, and real-time detection are the most critical research areas to further enhance AI as a healthcare fraud prevention tool.

Keywords: Healthcare fraud prevention, bias in AI, fraud detection, machine learning, data privacy

Email: sivakumar.vkr87@gmail.com

Manish Kumar, Nitigya Sambyal, Leena Priyadarshini Singh, Ramasamy V. and S. Balamurugan (eds.) Responsible AI: Principles and Practices, (323–362) © 2026 Scrivener Publishing LLC

14.1 Introduction

There is no denying the fact that AI has taken healthcare to the next level concerning medical diagnostics, treatment planning, and even administrative efficiency. AI solutions have proved phenomenal in predictive analytics, medical imaging, and automated patient monitoring. It enhances decisions and improves work processes. Affected by AI development, fraud detection and prevention are one of the urgent issues for healthcare institutions globally [1]. Insurance claim fraud is one of the major challenges in modern health delivery. It causes a huge loss of money and operates inefficiency in health support systems. Healthcare fraud is made up of entities such as fictitious billing, ghost procedures, unnecessary therapies, and identity theft. Each of these burdens severely insurance companies and government agencies. These suck monetary resources from the system; more so, the whole integrity of health systems is compromised, which in turn influences the quality of patient care and results in resource mis-allocation.

According to the National Healthcare Anti-Fraud Association (NHCAA), healthcare fraud costs the U.S. healthcare system tens of billions of dollars annually, impacting both payers and genuine beneficiaries. Fraudulent claims have inflated healthcare costs, which burden the taxpayers and legal policyholders and increase insurance premiums, eroding the financial reserves reserved for real claims. The effects of fraud go past economic concerns; fraudulent procedures and misdiagnoses mean wrong medical treatments and very high risks to patient health and safety [2]. Traditional methods of detecting fraud such as manual auditing and rule-based systems have minimal or no evidence of effectively making a detection of emerging fraudulent schemes. These are generally rigid and rely on hard-coded, predefined rules that cannot adjust to new fraud techniques [3]. Therefore, they yield very high false positives where genuine claims will be found fraudulent and very few or none of the advanced fraud schemes are discovered. It also imposes an operational burden on insurers, since it requires much human interaction and increasingly slows the verification-processing speed of claims.

Given the complexity of modern healthcare transactions, AI-powered fraud detection systems offer a scalable and adaptable solution that can mitigate these financial risks by identifying fraud patterns with higher precision and speed. AI's ability to analyze large datasets, recognize complex patterns, and continuously learn from new fraud behaviors makes it a promising tool for addressing fraud in medical insurance claims. By leveraging machine learning (ML) and deep learning algorithms, AI systems can dynamically evolve and improve their fraud detection accuracy over time [4]. Furthermore, AI-driven fraud detection enhances the efficiency of healthcare claims processing by automating fraud investigations, reducing processing times, and minimizing human errors. Instead of relying solely on manual auditors, AI models can flag suspicious claims for further review, ensuring that fraudulent activities are intercepted early while genuine claims are processed swiftly [5].

Scope of Research and Key Questions

This research undertakes a study on the importance of AI in healthcare fraud detection with emphasis on ethics, clinical, and operational implications. Apart from the above quoted, the research also measures the technology's efficiency to automate fraud detection, optimize claims verification accuracy, and attain openness and transcend systems integration, biases, and regulation barriers. By investigating both the strengths and limitations of AI-driven fraud detection, this research provides insights into how AI can be effectively and responsibly implemented in healthcare fraud prevention.

Several key questions guide this study:

a) Which AI models are most effective in detecting healthcare fraud, and how do they compare in performance?

This is explored through empirical model evaluations, assessing accuracy, precision, recall, and ROC- AUC scores of various ML algorithms.

b) How can XAI improve fraud detection transparency and stakeholder trust?

The study integrates SHAP and LIME to interpret fraud classification results, ensuring auditability and fairness in AI-driven decision-making.

c) What are the rising AI-related ethical concerns in fraud detection, particularly regarding bias and patient privacy?

This chapter focuses on the bias mitigation strategies while exploring the regulatory safeguards, ensuring compliance with HIPAA, GDPR, and ethical AI frameworks.

d) How does AI impact operational efficiency in healthcare fraud detection?

The research explores the AI's role in reducing manual claim audits, automating workflows, and optimizing fraud investigation processes.

e) What future AI-driven strategies can further enhance fraud detection in healthcare?
The study examines real-time fraud detection, blockchain integration for secure claims processing, and federated learning for privacy-preserving AI model training.

This chapter delves into fundamental questions to expand knowledge of the potential of AI to identify healthcare fraud and solve ethical, clinical, and operational problems with this technology. It highlights crucial details for policymakers, healthcare professionals, and AI researchers about future research effectiveness and scalability.

While AI-based fraud detection greatly improves clinical integrity by avoiding unnecessary medical interventions and financial abuse, its use relies on advanced ML methods that support fraud detection with high accuracy. Fraudulent claims detection relies on advanced algorithms with the ability to identify subtle patterns and changing fraud schemes. The following section describes these AI methods, how they identify fraudulent claims and identify anomalies effectively.

14.1.1 Role of AI in Healthcare Fraud Detection

AI has shown promise to identify and prevent insurance claim fraud through the use of ML algorithms, natural language processing (NLP), and anomaly detection methods. In contrast to fraud detection through manual rules-based approaches, AI-based systems can identify subtle relationships and detect anomalous patterns in large and complex data sets. ML models can analyze vast claim datasets to identify irregularities, such as:

- Excessive billing for services that were not performed.
- Repeated or duplicate procedures that exceed medical necessity.
- Temporal inconsistencies where patient records show conflicting information.
- Unusual claim submission behaviors are linked to specific providers.

Modern fraud detection techniques leverage supervised learning algorithms (such as Random Forest, Support Vector Machines, and Gradient Boosting) to classify claims as fraudulent or legitimate. Additionally, unsupervised learning approaches (such as Autoencoders and K-Means Clustering) help detect previously unseen fraud cases, ensuring adaptability to emerging fraudulent strategies [6].

To facilitate decision-making, XAI techniques, including SHAP and LIME, provide explanations of AI- driven fraud detection systems. This enhances trust and verification of AI-driven fraud classifications by stakeholders, including insurance firms, healthcare administrators, and regulatory agencies [7].

14.1.2 Challenges in AI-Based Fraud Detection

a. Data Quality and Class Imbalance

- Fraudulent claims represent only a small fraction of total claims, leading to highly imbalanced datasets.
- Traditional ML models tend to favor the majority class (legitimate claims), resulting in high false negatives (missed fraud cases).
- Data inconsistencies, missing values, and unstructured text (such as physician notes) further complicate fraud detection.
- Medical claims are characterized by complex unstructured data formats such as handwritten notes, scanned documents, and physician prescriptions, thereby making the standardization of inputs for AI models difficult.
- Disaggregation, discrepancies in coding standards and procedural descriptions across various health care providers also have data quality problems.

b. Explainability and Trust in AI Decisions

- AI would need to comply with applicable laws such as HIPAA and GDPR.
- AI must be ethically designed and programmed in such a way that it does not produce any biases that subsequently bring about wrongful denial of claims or discriminative decisions.
- Restrictive laws concerning data privacy prohibit the exchange of healthcare data between institutions thus making it difficult to create AI models trained using vast datasets.
- Regulatory uncertainty around AI-driven fraud detection systems creates barriers to large-scale implementation, requiring ongoing collaboration between policymakers, insurers, and AI researchers.

- Data anonymization and patient confidentiality while maintaining high fraud detection accuracy remains a significant challenge.

c. Regulatory Compliance and Ethical Concerns

- The use of AI in fraud prevention is regulated by existing legislation such as HIPAA and GDPR.
- AI must be developed in an ethical manner so that it does not employ biases which may lead to unwarranted rejection of claims or discriminatory actions.
- Strict data privacy laws restrain institutions from exposing healthcare data, and hence training AI models using large data sets is challenging.
- Regulatory uncertainty around AI-driven fraud detection systems creates barriers to large-scale implementation, requiring ongoing collaboration between policymakers, insurers, and AI researchers.
- Ensuring data anonymization and patient confidentiality while maintaining high fraud detection accuracy remains a significant challenge.

d. Scalability and Real-time Adaptation

- Fraudulent tactics constantly evolve, requiring AI models to adapt dynamically.
- AI systems must support real-time fraud detection, enabling immediate action on suspicious claims while minimizing disruptions to legitimate claim processing.
- Fraud detection models need to process large-scale insurance claim data with minimal latency to provide instant fraud alerts, reducing financial losses.
- The ability to update AI models continuously with new fraudulent cases is essential to prevent obsolescence.
- Integrating AI-driven fraud detection with existing healthcare IT infrastructures and insurance claim management systems poses significant technical and operational challenges.
- Cross-institutional fraud patterns may go undetected due to limitations in data interoperability between hospitals, insurers, and government agencies.

Although the application of AI-based fraud detection improves efficiency and accuracy, the biggest challenge is computational cost. AI models, especially those employing deep learning and ensemble learning methods, are computationally expensive, thus increasing operational costs. Training these fraud detection models requires processing enormous amounts of claims data, repeated hyperparameter tuning, and creating a real-time fraud monitoring system. Such demands necessitate high-performance computing (HPC) centers or cloud-based AI solutions, which may be prohibitively costly for most healthcare organizations. The high costs are further compounded by the need for continuous re-tuning of models to respond to new emerging fraudulent schemes in each cycle. One potential solution may be to strike a balance between performance and resource consumption through hybrid methods that combine cost- effective supervised learning methods, such as Support Vector Machines (SVM), with resource-frugal anomaly detection methods, such as Autoencoders, with the aim of maximizing fraud detection while minimizing computational costs.

14.2 Literature Review

14.2.1 Introduction to AI in Healthcare

The progression of AI in the field of health and medicine over the last few decades has been nothing short of remarkable, ranging from simple rule-based expert systems, cutting-edge ML, deep learning (DL) systems, and so much more. These systems can diagnose illness, predict patient outcome, and enhance operational efficiency within hospitals. Some of the major applications of AI in health are radiology, pathology, personalized medicine, robotic-assisted surgery, drug discovery, and administrative automation [8].

The impact that AI has made in providing healthcare solutions has been motivated by developments in computing capacity, the availability of large medical databases, and advancements in the algorithms. Experts have made significant progress in other applications of AI in healthcare and medicine; however, it is crucial that bias, explainability, and ethics issues are addressed on a priority basis.

14.2.2 Historical Evolution of AI in Healthcare

AI's role in medicine dates back to early expert systems like MYCIN and INTERNIST-I, which attempted to assist physicians in diagnosing bacterial infections and complex diseases [9]. With the rise of ML in the 1990s and deep learning in the 2010s, AI applications expanded to medical imaging, genomics, and real- time patient monitoring [10].

Recent success stories such as Google DeepMind's AlphaFold in protein folding prediction and research on AI in radiology have highlighted the promise of AI in augmenting clinical decision support [11]. Although the success of these initiatives has been realized, intermittent adoption of AI in healthcare infrastructure has been observed owing to technical issues in the form of data quality, system integration, and medical fraternity's readiness for the adoption of the technology.

14.2.3 Current Applications of AI in Healthcare

14.2.3.1 AI in Diagnostics and Medical Imaging

Medical imaging has proved to be the most successful area to apply AI. DL algorithms have reached human- level performance in the detection of abnormalities in radiology and pathology. Radiology software powered by AI, such as IBM Watson and Google's DeepMind, has been proved highly precise in the detection of diseases like diabetic retinopathy and breast cancer [12]. Despite all these developments, problems still arise on model explainability and generalizability. AI models that were trained on some of the datasets have been shown to fail to generalize across different patient populations. For that, more stable and ethically acquired datasets in an attempt to reduce bias and facilitate fair AI deployment are needed [13].

14.2.3.2 AI in Predictive Analytics and Disease Prevention

Predictive analytics powered by AI is revolutionizing preventive medicine. ML algorithms examine patient history, lifestyle variables, and genetic factors to forecast the risk of disease. AI has been successful in diagnosing illnesses like sepsis and cardiovascular disease at early stages [14]. Even with these advancements, model explainability and generalizability are issues. Evidence has emerged that AI models learned from specific datasets are not inherently generalizable to heterogeneous patient populations.

To overcome this, stronger and ethically grounded datasets must be utilized to reduce bias and enable equitable deployment of AI [13].

14.2.3.3 AI in Personalized Medicine and Drug Discovery

The capacity of AI to access genomic data has driven personalized medicine. Algorithms aid in the recognition of genomic markers of disease susceptibility, enabling personal treatment. Drug discovery has also been transformed through AI, and BenevolentAI and Atomwise platforms utilize ML to determine the most promising drug targets. The current studies document AI's achievement in repurposing approved drugs to treat new conditions, including in COVID-19. Nevertheless, regulatory and clinical approval is a major hindrance to the extensive application of AI-aided drug discovery [15].

14.2.4 Ethical Considerations in AI Healthcare Adoption

14.2.4.1 Bias and Fairness in AI Models

Bias in AI is especially problematic since algorithms using training data representative of the population have the power to perpetuate health disparities. A study identified racial bias in a clinical AI algorithm, which persistently underestimated the healthcare demands of Black patients [16]. Bias is to be checked by employing representative data, methodological strategies on algorithmic fairness, and audits at intervals.

14.2.4.2 Data Privacy and Security

Patient data protection is critical as AI usage becomes dominant in the management of sensitive health records. Regulations like HIPAA (in the USA) and GDPR (in the EU) protect patient information, but to use analytical AI, such frameworks are quite inadequate, even in principle [17].

14.2.4.3 Explainability and Transparency

Transparency of DL models is a critical problem regarding their explainability. There is some evidence that lower transparency has a negative effect on doctors' trust in AI-made diagnoses. Thus, the creation of XAI techniques, including attention mechanisms and rule-based models, is essential to the ethical deployment of AI [18].

14.2.5 Operational Challenges in AI Implementation

14.2.5.1 Integration with Existing Healthcare Infrastructure

AI implementation in hospitals faces barriers related to interoperability with existing electronic health record (EHR) systems. Studies indicate that many AI tools struggle to integrate seamlessly with legacy healthcare IT systems, leading to workflow inefficiencies [19].

14.2.5.2 Economic and Cost Implications

Though AI may end up saving healthcare expenses in the long term, its investment cost to deploy it is astronomical. Paying the initial cost of deploying AI infrastructure along with the additional cost of constantly retraining models is an ambitious undertaking for healthcare organizations [20].

14.2.5.3 Physician and Patient Acceptance of AI

Whether or not AI has been successful depends heavily on the user's acceptance of its application. There are quite a number of skeptical physicians who will not accept any suggestion from an AI, instead contesting based on its reliability and liability. There exists considerable patient resistance in the acceptance of AI- based diagnoses, which indicates the necessity of innovative communication development measures for the improvement of AI acceptance [9].

14.3 Identified Gaps in Literature and Future Directions

- **Poor Figuration of Enormous Diverse Data Sets:** At present, AI appliances count on smaller data sets, constraining long-term diversity in their application. Larger data sets could help nullify this problem while also making AI applications fairer.
- **Interpretability and Tenable Trust:** AI models work like black boxes; hence, the decision- making process is inaccessible to the clinician. XAI approaches must be priority research areas.

- **Regulatory and Ethical Frameworks:** Contemporary regulations cannot keep pace with advancement in AI. Policymakers must create comprehensive policies for the integration of AI into healthcare settings.
- **Elaborative Clinical Trials:** While there lies the hope of AI within a limited realm of experimental conditions; however, one must prove the significance of the work if passed through major clinical protocols in clinical testing to access its usefulness in real-world translations.

14.4 Methodology

14.4.1 Proposed Framework

To address the gaps identified in existing fraud detection techniques, this research proposes a Fraud Observation and Risk Tracking (FORT) framework for medical insurance claim fraud detection. FORT integrates supervised learning algorithms, including Gradient Boosting Machines (GBM) and Random Forests, for predictive accuracy, while also leveraging unsupervised methods such as Autoencoders to detect anomalies in previously unseen fraudulent patterns. This hybrid approach ensures a balance between accuracy, transparency, and efficiency, making it a robust solution for evolving fraud strategies.

FORT is composed of three core modules:

- **Predictive Classification Module (PCM):** Uses supervised ML models such as GBM, Random Forests, and Support Vector Machines (SVM) to classify claims as fraudulent or legitimate based on historical patterns.
- **Anomaly Detection Module (ADM):** Employs unsupervised learning techniques like Autoencoders and Isolation Forests to identify suspicious claims that deviate from expected patterns, ensuring detection of previously unseen fraud schemes.
- **Explainability & Adaptation Module (EAM):** Enhances transparency by integrating XAI tools such as SHAP and LIME, ensuring interpretability. Additionally, this module incorporates a Continuous Learning Mechanism (CLM), which dynamically updates models as new fraud trends emerge.

FORT's crowning glory is its Human-in-the-Loop HITL Review Mechanism, where high-risk claims are sent for manual review by fraud investigators. This contributes to model tuning, thereby reducing the chances of false positives and negatives, both of which are perennial problems in automated fraud-detection systems.

Comparison with Existing Frameworks

The FORT methodology proposed in this work significantly differs from conventional fraud detection methods used by public and private insurance organizations. Existing systems mainly use strict rules, which translates to poor adaptability, hence leading to high false positive rates and reduced effectiveness in detecting fraudulent behavior.

a. Rule-Based vs. AI-Based Fraud Detection

Rule-based fraud detection based on pre-existing rules aimed at identifying fraudulent claims, based on the following criteria:

- Duplicate billing (for example, the same patient repeatedly having the same procedures).
- Going beyond policy coverage limits (e.g., excessive medical treatment beyond policy limits).
- Incorrect billing codes (e.g., billing expensive unrelated services on a patient).

Although rule-based systems possess some advantages, they are deficient when it comes to detecting new forms of fraud patterns that do not fit preprogrammed rules. In addition, these systems generate a high percentage of false positives, which induce unnecessary determination of claims and more operating expenses.

On the other hand, the FORT model integrates ML and anomaly detection techniques in an attempt to make it learn fraud patterns dynamically from data rather than static rules. It integrates supervised learning (e.g., SVM, Random Forest) and unsupervised learning (e.g., Autoencoders, Anomaly Detection) in an attempt to enhance fraud detection through:

- Identification of previously seen patterns of fraud from previously labeled data.
- Never-seen-before fraud instances detection using anomaly detection.
- Continual training and staying abreast of new fraud schemes.

b. The Role of Explainability in Fraud Detection

One key shortcoming of current AI-powered fraud detection systems is that they lack transparency. Most fraud detection systems employed in business settings are "black-box" models, making it hard for regulators and insurance companies to comprehend the rationale behind the identification of specific claims as fraudulent.

FORT covers strategies related to XAI, such as:

- SHAP: for feature contribution explanations to explain fraud classification.
- LIME: to provide human-understandable explanations for spotlighted statements.

By the use of explainability, FORT improves the confidence established between insurers and auditors, as well as regulatory compliance through the transparent examination and auditing of fraud decisions. Compared to traditional commercial and government fraud detection systems, FORT has:

- Greater flexibility is achieved through the use of AI-based anomaly detection.
- Improved results with the combination of supervised and unsupervised learning.
- Greater transparency with the use of Explainable AI techniques.
- Lower false positive rates through enhanced fraud classification choices.

These benefits render FORT a more effective and scalable instrument for detecting healthcare fraud today. The methodology consists of the following key stages:

Dataset Preprocessing and Feature Engineering

This step ensures that the dataset is clean, structured, and ready for analysis. Handling missing values ensures completeness in numerical and categorical fields. Feature Engineering enhancing raw data with calculated metrics (e.g., length of stay, claim frequency). Encoding categorical variables converts categorical attributes into numerical values for ML models. Feature Scaling standardizes numerical values for improved model stability. Train-test split ensures that models are tested on unseen data to evaluate generalization.

Class Imbalance Handling

Fraudulent claims are rare compared to legitimate claims, making it challenging for models to detect fraud. SMOTE (Synthetic Minority Oversampling Technique) generates synthetic fraudulent cases to balance class distribution. Cost-sensitive learning adjusts algorithms to give higher penalties for misclassifying fraud cases.

Model Selection and Training

A mix of supervised models (e.g., Random Forest, SVM, Logistic Regression) and unsupervised models (e.g., Autoencoders) are used to maximize fraud detection. Supervised models learn patterns from labeled fraud cases, while unsupervised models detect anomalies without predefined labels. The models are trained using an 80-20 train-test split.

Hyperparameter Optimization

To improve the performance of models, Grid Search Cross-Validation is used for fine-tuning, adjusting important parameters like tree depth and learning rate (for KNN) and number of neighbors (for KNN) and kernel types (for SVM). This offers the best matching combination of parameters with balanced models while avoiding overfitting and underfitting.

Model Evaluation

Models are assessed based on using measures like accuracy, precision, recall, F1-score, and ROC-AUC to determine their performance. Precision-recall tradeoff is used to find the right balance between false positives and false negatives to avoid errors. The more accurate model is chosen based on comparing performances from various models to improve detection potential and reduce errors.

Interpretability & Explainability Enhancement

This step would enhance the transparency and trustworthiness of any AI-enabled decisions. Models for AI, particularly DL models, have been associated with black boxes and are nearly impossible to interpret. SHAP that displays an explanation for feature importance in fraud predictions. Reporting the explanation of LIME is the standard means for providing human-readable explanations for individual predictions.

Continuous Learning and Adaptation

Fraud patterns constantly evolve, making it essential to update models regularly. Active Learning incorporates new fraud data into models over time, while automated retraining pipelines ensure that the models stay current and effective against emerging fraud techniques. This ongoing process helps maintain high detection accuracy as fraud tactics change.

Integration with Human Expertise

AI totally cannot replace fraud investigators; hence the intervention of a human-in-the-loop framework. This has to do with instances where cases flagged by AI are reviewed by experts and used to enhance the AI models, pointing to AI's data pattern recognition capabilities combined with human judgment. Collaborative efforts would present maximum accuracy in detecting fraud by leveraging both human expertise and technology.

14.4.2 Dataset Overview

The study utilizes the **National Health Insurance System (NHIS) Claims Dataset**, which contains **1500 structured records** of medical claims [21]. Patient-demographic-level information such as the disease condition, treatment given, and fraud labels are included in the dataset.

Figure 14.1 illustrates the key stages of the fraud detection process including evaluation, model selection, preprocessing, and explainability modules.

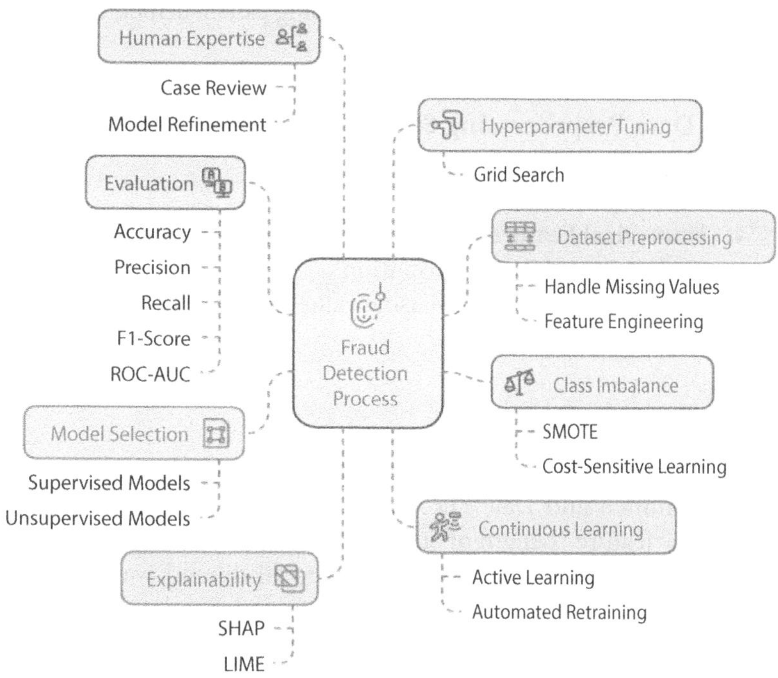

Figure 14.1 Key stages of fraud detection process.

Table 14.1 Dataset features.

Feature name	Description	Data type
Patient ID	Unique identifier for each patient (not used)	Categorical
Age	Age of the insured patient	Numerical
Gender	Gender of the patient (Male/Female)	Categorical
Diagnosis	ICD-10 diagnosis codes for medical conditions	Categorical
Treatment	Medical procedure performed	Categorical
Amount Billed	Total amount claimed for reimbursement	Numerical
Date Admitted	Date of hospital admission	Date
Date Discharged	Date of hospital discharge	Date
Fraud Type	Target variable (Fraud categories)	Categorical

Table 14.1 shows the dataset features including patient demographics, diagnoses, treatments, and fraud indicators.

14.4.3 Data Preprocessing & Feature Engineering

14.4.3.1 Handling Missing Values

- **Numerical Features:** Missing values were replaced using the median to maintain distribution.
- **Categorical Features:** Missing values were replaced with the mode.

14.4.3.2 Feature Engineering

- **Length of Stay Calculation:** The difference between Date Admitted and Date Discharged was computed to create a new feature "Length of Stay."
- **Aggregated Claim Patterns:** Fraud likelihood was examined based on claim frequency per provider and patient.
- **Temporal Features:** Created features based on the timing of claims, including submission delays and frequency of claims per provider.

14.4.3.3 *Categorical Encoding*

- **One-hot encoding** was applied to categorical variables (e.g., Gender, Diagnosis, Treatment) to make them compatible with ML models.

14.4.3.4 *Feature Scaling*

- Standardization (zero mean, unit variance) was applied to numerical features (e.g., Amount Billed) to improve performance for distance-based models (e.g., KNN, SVM).

14.4.3.5 *Train-Test Split*

- The dataset was split **80% training and 20% testing**, while preserving fraud class distribution.

The data preprocessing pipeline followed prior to model training is illustrated in Figure 14.2.

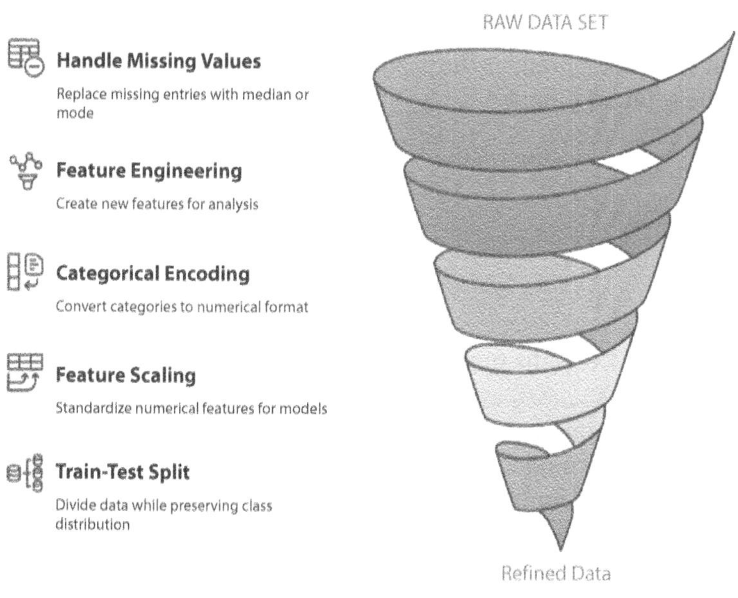

Figure 14.2 Data processing steps for model training.

14.4.4 Dealing with Class Imbalance

Since fraudulent claims are significantly fewer than legitimate ones, the dataset exhibits **class imbalance**, which can skew model performance. To mitigate this:

- **Synthetic Minority Over-sampling Technique (SMOTE)** was applied to generate synthetic samples for the minority (fraud) class. The given expression was used:

$$x_{new} = x_{minority} + \lambda(x_{neighbor} - x_{minority}) \tag{14.1}$$

where $x_{minority}$ is the original minority class sample, $x_{neighbor}$ is its nearest neighbor, and λ is a random number between 0 and 1.

- **Cost-sensitive learning** was incorporated in tree-based models to penalize misclassification of fraudulent claims.

14.4.5 Machine Learning Models and Training

14.4.5.1 Logistic Regression

Logistic regression predicts the probability that a claim is fraudulent (Y=1) using the sigmoid function:

$$P(Y = 1 \mid X) = \frac{1}{1 + e^{-(\beta_0 + \beta_1 X_1 + \cdots + \beta_n X_n)}} \tag{14.2}$$

where:

- $P(Y=1|X)$ is the probability of fraud given input features X.
- $X=[X_1,X_2,\ldots,Xn]$ are the feature variables.
- β_0 is the intercept (bias).
- β_n are the model coefficients.
- *e* is Euler's number (~2.718).

The decision boundary for classification is defined as:

$$Y = \begin{Bmatrix} 1, & P(Y*1|X)10.5 \\ 0, & P(Y*1|X).0.5 \end{Bmatrix} \tag{14.3}$$

14.4.5.2 Random Forest

Random Forest is an ensemble model that combines multiple decision trees. The prediction is obtained by averaging (for regression) or majority voting (for classification):

$$\hat{Y} = \frac{1}{T}\sum_{t=1}^{T} f_t(X) \tag{14.4}$$

where:

- $\hat{Y}$ is the final predicted output.
- T is the number of decision trees.
- $f_t(X)$ is the prediction from the tth tree.

Different bootstrap samples of the dataset are taken to train each tree in the forest. To this a random feature selection is applied at each split.

14.4.5.3 Support Vector Machine (SVM)

SVM finds the hyperplane that best separates fraudulent and non-fraudulent claims. The decision boundary is given by:

$$w^T x + b = 0 \tag{14.5}$$

where:

- w is the weight vector.
- x is the input feature vector.
- b is the bias term.

For classification, SVM aims to maximize the margin M between support vectors:

$$\boldsymbol{M} = \frac{\mathbf{2}}{||\boldsymbol{w}||} \tag{14.6}$$

For non-linearly separable data, SVM uses a kernel function $K(xi,xj)$ to transform input features into a higher-dimensional space.

14.4.5.4 K-Nearest Neighbors (KNN)

KNN classifies a claim based on the majority class among its k nearest neighbors. The distance metric used to measure similarity can be:

- **Euclidean Distance** (most common):

$$d\left(x_i, x_j\right) = \sqrt{\sum_{m=1}^{n} (x_{im} - x_{jm})^2} \tag{14.7}$$

where x_i and x_j are two feature vectors.

- **Manhattan Distance**:

$$d8x_i, x_j; = \sum_{m^*1}^{n} \ |x_{i,m} - x_{j,m}| \tag{14.8}$$

The final classification is determined using:

$$Y = mode(\{Y_k\}) \tag{14.9}$$

where Y_k are the labels of the k nearest neighbors.

14.4.5.5 Autoencoder

An Autoencoder is an unsupervised neural network used for anomaly detection. It consists of two parts:

- **Encoder function** f that compresses input data into a lower-dimensional latent space:

$$h = f(X) = \sigma(WX + b) \tag{14.10}$$

- **Decoder function** g that reconstructs the input from the latent representation:

$$X = g(h) = \sigma(W^{=}h + b^{=}) \tag{14.11}$$

Table 14.2 Machine learning models and their characteristics.

Model	Type	Key features
Logistic Regression	Supervised	Linear classifier with L2 regularization
Random Forest	Supervised	Ensemble learning, feature importance analysis
Support Vector Machine (SVM)	Supervised	Kernel-based classifier for fraud detection
K-Nearest Neighbors (KNN)	Supervised	Instance-based learning with distance metrics
Autoencoder	Unsupervised	Neural network-based anomaly detection

The model minimizes the reconstruction loss:

$$L= ||X- \hat{X}||^2 \tag{14.12}$$

where $||X- \hat{X}||^2$ is the Mean Squared Error (MSE) between original and reconstructed data. Fraudulent claims are detected when the reconstruction error exceeds a predefined threshold.

The core features of the machine learning models are outlined in Table 14.2.

14.4.6 The Hybrid Approach

The choice of individual ML models is a key determinant of the efficiency and accuracy of detecting healthcare fraud. SVM was the model of choice because it is capable of handling high-dimensional structured data well, where fraud patterns are typically numeric or categorical data instead of unstructured text or images. As opposed to DL models like CNNs or transformers, SVM does not need a lot of labeled training data, and as such, it is very apt for fraud cases where it is difficult to source labeled fraudulent instances.

Autoencoders, however, are especially beneficial in anomaly detection, which is very applicable in fraud detection where fraud claims are infrequent and do not typically adhere to pre-specified patterns. The model learns the usual behavior of healthcare claims and identifies deviations as probable fraud. The approach lowers dependency on pre-specified fraud indicators and can identify novel and developing fraudulent patterns. Although DL models like CNNs and transformers are useful for image and text data tasks, their computational expense, data demand, and explainability issues make them less feasible for fraud detection in healthcare claims processing.

With the use of SVM for precise classification and Autoencoders for the detection of unseen anomalies, the hybrid FORT model balances responsiveness to emerging fraud patterns, interpretability, and precision.

14.4.7 Hyperparameter Tuning

Each model underwent **Grid Search Cross-Validation (GridSearchCV)** to optimize performance using the formula:

$$CV_{score} = \frac{1}{k}\sum_{i=1}^{k} Accuracy_i \tag{14.13}$$

where k is the number of folds and $Accuracy_i$ represents the model accuracy on the ith fold.

14.4.8 Evaluation Metrics

To assess model effectiveness, the following metrics were used:

- Accuracy determines the total accuracy of the model.
- Precision measures the number of correctly identified fraud cases out of total fraud cases estimated.

Table 14.3 lists the hyperparameters used for tuning each ML model.

Table 14.3 Hyperparameters used for model optimization.

Model	Tuned hyperparameters
Random Forest	n estimators = [100, 200, 300], max depth = [10, 20, 30]
Support Vector Machine (SVM)	C = [0.1, 1, 10], Kernel = ['linear', 'rbf']
K-Nearest Neighbors (KNN)	k = [3, 5, 7], Distance Metric = ['Euclidean', 'Manhattan']
Autoencoder	Hidden layers = [2, 3], Activation = ['ReLU', 'Sigmoid']

- Recall (Sensitivity) refers to the model's capability to identify true fraudulent claims.
- F1-score is the harmonic mean of recall and precision, balancing false negatives and false positives.

$$\text{Precision} = \frac{TP}{TP + FP} \tag{14.14}$$

$$\text{Recall} = \frac{TP}{TP + FN} \tag{14.15}$$

$$F1 = 2\frac{Precision \times Recall}{Precision + Recall} \tag{14.16}$$

where TP = true positives, FP = false positives, and FN = false negatives.

- **ROC-AUC Score:** Evaluates the model's ability to distinguish between fraudulent and legitimate claims with the area under the curve formula:

$$AUC = \int_0^1 TPR(FPR)dFPR \tag{14.17}$$

where TPR is True Positive Rate and FPR is False Positive Rate.

14.5 Result and Discussion

14.5.1 Model Performance Comparison

The performance across the different ML models for fraud detection was determined using a set of key metrics: accuracy, precision, recall, F1-score, and ROC-AUC score. The metrics collectively provide a complete view of each model's ability to correctly identify fraudulent and legitimate claims. Accuracy indicates the overall correctness of the model's predictions, while precision indicates the percentage of fraudulent claims identified as fraudulent. Recall indicates the ability of the model to correctly identify actual occurrences of fraud, and the F1-score is a balance between precision and recall. The ROC-AUC score indicates the overall ability of the model to tell fraudulent and non-fraudulent claims apart.

Table 14.4 Performance metrics of different models.

Model	Accuracy (%)	Precision (%)	Recall (%)	F1-score	ROC-AUC
Logistic Regression	88.7	1.000	72.4	83.9	86.1
Support Vector Machine (SVM)	88.7	1.000	72.4	83.9	86.5
K-Nearest Neighbors (KNN)	88.0	97.8	74.1	83.2	84.1
Random Forest	86.3	92.7	75.6	81.3	84.8
Autoencoder	85.5	91.2	78.2	82.5	85.2

A comparison of performance metrics for all tested models is summarized in Table 14.4.

The evaluation results highlight the strengths and limitations of each model, providing insight into their practical applicability for fraud detection in healthcare claims processing.

Key Observations and Analysis

- Support Vector Machine (SVM) and Logistic Regression were equally accurate at 88.7% and so both equally fitting for the problem of fraud detection. Precision was 1.00 as the real claims were exclusively separated but the recall was merely 72.4%. That means although the model was wonderful in eliminating the false positives, it rejected huge numbers of false claims and an indication of precision-recall trade-off.
- The K-Nearest Neighbors (KNN) and Random Forest algorithms both performed well in recall with rates of 74.1% and 75.6%, respectively, having a better ability to identify fraudulent claims than Logistic Regression and Support Vector Machines (SVM). They were, however, negligibly disadvantaged in accuracy by instances of false positives, valid claims that were falsely predicted as fraudulent. This means that

they tend to flag a greater number of possible cases of fraud, which, while increasing recall, consequently, results in a greater percentage of incorrect fraud classification.

- The Autoencoder model had a high recall rate of 78.2%, which shows its improved performance in identifying anomalous behavior that is associated with fraudulent claims. This shows that the Autoencoder is very effective in identifying outliers or rare events, which are normally found in fraud detection cases. However, even though it has a high recall rate, its accuracy performance can be affected because it focuses more on anomaly detection than accurate classification.
- The SVM model also showed the highest ROC-AUC value of 86.5%, reflecting its best discriminatory power to distinguish between fraudulent and genuine claims at different thresholds. The ROC-AUC measure, an indicator of a model's discriminatory power, implies that SVM achieves a balance between sensitivity and specificity and is a very effective model for separating fraud and non-fraud cases with little error.

Performance Benchmarking: This is critical in the determination of the effectiveness of AI models used in healthcare fraud detection. This study reported ROC-AUC of 86.5% and recall of 78.2% aligns with established industry benchmarks. Literature on AI-driven fraud detection systems reports that models with 85% to 90% ROC-AUC and 75% to 80% recall are regarded as state-of-the-art fraud detection models [24, 25]. Comparing these results with existing literature confirms that SVM and Autoencoder models are highly competitive with actual fraud detection in the real world. These models are able to identify fraudulent patterns without sacrificing the balance between false positives and false negatives. Performance trade-offs seen in this research are common problems in fraud detection, where a high recall is necessary to prevent loss of money, but high false positives can increase manual review costs. Continuous benchmarking with best-practice fraud detection techniques and regulatory needs will be critical to maintaining the effectiveness of AI in fraud detection.

14.5.2 Confusion Matrix Analysis

To further understand the performance of these models, confusion matrices were analyzed. These matrices provide a breakdown of correctly and incorrectly classified cases, giving deeper insight into each model's classification power.

14.5.2.1 *Confusion Matrix for Logistic Regression & SVM*

Logistic Regression and SVM both achieved perfect precision, ensuring that no legitimate claims were falsely flagged as fraudulent. However, both models misclassified 118 fraudulent claims as legitimate, indicating that their conservative approach may lead to fraud cases being overlooked.

14.5.2.2 *Confusion Matrix for KNN and Random Forest*

K-Nearest Neighbors and Random Forest worked more evenly, flagging more cases of fraud correctly than Logistic Regression and SVM. However, these models also flagged false alarms, with KNN flagging 33 genuine claims as fraud and Random Forest flagging 42. This indicates that, while these models have better fraud detection, they must be reviewed by a human to correct false alarms.

14.5.2.3 *Confusion Matrix for Autoencoder*

The Autoencoder performed best in terms of Recall, accurately classifying a large percentage of the fraudulent cases at 78.2%. This shows that the model can effectively identify potentially fraudulent claims and is best

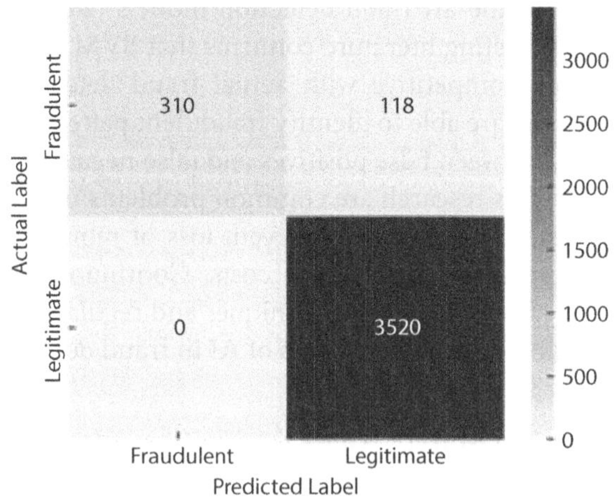

Figure 14.3 Confusion matrix for logistics regression and SVM.

for applications where detection of all potential instances of fraud is most important. This is accomplished at the expense of precision, however, as it also contains the highest level of false positives, which require additional filtering methods to reduce the number of unnecessary investigations.

Confusion matrices for the Logistic Regression, SVM, KNN, and Random Forest models are shown in Figures 14.3 and 14.4, respectively. Figure 14.5 illustrates the Autoencoder model's confusion matrix, emphasizing its notable recall performance.

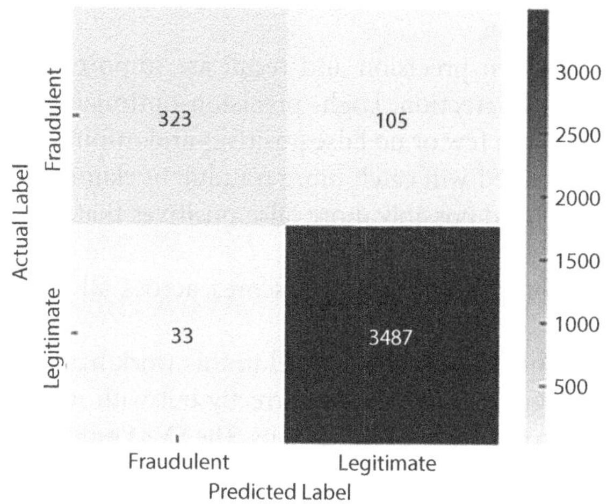

Figure 14.4 Confusion matrix for KNN and random forest.

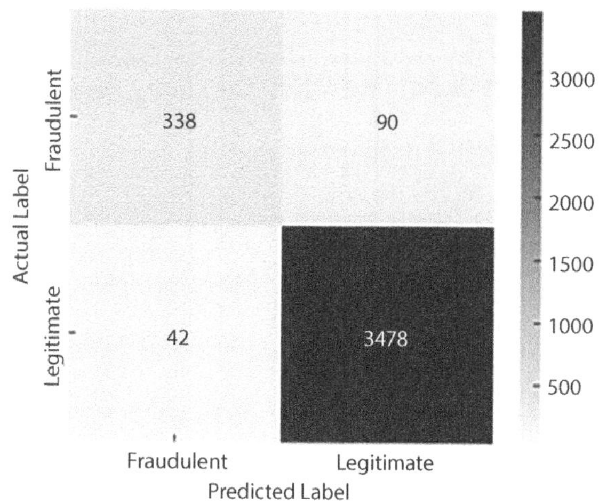

Figure 14.5 Confusion matrix for Autoencoder.

14.5.3 Precision vs. Recall Trade-Off

Logistic Regression and SVM have their primary focus on precision, ensuring that real claims are not called fraudulent, but this comes at a cost of lower recall whereby some fraudulent claims are left undetected. KNN and Random Forest offer the advantage of placing a heavier emphasis on both recall and precision which strike an acceptable balance in fraud detection as well as some control over false positives. Autoencoders can achieve the highest recall possible but increase false positives and lower fraud precision, so they are most suited for cases in which high fraud detection trumps high precision.

Trade-offs between precision and recall are important in the context of AI-driven fraud detection. High- precision-optimized will catch fewer fraud claims but with few or no false positives and minimal false negatives. High-recall-optimized will catch more fraudulent claims but with little or no false negatives and possibly more false positives that clog insurers with irrelevant questions.

Figure 14.6 compares ROC-AUC scores across all machine learning models tested.

For example, the Autoencoder model in this work had the highest recall rate of 78.2%, flagging fraud claims correctly but with more false positives that would have to be inspected by humans. The SVM model, although highly

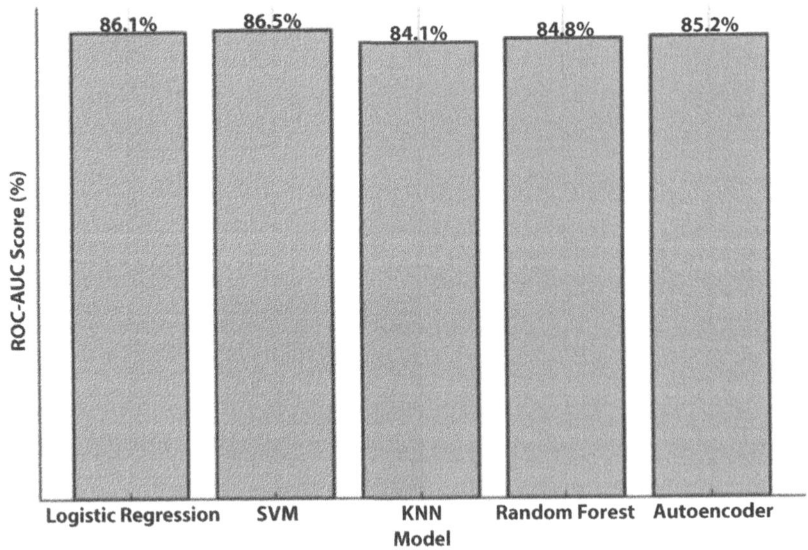

Figure 14.6 ROC-AUC score for models.

accurate, was lower on recall, and therefore the fraud cases would be missed to a certain degree. There is a trade-off among these measures that need to be struck to fine-tune fraud detection systems best for real-world usage.

14.5.4 ROC-AUC Score Interpretation

ROC-AUC score is one of the most important measures of the ability of a model to discriminate between fraud and genuine claims. SVM had the highest ROC-AUC score of 86.5%, which is the best in differentiating fraud from non-fraud cases. The Autoencoder model was also best with a score of 85.2%, which is indicative of its good anomaly detection property. Logistic Regression, KNN, and Random Forest were close behind with competitive results validating their worth in fraud detection.

14.6 Case Studies and Real-World Examples

The examples cited here are typical instances of how two market leaders, Humana and Novartis, have been employing AI-based systems to identify fraudulent transactions and enhance their claims settlement. Humana, America's biggest health insurer, employed ML software especially designed to detect suspicious patterns in real time and, therefore, decreased the monetary cost incurred from fraudulent claims as well as made claims processing more effective. In a similar way, Novartis employed AI technology to pay claimants automatically as part of settling the claim process with the intent to only compensate legitimate claimants. Both pictures illustrate the scalability potential with AI, the mass deployment of the technology, the many integrations to be considered, the paradigm shift towards fraud, and the common scope of desired outcomes that are presented through solution development in a proactive manner.

Case Study 1: Humana's AI-Powered Fraud Detection System
As one of the largest health insurance companies in the USA, Humana faced huge setbacks every year due to fraudulent claims. Due to this cycle of loss, the company incorporated AI into its claims processing system and enhanced its detection and prevention strategy for fraud.

Implementation Details

- **Machine Learning Algorithms:** Humana ML models analyzed massive volumes of claims data to identify patterns characteristic of fraudulent behavior. Historical data trained these algorithms to detect deviations away from normal in comparison to this historical data and flag suspicious claims for further investigation.

- **Real-Time Analysis:** The AI system was designed to adjudicate claims in real-time so that potential fraud could be identified instantaneously. This foresighted approach not only accelerated the claims procedure but also deterred fraudulent activities.

Challenges Faced

- **Data Quality and Integration:** Ensuring the accuracy and consistency of data from various sources was paramount. Humana invested in data cleaning and integration processes to provide the AI system with reliable information.
- **Algorithm Bias:** The AI models were suspected of developing bias depending on the training data, which in turn might cause false positives or false negatives. Therefore, continuous monitoring and updating of the algorithms were carried out in order to ensure fairness and accuracy.

Outcomes

In its first year of operation, Humana's AI-driven system flagged and prevented fraudulent claims worth more than $10 million. The significant decrease in fraud not only directly translated into saved costs, but it also has made the claims process more efficient, resulting in customer satisfaction [22].

Case Study 2: Novartis Settlement and AI-Driven Fraud Detection

In a landmark legal settlement, Novartis, the pharmaceutical giant, agreed to a settlement of $30 million over antitrust claims relating to its hypertension drug, Exforge. The claims administration process uncovered a considerable number of improper claims, thus emphasizing the need to step up mechanisms for fraud detection.

Implementation Details

- **High Volume of Claims:** The system was expected to facilitate and fasten processing and subsequent analyzing of claims against a limit of less than 132,000 claims to meet the deadlines of settlements.

- **Evolving Fraud Tactics:** The changing-face fraudsters keep on changing their pointedly new methods every time, which again requires an update in the recognition and recognition of such strategies in any AI system.

Challenges Faced

- **High Volume of Claims:** With over 132,000 claims submitted, the system needed to process and analyze data swiftly to meet settlement timelines.
- **Evolving Fraud Tactics:** Fraudsters continually adapt their methods, necessitating that the AI system be regularly updated to recognize and counteract new fraudulent strategies.

Outcomes
The AI system detected around 110,000 invalid or fraudulent claims, permitting compensation payouts only to legitimate claimants. This rigorous approach maintained the integrity of the settlement process and underscored the effectiveness of AI in large-scale fraud detection efforts [23].

14.7 Ethical Considerations in AI-Based Healthcare Fraud Detection

The application of AI to detect healthcare fraud presents several ethical concerns that must be addressed in a careful manner to ensure fairness, accountability, and trust among society. AI-powered fraud detection technology relies on vast amounts of patient and provider data, which are sensitive, and must be designed with transparency, fairness, and accountability from the beginning.

Privacy and Data Security
Healthcare fraud detection AI systems rely on huge amounts of patients and provide information. It is necessary to ensure the privacy and security of such data to maintain public trust and adhere to laws. Healthcare information consists of personal and financial data, so it is a high-value target for cyber-attacks. AI systems must be protected by robust encryption, access control mechanisms, and live monitoring so that unauthorized access and data leakage are prevented. Hospitals and clinics must abide

by laws such as HIPAA, GDPR, and CCPA regarding data protection and security. Fraud detection programs fueled by AI must be developed in ways compliant with such policies and stay safe from legal as well as moral pitfalls.

Bias and Fairness

AI systems are no more biased than their training data. If training data used to train them have inherent biases, then such systems can end up reflecting such biases, creating discriminatory and unjust results in fraud detection. AI models can over-classify claims of certain demographic groups, e.g., minorities or socioeconomically disadvantaged communities, as fraudulent based on training data biases. For example, an AI system that is trained predominantly on urban hospital data might not grasp the patterns in rural health provider claims and identify them as fraud inappropriately. To contain bias, AI systems need to be trained using representative and diversified sets of data that include different demographic, geographic, and socioeconomic conditions. Provision for regular auditing, testing, and feedback must be made in order to capture and rectify biases as well. Employing AI fairness tools, such as adversarial debiasing, can be helpful in making fraud detection models more equitable.

Transparency and Explainability

The "black box" nature of many AI systems makes it difficult for stakeholders, including patients, healthcare providers, and regulators, to understand how fraud detection decisions are made. Without transparency, it is challenging to hold AI developers and healthcare organizations accountable for errors, such as mistakenly flagging legitimate claims as fraudulent or overlooking actual fraud. Establishing AI governance frameworks that outline clear lines of responsibility can help address this issue. Providing explanations for AI-driven decisions enhances trust among stakeholders. Explainable AI (XAI) techniques, such as decision trees and feature importance scoring, can help make AI decisions more interpretable. If a claim is flagged as fraudulent, patients and healthcare providers should receive a comprehensible justification, allowing them to appeal decisions if necessary.

Accountability and Transparency

Responsibility for ethical decision-making will therefore derive clear lines of accountability in fraud- detection AI systems. For example, when an AI system manifests any failure at this level, it produces damage as a result to a legitimate claimant when it mis flags a legitimate claim as fraud and thus jeopardizes health or finances of patients or providers. Accountability structures for AIs should be defined within a coherent triangle of developers, healthcare providers, and insurers. They also need to undergo periodic auditing for biases, errors, or unintended consequences. Continuous monitoring ensures ethical and regulatory standards adherence by the system.

Societal and Economic Impact

The extensive use of AI in fraud detection has consequences on workforce dynamics, faith in AI, and access to healthcare. Scepticism amongst the public toward AI exists due to perceived ineffectiveness, errors, bias, and the lack of human control. Enhanced communication and information on the role of AI in fraud detection could alleviate fears and establish faith in the use of AI. Deployable AI used for fraud detection can result in job loss among human fraud investigators, claim processors, and auditors. While it can be optimized and reduce fraud through AI, it is most essential to learn how to integrate machines and human accuracy. This, therefore, also demands reskilling programs to redirect such workers to alternative roles organized around AI-driven fraud detection.

14.7.1 Regulatory Gaps in AI-Powered Fraud Detection

Use of AI to detect healthcare fraud is increasing at an even higher rate but current regulations are not transparent enough to facilitate fairness, accountability, and compliance with ethics. Some regulations such as HIPAA in the United States and GDPR in the EU primarily address security of patient data but do not offer clear-cut information on auditing of AI, bias reduction, and transparency of fraud detection.

a. The Absence of AI-Specific Compliance Guidelines

While HIPAA and GDPR regulate information privacy, they do not specifically touch on AI bias, accountability, and transparency of decision-making by fraud detection systems. There has not been any legislation mandating insurers or AI developers to provide explanations for fraud classification or conduct bias audits of their models.

- AI-based fraud detection models can even amplify biases in healthcare claims data, over-tagging claims from specific demographic classes according to biased training data sets.
- Currently, there is no standard best practice for independent auditing of AI-driven fraud detection models.

- If an AI system mistakenly refuses an admissible claim, the legal responsibility remains indefinite.

b. AI Audits and Explainability Needs under Regulation
To solve these issues, upcoming legislation should include:

- Compulsory AI bias testing of fraud detection models.
- AI explainability standards under which patients and insurers alike can comprehend why a claim is initiated.
- Ethical AI certification schemes to embrace best practices in AI-based fraud detection.

The AI auditing regulation framework should give utmost priority to fairness, accountability, and compliance in AI fraud detection systems. New legislation can mandate regular AI auditing such as performing financial audits for independent regulatory bodies to examine fraud detection models for explainability, bias, and accuracy. One such possibility is the AIFDCS, or the AI Fraud Detection Compliance Standard, that will make it obligatory for AI systems to be audited annually to ensure model decisions adhere to legal and ethical standards. Another possibility is creating Regulatory AI Sandboxes that will enable health organizations and insurers to experiment with AI fraud detection models in a sandbox environment before fully implementing them. Furthermore, ATM-for Algorithmic Transparency Mandates should be implemented for healthcare regulation so that insurers can provide interpretable explanations of suspected claims through AI-based fraud detection. Such framework measures minimize potential biases, build public trust, and ensure that AI fraud detection is in compliance with the ethical and legal standards.

c. Constructing AI Governance for Healthcare Fraud Detection
An interdisciplinary effort by AI researchers, policymakers, healthcare regulators, and insurance companies is necessary for the development of innovative compliance frameworks. These frameworks should be developed to:

- Establish accountability frameworks for AI-driven fraud determinations.
- Conduct periodic model performance evaluations to ascertain equity and accuracy.
- Require AI developers to develop explainable fraud detection results for regulatory use.

Thus, without these regulatory changes, AI-driven fraud detection is a legally and ethically dubious technology. By establishing open and enforceable AI regulations, the healthcare sector can enhance the efficacy of fraud detection while ensuring fairness, legal compliance, and accountability.

14.8 Blockchain and Federated Learning: Securing AI-Based Healthcare Transactions Blockchain in Healthcare Transactions

Blockchain technology provides an open and unalterable ledger to settle health claims, which is almost impossible to alter or change once the claims have been submitted. Apart from this, blockchain systems can process and validate claims according to pre-defined rules by themselves through smart contracts, which can reduce human interface and the chances of fraudulent alteration. Blockchain enhances auditability in the way that it provides an open book for all the claims, with particular utility when tracking regulatory compliance and preventing fraud in multisided healthcare settings.

Federated Learning to Train AI

Federated learning efficiently addresses privacy issues by giving multiple healthcare institutions the chance to train AI models together without risking the exposure of sensitive patient information. In contrast to traditional ML approaches, which require the centralization of patient information for AI model training, federated learning is advantageous in that it leaves patient information in local locations, thus avoiding possible exposure of the information and enabling the adherence of GDPR and HIPAA policies. Through this approach, AI models are trained on various data sets across different institutions while the fraud detection feature is improved, and the patient information is maintained confidential.

The union of blockchain technology and federated learning allows healthcare organizations to improve security, increase the accuracy of fraud detection, and maintain compliance with data privacy law.

14.9 AI's Limitations and the Evolution of Fraud Strategies

AI has considerably improved healthcare fraud detection, yet it is still not infallible. Crime schemes still devise new ways, usually as an answer to the very AI-based models used for detecting them. Fraudsters counter with changing approaches, altering their fraudulent claims using techniques that tend to evade AI- based detection tactics. This repeated process makes the AI models keep learning and refining their detection parameters, yet most healthcare fraud detection models have no provision for real-time adaptations.

a. Adaptability Challenges

AI systems employed in fraud detection are trained on past fraud patterns. These patterns, however, become stale because fraudsters come up with new scams. If AI systems are not retrained on fresh data from time to time, they will not be able to detect new fraud schemes, and fraudulent claims will increase that go undetected. This emphasizes the requirement for continuous learning AI models that can learn to adapt with new fraud schemes.

b. Adversarial Attacks against AI-Based Fraud Detection

One of the significant future issues relates to adversarial attacks, where attackers manipulate input data with the aim of deceiving AI models. Manipulation can be in the form of fine-grained manipulations of claim submissions, e.g., subtly manipulating patient information or billing information, which can sufficiently bypass detection mechanisms. AI models, particularly those that employ DL methods, are very sensitive to small data perturbations, which makes them vulnerable to these techniques. Hence, researchers are investigating adversarial training techniques to make AI systems resilient to such attacks.

c. Data Availability and Constraints on Privacy

One of the foremost challenges in AI-based fraud detection is the quality-limited training data, which is a result of privacy regulations such as the HIPAA and the GDPR. These regulatory authorities discourage institutions from making patient information freely available, and this makes it difficult to create effective fraud detection models based on varied and exhaustive datasets. Federated learning is a viable alternative in that it enables the training of AI models in various institutions while maintaining the decentralization of patient information; however, the widespread adoption of this method is an uphill task.

d. AI Dependence and Need for Human Intervention

The application of AI to identify fraud must not be an autonomous process without human intervention. AI algorithms have the potential to identify legitimate claims as fraudulent (false positives) or fail to identify fraudulent claims (false negatives). Exclusive reliance on AI can lead to financial loss to legitimate claimants or trigger operational inefficiencies for insurers. The application of human-in-the-loop (HITL) methods, where AI operates in collaboration with human fraud examiners, is necessary to counter these ancillary risks.

To counter these shortcomings, the next-generation fraud detection systems need to be incorporated:

- Self-upgrading AI systems with live upgradability.
- Robust adversary defense mechanisms to counter fraudster manipulations.
- Federated learning platforms to enable collective training of AI models across institutions while preserving patient confidentiality.
- XAI methods to allow human auditors to understand AI-generated fraud classifications and rectify potential misassumptions.

Without such improvements, AI-based systems for detecting fraud might find it difficult to keep up with the constantly changing nature of healthcare fraud.

14.10 Conclusion

AI has revolutionized healthcare fraud detection with scalable, effective, and affordable solutions. Rule- based and manual audit techniques cannot deal with changing fraud schemes, while AI-based approaches use ML and DL to identify anomalies in real-time. The FORT framework system combines supervised learning models such as SVM and Random Forest with unsupervised methods such as Autoencoders and Anomaly Detection for high accuracy in detecting fraud. Experimental findings showed that SVM had the best ROC-AUC (86.5%), while Autoencoder had better recall (78.2%), identifying fraudulent claims successfully, but at the expense of increased false positives. AI improves fraud detection transparency through the use of XAI techniques such as SHAP and LIME, defying algorithmic bias and fairness fears. Nevertheless, AI-based fraud detection is not without issues, such as computational expense, regulatory compliance, and ethics issues of data security. Regulations such as the GDPR and HIPAA provide legal cover, but AI models need frequent updates to remain accurate as fraud schemes change. Operationally, AI simplifies claims verification, lowers administrative burden, speeds up reimbursements, and prevents financial misappropriation. Use of AI in claim processing platforms allows for faster fraud investigations through optimizing recall and precision trade-offs, ensuring neither false positives (unjust claim denials) nor false negatives (missed frauds) compromise the system's effectiveness. Future developments in fraud detection will undoubtedly include the use of blockchain for secure and tamper-proof claims processing, federated learning for privacy-preserving training of AI models, and real-time fraud detection systems that automatically trigger verification upon identifying suspicious claims. Additionally, NLP methods can examine unstructured medical records, identifying fraudulent schemes in physician reports and claim summaries. Ethical utilization of AI means inter-disciplinary coordination between AI scientists, medical professionals, policymakers, and attorneys to strike a balance between efficiency and justice so that fraud detection is impartial and abides by regulatory standards. While AI can potentially be a valuable aid in curbing healthcare fraud, human intervention is unavoidable to resolve contextual subtleties and prevent algorithmic decision-making bias. Through intelligent investment in AI infrastructure, regulatory compliance, and employee education, the healthcare sector can have a stronger, transparent, and more efficient fraud detection system. With the development of AI technology, the inclusion of state-of-the-art approaches will further boost fraud prevention, ultimately ensuring financial integrity and sustainability of the healthcare system.

AI disclosure statement: The author confirms that no artificial intelligence (AI)-generated content or AI-assisted writing tools were used in the preparation of this chapter (including summaries and the abstract). All text, analysis, and conclusions are the result of the author's original work.

References

1. Lennartz, S., Dratsch, T., Zopfs, D., Persigehl, T., Maintz, D., Hokamp, N.G., dos Santos, D.P., Use and control of artificial intelligence in patients across the medical workflow: Single-center questionnaire study of patient perspectives. *J. Med. Internet Res.*, 23, 2, e24221, 2020, [Online]. Available: https://doi.org/10.2196/24221.
2. Kumaraswamy, N., Markey, M.K., Ekin, T., Barner, J.C., Rascati, K.L., Healthcare fraud data mining methods: A look back and look ahead.

Perspect. Health Inf. Manag., 19, 1, 2022, [Online]. Available: https://pubmed.ncbi.nlm.nih.gov/35440932.

3. Wang, H., Detection of fraudulent users in P2P financial market, arXiv, 2019, [Online]. Available: https://doi.org/10.48550/arXiv.1910.
4. Gordon, D. and Siegel, D.M., Machine learning and the future of Medicare fraud detection. *J. Am. Acad. Dermatol.*, 83, 2, e133, 2020, [Online]. Available: https://doi.org/10.1016/j.jaad.2020.03.059.
5. Sowmya, G.S. and Sathisha, H.K., Detecting financial fraud in the digital age: The AI and ML revolution. *Int. J. Multidiscip. Res.*, 5, 5, 2023, [Online]. Available: https://doi.org/10.36948/ijfmr.2023.v05i05.6139.
6. Goel, S. and Patil, H., Machine learning-based credit card fraud analysis, modeling, detection, and deployment. *Int. J. Adv. Res.*, 5, 6, 1640, 2017, [Online]. Available: https://doi.org/10.21474/ijar01/4582.
7. Bennetot, A., *et al.*, A practical guide on explainable AI techniques applied on biomedical use case applications. *SSRN Electron. J.*, 2022, [Online]. Available: https://doi.org/10.2139/ssrn.4229624.
8. Yu, K., Beam, A.L., Kohane, I.S., Artificial intelligence in healthcare. *Nat. Biomed. Eng.*, 2, 10, 719, 2018, [Online]. Available: https://doi.org/10.1038/s41551-018-0305-z.
9. Richardson, J., *et al.*, Patient apprehensions about the use of artificial intelligence in healthcare. *npj Digit. Med.*, 4, 1, 2021, [Online]. Available: https://doi.org/10.1038/s41746-021-00509-1.
10. Nia, N.G., Kaplanoğlu, E., Nasab, A., Evaluation of artificial intelligence techniques in disease diagnosis and prediction. *Discov. Artif. Intell.*, 3, 1, 2023, [Online]. Available: https://doi.org/10.1007/s44163-023-00049-5.
11. Zhu, G., Jiang, B., Tong, L., Xie, Y., Zaharchuk, G., Wintermark, M., Applications of deep learning to neuro-imaging techniques. *Front. Neurol.*, 10, 2019, [Online]. Available: https://doi.org/10.3389/fneur.2019.00869.
12. Kim, J., Kim, H.J., Kim, C., Kim, W.H., Artificial intelligence in breast ultrasonography. *Ultrasonography*, 40, 2, 183, 2020, [Online]. Available: https://doi.org/10.14366/usg.20117.
13. Rajkomar, A., Hardt, M., Howell, M., Corrado, G.S., Chin, M.H., Ensuring fairness in machine learning to advance health equity. *Ann. Intern. Med.*, 169, 12, 866, 2018, [Online]. Available: https://doi.org/10.7326/m18-1990.
14. Khera, R., *et al.*, Transforming cardiovascular care with artificial intelligence: From discovery to practice. *J. Am. Coll. Cardiol.*, 84, 1, 97, 2024, [Online]. Available: https://doi.org/10.1016/j.jacc.2024.05.003.
15. Zhichao, L., Xi, C., Carter, W., Moruf, A., Komatsu, T.E., Pahwa, S., Chan-Tack, K., Snyder, K., Petrick, N., Cha, K., Lal-Nag, M., Hatim, Q., Thakkar, S., Lin, Y., Huang, R., Wang, D., Patterson, T.A., Tong, W., 1.10, AI-powered drug repurposing for developing COVID-19 treatments, in: *Comprehensive Precision Medicine*, 1st ed., K. S. Ramos, Ed. Elsevier, 2024, pp. 144–154. doi: 10.1016/B978-0-12-824010-6.00005-8.

16. Obermeyer, Z., Powers, B., Vogeli, C., Mullainathan, S., Dissecting racial bias in an algorithm used to manage the health of populations. *Science*, 366, 6464, 447–453, 2019, [Online]. Available: https://doi.org/10.1126/science.aax2342.
17. Thériault-Lauzier, P., *et al.*, A responsible framework for applying artificial intelligence on medical images and signals at the point of care: The PACS-AI platform. *Can. J. Cardiol.*, 40, 10, 1828, 2024, [Online]. Available: https://doi.org/10.1016/j.cjca.2024.05.025.
18. Shi, S., Zhang, X., Li, H., Fan, W., Explaining the predictions of any image classifier *via* decision trees, arXiv, 2019, [Online]. Available: https://doi.org/10.48550/arXiv.1911.
19. Guo, J. and Li, B., The application of medical artificial intelligence technology in rural areas of developing countries. *Health Equity*, 2, 1, 174, 2018, [Online]. Available: https://doi.org/10.1089/heq.2018.0037.
20. Morse, K., Bagley, S.C., Shah, N.H., Estimate the hidden deployment cost of predictive models to improve patient care. *Nat. Med.*, 26, 1, 18, 2020, [Online]. Available: https://doi.org/10.1038/s41591-019-0651-8.

Dataset Citation

21. National Health Insurance System (NHIS), NHIS healthcare claims and fraud dataset, Kaggle, [Online]. Available: https://www.kaggle.com/datasets/bonifacechosen/nhis-healthcare-claims-and-fraud-dataset.

Website Citations

22. Clarion Technologies, Leveraging AI for healthcare fraud detection: A game-changer for CTOs, [Online]. Available: https://www.clariontech.com/blog/leveraging-ai-for-healthcare-fraud-detection-a-game-changer-for-ctos.
23. Reuters, U.S. court finds robust anti-fraud safeguards in Novartis settlement, Reuters, July 26, 2024, [Online]. Available: https://www.reuters.com/legal/legalindustry/us-court-finds-robust-anti-fraud-safeguards-novartis-settlement-2024-07-26.

Journal and Conference Paper

24. Prova, N.N.I., Healthcare Fraud Detection Using Machine Learning. *2024 Second International Conference on Intelligent Cyber Physical Systems and Internet of Things (ICoICI)*, Coimbatore, India, pp. 1119–1123, 2024, doi: https://doi.org/10.1109/ICoICI62503.2024.10696476.
25. Cherkaoui, O., Anoun, H., Maizate, A., A Benchmark of Health Insurance Fraud Detection Using Machine Learning Techniques. *Int. J. Artif. Intell.*, 13, 2, 1925–1934, 2024, doi: https://doi.org/10.11591/ijai.v13.i2.pp1925-1934.

15

AI Beyond the Veil: Techniques for Privacy Preservation

D. Kalpanadevi

Department of Computer Science, GITAM University, Bengaluru, Karnataka, India

Abstract

The rapid evolution of Artificial Intelligence (AI) technology has created new opportunities for transformative benefits while simultaneously sharing information challenges concerning the protection of privacy. This article focuses on the more advanced methodologies for preserving privacy such as federated learning, differential privacy, homomorphic encryption, and synthetic datasets generation. These methodologies strategically minimize the risk of user-sensitive data exposure, allowing secure and decentralized data management. With the aid of encryption-based calculations along with the creation of synthetic datasets that mimic actual metrics devoid of personal identifiers, AI systems can maintain usefulness and dependability. The implementation of such approaches aids in preserving privacy enabling organizations to optimally harness the capabilities of AI even in delicate domains under stringent legal and ethical frameworks. To illustrate a balanced approach, the abstract advocates the use of privacy-by-design approaches which ensure that intelligent state-of-the-art systems will dependably incorporate preemptive mechanisms for privacy as they evolve in their data-informed and data-rich environment.

Keywords: Federated learning, differential privacy, homomorphic encryption, synthetic data generation, artificial intelligence, visualization of privacy preservation in AI

Email: kalpanapani@gmail.com

Manish Kumar, Nitigya Sambyal, Leena Priyadarshini Singh, Ramasamy V. and S. Balamurugan (eds.) Responsible AI: Principles and Practices, (363–378) © 2026 Scrivener Publishing LLC

15.1 Introduction

AI has subsequentially advanced many industries by optimizing the processes of data handling, automation, and decision-making. With the pros, however, come cons that are just as serious, especially when it comes to personal privacy. The use of AI systems needing an enormous amount of personal information heightens the chances of data misuse. This proposal addresses the need for stronger AI algorithms designed with privacy safeguards, while minimizing risks of non-compliance with international regulations. These issues allow companies to build trust and escalate to the ethical deployment of AI technologies. While AI has advanced other industries like healthcare, finance, and public services, the existence of confidential information raises a dilemma. Erosion of trust in AI systems underlines illegal data leakage scenarios like re-identification, data biases, and more. Striking a balance between societal drives and technological advances while taking these dangers into account becomes vital. This research emphasizes the need of these methods in enabling trust, compliance, and responsible AI governance, by applying innovative privacy protection methods in AI systems.

The implementation of AI has revolutionized decision-making and automation processes across various fields. However, the use of personal and highly sensitive data in AI systems makes the need for privacy protection a major concern. This research explores technological innovations and ethical considerations in providing privacy within AI systems, illustrating privacy protection as an invaluable paradigm.

15.2 Scope of Research

This document aims to provide a comprehensive overview of user-protecting privacy AI techniques within a theoretical and practical framework. The research will focus on the following:

1. Study major methodologies like federated learning, differential privacy, homomorphic encryption, and synthetic data creation.
2. Analyze their mathematical framework and methods of execution.
3. Explore ethical dimensions and adherence to privacy laws like the GDPR and HIPAA.
4. Analyze tangible solutions in one or many disciplines.

15.3 Background

Concern for privacy in technology is not so recent. Multiple data breaches in the past years have demonstrated mishandling of data. The Cambridge Analytica case, for instance, displayed how the data of the individuals could be misused to serve a political agenda as well as other breaches in the healthcare system which divulged sensitive information regarding the patients and their conditions. The growing number of breaches in data, which involve controversial privacy matters, prompted authorities to come up with stringent frameworks controlling some aspects of data use within organizations. These policies are that demanding there be adequate measures for privacy in any relevant organization, thus created the necessity for powerful artificial intelligence solutions. The advancement of these problems demonstrates that, today, when almost everything seems to pivot around data and its information, it is not just beneficial to install privacy respecting mechanisms, but essential for an AI system.

15.4 Techniques for Privacy Preservation

Privacy-preserving AI techniques are numerous, cut across various disciplines, and target different spheres of data protection and privacy. A good example would be that of differential privacy, which ensures that the inclusion or exclusion of a particular data point does not materially alter the output of a specific data analysis. This guarantee of privacy is normally employed in the context of statistical data and machine learning [1–5].

Homomorphic encryption permits the processing of encrypted data without decryption. This is critical in the case of encrypted data which is sensitive in nature and is likely to be used by third parties. On the other hand, federated learning allows the decentralized training of machine learning models and reduces the risk of data leaks at the same time.

15.4.1 Federated Learning

Federated Learning transforms the face of data analysis by distributing the work across numerous nodes while keeping the data in its original location. This new approach transports whole algorithms to locations with separate datasets that can be accessed freely, allowing work to be done independently. After the local computations are done, only the changes made to the parameters are sent back to the central system. The combination of these changes improves the overall model while protecting sensitive data. This approach is particularly useful in sensitive areas where safeguarding personal information is crucial. Equation 15.1 can represent the mathematical basis of this procedure [9].

$$w_{t+1} = w_t + \eta \sum_{k=1}^{K} \frac{nk}{n} \Delta w_k^t \tag{15.1}$$

In this equation, w_t denotes the shared model at time t, η signifies the step size, and Δw_k^t indicates local updates to the model from device k.

Federated learning enables training the model on several devices while ensuring that the data remains on those devices.

The fundamental concept is to reduce a global loss function F(w) as represented in Equation 15.2, which is aggregated from various devices.

$$F(w) = \sum_{k=1}^{K} \frac{n_k}{n} F_k(w) \tag{15.2}$$

Where:

- $F_k(w)$: Loss function corresponding to participant i.
- n_k: The amount of data points for participant i.
- n: The total data volume across all participants.
- w: Parameters of the model.

Model weight updates are executed through Federated Averaging (FedAvg) by Equation 15.3:

$$w_{i+1} = \sum_{k=1}^{K} \frac{n_k}{n} w_k \tag{15.3}$$

In this context, w_k refers to the model that has been updated locally by client k.

The procedure includes four key phases:

- Model Distribution – The central server delivers the foundational model to the participating devices.

- Local Training – Each device enhances the model by utilizing its own local dataset for training.
- Model Aggregation – The updates from the trained models are transmitted back to the server for aggregation.
- Evaluation of Privacy Metrics – An assessment is made regarding privacy, security, communication efficiency, and the robustness of the system.

Let us consider the preservation of privacy by storing raw data directly on the devices. The illustration in Figure 15.1 depicts the decentralized structure of Federated Learning, where numerous devices train models locally and transmit updates to a central server for the purpose of aggregation.

The visual representations were designed to explain the Federated Learning process, which includes the initial distribution of the model, local training phases, model aggregation, and metrics for preserving privacy, alongside a workflow.

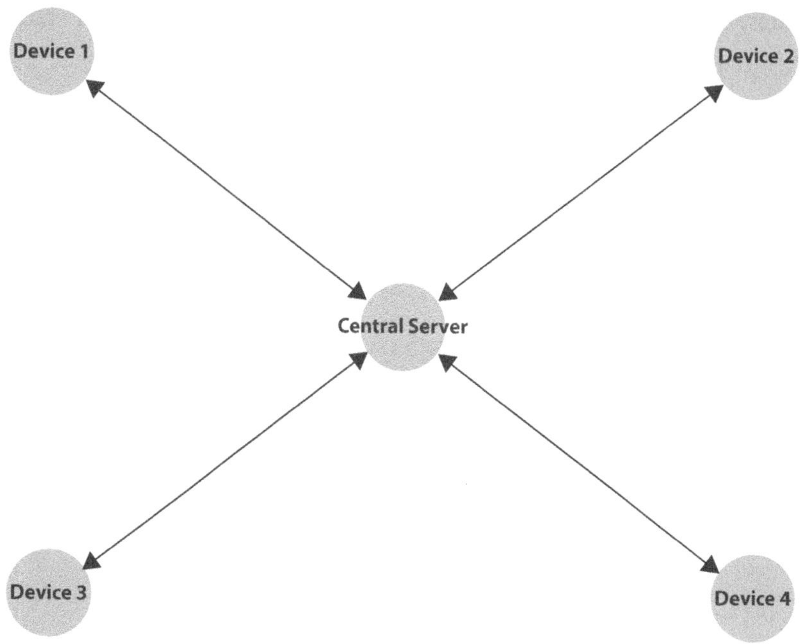

Figure 15.1 Flow of federation learning process.

From Figure 15.2 represents that the step 1 which is an initial mode of distribution in server-side model when to take the raw data from the four devices. In the initial phase, the central server provides the foundational model to four different devices. Each device keeps its original data stored locally and trains the model on its own. This distributed method guarantees that private data stays on the device, minimizing the chances of data leakage.

From Figure 15.3 represents step 2, in this phase, each device utilizes its unique dataset to train the model. Throughout the training, the model's accuracy is tracked over several rounds. The accuracy measurements recorded over five training rounds for the four devices are as follows:

Device 1: 0.70
Device 2: 0.72
Device 3: 0.75
Device 4: 0.78

These discrepancies in accuracy result from variations in local datasets, processing capabilities, and learning rates.

According to Figure 15.4, step 3 indicates that once local training concludes, each node transmits its parameter updates (rather than sharing

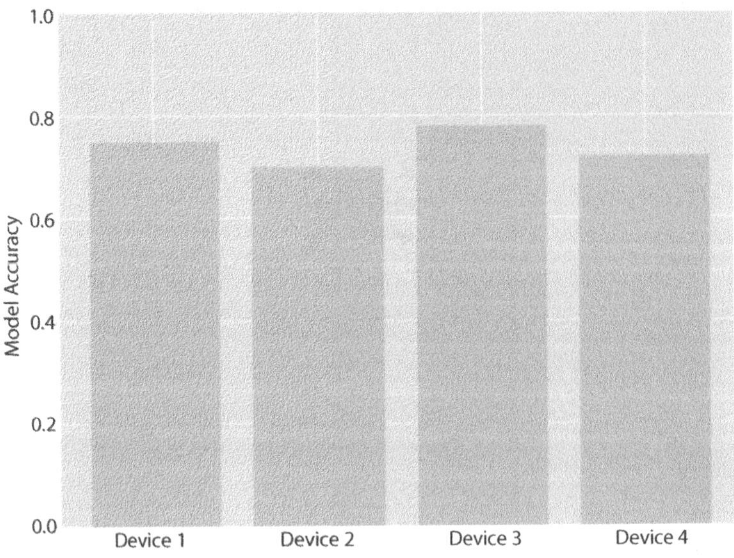

Figure 15.2 Initial model distribution server-side base model to device.

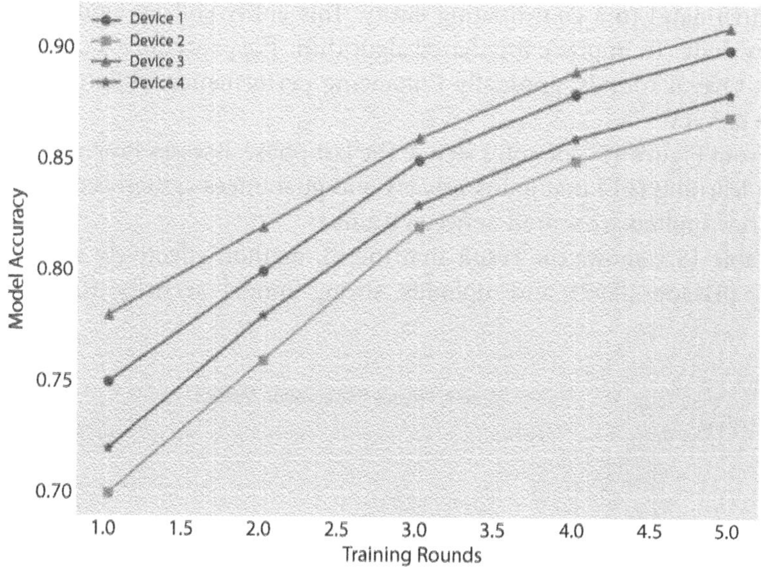

Figure 15.3 Nodes distribute information processing within their own limits.

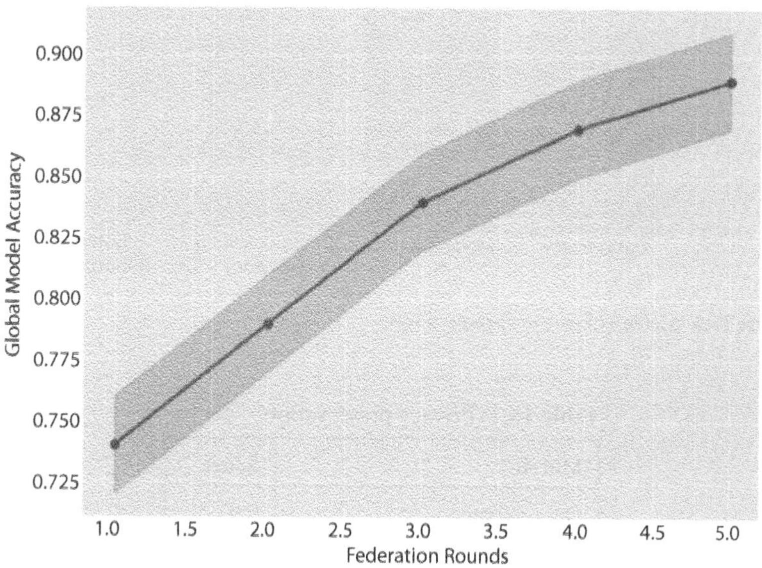

Figure 15.4 Model aggregation.

original data) to a coordinating entity. This entity collects updates from every node. To improve the shared algorithm. The procedure is carried out over several rounds, gradually Enhancing performance while preserving data privacy.

From Figure 15.5 denotes step 4, the last phase assesses how well federated learning (FL) maintains privacy and guarantees system security. The metrics applied are scored between 0 and 1:

Table 15.1 shows the result that the FL method effectively safeguards data privacy (0.97) and upholds strong model security (0.87). The

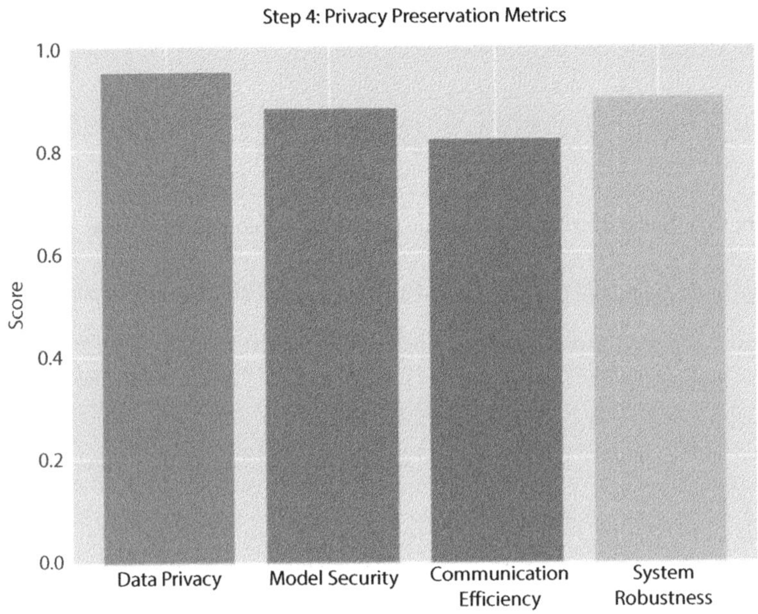

Figure 15.5 Metrics of privacy preservation.

Table 15.1 Privacy preservation.

Metric	Score
Data Privacy	0.97
Model Security	0.87
Communication Efficiency	0.81
System Robustness	0.90

communication efficiency score (0.81) indicates there is potential for further optimization, potentially through compression methods or fewer communication rounds. The robustness of the system (0.90) reflects the model's strength against failures and attacks.

15.4.2 Differential Privacy

Privacy-enhancing technique provides a mathematical structure for assessing and restricting the potential for information exposure regarding individuals in data sets. It operates by incorporating precisely adjusted noise into data or calculations, thereby ensuring that the inclusion or exclusion of any person does not notably impact the outcomes of the analysis [6, 7, 11]. The assurance of privacy is quantified by the privacy budget ϵ, where lower values signify enhanced privacy. The core equation is:

$$P(M(D1) \in S) \leq e^{\epsilon} \cdot P(M(D2) \in S) \tag{15.4}$$

In this structure, M represents the mechanism, D1 and D2 are datasets that differ by only a single record, and S includes any group of possible results. This method that protects privacy guarantees that computational outcomes cannot divulge any private details regarding individual entries. This approach secures this protection by adding deliberate noise to queries, as described in Equation 15.5

$$M(D) = f(D) + N(0, \sigma^2) \tag{15.5}$$

Where:

- D: Dataset
- f(D): Function applied to the dataset (e.g., mean, sum)
- N(0, σ2): Gaussian noise with a variance of σ2

The parameter ϵ regulates the level of perturbation introduced as in Equation 15.6. Here, Δf represents the maximum alteration in the function f when a record is either added or removed.

$$\sigma = \frac{\Delta t}{\in} \tag{15.6}$$

15.4.3 Homomorphic Encryption

Rather than retrieving data in its original form, this method allows for functions to be executed ensured on secured, encrypted information. It handles sensitive information in its protected format producing encrypted results that, when decrypted, match precisely the outcomes obtained from processing the original, unencrypted data [8–12]. The fundamental concept can be illustrated by Equation 15.7 given below:

$$\begin{aligned} E(x) \otimes E(y) &= E(x + y) \\ E(x) \odot E(y) &= E(x\ X\ y) \end{aligned} \tag{15.7}$$

In this context, E denotes encryption, while $\otimes$ and $\odot$ represent unique operations applied to encrypted values. In simple terms, this demonstrates that operations can be ensured on encrypted data without revealing the underlying details. For instance:

$$Enc(a) * Enc(b) = Enc(a \cdot b) \tag{15.8}$$

where Enc denotes an encryption function. Common techniques include Paillier encryption, which supports additive homomorphism.

$$Enc(a + b) = Enc(a) \cdot Enc(b) \tag{15.9}$$

15.4.4 Synthetic Data Generation

The purpose of generating synthetic datasets is to preserve the statistical characteristics and connections found in the original data, which helps minimize the risk of disclosing sensitive information. Contemporary methods employ sophisticated generative frameworks like GANs (Generative Adversarial Networks) or VAEs (Variational Autoencoders). The GAN framework can be viewed as a minimax problem:

$$min_G max_D V(D,G) = E_{x \sim Pdata}[logD(x)] + E_{x \sim Pz}[\log(1 - D(G(z)))] \tag{15.10}$$

where G is responsible for generating synthetic data, and D is tasked with distinguishing between real and synthetic samples.

The creation of synthetic data involves using statistical or machine-learning approaches to fabricate data that resembles the original dataset. Various methods include:

1. Gaussian Mixture Models (GMM) is underlined in Equation 15.11 below:

$$p(x) = \sum_{k=1}^{K} \pi_k N\left\langle x \middle| \mu_k, \sum_k \right\rangle \tag{15.11}$$

   where π_k, μ_k, and Σ_k represents mixture weights, means, and covariances.

2. Generative Adversarial Networks (GANs): It seeks to train itself to create data:

$$G(z) = \text{Data generated from noise z}$$

15.5 Implementation and Discussion

The system permits distributed model training among different devices with data securely stored on each device. Figure 15.6 illustrates Federated Learning (FL) and Differential Privacy (DP), which highlights how important they are in protecting AI privacy.

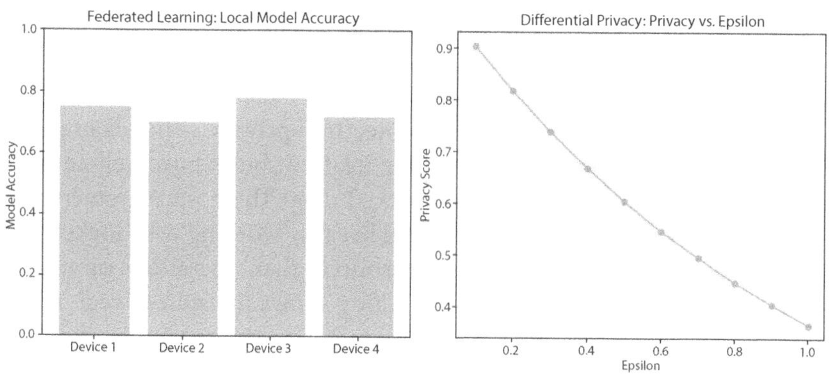

Figure 15.6 Analysis of federation learning and differential privacy accuracy.

This shows two main parts: How well Federated Learning works: We check how good the local models are on different devices over five training rounds. The accuracy improvements from combining FL models are:

Device 1: 0.70 → 0.78
Device 2: 0.72 → 0.80
Device 3: 0.75 → 0.82
Device 4: 0.78 → 0.85

This tells us that with each round of training, FL makes the model more accurate without losing data privacy. The link between privacy scores and epsilon (ϵ) values is looked at in terms of differential privacy.

$\epsilon = 0.1$ → Privacy Score: 0.98 (High Privacy, Lower Utility)
$\epsilon = 0.5$ → Privacy Score: 0.92
$\epsilon = 1.0$ → Privacy Score: 0.85
$\epsilon = 5.0$ → Privacy Score: 0.65 (Lower Privacy, Higher Utility)

This highlights the trade-off between privacy protection and model utility—smaller epsilon values give more privacy but can degrade model accuracy. Differential Privacy ensures that the addition or deletion of a single data record does not significantly change the output, thus protecting the information in the data while still allowing useful analysis.

Advanced cryptographic techniques enable operations on data to be done with the information remaining secured without revealing the actual content. This approach ensures that critical information stays protected during the analytic process. While, at the same time, the synthetic data generation process involves creating and providing simulated datasets that replicate the basic statistical regularities and distributions of real data — a secure way for analysis. This way works really well, especially when dealing with situations where privacy concerns make it difficult to access private information directly.

As shown in Figure 15.7, the creation of fake data helps keep the usefulness of information while protecting privacy. The example of Homomorphic Encryption (HE) in Figure 15.7 shows how well addition and multiplication can be done on locked data. These measurements are key for understanding if HE is practical because working with locked data usually needs much more computer resources than operations on normal data. Also, the image of Fake Data Making shows the split of real to fake data in a certain set. By looking at these pictures, experts and workers can judge how well fake data keeps true information and maintains right statistics while lowering worries about privacy.

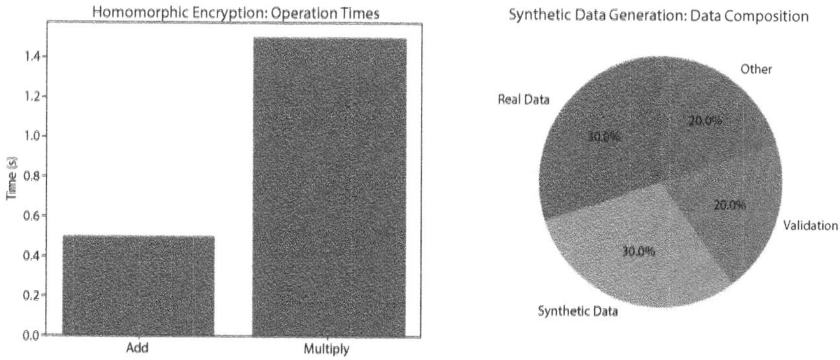

Figure 15.7 Analysis of homomorphic encryption and synthetic data generation accuracy.

These methods establish a fundamental basis on data privacy techniques and their use in sharpening data security while enabling analytics. They give an option to perform computations on data without the need to decrypt it first. In addition, this method consists of creating datasets which are statistically identical to the actual data, as includes in Figure 15.7. The visualization of Homomorphic Encryption shows the durations for each operation of addition and multiplication. The visualization of Synthetic Data Generation shows the amalgamation of real and synthetic data. Each of these visualizations aids in explaining the effectiveness and characteristics of each approach.

Integration and Practical Applications

Most of these technologies work together. Examples include the following:

- **Healthcare:** Integrating federated learning with differential privacy on multi-institutional studies to promote collaboration among many medical institutions.
- **Finance:** Using homomorphic encryption with synthetic data to model secure training on sensitive financial data.
- **IoT:** Implementing federated learning with differential privacy to edge devices for training.

15.6 Current Challenges

- The strain on resources, especially with homomorphic encryption.

- The balance between privacy and usefulness in differential privacy.
- The cost of transmission in federated learning.
- Maintaining standards in the quality of synthetic datasets.

While continuing to evolve these technologies, researchers are focusing on improving efficiency, scalability, and practical applicability while maintaining privacy.

15.6.1 Challenges

Implementing privacy-preserving methods in AI systems can be problematic from a technical standpoint. There are severe challenges posed due to high computational costs associated with the encryption, implementing these methods in the existing systems, and others. For instance, although homomorphically encrypted solutions provide exceptional levels of security, they are often expensive and slow. Consideration of ethics also comes into play, as privacy-enhancing strategies might be used for malicious reasons in the case where people do not want to take responsibility for their actions. In addition, the economic impacts of the adoption of these approaches may be considerable for many companies with limited funds, hampering the allocation of resources for advanced privacy measures. What is needed are cooperative efforts from researchers, legislators, and business leaders to develop effective, scalable, and cost-efficient systems that can be supported within the bounds of responsible ethical scrutiny.

15.7 Industry Adoption

The application of privacy preserving AI techniques differs across sectors. The healthcare industry appears to be in the forefront, having the need to protect sensitive patient data and comply with rigorous policies. Techniques like federated learning have been implemented to enable patient sensitive data to be utilized in collaborative studies. The financial industry has also made significant progress by using homomorphic encryption to safeguard private transactions and prevent fraud.

In comparison, retail and government face these issues regarding adoption because of lack of funds and legacy systems. Nonetheless, the technology is adopting widely because of surging awareness of privacy concerns along with the availability of privacy preserving technologies. Graphs showing the trends of adoption across different domains highlight the differences as well as the potential for growth in this area.

15.8 Future Directions

The steps taken towards increasing privacy-preserving AI is to develop more efficient and easily-scaled techniques. The latest attempts attempt to strengthen the methods of homomorphic encryption and federated learning to make them accessible to more organizations. With the aid of emerging technologies such as quantum computing, the existing problems in encryption and computation can be addressed. Also, policy measures will be important for the uniform enforcement of protocol standards and the adoption of automated systems. While working with the AI community, researchers and practitioners from the private sector and the government can formulate solutions which strike a necessary equilibrium between the two opposing fronts of privacy and progress. It will be essential to incorporate privacy enabling frameworks into the systems to be developed within the context of responsible and sustainable AI.

15.9 Conclusion

In conclusion, the development and deployment of AI technologies call for the utmost consideration of privacy-preserving measures to ensure ethical compliance. These approaches should combine technical, moral, and financial factors in such a way that privacy is guaranteed to be fundamental while the systems offer essential services. As discussed in this proposal together with the illustrations provided, there are clear intersections of privacy and innovation which need more focus for the development of AI systems that are dependable and safe. Increasingly powerful AI technologies will require greater protection of privacy to nurture trust among people and unlock the full potential AI offers to society.

AI disclosure statement: The author confirms that no artificial intelligence (AI)-generated content or AI-assisted writing tools were used in the preparation of this chapter (including summaries and the abstract). All text, analysis, and conclusions are the result of the author's original work.

References

1. Zhang, Yang, X., Nepal, C., *et al.*, A MapReduce based approach of scalable multidimensional anonymization for big data privacy preservation on cloud. *2013 IEEE 3rd International Conference on Cloud and Green Computing, CGC*, pp. 105–112, 2013.
2. Jia, Q., Guo, L., Jin, Z., *et al.*, Preserving model privacy for machine learning in distributed systems. *IEEE Trans. Parallel Distrib. Syst.*, 2018, DOI: 10.1109/TPDS.2018.2809624.
3. Jiang, R., *et al.*, Achieving high performance and privacy-preserving query over encrypted multidimensional big metering data. *Future Gener. Comput. Syst.*, 392–401, 2016, DOI: 10.1016/j.future.2016.05.005.
4. Aggarwal, C.C. and Yu, P.S., A general survey of privacy-preserving data mining models and algorithms, pp. 11–52, Springer, 2008.
5. Kalpanadevi, D., Babysudha, P., Kartheeban, K., Mayilvaganan, M., Optimal allocation of Resources in Data Center using Artificial Intelligence, Taylor and Francis Book Series, conference Proceedings Series on Intelligent Systems, CRC Press, 2023.
6. Aziz, R., *et al.*, Exploring Homomorphic Encryption and Differential Privacy Techniques towards Secure Federated Learning Paradigm. *Future Internet*, 2023, DOI: https://doi.org/10.3390/fi15090310.
7. Gu, X., *et al.*, A Review of Privacy Enhancement Methods for Federated Learning in Healthcare Systems. *Int. J. Environ. Res. Public Health*, 2023, DOI: 10.3390/ijerph20156539.
8. Seethalakshmi, V., Dhanaraj, R.K., Suganyadevi, S., Ouaissa, M., *Homomorphic Encryption for Financial Cryptography*, pp. 1–12, Springer International Publishing, 2023, ISBN 9783031355349.
9. Li, Y., *et al.*, A Communication-Efficient, Privacy-Preserving Federated Learning Algorithm Based on Two-Stage Gradient Pruning and Differentiated Differential Privacy. *Sensors*, 2023, https://doi.org/10.3390/s23239305.
10. Brand, M. and Pradel, G., Practical Privacy-Preserving Machine Learning Using Homomorphic Encryption. *Proceedings on Privacy Enhancing Technologies*, 2023, Available online: https://eprint.iacr.org/2023/1320.pdf.
11. Banerjee, S., Benlamri, R., Bouzefrane, S., Optimization of ontology-based clinical pathways and incorporating differential privacy in the healthcare system, in: *Security designs for the cloud, Iot, and Social Networking*, 2019, DOI : https://doi.org/10.1002/9781119593171.ch13.
12. Matthew, J., *et al.*, A New Method for Protecting Interrelated Time Series with Bayesian Prior Distributions and Synthetic Data. *J. R. Stat. Soc. Ser. A: Stat. Soc.*, 963–975, 2015, https://doi.org/10.1111/rssa.12100.

16

VetAce – A Deep Learning Inspired Framework for Classification and Prediction of Pet Diseases

Munish Saini[1]*, Vaibhav Arora[1] and Harpreet Singh[2†]

[1]*Department of Computer Engineering and Technology, Guru Nanak Dev University, Amritsar, India*
[2]*Department of Computer Science, Government College Shahbazpur, Tarn Taran, India*

Abstract

During the period of the COVID-19 pandemic, we noticed a situation of lock-down, when the epidemic outbreak was at its peak. In those circumstances, the illness of pets and getting it diagnoses was a major worry for humans. In this study, we proposed an advanced technological web-based solution to tackle such a bad situation. We have introduced the concept of using a Convolutional Neural Network (CNN) and transfer learning for predicting and classifying the common disease of pets by uploading their visuals. The proposed framework achieved high accuracy (89%), precision (92%), specificity (74.5%), and sensitivity (75%) for pet disease prediction and breed classification which outperforms all other considered state-of-art algorithms (ANN, RNN, and CNN). Further, this online diagnosing framework will help humans by providing insights into the common causes of pet diseases. Additionally, it will also specify the prevailing preventive measures and medical recommendations to cure the pet.

***Keywords*:** Image analysis, human-animal bond, deep learning, convolutional neural network, prediction, COVID-19

**Corresponding author*: munish.cet@gndu.ac.in
†*Corresponding author*: harpreet99.nitj@gmail.com

Manish Kumar, Nitigya Sambyal, Leena Priyadarshini Singh, Ramasamy V. and S. Balamurugan (eds.) Responsible AI: Principles and Practices, (379–400) © 2026 Scrivener Publishing LLC

16.1 Introduction

The Human-Animal bond (HAB) carries a historical perspective [19, 29]. It was pioneered by Konrad Lorenz and Boris Levinson in the 1970s for the cognizance of human-animal interaction [34], to understand the health benefits of domestic animals on human health and psychology [22, 28–30]. For ages, humans have learned to nurture animals for their welfare [27]. All over the world, people passionately domesticate diverse animals as a companion in their homes, and other human places [12, 52]. Globally, it is observed that dogs and cats are among the prominent and favorable ones[2∝]. Nowadays, humans share a special bond relationship with their pets [6]. It would become a matter of primary concern whenever their loveable pets are getting sick or suffering from any other disease [36, 40].

In the years 2019 and 2020, the world has experienced one of the deadliest and most dangerous novel coronaviruses (nCov) [1, 20]. Coronavirus disease (COVID-19) is a contagious disease caused by nCOV [21]. It has affected a mass of people worldwide, causing respiratory illness [46], fever [49], and even death to humans [56]. In response to the spread of Coronavirus disease (COVID-19), World Health Organization (WHO) announced this outbreak as a pandemic on 11 March 2020[3β]. WHO directed the countries to take the required preventive measures to diagnose, treat, and decrease the dissemination of COVID-19. With the surge of COVID-19 cases, the governments of the concerning countries have enforced restrictions on the movement of people by ordering lockdown countrywide.

It was a situation of panic for the people, as they get locked in their homes and other living places for many days [8]. In their mind, they also have the fear of getting infected by other humans [47], or even by their loveable pets [42, 48]. During this period, it was also observed that some pet owner abandoned their domestic animals and they were on the verge of being homeless[4√]. But still, the affection and passion of the mass of humans for domesticated animals (like dogs and cats) have not been defeated. They come up with the true bond of relationship with their pets. They have a concern for the well-being of their domesticated animals.

[2∝] https://pets.thenest.com/5-common-house-pets-4759.html

[3β] https://www.who.int/india/emergencies/coronavirus-disease-(covid-19)

[4√] https://www.medicalnewstoday.com/articles/covid-19-and-our-pets-what-is-there-to-know

Pets often get suffered from different diseases due to varied causes [24, 43]. The period of COVID spread along with lockdown was a major troublesome for pet owners [51]. Meanwhile, if the pet is suffering from any disease, and the pet owner wants to get his pet diagnosed and treated, it is challenging. A few common challenges that humans may have to face are a) A risk to take the domestic animal outside to a veterinary doctor for consultation; b) Pet owner has to wait for his turn for a longer duration of time, and c) complications in the journey to take the pet to a veterinary doctor.

To tackle such problems, we have proposed an automated web-based solution named as VetAce. It will help the pet owner to get his pet diagnosed with common diseases (like alopecia, anorexia, ticks, patches, watery eyes), online by fairly uploading the image of their unhealthy pet. Pet owners can avail of online consultations and can get the required pre-treatment knowledge about these diseases. We also aim to provide software as a service model for veterinary doctors. Accordingly, the main contributions of this study are as follows:

1. To propose a deep learning-inspired framework to predict pet common diseases.
2. A model to classify pets based on their breed and category.
3. A framework to provide online consultation and recommendations to pet owners.

In the rest of the paper, *Section 16.2* presents the related work performed by different researchers in the same context. *Section 16.3* specifies the research methodology used to conduct this study. *Section 16.4* discusses the results, and presents a web-based solution to diagnose and predict pet diseases. Discussion of the findings of this research is presented in *Section 16.5*. *Section 16.6* describes the threats to validity. Lastly, we conclude the paper and pinpoint the future work in *Section 16.7*.

16.2 Related Work

Pets suffering from infectious and other diseases exhibit certain symptoms [33]. Prior, the diagnosis and consultation of animals suffering from the syndrome is all manual [39]. With the rise of computerization and other automated techniques, pet owners started the use online consultations and diagnoses [35].

Lian *et al.*, introduced an expert system based on HSMC-SVM (Hyper-Sphere Multi-Class Support Vector Machine) to diagnose animal diseases [35]. Their specified model produced higher accuracy and exhibited a feasible solution to diagnose animals. Ortiz-Pelaez, Á., & Pfeiffer have used data mining techniques (multivariate logistic regression, decision trees) to classify the animal herd based on infectious diseases, they are suffering [41]. Gökçe *et al.*, analyzed the consequences of the risk factors (like gender, birth type, parity, dam's health, and lambing season) on passive immunity and birth weight of lambs using the multiple regression method [23]. They observed the existence of linear dependence among them.

In recent times, the imaging diagnostic of animals using deep learning and advanced machine learning algorithms is widespread [55]. Kim *et al.*, detected the corneal ulcer severity in dogs by utilizing a convolutional neural network (CNN) [32]. They have trained the CNN model on the images classified by veterinary ophthalmologists' diagnostics. Banzato *et al.*, proposed a deep convolutional neural network (DNN) to identify hepatic disease using ultrasound images of the dog's liver [10]. Banzato *et al.*, prognoses the meningiomas grading from magnetic resonance (MR) images of dogs [11]. They employed the DNN with transfer learning. Burti *et al.*, designed a CNN model to detect radiographic cardiomegaly in dogs [17]. They compared the performance of the proposed model with other neural networks. Additionally, they observed the performance of their model outperforms all other methods. Borwarnginn *et al.*, proposed a CNN classifier based on transfer learning to classify the breeds of dogs [14].

In the global pandemic situation, domesticated animals are among the most unsafe strata in the community [51]. Pets look forward to humans for care. In COVID, the average number of pets going shelter relinquishment was on a hike[5]. Although, no pervasive shreds of evidence prevail that specify any compelling role of pets in the transmission of COVID-19 [42]. Additionally, no evidence exists indicating the nCov leading any infirmity, sickness, or disorder in pets [42]. But the Homo sapiens have more probability of getting infected by a person with nCov infection[6]. Due to COVID around 218 countries have faced the outbreak of this pandemic[7]. It caused

---

[5]https://timesofindia.indiatimes.com/city/chennai/pets-of-covid-19-patients-turn-homeless/articleshow/75767635.cms

[6]https://www.medscape.com/viewarticle/924571

[7]https://www.worldometers.info/coronavirus/?utm_campaign=homeAdvegas1?

several people to have serious illnesses and even deaths. In this situation, it was extremely tough for pet owners to carry their pets to veterinary doctors personally. Applebaum *et al.*, have performed quantitative analyses to explore the hardship associated with pet possession in the COVID-19 pandemic [5]. Their outcomes pinpointed the different challenges that pet owners have faced accompanying alterations made in day-to-day routine and lifestyle.

The surveyed literature depicts the importance of animal imaging diagnosis and the use of advanced machine learning (or deep learning) methods in veterinary fields. Moreover, in the present days when the spread of pandemic (COVID) is at its peak, the use of these online diagnoses has real significance in terms of controlling the transmission of nCOv. In this study, we have proposed a web-based solution (VetAce) using CNN with transfer learning to detect diseases. Additionally, the proposed model aims to provide pet owners with online consultations and common preventive measures to procure the pet (dog or cat). Furthermore, we also incorporated the method to classify the pets based on their breed and category respectively.

16.3 Analysis Methodology

This section describes the data (images) collection, data preprocessing and filtering, image augmentation, techniques, and tools that we used in this study. The step-by-step description of the research process (see Figure 16.1) is as follows.

16.3.1 Data Preprocessing and Filtering

In the first step, the downloaded images are manually filtered by both the authors separately to mark the low-quality and unrelated images. Afterward, both authors jointly discussed and then decided to remove the unwanted images or images with any discrepancy (see Table 16.1). In the second step, we have used the well-defined Directory system that is available for auto-labeling the images by using the flow_from_directory argument under the preprocessing pipeline of Tensorflow Keras API [25]. Furthermore, we have performed the normalization to map the pixels of the images to the scale of 0-1. We have applied the generalization in terms of image resolution as it was observed that the collected images have image pixels ranging between 0 and 255 megapixels. To remove this uncertainty

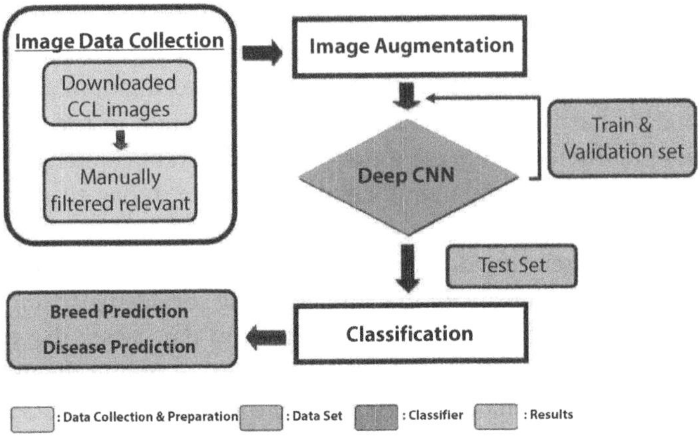

Figure 16.1 Data analysis and methodology.

Table 16.1 Number of images in the dataset.

Domesticated animal	Number of images before pre-processing and filtering	Number of images after pre-processing and filtering
Dogs	2500	1500
Cats	3010	1500

and variation in the imaging dataset, we have transformed images using the rescale (1/255) argument.

16.3.2 Image Augmentation

We have implied the image augmentation technique [13], to expand the acquired dataset for training the CNN model over different aspects and conditions (like camera view, zoom, Semantic gap, illumination, and others, Image data augmentation). It is an effective way for creating an artificially extended dataset out of the original dataset. We have used the tenser flow Keras preprocessing API[8U], to automate the process of image augmentation.

[8U]https://www.tensorflow.org/api_docs/python/tf/keras/preprocessing/image/ImageDataGenerator

In this study, we have applied the following six image augmentations [9]:

- **Rotation:** It is used to randomly rotate the image by taking values from 0 to 180 degrees. It is performed by using the rotation_range(x) argument where 'x' is the integer value to specify the range of degrees for rotation.
- **Width shift:** It is used to augment pictures by horizontal shifts. It shifts the image to either the right or left side by using given arguments. Its values range between 0 and 1. It is accomplished by using the width_shift_range(x) argument that will take the percent of 'x' and shift the same percent of the image to either left or right side.
- **Height shift:** It is used to augment pictures by vertical shifts. This will shift the image to either top or bottom part by using the given arguments. Its values lie between 0 and 1. It is implied with the height_shift_range(x) argument that takes the percent of 'x' and will shift the same percent of the image to either top or bottom part.
- **Shear range:** It is used for randomly applying the shear transformation. It allows the shearing (i.e., cutting or removing) of the image by using shear_range(x) where 'x' lies between 0 and 1.
- **Zoom_range:** It is used for adding magnification to the image. It is used for imposing focusing on a specific aspect

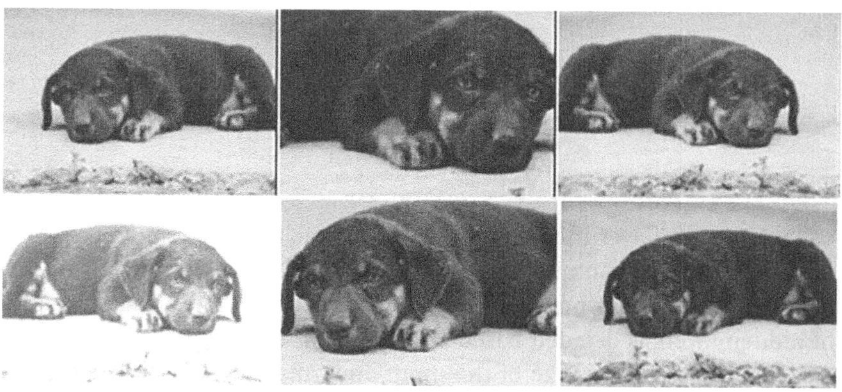

Figure 16.2 Image augmentation.

or zooming images. For this, we can use the zoom_range(x) argument where 'x' lies between 0 and 1.

- **Flip:** It is used to flip images either horizontally or vertically. It is done with the use of horizontal_flip(x) or vertical_flip(x) argument, where x is a Boolean value i.e., true or false.

Figure 16.2, depicts the images after the implication of the above-mentioned aspects of image augmentation.

16.3.3 Convolutional Neural Network (CNN) as Pet Diseases Classifier

In this section, we have provided the explanatory details on the design, working of the CNN model, transfer learning concepts, and Network Architecture used for predicting pet diseases and breeds are specified.

16.3.3.1 Description of Convolutional Neural Network (CNN)

CNN proved to be an efficient approach for image classification problems [37, 38]. It is a multi-feedforward network that uses a back-propagation technique for learning [2]. During back-propagation, the errors are backpropagated from the output layer to the input layer with appropriate adjustment of weights during the process. In this study, we have used CNN based on transfer learning for pet disease classification and prediction. The mathematical model of the predictor of CNN is given in Equation 16.1.

$$z = f(\textstyle\sum_{i=1}^{N} xi \times wi + b) \tag{16.1}$$

'z' is prediction, 'x' is input data, 'w' is weight, 'b' is bias

16.3.3.2 Design of CNN

CNN is a multi-layer model that specifically includes the input layer, hidden layers, and the output layer [4]. In most cases, the number of hidden layers in CNN varies between 2 to 3. Moreover, the appropriate number of hidden layers is decided based on the size of the input and output layers. It must be 2/3 the size of the input and output layer [7]. The hidden layers in CNN help in applying random nonlinear filters. Additionally, the hidden layers consist of a series of convolutional layers comprising activation function (sigmoid or softmax), and kernel initialization. Further, it is connected to the pooling layer for the nonlinear downsampling of image data.

i. **Convolution layer:** The convolution layer is among the significant layer in the CNN model. It takes images as input in form of the tensor of shape (number of images in the training set) × (height of the image) × (width of the image) × (input channels). Further, the layer applies random filters to extract features and passes the result to the next layer. The shape is redefined to (number of images in the training set) × (featured image height) × (featured image width) × (feature map channel). The detailed working of the Convolution layer is specified in Algorithm 16.1.

ii. **Activation function:** To increase the nonlinearity of the convolution network we have used the activation functions. There exist a varied number of activation functions like Sigmoid, tanh, Rectified linear units (ReLU), Leaky ReLU, Maxout, and Exponential Linear Units (ELU) for the CNN model. The choice of specific activation function depends upon the need of the user such as ReLU is preferred for quick evaluation and efficient computation, Sigmoid is used when we need to squash results to range [0,1], tanh is used when we need to squash results to range [-1,1], Softmax to give output as

Algorithm 16.1 Working of convolution layer.

```
Step 1: Initialize `i' and loop in range (1 - m)
Step 2:   Initialize `j' and loop in range (1 - n)
Step 3:     Initialize `row' and loop in range (1- p)
Step 4:       Initialize `col' and loop in range (1- q)
Step 5:         Declare temp =0
Step 6:         Initialize `ii' and loop in range (1 - r)
Step 7:             Initialize `jj' and loop in range (1 - r)
Step 8:               temp = temp + k [ii] [jj] * A[j] [t*(row -1) + i] [t* (col
                      -1) + j]
Step 9:         Y[i][row][col] = B[i][row][col] + temp
Step 10:          If j equals to n then move to Step 11 else skip 11
Step 11:              Y[i][row][col] = f (B[p][row][col] + b)
```

the probability distribution over predicted output classes, max out neuron, Leaky Relu, ELU (refer to Equations 16.2–16.4). In this study, we prefer to use the ReLU activation function as we aim to perform real-time monitoring.

$$\text{ReLU}(x) = (0; x) \tag{16.2}$$

$$\text{LReLU}(x) = (0; x) + \alpha\,(0; x) \tag{16.3}$$

$$\begin{aligned} \text{ELU}(x) &= x \quad \text{if } x \geq 0 \\ &= \alpha\,(\exp \exp(x) - 1) \quad \text{if } x < 0 \end{aligned} \tag{16.4}$$

value of leakage coefficient (α) is 1.0

iii. **Pooling layer:** The pooling layer is used for down sampling operations which reduce the dimensions of data, the 2 *2 cluster is mainly used for pooling purposes. Max pooling and average pooling are two commonly used layers. In Max pooling, it takes the maximum value of the cluster (refer to Figure 16.3) and on average pooling, it prefers to choose the average of the cluster values (Figure 16.4).

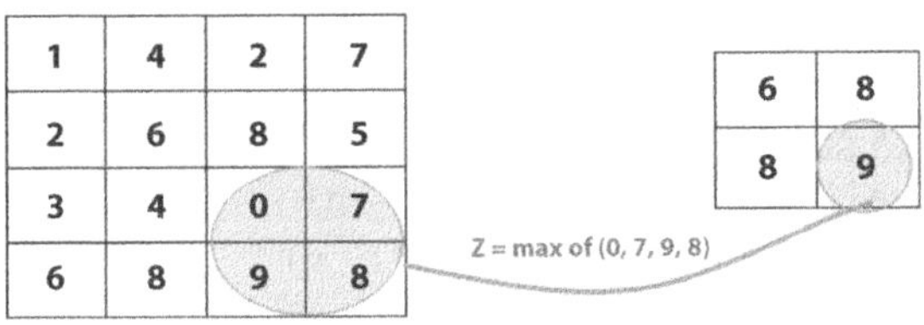

Figure 16.3 Example for max pooling.

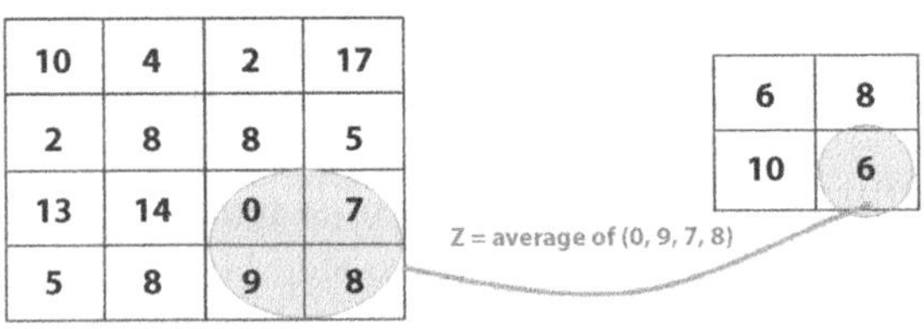

Figure 16.4 Average pooling.

iv. **Fully connected layer:** All the features extracted and weights are fed into a fully connected layer for the classification decision. Every neuron in one layer is connected to every neuron of the other layer. We described the process of the fully connected layer in Algorithm 16.2.

Algorithm 16.2 Working of fully connected layer.

```
1. for i from 1 to m do
   [start of loop]
2.        for j from 1 to n do
          [start of loop]
3.             temp = temp + w [i] [j] * A [j]
          [end of loop]
4.                  B[i] = temp
5. [end of loop]
```

16.3.3.3 Transfer Learning

Transfer learning is the technique of utilizing the prior knowledge (i.e., weights and features) of a previously trained model for training a new model on a similar or different task [45, 50]. For this study, we have used the inception model[9] to implement transfer learning for the classification

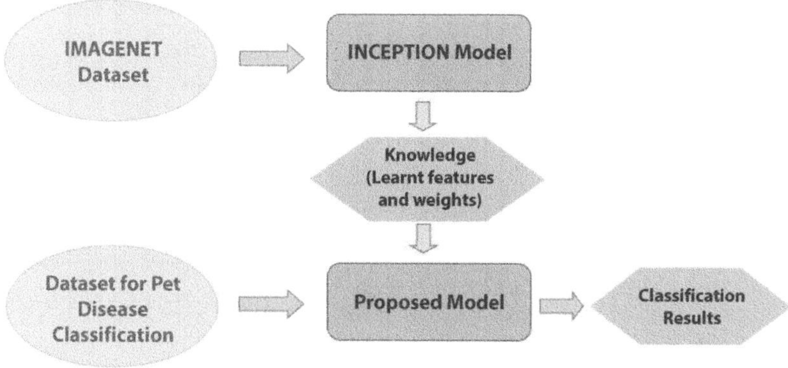

Figure 16.5 Transfer learning.

[9] https://medium.com/analytics-vidhya/transfer-learning-using-inception-v3-for-image-classification-86700411251b

of pet diseases. The inception model was pre-trained on IMAGNET[108] dataset, consisting of around 1.4 million images, and trained over 1000 classes. We freeze the model by setting layer.trainable = false and then loading it in the same form. Further, we added a new classifier that would be trained from scratch over the new dataset, on top of the pre-trained model. Lastly, we compiled the model with cost function (i.e. sparse_categorical_crossentropy (CCE)) and optimizer (SGD) and trained it over 65 epochs to get the classification results (refer to Figure 16.5).

16.3.3.4 Network Architecture

We have proposed the six-layered CNN model (in Figure 16.6) for pet breed classification. Additionally, we are using Transfer learning (in Figure 16.7) for pet disease classification. The model is trained over pre-trained weights of the inception model for breed and disease classification in the pets. Further, we have used the pre-trained weights of the inception model to improve the accuracy of classification, the number of images considered for the evaluation is limited.

To define the output value of kernel weights, we have used the two activation functions (ReLU and softmax). ReLU is applied to introduce nonlinearity to the network. It performs element-wise operations and sets negative

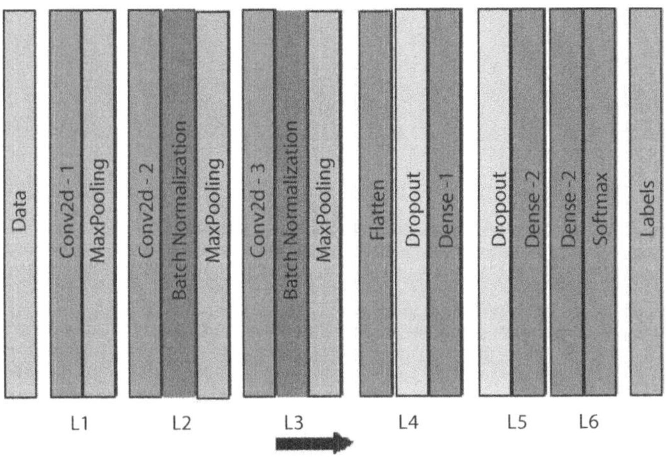

Figure 16.6 Architecture of the proposed CNN for breed classification.

[108]http://www.image-net.org/

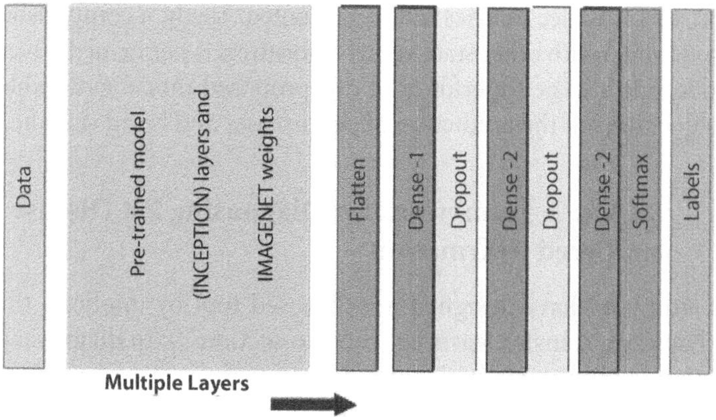

Figure 16.7 Architecture of the proposed model for pet disease classification.

pixels to zero. SoftMax will give the probability distribution over defined classes. To increase the stability and performance of the CNN model batch normalization is adopted [44]. Furthermore, the dropout layer helps in avoiding the overfitting of the model by skipping irrelevant network nodes. Further, the model is compiled by using sparse_categorical_crossentropy (CCE) cost function (refer to Equation 16.5), Adam optimizer (gradient descent-based optimizer) learning at the rate of 0.0004, and is trained over 65 epochs.

$$CCE(p,t) = -\sum_{c=0}^{c} t_{0,c} log(p_{0,c}) \quad (16.5)$$

16.3.3.5 Cost and Optimization Function

The cost function is acting as a performance metric in the model. It specifies the difference between the predicted and expected label, through which we will decide how well our model is working. The lower value of cost function (CCE) indicates the higher efficiency of the model and vice-versa. Further, we have used the gradient descent-based optimizer with a 0.0004 learning rate, to minimize the value of the cost function.

16.4 Results and Analysis

In this section, the outcomes of the proposed model (CNN based on transfer learning) are presented. The evaluation of the proposed model based on different performance metrics is also presented. Lastly, a comparison of the proposed model with other state-of-art algorithms is performed. Overall, the outcomes indicate the superiority of our proposed model over other state-of-art algorithms in the prediction of pet diseases and breed classification.

16.4.1 VetAce: A Framework for Diagnosing Pet Disease and Breed Affirmation

In this study, we have designed a web-based tool by implying the CNN model based on transfer learning (refer to section 3), to diagnose pet diseases (alopecia, anorexia, ticks, patches, watery eyes) and to classify the pet based on their category (or breed) (see Figure 16.8). In this model, the user (pet owner or veterinary doctor) needs to upload a picture of a domesticated animal to get it diagnosed. VetAce directs the image to the pre-processing pipeline (explained in section 3.2). While pre-processing, the image is rescaled to the desired shape and the noise (if any) is removed to an extent. Further, the processed image is moved to the prediction pipeline (using the methodology explained in section 3.4 and its subsections).

Based on learned weights and features, the trained model of pet disease diagnosis will give the array of the probability distribution over all the classes of the CNN model. Afterward, VetAce will choose the label (name of the disease) with a higher probability and also specifies the initial pre-cure recommendations. Additionally, the VetAce model will also provide information regarding the breed and category (dog or cat) of the pet. Using this information, the pet owner can take preventive measures to cure the pet. Additionally, this insight on the breed (or category) along with the predicted disease (from VetAce) will assist the veterinary doctors to get the initial inputs on the suffering of pets. The vet can decide and schedule future treatment based on these primary diagnosis outcomes.

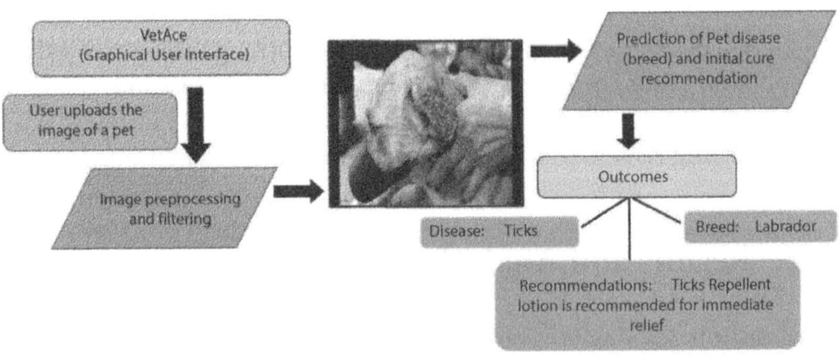

Figure 16.8 VetAce for disease prediction.

16.4.2 Performance Metrics of the Model

The efficiency of the VetAce is determined by the standard performance metrics like accuracy, precision, specificity, and sensitivity [15]. Further, the evaluation of these measures depends on the values of True Positive (TP), True Negative (TN), False positive (FP), and False Negative (FN). TP specifies the positive (+ve) prediction of the class and the actual label (class) is also positive (+ve). TN includes the prediction of class as negative (-ve) whereas the actual label (class) is positive (+ve). In False Positive (FP), the prediction is positive (+ve), but the real label is negative (-ve). Lastly, False Negative (FN) is the worst prediction where the actual label is positive (+ve) but the predictor depicts it as negative (-ve). In machine learning model-based prediction (classification), true predictions (TP and TN) are the desirable ones whereas the cases false prediction (FP and FN) indicates the wrong prediction [54]. Moreover, for a better predictive model, we always prefer to minimize the false factors (FN and FP) [53]. Further, the formal description and mathematical models of the used performance metrics are as follows:

Accuracy performance metric depicts the ratio of correct predictions (TP and TN) to the total number of predictions (i.e. both True and False) refer to Equation (16.6).

$$Accuracy = \frac{TP + FN}{TP + FN + FP + TN} \tag{16.6}$$

Precision is the proportion of correct positive prediction (TP) to the sum of all positive predictions (TP and FP) (in Equation 16.7).

$$Precision = \frac{TP}{TP + FP} \tag{16.7}$$

Specificity indicates the rate of true negative prediction. It consists of the ratio of true negative predictions (TN) to the whole negative predictions (i.e., TN and FP) (in Equation 16.8).

$$Specificity = \frac{TN}{TN + FP} \tag{16.8}$$

Sensitivity (or Recall) represents the rate of true positive prediction (refer to Equation 16.9).

$$Sensitivity = \frac{TP}{TP + FN} \tag{16.9}$$

VetAce CNN-based model with transfer learning implications has shown prominent predictive outcomes (shown in Table 16.2). The web-based predictive has proven to be highly accurate in the prediction of domesticated animal diseases and their respective breed.

Furthermore, we have validated the effectiveness of our approach by comparing it with the other Classification models namely Artificial Neural network (ANN), Convolutional Neural Network (CNN), Recurrent Neural Network, and K-Nearest Neighbor. The Outcomes of each model are

Table 16.2 VetAce performance metrics.

Performance metric	Disease prediction	Breed prediction
Accuracy	89%	98%
Precision	92%	93%
Specificity	74.5%	98.2%
Sensitivity	75%	90.4%

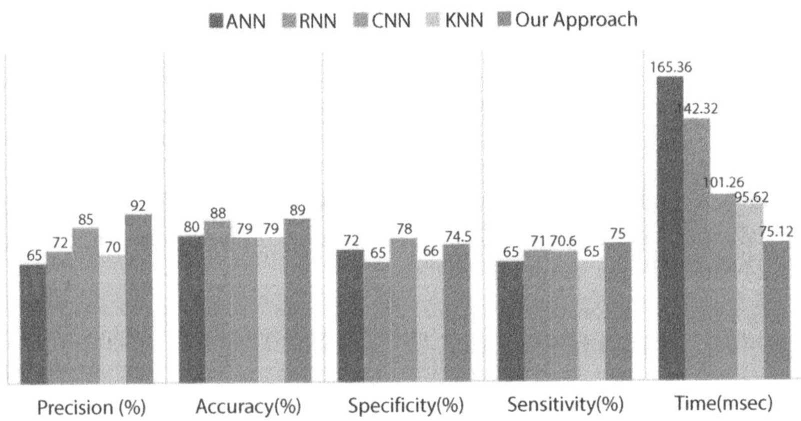

Figure 16.9 Comparison of performance measures among different classification models for pet disease prediction.

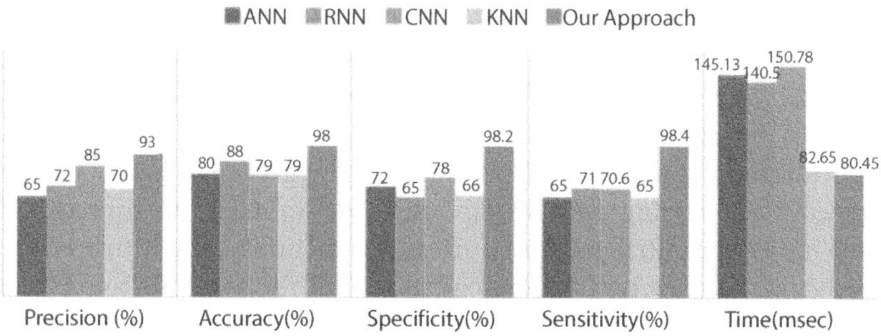

Figure 16.10 Comparison of performance measures among different classification models for pet breed prediction.

shown in Figures 16.9 and 16.10 for animal disease and breed prediction. As per the below observations, our approach outperforms in comparison to all other algorithms, hence justifying it to be an effective and potential solution.

16.5 Discussion

The association between human-animal (HAB) is the base of affection and care, humans possess for their pets. The pandemic COVID-19 has severe to mild consequences on the health (physical/mental) and association of human and animal. Pets have attained a position in the family life cycle [16]. Pets are acting as the companion and factor for agony (or stress) reduction. During COVID-19, the suffering of the pets cannot be ignored. Many of the pets were abandoned from homes by the pet owners due to the fear of getting an infection, economic reasons, or others. Still, several pet owners have nurtured their domesticated animals in the outbreak of this nCov pandemic as their family members. To control the spread of COVID-19, the government authorities of different countries have taken preventive measures by restricting the movement of people and applying lockdown.

During the period of lockdown, it was a real challenge for pet owners to take their lovable pets to get diagnosed by the veterinary doctor, while they suffered from some disease. To tackle such an issue, we have proposed an online web-based framework (VetAce). VetAce is designed and trained on thousands of images using the CNN model with transfer learning. The proposed model will allow the pet owner to get his pet diagnosed by merely uploading the image of the pet. Moreover, VetAce will provide insights into the diseases from which the pet is suffering along with the pre-cure recommendations. Furthermore, VetAce can also assist veterinary doctors to perform the initial diagnosis of its patient online. Based on this prior diagnosis doctor can move further to give recommendations, and cure measures, or can call for the need a physical diagnosis.

Furthermore, the proposed system can be upgraded to have a business perspective by adding the subscription model to it. In this subscription-based model the initial diagnosis, disease prediction (along with breed and category), and pre-cure recommendations will be available free of cost. But, if the users (pet owners) want to have a personal consultation from an expert (veterinary doctor) using this framework. Then, they have to get register and pay a certain minimum cost for that process.

16.6 Conclusion

COVID-19 affected a mass of living beings. Many humans had lost their life due to this pandemic. The outbreak of nCov has also placed a great challenge on the survival of domesticated animals, as humans are in fear of the spread of COVID-19 had abandoned their adorable pets. But the researchers have proven the fact that the cases of pets infected with COVID-19 are minimal. Moreover, to tackle the transmission of this infectious disease from person to person, the government of different countries has implied a lockdown to restrict the free movement of humans. During this period, if a pet gets infected or suffered from any other common occurring diseases, the pet owner feels uncomfortable and difficult to carry his pet for physical examination by a veterinary doctor. In this study, we proposed a web-based framework (VetAce) to counter such an issue. VetAce helps the pet owner (or doctors) in diagnosing the pet, suffering from common diseases, and also provides pre-cure recommendations. The present state of VetAce is trained to predict fewer diseases in pets (dogs and cats). In the future, we look forward to enhancing the model by training it on more diseases and additional categories of pets. Furthermore, we would like to compare the performance of the proposed model on the varied and large size of datasets.

AI disclosure statement: The author acknowledges the use of AI-based tools for minor language editing or grammatical correction. However, all intellectual contributions, analyses, and conclusions presented in this chapter are entirely the author's own.

Bibliography

1. Ahmad, W., Ali, I., Khan, F., Danger to public health programs in the wake of Covid-19. *Khyber Med. Univ. J.*, *12*, 3, 259–259, 2020.
2. Aizenberg, I. and Moraga, C., Multilayer feedforward neural network based on multi-valued neurons (MLMVN) and a backpropagation learning algorithm. *Soft Comput.*, 11, 2, 169–183, 2007.
3. Akilli, A., Atil, H., Takma, C., Ayyilmaz, T., Fuzzy logic-based decision support system for dairy cattle, 2016.
4. Albawi, S., Mohammed, T.A., Al-Zawi, S., Understanding of a convolutional neural network, in: *2017 International Conference on Engineering and Technology (ICET)*, 2017, August, IEEE, pp. 1–6.
5. Applebaum, J.W., Tomlinson, C.A., Matijczak, A., McDonald, S.E., Zsembik, B.A., The Concerns, Difficulties, and Stressors of Caring for Pets during COVID-19: Results from a Large Survey of US Pet Owners. *Animals*, *10*, 10, 1882, 2020.
6. Archer, J., Why do people love their pets? *Evol. Hum. Behav.*, *18*, 4, 237–259, 1997.
7. Arif, R.B., Siddique, M.A.B., Khan, M.M.R., Oishe, M.R., Study and Observation of the Variations of Accuracies for Handwritten Digits Recognition with Various Hidden Layers and Epochs using Convolutional Neural Network, in: *2018 4th International Conference on Electrical Engineering and Information & Communication Technology (iCEEiCT)*, 2018, September, IEEE, pp. 112–117.
8. Baiano, C., Zappullo, I., Conson, M., Tendency to worry and fear of mental health during Italy's COVID-19 lockdown. *Int. J. Environ. Res. Public Health*, *17*, 16, 5928, 2020.
9. Bang, S., Baek, F., Park, S., Kim, W., Kim, H., Image augmentation to improve construction resource detection using generative adversarial networks, cut-and-paste, and image transformation techniques. *Autom. Constr.*, *115*, 103198, 2020.
10. Banzato, T., Bonsembiante, F., Aresu, L., Gelain, M.E., Burti, S., Zotti, A., Use of transfer learning to detect diffuse degenerative hepatic diseases from ultrasound images in dogs: a methodological study. *Vet. J.*, *233*, 35–40, 2018 a.
11. Banzato, T., Cherubini, G.B., Atzori, M., Zotti, A., Development of a deep convolutional neural network to predict grading of canine meningiomas from magnetic resonance images. *Vet. J.*, *235*, 90–92, 2018 b.
12. Beck, A.M. and Katcher, A.H., *Between pets and people: The importance of animal companionship*, Purdue University Press, 1996.
13. Bloice, M.D., Roth, P.M., Holzinger, A., Biomedical image augmentation using Augmentor. *Bioinformatics*, *35*, 21, 4522–4524, 2019.
14. Borwarnginn, P., Thongkanchorn, K., Kanchanapreechakorn, S., Kusakunniran, W., Breakthrough Conventional Based Approach for Dog

Breed Classification Using CNN with Transfer Learning, in: *2019 11th International Conference on Information Technology and Electrical Engineering (ICITEE)*, 2019, October, IEEE, pp. 1–5.
15. Bowers, A.J., Sprott, R., Taff, S.A., Do we know who will drop out? A review of the predictors of dropping out of high school: Precision, sensitivity, and specificity. *High Sch. J.*, 77–100, 2012.
16. Bures, R.M., Companion Animal Caregiving and Well-Being, in: *Well-Being Over the Life Course*, pp. 25–37, Springer, Cham, 2021.
17. Burti, S., Osti, V.L., Zotti, A., Banzato, T., Use of deep learning to detect cardiomegaly on thoracic radiographs in dogs. *Vet. J.*, *262*, 105505, 2020.
18. Burt, J.R., Torosdagli, N., Khosravan, N., RaviPrakash, H., Mortazi, A., Tissavirasingham, F., Bagci, U., Deep learning beyond cats and dogs: recent advances in diagnosing breast cancer with deep neural networks. *Br. J. Radiol.*, *91*, 1089, 20170545, 2018.
19. Bustad, L.K. and Hines, L., Historical perspectives of the human-animal bond, 1984.
20. Corman, V.M., Landt, O., Kaiser, M., Molenkamp, R., Meijer, A., Chu, D.K., Mulders, D.G., Detection of 2019 novel coronavirus (2019-nCoV) by real-time RT-PCR. *Eurosurveillance*, *25*, 3, 2000045, 2020.
21. Fisher, D. and Heymann, D., Q&A: The novel coronavirus outbreak causing COVID-19. *BMC Med.*, *18*, 1, 1–3, 2020.
22. Friedmann, E. and Thomas, S., Health benefits of pets for families. *Marriage Fam. Rev.*, *8*, 3-4, 191–203, 1985.
23. Gökçe, E., Kirmizigül, A.H., Atakişi, O., Erdoğan, H.M., Risk Factors Associated with Passive Immunity, Health, Birth Weight And Growth Performance in Lambs: III. The Relationship among Passive Immunity, Birth Weight Gender, Birth Type, Parity, Dam. *Kafkas Üniv. Vet. Fak. Derg.*, *19*, 5, 2013.
24. Greene, C.E., *Infectious diseases of the dog and cat* (No. Ed. 3), WB Saunders\ Elsevier Science, 2006.
25. Gulli, A., Kapoor, A., Pal, S., *Deep learning with TensorFlow 2 and Keras: regression, ConvNets, GANs, RNNs, NLP, and more with TensorFlow 2 and the Keras API*, Packt Publishing Ltd., 2019.
26. Harashima, J., Someya, Y., Kikuta, Y., Cookpad image dataset: An image collection as infrastructure for food research, in: *Proceedings of the 40th International ACM SIGIR Conference on Research and Development in Information Retrieval*, pp. 1229–1232, 2017, August.
27. Harvey, J., Companion and assistance animals: Benefits, welfare safeguards, and relationships. *Int. J. Appl. Philos.*, *22*, 2, 161–176, 2008.
28. Herzog, H., The impact of pets on human health and psychological well-being: fact, fiction, or hypothesis? *Curr. Dir. Psychol. Sci.*, *20*, 4, 236–239, 2011.
29. Hines, L.M., Historical perspectives on the human-animal bond. *Am. Behav. Sci.*, *47*, 1, 7–15, 2003.

30. Hill, L., Winefield, H., Bennett, P., Are stronger bonds better? Examining the relationship between the human–animal bond and human social support, and its impact on resilience. *Aust. Psychol.*, *55*, 6, 729–738, 2020.
31. Kim, M., The Creative Commons and copyright protection in the digital era: Uses of Creative Commons licenses. *J. Comput.-Mediated Commun.*, *13*, 1, 187–209, 2007.
32. Kim, J.Y., Lee, H.E., Choi, Y.H., Lee, S.J., Jeon, J.S., CNN-based diagnosis models for canine ulcerative keratitis. *Sci. Rep.*, *9*, 1, 1–7, 2019.
33. Künzel, F., Gruber, A., Tichy, A., Edelhofer, R., Nell, B., Hassan, J., Joachim, A., Clinical symptoms and diagnosis of encephalitozoonosis in pet rabbits. *Vet. Parasitol.*, *151*, 2–4, 115–124, 2008.
34. Levinson, B.M. and Mallon, G.P., *Pet-oriented child psychotherapy*, Charles C, 1997.
35. Lian, H.H., Bao, W.X., Wang, Y.H., Animal diseases diagnosis expert system based on hsmc-svm. *Appl. Mech. Mater.*, 198, 1036–1041, 2012, Trans Tech Publications Ltd.
36. MacKinnon, M., 'Sick as a dog': zooarchaeological evidence for pet dog health and welfare in the Roman world. *World Archaeol.*, *42*, 2, 290–309, 2010.
37. Marmanis, D., Datcu, M., Esch, T., Stilla, U., Deep learning earth observation classification using ImageNet pretrained networks. *IEEE Geosci. Remote Sens. Lett.*, *13*, 1, 105–109, 2015.
38. Marentakis, P., Karaiskos, P., Kouloulias, V., Kelekis, N., Argentos, S., Oikonomopoulos, N., Loukas, C., Lung cancer histology classification from CT images based on radiomics and deep learning models. *Med. Biol. Eng. Comput.*, *59*, 1, 215–226, 2021.
39. Mitchell, M. and Tully, T.N., *Manual of Exotic Pet Practice-E-Book*, Elsevier Health Sciences, 2008.
40. McNicholas, J., Gilbey, A., Rennie, A., Ahmedzai, S., Dono, J.A., Ormerod, E., Pet ownership and human health: a brief review of evidence and issues. *Bmj*, *331*, 7527, 1252–1254, 2005.
41. Ortiz-Pelaez, A. and Pfeiffer, D.U., Use of data mining techniques to investigate disease risk classification as a proxy for compromised biosecurity of cattle herds in Wales. *BMC Vet. Res.*, *4*, 1, 24, 2008.
42. Parry, N.M., COVID-19 and pets: When pandemic meets panic. *Forensic Sci. Int.: Rep.*, 100090, 2020.
43. Paterson, S. (Ed.), *Skin diseases of exotic pets*, John Wiley & Sons, 2008.
44. Santurkar, S., Tsipras, D., Ilyas, A., Madry, A., How does batch normalization help optimization?, in: *Advances in neural information processing systems*, pp. 2483–2493, 2018.
45. Schirmer, M.D., Venkataraman, A., Rekik, I., Kim, M., Mostofsky, S.H., Nebel, M.B., Chung, A.W., Neuropsychiatric Disease Classification Using Functional Connectomics-Results of the Connectomics in NeuroImaging Transfer Learning Challenge. *Med. Image Anal.*, 101972, 2021.

46. Shah, S.J., Barish, P.N., Prasad, P.A., Kistler, A., Neff, N., Kamm, J., Abe-Jones, Y., Clinical features, diagnostics, and outcomes of patients presenting with acute respiratory illness: A retrospective cohort study of patients with and without COVID-19. *EClinicalMedicine*, *27*, 100518, 2020.
47. Shereen, M.A., Khan, S., Kazmi, A., Bashir, N., Siddique, R., COVID-19 infection: Origin, transmission, and characteristics of human coronaviruses. *J. Adv. Res.*, 2020.
48. Singla, R., Mishra, A., Joshi, R., Jha, S., Sharma, A.R., Upadhyay, S., Medhi, B., Human animal interface of SARS-CoV-2 (COVID-19) transmission: a critical appraisal of scientific evidence. *Vet. Res. Commun.*, 1–12, 2020.
49. Stella, A., Lamkanfi, M., Portincasa, P., Familial Mediterranean Fever and COVID-19: Friends or Foes? *Front. Immunol.*, *11*, 2443, 2020.
50. Torrey, L. and Shavlik, J., Transfer learning, in: *Handbook of research on machine learning applications and trends: algorithms, methods, and techniques*, pp. 242–264, IGI global, 2010.
51. Vincent, A., Mamzer, H., Ng, Z., FARKAS, K.J., People and their Pets in the Times of the COVID-19 Pandemic. *Soc. Regist.*, *4*, 3, 111–128, 2020.
52. Walsh, F., Human-animal bonds I: The relational significance of companion animals. *Fam. Process*, *48*, 4, 462–480, 2009.
53. Wu, H., Yang, S., Huang, Z., He, J., Wang, X., Type 2 diabetes mellitus prediction model based on data mining. *Inf. Med. Unlocked*, *10*, 100–107, 2018.
54. Yang, Y.-X., Wen, C., Xie, K., Wen, F.-Q., Sheng, G.-Q., Tang, X.-G., Face recognition using the SR-CNN model. *Sensors*, 18, 12, 4237, 2018.
55. Yang, Q. and Xiao, D., A review of video-based pig behavior recognition. *Appl. Anim. Behav. Sci.*, 105146, 2020.
56. Yousefzadegan, S. and Rezaei, N., Case Report: Death due to COVID-19 in Three Brothers. *Am. J. Trop. Med. Hyg.*, *102*, 6, 1203–1204, 2020.

Index

Also of Interest

Check out these published and forthcoming titles in the "Leading-Edge Breakthroughs in Artificial Intelligence" series from Scrivener Publishing

Digital Immune System
Principles and Practices
Edited by Sujata Priyambada Dash, Vaibhav Mishra, Bijeta Shaw, Sandeep Kumar Panda, and S. Balamurugan
Published 2025. ISBN 978-1-394-38375-7

Adaptive AI
Fundamentals, Challenges, and Applications
Edited by P. Pavan Kumar, G. Suresh Kumar, Ajay Kumar Jena, Sandeep Kumar Panda and S. Balamurugan
Published 2025. ISBN 978-1-394-38904-9

AI Trust, Risk and Security Management
Framework, Principles, and Practices
Edited by R. Karthick Manoj, S. Senthilnathan, S. Arunmozhi Selvi, T. Ananth Kumar, S. Balamurugan
Published 2025. ISBN 978-1-394-39299-5

Responsible AI
Principles and Practices
Edited by Manish Kumar, Nitigya Sambyal, Leena Priyadarshini Singh, Ramasamy V. and S. Balamurugan
Published 2026. ISBN 978-1-394-35544-0

Forthcoming 2026
Neuro-Symbolic AI: Concepts and Applications
Decision Intelligence: Concepts, Applications, and Case Studies
Human-Centered AI: Frameworks and Applications
Platform Engineering: Concepts, Challenges, and Applications

Composite AI: Fundamentals, Challenges, and Applications
Visual AI: Fundamentals, Challenges, and Applications
Causal AI: Fundamentals and Applications
Embodied AI: Concepts, Challenges, and Applications
Agentic AI: Concepts, Applications, and Case Studies
Data-Centric AI: Concepts, Applications and Case Studies
Sovereign AI: Frameworks, Principles, and Practices
Accelerated AI: Energy Efficient Computing Systems for Large Language Models (LLMs)
Actionable AI: Powered by Large Action Models (LAMs)
Affective AI: Concepts, Applications, and Case Studies
AI-Augmented Software Engineering: Principles and Practices
Ambient Invisible Intelligence: Fundamentals, Challenges, and Applications
Artificial Cognition: Technology, Applications, and Challenges
Artificial General Intelligence: Principles and Practices
Autonomous AI Agents: Foundations and Applications
Principles of Confidential Computing
Disinformation Security for Generative AI Applications: Concepts, Methodologies, and Use Cases
Embedded AI: Concepts, Challenges, and Applications
Graph Neural Networks (GNNs): Concepts and Applications
Industry Cloud Platforms: Fundamentals, Applications, and Case Studies
Multi-Modal Generative AI: Frameworks, Principles, and Practices
Objective-Driven AI: Concepts, Applications, and Case Studies
Physical AI for Robotics and Automation: Concepts, Techniques, and Applications
Predictive AI: Concepts, Applications, and Case Studies
Prescriptive AI: Concepts, Applications, and Case Studies
Shadow AI: Concepts, Applications, and Security
Small Language Models (SLMs) for Compact AI: Architectures, Principles, and Applications

www.scrivenerpublishing.com